OPENING THE

Ark of the Covenant

The Secret Power *of the* Ancients,
The Knights Templar Connection,
and the Search *for the* Holy Grail

Frank Joseph *and* Laura Beaudoin

NEW PAGE BOOKS
A division of The Career Press, Inc.
Franklin Lakes, NJ

OPENING THE ARK OF THE COVENANT
EDITED BY KARA REYNOLDS
TYPESET BY EILEEN DOW MUNSON
Cover design by Lu Rossman/Digi Dog Design
Printed in the U.S.A. by Book-mart Press

To order this title, please call toll-free 1-800-CAREER-1 (NJ and Canada: 201-848-0310) to order using VISA or MasterCard, or for further information on books from Career Press.

The Career Press, Inc., 3 Tice Road, PO Box 687,
Franklin Lakes, NJ 07417
www.careerpress.com
www.newpagebooks.com

Library of Congress Cataloging-in-Publication Data

Joseph, Frank.
    Opening the ark of the covenant : the secret power of the ancients, the Knights Templar Connection, and the search for the Holy Grail / by Frank Joseph and Laura Beaudoin.
        p. cm.
    Includes bibliographical references and index.
    ISBN-13: 978-1-56414-903-9
    ISBN-10: 1-56414-903-X
    1. Ark of the Covenant—Miscellanea. 2. Knights Templar (Masonic order)—Miscellanea. 3. Grail—Miscellanea. 4. Templars—Miscellanea. 5. Freemasonry—Miscellanea. I. Beaudoin, Laura. II. Title.

BM657.A8J67 2007
296.4´93--dc22

                                                                                        2006031941

To Laura's father,
Judge Irving W. Beaudoin,
a linear descendent of the king
who founded the Knights Templar,
remembered fondly
for his regal cast of mind
and human kindness.

Contents

The Golden Paradox

You shall have the illumination of the world, and darkness will disappear.

—Thoth-Hermes on his Emerald Tablets[1]

"The Ark of the Covenant is something everyone has heard about, but no one is sure what it was." Her trite response to my question was disappointing. I felt like getting up and leaving right then, but didn't. You know how it is: You don't want to seem rude to a kindly stranger, especially one claiming personal connections—however dubious—with the Other Side.

"Which seems all the more remarkable," she went on, "because everybody's fascinated by it."

I obediently concurred, then thought of a credibly urgent excuse that would set me on my merry way without offense. As I got up to go, she essayed a last attempt to snag me. "Hey, why are you so interested in the Ark, anyway?"

"You're the psychic," I answered good-naturedly, but with an inadvertent tinge of cynicism. "You're the one with all the answers. You tell me."

My flippant reply didn't faze her, judging from the woozy expression that began to rapidly suffuse her features and half-lower her eyelids, as the lady's consciousness supposedly slipped back into that etheric realm she accessed for the greater good of all mankind. I couldn't walk out on such an uncomfortable moment, so I paused, impatient for her to get on with it so I could leave without feeling like a heel.

"Ah," she intoned with some revelation I was sure to learn, like it or not. "I see. You've been looking for the Ark a long time." Well, she was certainly right on that score. Five years did indeed seem like "a long time" to be investigating just one subject. She might have told me then I had another 21 years to go. Come to think of it, better that she didn't tell me.

"No," she raised her voice, her brow furrowed in vexation. "For many *life-times*." The feeling that she had just read my thoughts produced an abruptly galvanizing effect on my attention.

"You found it and lost it, found it and lost it—just like the others. That's why you're still looking. Now you have to try and remember everything you found before and put it all together with the new stuff you find. Quite an assignment!"

There was a suggestion of mirthful mockery in her low, slow-spoken words, as though referring to something she suddenly discovered and I should have known, but did not.

"What 'others'?" I asked, "What 'assignment'?" But she ignored me.

"I'm quoting now: 'The seat of the soul is where the inner and outer worlds meet. That is where you will find the Ark'."

"Could you be a little more specific?" I was unable to resist, but her inward concentration remained unbroken. As though in defiance of my question, she responded, still "quoting," I presumed, "'It is an intelligible sphere whose center is Everywhere and circumference is Nowhere. Search Everywhere. Not Nowhere.'" I could hear the capital "E"s and "N"s in her deliberate pronunciation. "In other words," she carefully explained as would a testy teacher to her slow-witted student, "do not waste your time in the wrong place. Follow the breadcrumbs so someday you can sing, 'Oh, sweet mystery of life, at last I've found you!'"

Her unexpected outburst into the old Victor Herbert song made me jump, and attracted the alarmed stares of other, "psychic faire" visitors within earshot. I sheepishly smiled back at them, implying everything was under control, though I wasn't entirely sure.

"Oh, at last I know the meaning of it all! All the yearning, striving, waiting, yearning, longing, the idle hopes that...."

Her singing sputtered out, as she seemed to have forgotten the rest of the words, or so I hoped she had. At any rate, I got the point—maybe. She nodded once on her ample chest, then appeared to doze

off in that position for a few moments before snapping back into full consciousness.

"There! I'm in the so-called 'real world' again," she said sweetly and sighed. "That will be 20 dollars, please. Just kidding!"

I gave her a five-dollar bill anyway, and thanked her for the reading.

"Good luck," she said sincerely. "Let me know if you find it!"

Contrary to any false impressions my 1985 encounter may give, this book is not the result of any paranormal insights. Nothing has been "channeled," at least not consciously. I had no further recourse to psychics, and I mention meeting the self-described intuitive lady only because she brought up some points still worthy of consideration. As she said, it does indeed seem "remarkable" that the Ark of the Covenant should have such an enduring popular allure, when so little is known about it. The sibyl's reputation as a genuinely gifted seer had prompted me to consult her about it at a time when the sacred object seemed about to disclose its secrets, only to fade back behind its veil of uncertainty. At that point, I was open to any guidance, whatever the source.

Although she gave me no useful details to check out, I did follow the breadcrumbs. They led me to many of the places described in this book: Tenerife, Delos, Delphi, Ilios, Giza, Cuzco, Teotihuacan, Nara, and dozens more; largely unfamiliar names spread around the globe, but all known at one time or another as "the Navel of the World." The term surfaced early during my research (read: "obsession") into the lost civilization of Atlantis, beginning in the spring of 1980. At that time, few believed the place had actually existed, and I was not entirely sure myself. In the years since then, my four books on the subject were published in a dozen foreign editions, joining the deluge of material released about Plato's sunken city since he first spoke of it 2,300 years ago. These numerous volumes, compact discs, magazines, lectures, television productions, and feature films reflect unprecedented, international interest in Atlantis and the Ark itself.

Truly, no object on Earth, throughout history, has captured human imagination more thanthe Ark of the Covenant. It is traditionally thought to contain the power of God, and built according to the divine specifications Moses received personally from the Almighty atop Mount Sinai. Everyone—Christian, Jew, Muslim, and nonbeliever—pictures the Ark as a golden box, surmounted by two sculpted angels, which cannot be touched, and can only be transported with a pair of long carrying poles. But no one knows its precise function, why it was valued as ancient Israel's most prized possession, or what finally became of it. Many scholars are convinced the artifact never existed, yet it is mentioned more often in the Bible than any other single item. Surprisingly, I have noticed that the merest mention of the Ark in my public presentations galvanizes audiences more than any other subject. Why should people be so intensely interested in something they know so little about? It has the universal allure of a powerful archetype.

In 1980, I was as ignorant of this fascinating item as the next person. It has taken me all this time, traveling the world and collecting stacks of research materials, to have unlocked its mysteries, identified its intended purpose, its real origins—and possibly, its present whereabouts. Clues leading to the Ark were as bizarre as the sacred object itself: a Jesuit priest, the Great Pyramid of Egypt, a deformed pharaoh, Canada, a Japanese scuba diver, a thousand-year-old tree, a famous Russian explorer, a famous French painter, an infamous French cardinal, American Indians, secret societies, and an Illinois woodworker. Individually incongruous, they nevertheless comprise a vast mosaic spanning not only the world, but the entire history of man. The image emerging from their interrelationship is both wonderful and horrible, filled with transfiguration, heroism, genius, and beauty, contrasted by deceit, terror, madness, and mass murder. It is an unexpected picture I did not paint. I only found it after 26 years of continuous investigation. This book is the summary and outcome of that long labor of love.

I was aided in my discovery of the Ark's story by someone without whom my work would have been woefully incomplete. If there is such a thing as destiny, her appearance was perfectly timed. While in the midst of researching the man who established the Order of the Knights Templar in Jerusalem, both Laura Beaudoin and I learned that she is his linear descendant. We then found that she is directly related to several other key players in the Ark drama, from a figure in the Old Testament to what may have been the sacred object's 17th century steward. Never interested in genealogy, and emotionally incapable of boasting about her family tree, she provided unique insight into the darkest corners of medieval politics. Laura also owned a rare document, a privately published Beaudoin family history, preserved by her mother, Dolores. Thanks to this one-of-a-kind manuscript, we may find a hitherto unknown chapter in the lost history of the Ark of the Covenant. And that, in essence, is the result of our combined efforts: the first history of this supremely enigmatic artifact.

CHAPTER 1

The World's
Most Valuable Object

*Yet, what mysteries! The more difficult to clarify, because
there is a hiatus between the men of that time and ourselves, a
gulf in which a form of civilization has disappeared. What
was a civilization has gone up in a dust-cloud of particulars.*

—Louis Charpentier[1]

The great city gleamed white in the desert sun. Stucco structures, clean, but small and indistinguishable from each other, clustered haphazardly together, remininiscent of herds of sheep waiting around the base of the mountain and partially climbing its slopes. A maze of unmarked streets—more alleys than thoroughfares—snaked their way into the urban center like a ceremonial labyrinth challenging pilgrims to enter its ritual path. Once inside, noisy crowds of wary buyers and animated sellers mixed amid a swift current of passing men and women urged on by their own personal agendas, while heedless children played underfoot.

Emerging from this din of everyday concerns, a well-trodden track led up the mountainside, the busy sounds of the capital growing increasingly muted, until travelers could look down on the tops of its scrubbed buildings and beyond to the vast extent of its metropolitan limits, stretching far toward the sandy horizon. The upward trek was not difficult, even on a windless, summer morning, and there were many travelers, young and old, coming and going, all of them light-hearted, along the same trail.

Progress was nonetheless slow, deliberately so, to impart a sense of sanctified pilgrimage as the low, powerful murmur of many voices grew more distinct. At the top was a paved plaza spreading far in all directions, and vast enough to accommodate throngs of visitors from all over the world. It was as though the entire mountaintop had been sheared off, its former place perfectly leveled to make way for this immense public square. It held a 30-ton basin, 12 feet tall and 20 feet wide at the lip, mounted on the life-size representations of a dozen cast-bronze bulls. The basin itself was burnished bronze, and almost too bright to behold directly in the reflected sunlight of high noon. A priest atop an abutting platform scooped water from the brim of his gargantuan receptacle with a bucket, which he handed to an attendant for pouring into several wash-bowls mounted on metal stands, each pushed about on four wheels. The imposing temple of polished stone at the center of the expansive precinct was 135 feet long, 35 feet wide, and stood upon its own platform, which elevated the entire structure to 50 feet above the plaza.

A broad staircase of 10 steps led to its recessed entrance, flanked on either side by a pair of ornate pillars, each nearly 6 feet thick and 27 feet tall. The capitals on top of each column were 8 feet high and decorated with a lily motif. Nets of checkerwork covered each capital, which was festooned with rows of 200 representational pomegranates, wreathed in seven chains for each capital, and topped by lily designs. Both columns were brass, in bold contrast to the pale white blocks of stone before which they stood on either side of twin, cedar doors 23 feet tall and inlaid with gold images of cherubim. Through these imposing portals visitors passed into the Temple's small anteroom, where they paused to adjust their vision.

Another, equally imposing set of doors opened to the main hall. Exposed beams criss-crossed the ceiling just above five square windows on either wall adorned with golden lily motifs ending near the cedar floor in oversized images of cherubim. The high windows allowed shafts of sunlight, clearly defined by translucent clouds of frankincense rising from a large censer, to angle down through the sacred space. At its center was a low table bearing 12 loaves of bread, while 10 tripods hung with oil lamps stood around the hall for evening ceremonies.

At the far end, a final fight of steps rose to another pair of gold-inlaid doors. These were locked 364 days each year, and

perpetually guarded by armed sentries under strict orders to forbid approach by anyone, save only the high priest, on pain of death. After sunset each October 1st, he donned a protective, full-length garment, while attendants shackled his right ankle with a heavy manacle. They attached it to a length of chain with which his body might be retrieved in the event of a mishap when the priest stepped behind the doors leading to the otherwise forbidden chamber.

This was the holy-of-holies, a dark, windowless, cube-shaped room 30 feet high, wide, and long, with olive wood-paneled walls of inlaid gold floral designs. Its only source of illumination was the main hall's lamplight streaming through the annually opened portals, behind which attendants crouched in fear for the fate of their high priest. Entering the shrine, he was confronted by a colossal pair of winged sphinx. Masterfully sculpted from olive wood and set with gold, their outstretched wings brushed the walls of the chamber and met 17 feet overhead.

Between them, sitting alone on the floor, was a rectangular chest nearly 4 feet long, and more than 3 feet high and wide. Its acacia wood frame was entirely sheeted in beaten gold, including two carrying poles slipped through a pair of rings on either side of the casket. An identical pair of cherubim, the tips of their arching wings almost touching each other, bent over a shallow platter mounted in the middle of the coffer lid, which no one ever dared to remove. From this small, seldom-seen tabernacle, not only the temple building but also the entire mountaintop derived their unique sacredness.

The source of its pervasive mystical potency appeared irregularly and beyond human control, when the gold container unexpectedly shone with a bright radiance, and an otherworldly flame danced above the lid, between the shallow dish and the outstretched wings of the kneeling cherubim. These were moments when the Deity himself was said to appear in the form of light, and make his will known to the high priest in a spiritual experience without parallel. Occasionally, the Lord showed his displeasure with mankind by striking his servant with a blast of power from the glowing vessel. Then his assistants, watching from behind the doors of the main hall, would have to heave on the chain to which his ankle was fastened, pulling the current high-priest's unconscious—sometimes lifeless—body from the shrine room, then close and bolt the great doors of the holy-of-holies, locking it in utter darkness for another year, until the next high priest would enter alone to learn the will of God. As is the natural world he made, the Creator is at once beautiful and terrible.

So a visitor to King Solomon's temple might have described the Ark of the Covenant nearly 3,000 years ago, a portrayal based almost entirely on the Old Testament. Some three centuries after the object was installed atop Jerusalem's Mount Moriah, it vanished, never to be seen again.

Perhaps.

While most modern scholars believe the Ark did actually exist, they are unsure of its real identity. They are puzzled by its biblical description as nothing more than a depository for the Ten Commandments (also known as the Decalogue), a characterization at odds with its reputation depicted by the same source as a weapon of mass destruction and a direct communication hookup to heaven. These diametrically opposed functions are usually dismissed by conventional investigators as mythic qualities the Old Testament writers undoubtedly wove around a mundane item to imbue its memory with an air of potent, if ambivalent, mysticism. But this supposition is superficial, because it assumes, without looking further into the subject, that the Ark, admittedly important for its preservation of the Decalogue, was, after all, just a fancy container.

A glimpse behind the veil of assumption, however, reveals something vastly more significant than previously imagined. The resultant insight is truly mind-boggling, a multifaceted revelation that throws our origins and potential into a bright new light. The discovery is, to put it bluntly, the most important of its kind ever made. Appreciation of its consequences for human understanding and destiny alone is life-changing. Once comprehended, we are never the same afterward, and for the better. By merely beginning to understand the world's supremely important object we tune into its eternal energies. It grabs hold of us, and we begin to possess it, as much as we are possessed by it. It touches many faiths, but none may claim it as sole owner. It is mankind's foremost spiritual power, but it is entirely nondenominational, even nonreligious. It is extremely ancient, yet far in advance of anything today's technology has so far produced—although, as we will see, 21st century science has achieved a degree of proficiency allowing for its present replication—the reason, perhaps, why the "Perfection of Paradise," as it was once called, has not been forgotten. It is most famous as the Ark of the Covenant, but was known by many other names in different lands long before it passed to the Hebrews, and for centuries after they lost it. If used as designed, it still has the power to save our civilization from catastrophe, heal our bodies, expand our consciousness, and transform our souls. If abused, it will cause cancer, kill, and drive us mad. It has caused all these things in the past, and it still has the undiminished capacity to repeat them.

The Ark is not just a container. Nor is it a biblical oddity whose questionable existence is of little concern. Instead, its powers are as vast as its history, which is as old as civilization itself. Consequently, understanding its origins, passage among various peoples, true identity, and ultimate importance to modern society is challenging. The magnitude of relevant information needed to appreciate its core significance can be overwhelming. Its enormous time-scale, far-flung interaction with disparate cultures, and sheer scale of operation are difficult to grasp.

To make sense out of so vast a subject, we present its story from its earliest beginnings to our own time. As such, *Opening the Ark of the Covenant* is that object's first, real history, in the course of which its actual functions, inestimable value, and present whereabouts become accessible. The result is a straightforward offering of an otherwise complex tale aimed at clarity of comprehension. We've used facts to support recurrent themes that more lucidly explicate the enigma, expose its secret workings, and make sense out of the continuing fascination countless generations have had for it.

Despite the title of this book, the artifact described here only appeared as the "Ark of the Covenant" when Moses descended from Mount Sinai. In fact, it existed long before that event, under different names, in different places. And after the Ark disappeared with the destruction of Solomon's Temple, it was referred to by new titles, in new lands. Accordingly, our investigation follows its pre-Near Eastern origins and progress in other parts of the world, sometimes far removed from its biblical settings in both time and geography. Throughout all its changes in name, place, and ownership, however, it remained the same powerful phenomenon. The various environments through which it traveled, and the human influences that carried it throughout the past all brought out its inner nature and defined it far better than any plain description—as ark or power stone—ever could.

In the process, many wonderful revelations—some apparently disconnected, but all ultimately interrelated—come to light. Just a few include the sacred object's medieval rediscovery, its role as part of the Great Pyramid, and its impact on Christianity. It affected not only millions of common men and women, but also some of history's most prominent players on the world stage. Along with Moses and King Solomon, some of the famous personalities surrounding it included such diverse characters as Herod the Great, Pharaoh Akhenaton, Joseph of Arimathea, Jesus, Saint Bernard, Nebuchadnezzar, Cardinal Richelieu, Jacques Cartier, Samuel de Champlain, and Sieur de LaSalle. It was supposedly carried along by Lemurians, Atlanteans, Canary Islanders, ancient Egyptians, Israelites, Ethiopians, Crusaders, Knights Templar, Cathars, Nazis, the Japanese, Jesuit missionaries, English monks, and American Indians.

But the fundamental purpose of *Opening the Ark of the Covenant* is to discover the secret of its power, as revealed in its history, and thereby suggest its likely whereabouts. For the Ark does indeed still exist, and it's much closer than we suspect.

CHAPTER 2

The Jewel That Grants All Desires

Om mani padme hum. "*Behold! The jewel is in the lotus.*"
—Tibetan Buddhism's foremost mantra

Set like an almond-shaped opal in a turquoise ocean, the island of Yonaguni is last in a chain of isolated territories—known as the Ryukyus—extending southwest from Japan into the East China Sea, just above the Tropic of Cancer. But in 1986, the remote, 6-mile-long island with its 2,000 residents—mostly farmers and fishermen—was not an easy place for Kihachiro Aratake to make a living. As a teacher at the local scuba school, he was finding it difficult to attract students from faraway Tokyo or Kyoto.

One afternoon in early spring, he began cruising the seldom-visited waters off Yonaguni's southern coast for a new dive site. There, some 300 feet parallel to a rough, remote area known as Arakawa-bana, underwater clarity was extraordinarily good; an ideal place for new students or tourists. As Aratake completed his dive, he noticed a massive shadow just beyond the periphery of his 100-foot vision. Low on air, he nevertheless swam toward it, his curiosity peaked.

"Maybe it's an old shipwreck," he hoped. "What a terrific draw *that* would be!"

But the indistinct, solid black form less resembled any sunken vessel the closer he approached. He would have to descend deeper than safety precautions advised if he wanted to reach the hulking shape. From 20 feet, he dove to 40, then 60. "That's two atmospheres," he thought to himself (a term used to define increasing levels of pressure at depth). At 75 feet, in shadow more than light, the massive block suddenly emerged from its obscurity. Aratake stopped in mid-kick. Peering in disbelief through his partially fogged facemask, he found himself suddenly hovering near a full-size building sitting squat on the ocean floor.

The Place of the Ruins

In all his years as a dive-master, he had never seen nor heard of anything like this. It resembled an immense, flat-topped pyramid of stone steps only a titan could climb, together with a smaller staircase and broad, semicircular plazas surmounted by a pair of tall pylons. It seemed adorned with strange configurations resembling an oversized hourglass; a giant, sculpted human head; and a monstrous turtle carved in relief—each one eroded almost beyond recognition by unguessed centuries of swift currents. Nearby, a huge, egg-shaped boulder had been set on its own plinth (a low platform), similar to some megalith from Stone Age Europe. Slanting walls of fitted stone skirted a kind of loop-road going around the base of the structure through a colossal arch resembling photographs Aratake had seen of the pre-Inca "Gateway to the Sun," on the other side of the Pacific at Tiahuanaco, high in the Bolivian Andes Mountains.

Recreation of the sunken monument discovered in 1986 by diver Kihachiro Aratake near the Japanese island of Yonaguni.

Something near the north end of the building stirred, an indefinable form that first intrigued, and then alarmed him. The cloud-like apparition was an unexpectedly large school of hammerhead sharks. He drew in a deep breath, but it was the last his tank had to offer. His right hand fumbled around his back, anxiously feeling for the valve to the reserve tank. He found it, yanked the switch, and gratefully filled his lungs with a fresh gush of air. It was only enough to enable his escape, however, and he slowly ascended, eyeing the dozens of congregating killers that so far had failed to notice him.

Breaking the surface, he swam as quickly as he dared in the direction of his waiting dive-boat, and felt grateful to haul himself aboard in one piece. A mate helped him unstrap the empty air tanks and peel off his dripping wet-suit.

"See anything worthwhile down there?"

"You wouldn't believe it!" Aratake answered.

Believe it or not, Aratake's find electrified Japan, and news of it spread around the world. Yonaguni basked in a fame it had never known, as the divers he once hoped to attract now flocked to the obscure little island from as far away as Europe and America. They shared his initial awe of discovery, as Aratake personally escorted them in guided tours to the sunken structure. Most observers, Japanese and foreign alike, were struck by its evidently man-made appearance, and sure that it must be the remnant of some ancient civilization. Hence, the new name for its location: Iseki Point, or "Place of the Ruins."

Far less certain of its artificial origins were mainstream archaeologists. To them, civilization began 55 centuries ago in the Near East—not the western Pacific Ocean. Judging from the depth at which the Iseki Point site lies and given rises in sea level since the close of the last ice age, the so-called ruin was last on dry land about 12,000 years ago, far earlier than the first city-states of Mesopotamia (today's Iraq) some 9,000 years later.[1] So the underwater feature, they said, had to be a natural formation that just happened to resemble some cultural edifice, thanks to the erosional effects of swiftly moving currents on sandstone over the course of time. Convincing as such a conclusion might sound issuing from the revered halls of Academia, few of the skeptical scholars troubled themselves to actually visit Yonaguni before passing judgment on the controversial site.

A scientist who did bother to personally investigate it was a marine seismologist with an international reputation. Aided by fellow instructors and student volunteers, Professor Masaaki Kimura launched a thorough investigation of Iseki Point, using cutting-edge technology put at his disposal by the University of the Ryukyus, where he taught geology. Beginning in 2000, they used narrow beam lasers to take thousands of super-accurate measurements, thousands of underwater and aerial photographs, and abundant sample materials. They also produced numerous computer simulations and operated the most advanced sonar instruments available for nonmilitary purposes.

Dr. Kimura supplemented these exhaustive surveys by consulting board-certified archaeologists, other geologists, and even local craftsmen, especially stone-cutters who worked in traditional methods. He had undertaken the investigation as a true scientist, with no preconceived opinions one way or the other, determined to arrive at conclusions regarding the sunken structure based exclusively on the physical evidence collected. After three years of intensive study, he publicly announced his findings concerning the sub-surface feature off the south coast of Yonaguni: It was unquestionably man-made.

Although the ruined structure's original purpose could not be determined with certainty, clear evidence of tool marks and even glyphs carved on its exterior proved that the Iseki Point enigma had been terraformed, or deliberately modified by human hands from what was once a natural rock outcropping standing above sea level before the end of the last ice age. Coming as such an assertion did from an investigator of Dr. Kimura's professional background, it sent shockwaves of disbelief throughout Japan's scholarly community. Later, he was able to present his findings for peer review in Tokyo, where his colleagues overwhelmingly endorsed the correctness of his research at Yonaguni.

Dr. Masaaki Kimura (Professor of Geology, University of the Ryukyus) describes his investigation of Yonaguni's underwater structure at a meeting of the Japan Petrograph Society in Fukuoka, May, 2000.

The People of Mu

Aratake's underwater find did not stand alone. Equally stupendous and enigmatic structures are scattered from Polynesia to Melanesia. The Micronesian city of Nan Madol, built with 280 million tons of magnetized basalt, Luzon's gargantuan food factories in the Philippines, Tonga's 109-ton coral gate, and Tahiti's

267-foot-long pyramid are all remnants of a vanished civilization. Its physical outlines appear in these and numerous other, ancient engineering feats, especially when highlighted by indigenous traditions and ongoing archaeological finds. Despite the often thousands of miles separating the locations of such prehistoric marvels, they share several revealing commonalities: Native peoples residing in their vicinity make no claim to them, but almost invariably insist the structures were built by "sorcerers" or demigods of some foreign, preancestral race from a formerly splendid kingdom either some time before or shortly after it sank to the bottom of the sea.

Although mainstream archaeologists are loathe to place much stock in folk traditions of any kind, the fundamental uniformity of such oral accounts shared by linguistically and racially dissimilar islanders, isolated from each other by vast distances, powerfully underscores the culturally anomalous remains themselves. A leading motif running through these accounts is a name familiar to countless generations of native peoples: Mu. The chiefs who built Tonga's gigantic canal and public works projects are remembered as the Mu'a, literally "men from Mu." Hawaii's original inhabitants were the Mu, who arrived before the Polynesians from a large island that succumbed to a "warrior-wave." According to the *Kumulipo*, Hawaii's oldest and most important oral tradition, the Mu originated in Helani, "the unstable land in the deep blue sea."

Coastal civilizers of northern Peru predating the Incas were the Chimu—literally, the "People of Mu." Surviving among the ruins of Chan-Chan, outside the modern city of Trujillo, is a mural depicting their lost homeland as a sunken city with fish swimming over the tops of its pyramids.

Far beyond the western Pacific, into Asia, on the other side of the Himalayas, an 18th century Tibetan scholar, gSum-pam-Khan-po, described the arrival of Byamspa, Tibet's first king in Yarling—then the nation's capital—from "the Land of Mu." Byamspa belonged to a pre-Buddhist people, the Mu, who introduced the tenets of the Boen religion, which still underlie Tibetan spirituality today. A Taiwanese version of the Great Flood, the *Tsuwo*, tells how the Pacific Ocean long ago swallowed a magnificent kingdom. Its former seat of power was a splendid palace ringed with great walls of red stone. The vanished realm is remembered as Mu-Da-Lu.

The recurrence of this name associated with a civilization that foundered long ago in the Pacific Ocean, amid so many widely disparate folk traditions, persuasively underscores Dr. Kimura's belief that "the Yonaguni Monument may be considered as evidence signifying that Mu existed."[2] The same land was known as far afield as ancient Rome, where its fate was commemorated every May 9th, 11th, and 15th. As a Roman ceremony, the Lemuria appeased the souls of men and women who perished when the distant kingdom was destroyed by a natural catastrophe, which occurred over the three festival days. The ceremony was traditionally instituted by Romulus, the mythic founder of Rome, as atonement for murdering Remus, his twin brother. Celebrants walked barefoot, as though escaping unprepared from some disaster that drove them from their homes. In the course of the observance, they proceeded from room to room, throwing handfuls of black beans nine times as a gesture of rebirth: Ghosts were symbolized by black beans, while the number 9, paralleling the nine months of pregnancy, stood for birth. Such ritualistic behavior was designed to honor, and hence exorcise, any unhappy spirits that may haunt one's residence. A graphic reenactment of the deluge would occur on the third day of the Roman Lemuria, when celebrants cast 30 images made of rushes and representing human victims of the flood into the Tiber River.

The name "Lemuria" echoes far from ancient Rome to the other side of the world, among southern California's Chumash Indians: San Miguel Island, site of a very un-Indian megalithic wall, was known to them as Lemu. And in the Maldives of the Indian Ocean, Laamu Atoll features the islands' largest *hawitta,* or stone mound, said to have been constructed by a foreign, red-haired, seafaring people in remote prehistory. On Tonga, Lihamui is the name of the month of May, just when the Roman Lemuria was celebrated. In transpacific myth, Mu-ri-wai-hou is a sunken realm reigned over by Limu, the ubiquitous Polynesian god and guardian of the dead, from his huge palace at the bottom of the sea.

Lemuria as it probably appeared 4,000 and more years ago—a series of mostly low-lying islands and archipelagoes strung out across the Central Pacific.

Easter Island

The single most obvious survivor of this lost civilization is Easter Island, separated from the South American coast by 2,485 miles of open water. The nearest inhabited landfall to the 7-mile-wide, 15.5-mile-long Chilean "protectorate" is Pitcairn Island, 1,242 miles to the west, and the scene of the famous novel *Mutiny on the Bounty.* Easter Island knew its own tragedies—prehistoric and 19th century acts of genocide—but is more famous for its austere, colossal statues and inscrutable written language. Far less well-known is the native account of how the first humans found their way to this tiny speck of dry land in the middle of the world's most vast ocean.

"There was a big country," the islanders' oral tradition begins, "a land of abundance, a land of temples." Rich in agriculture, its people traveled to every corner of Hiva—revered in numerous folk traditions as an ancestral homeland that was overcome by a terrible deluge—along an extensive road network, passing under stone gateways to cities with broad ceremonial plazas fronted by colorfully decorated, cyclopean buildings. Its capital province was Marae Renga, ruled by King Haumaka. Warned by a prophetic dream of Hiva's coming destruction, he ordered six of his most skilled mariners to find a distant place of refuge. They immediately set sail aboard their ship, the Oraorangaru, or "Saved-from-the-Billows," but were many weeks at sea until they discovered an island too small for the relocation of Hiva's entire population, but large enough to accommodate the rulers, their families, and retainers from Marae Renga.

After preparing the deserted island for settlement, the explorers returned to chief Haumaka, made their report, and were assigned as pilots for the evacuation. In charge of the operation was Hotu Matua, the "Prolific Father," who disembarked with his family and 300 followers in a pair of "mile-long canoes" stockpiled with provisions, water, and cargo. Two months later, they arrived at their new home, where they offloaded numerous trees, tubers, and plants, plus a library of 67 bark-cloth-covered tablets inscribed with genealogies and histories, together with religious, agricultural, botanical, medical, and astronomical texts. Their most treasured possession, however, was the Te-pito-te-Kura, the "Navel of Light," a sacred stone from Hiva. So revered was this holy object that Hotu Matua christened the island Te-pito-te-henua, the "Navel of the World."

Back at Marae Renga, the terrible god of earthquakes suddenly shook great stretches of territory into the sea. Uvoke "lifted the land with his crowbar. The waves uprose, the country became small...the waves broke, the wind blew, rain fell, thunder roared, meteorites fell on the island." Haumaka lived to see the fulfillment of his prophetic dream: "The king saw that the land had sunk in the sea. As the sea rose, the land sank. Families died, men died, women, children, and old people. The Earth is drowned." Returning to Te-pito-te-henua, the six original discoverers who prepared the island for settlement begged Hotu Matua for permission to return home. But the mournful king told them, "The sea has come up and drowned all people in Marae Renga."[3]

Over the following generations, he and his people made a success of their little island. Rock art flourished in harmony with agricultural prosperity, while stone platforms (*ahu*) supporting colossal statues (*moai*) stood amid lofty towers surrounded by massive walls. There were public recitation contests and religious festivals, but the most important competition occurred every Vernal Equinox, when young athletes risked their lives for an egg. On the first day of spring, they swam for a mile through shark-infested waters to the offshore islet of Mutu Nui (known today as Motunui), where frigate birds laid their clutch amid sharp rocks. The first volunteer who returned with one of their unbroken eggs was venerated as the man of

the year, and accorded holy status. His triumph signified rescue of the egg-shaped "Navel of Light," a sacred souvenir from old Hiva, the strange artifact believed to emanate the power of creation. Given its suggestive name, Mutu Nui was intended to symbolize the lost motherland, known to various Pacific Ocean islanders as Horaizan, Haiviki, Hiva, and numerous other cultural inflections on the memory of Mu.

The first modern European to sight Te-pito-te-henua was Jakob Rogeveen, who found it in 1772 on Easter Sunday; hence its modern name: Easter Island. Ironically, eggs signified the core meaning of both the Christian holiday and the Pacific ritual race, in that both were celebrations of spiritual birth or rebirth.

As he was about to die of old age, Hotu Matua ascended a volcano at the southwestern corner of Easter Island. John Macmillan Brown, an Oxford scholar and founding professor at New Zealand's University of Canterbury in Christchurch, described the king's last day:

> *Looking out westward, he called to the spirits that hovered round his old submerged home to bid the cocks crow, and when the cocks crew he gave up the ghost. In this tradition, we have clearly expressed the consciousness of archipelagoes to the west of Easter Island having gone down, and the submersion being the cause of ocean-voyaging immigrants settling on its infertile soil.*[4]

This and other oral traditions describing Hotu Matua—his flight from doomed Marae Renga and its destruction in earthquake and flood—are not unlike many similar Polynesian accounts of a powerful realm said to have dominated the Pacific long ago, before succumbing to a cataclysm of unique violence. But the Easter Island rendition differs from most other versions primarily in the addition of a supremely sacred heirloom. The Navel of Light was the most valuable treasure Hotu Matua and his people owned. But it was far more than some sentimental keepsake from the drowned motherland. They revered the Te-pito-te-Kura as the very power-center of their lives, and named their entire island after it.

Incredibly, this formerly paramount object still survives, unworshiped and largely ignored, on the north coast in La Perouse Bay, between a mantle of loose stones and pavement in the southwest corner of the west wing of an ahu. In fact, the monumental platform takes its name from the artifact. At 75 centimeters across and 45 centimeters thick, with a circumference of 2.53 meters, the oblate spheroid of dense, crystalline volcanic rock is gray in color, with some tones fading to black. It was never cut into a gem, but shows evidence of having been deftly shaped and repeatedly polished. How this unprepossessing stone could have continuously elicited the chief veneration of an entire people over the long course of their cultural existence is not at all obvious from its rather ordinary physical appearance. In any case, the setting for the crystal Navel of Light was considered the foremost sacred center, the Navel of the World. Wherever it appeared, in either its original home at sunken Hiva, or later in Easter Island, was the most important place on Earth.

The Navel of Light in Hawaii

Its only other location throughout the entire Pacific was in Hawaii, formerly known as Ka-houpo-o-Kane, literally, the "Navel of Light." Kane (pronounced "kah-nay") was the god of illumination, as well as the deified personification of health and life itself. According to indigenous tradition, another divinity, the goddess Pele, arrived from the province of Honua-mea, or the "Navel," in the sunken kingdom of Kahiki, yet another variant on the theme of the lost motherland. A native chant, "The Era of Overturning," or Po-au-huliha, tells:

From Kahiki came the woman, Pele. Lo, an eruption in Kahiki! A flashing of lightning, O Pele! Belch forth, O Pele! The phosphor burns like the eye of Pele, or a meteor-flash in the sky. The heavens shook, the Earth shook, even to the sacred places. The Earth is dancing. The heavens are enclosing. Born the roaring, advancing, and receding of waves, the rumbling sound, the earthquake. The sea rages, rises over the beach, rises to the inhabited places, rises gradually up over the land.

Then followed the Kai-a-ka-hina-li'i, the "Flood that caused the downfall of the chiefs." They fled:

in crowds from the vanishing isle on the shoulders of Moanaliha [the ocean]: Ended is the line of the first chief of the dim past. Dead is the current sweeping in from the navel of the world. That was a warrior-wave. Many who came vanished, lost in the passing night. The swirling, shifting ocean climbed the mountains, sucked in and swallowed up life as it climbed higher and higher above the homes of the inhabitants. The swelling sea, the rising sea, the boisterous sea, it has enclosed us. O, the overwhelming billows in Kahiki! Finished is the world of Haiviki.[5]

Thereafter, the west, where Kahiki was overwhelmed, was known as He-ala-nui-o-ka-make, "the great road of death or the dying." The sunken motherland itself was renamed once more, as Kahiki-ho-nua-kele, "the divine homeland going down into the deep, blue sea."

In escaping this world-class cataclysm, Pele rescued her sacred crystal, the Pohaku-o-Kane, or "Stone of Kane," so called because it gave off a luminescence of the utmost spiritual power, known throughout Polynesia as *mana*.

Landing on the island of Kauai, Pele excavated two subterranean places of worship, their entrances resembling the mouths of frogs. These animals were symbolic of rebirth, and therefore properly signified the Pohaku-o-Kane set up inside the Waikanaloa and Waikapalae sea caves. Both may still be visited, although the "Navel of Kane" was magically transfigured long ago into a large rock formation towering over its earlier position below, at the shore. Local legend repeats an old tradition that warns natives to persist in their veneration of the site, else all Kauai will follow Kahiki, where the Pohaku-o-Kane originated, to the bottom of the ocean.

Before the islanders' conversion to Christianity, every Hawaiian household featured a simulacrum, or model, of the Navel of Kane as the family altar, just as Catholics set up crucifixes in their homes. The conical or sometimes egg-shaped object could stand from 1 to 8 feet high, and was the domestic focus of spiritual life. During ceremonies, the stone was anointed with water in commemoration of the great flood from which it came, then covered with a piece of bark cloth to signify its safe arrival and continued worship in Hawaii.

After Pele set up the original Pohaku-o-Kane, she renamed the entire island after her birthplace, Ka-Piko-o-ka-Honua: the "Navel of the World." It was there that she had learned the secrets of mana from Ha-Mu-ka, which were passed on to the pre-Polynesian islanders, the fair-haired Mu.

General resemblances between the Easter Island and Hawaiian versions are remarkable, suggesting both locations were recipients of a shared experience; namely, the arrival of some extraordinarily holy object revered as a repository for the most potent mana. Their parallels are not altogether unique, however.

Native Americans Remember the Deluge

Arizona's Pima Indians, the self-styled "River People," recount that their ancestors came from an island "at the center of the world," before it sank beneath the waves. Leading the relatively few survivors was the heroic progenitor of their tribe, a powerful medicine man. Pima elders still recall how "South Doctor held magic crystals in his left hand," as he guided them to their traditional living spaces between the Gilla and Salt Rivers.[6]

The neighboring Mohave Indians tell of sacred Mount Avikome, in the Pacific Ocean. Just below its summit stood the Dark House (in other words, the holy-of-holies) with four doors opening to the cardinal directions, defining its location at the middle of the world. Inside the Dark House was a mysterious object, the Hawlopo, given to the ancestral Mohave as a potent gift from God, and after which the entire island had been named (just as Easter Island was known as the Navel of the World after its sacred stone, the Navel of Light). But even the Hawlopo could not save them from being engulfed by a terrible deluge. As the waters rose, people climbed to the top of Mount Avikome, where the Hawlopo "became a pinnacle of rock in the midst of the stream."[7] There, it still protrudes above the surface of the sea as a tombstone marking the precise location of their lost homeland. The Yuma Indians know of a similar mountain, called Aviqame, from which their forefathers escaped in all directions to repopulate the world.

South of the Rio Grande, in Central Mexico, the Toltecs worshiped a powerful demigod, Tezcatlipoca, also known as Hurakan, from which our "hurricane" derives, because he arrived on the west coast of Mexico during a global cataclysm. Referred to as the Ocelotonatiuh, or "Jaguar Sun," it obliterated mankind's first of four worlds, or ages before the present time. Tezcatlipoca means "Smoking Mirror," after his magic crystal, which supposedly reflected the past, present, and future.

Remarkably, a similar myth was repeated a thousand miles away in Peru, with the story of Pachacutec, legendary founder of the Inca Empire. He too was named after his most precious possession, the "Transformer of the World," a prognosticating crystal that revealed the destiny of his imperial lineage. The sacred object was a family heirloom handed down over generations from Kon-Tiki-Viracocha, or "Sea Foam," the red-haired culture-bearer from a terrific flood who appeared at Lake Titicaca, where he established the Andean civilization. Pachacutec's crystal Transformer of the World was lost when the Incas were overthrown by Francisco Pizarro and his Spanish Conquistadors, but its former existence is suggested by a surviving pair of carved crystal condors—emblems of Inca royalty—still displayed at Lima's Museo Arqueológico.

The Enclosure of Gold

Near Lake Titicaca, where Kon-Tiki-Viracocha was said to have arrived with his own Transformer of the World after the Great Deluge, sprawls one of South America's most important archaeological sites: Tiahuanaco. Tiahuanaco is a pre-Inca ceremonial center of spacious plazas, broad staircases, towering statuary, and monumental gates. These larger-than-life-size figures memorialize the race of giants who built Tiahuanaco "in a single night after the Flood," according to a native Bolivian oral tradition recorded by the 16th century Spanish chronicler Pedro de Cieza de Leon.[8] They were led, he was told, by Ayar Cachi, who landed on the Peruvian coast after their homeland, Pacaritambo (described as a Huagaiusa, or "Holy City") was engulfed by the sea. Among his first orders of business was the construction of a memorial, known as the Pacarina, or "Hill of Appearance," to their lost "Origin Place." Once this was accomplished, he relocated to a cave on a mountain christened after his own familiar name, Huanacauri, or "Rainbow," symbolic of the Deluge, the cause of his coming. At its summit, he set up a *huaca*, or sacred structure.

"After this monumental oracle, from which all Inca history was to follow," writes archaeologist Henry Brundage, "Ayar

The Incas' former "Navel of the World," at Cuzco, Peru, is not unlike the stone "sarcophagus" in the King's Chamber of Egypt's Great Pyramid.

A Catholic cathedral superimposed on a surviving wall of the Coricancha, the "Enclosure of Gold," location of the Incas' "Navel of the World."

Cachi was transformed into a rude stone, perhaps the most holy, single object in Inca ritual."[9] This was the Paypicala—the "Stone-in-the-Middle," "Bellybutton," "Transformer of the World," or "Navel," the original name for Isola del Sol, the "Isle of the Sun," in Lake Titicaca. The Paypicala was enshrined in an ornate temple, which fell into ruin centuries before it was shown to Cieza de Leon. "When the Indians of the district are asked who made the ancient monument," he reported, "they reply that they were made by other peoples, bearded and white like ourselves, who came to that region and settled there many ages before the reign of the Incas."[10] In time, the leader of the local Indians "entered the larger of the two islands in Lake Titicaca [the smaller is Isola del Luna, the "Island of the Moon," where a lesser lunar goddess was worshipped], and found there a race of white people with beards, and fought with them until he had killed them all."[11]

About 3,000 years ago, Lake Titicaca began to dry up, or some seismic event more suddenly withdrew Titicaca's shores to their present 12 miles from Tiahuanaco. In either case, the Paypicala was moved

again, this time to Cuzco, literally, the "Navel of the World," and installed at the center of a Maltese Cross design marking the convergence of the four cardinal directions. It was housed in the Incas' most "Holy Place," the Huacapata, surrounded by a larger structure, the Coricancha, or "The Enclosure of Gold," also known as the Inticancha, "The Enclosure of the Sun." A priestess alone inside the Huacapata would enter into a deep trance-state, allowing her consciousness to resonate with energy given off by the "power stone," thereby channeling the gods for oracular advice. Before assuming her role as the Sarpay, the Paypicala's sybil, she had been selected for her outstanding psychic gifts from members of the Accla Cuna, the "Little Mothers," a mystery cult composed exclusively of the Inca Empire's most beautiful, virtuous, and intelligent women.

The Land of Perfection

On the other side of the Pacific, *punamu*, literally, the "stone from Mu," or "green stone," was highly prized by the New Zealand Maoris for its association with the sea that overwhelmed their ancestral homeland. A slight variant, *pounamu*, was another "green stone" mythically associated with the Waitahanui folk, members of New Zealand's oldest known tribe, renowned as prodigious mariners who navigated the world in oceangoing sailing ships, and who raised colossal stone structures across the island. Also known as the Waitaha, or Urukehu, the "People of the West" were fair-skinned, hazel-eyed redheads, who came from a splendid kingdom obliterated by a natural catastrophe. Although the Waitahanui long ago dominated all of New Zealand, only 140 mixed descendants were still alive by 1988.

In neighboring Australia, the aboriginal people still speak of the "Land of Mystery," or the "Land of Perfection," a huge city surrounded by four walls, their exterior covered entirely in white quartz. The Land of Mystery was supposedly mountainous, volcanic, and luxuriant in plant growth, among which stood massive buildings of domes and spires. Entrance to the gleaming metropolis was flanked by a pair of cone-shaped crystals 200 feet high and 600 feet across at the base. Each was coiled round by the colossal representation of a great serpent. But one day, a great storm "raised the water of the ocean with tremendous force, and drove it through the wall of the Land of Perfection."[12] This tradition is all the more remarkable for a preliterate people supposedly unacquainted with cities or architecture until 18th century contacts with modern Europeans.

In China, it is said in the *Chou-li*, an ancient book of rites, that Mu Kung ruled the world at the beginning of time from an antediluvian realm far to the east and over the sea. Chien-Mu was the name of his golden palace located beside the Lake of Gems, where Earth and sky met at the *axis mundi*. Later, this earthly midpoint shifted toward the west, when the lake overflowed, drowning his kingdom, from which he carried the jewels to China's Kunlun Mountains. Mu Kung's relocation was recognized even in Japan, where the oldest known name for China was Chugoku, the "Navel of the World."

In Japanese myth, the dragon-king Sagara dwelt on the ocean floor amid the ghostly ruins of a former kingdom, from which he obtained a huge, translucent pearl with the power to cause floods akin to those that long ago destroyed the sunken realm. This was the Chintamani, the "Jewel That Grants All Desires." Later renditions of a much older version tell how an abbot from northeastern India who called himself "Buddha's Vow" went in search of the Chintamani "for the good of all sentient beings." He outfitted a sailing expedition, which, after many months, took him to the very midpoint of the ocean. There, the abbot used his psychic powers to summon the dragon-king from the sea bottom, and bound him with a powerful spell. "By the power of my own name, I will release you," he promised, "but only after you have given me the Chintamani."[13] Unable to escape, Sagara removed the Jewel That Grants All Desires from his forehead, and was in the process of surrendering it when the priest grasped for the pearl with his hand, inadvertently breaking the enchantment. Thus freed, the dragon immediately replaced the Chintamani in its forehead, and sank the ship with all aboard, save the abbot. He was eventually cast ashore on the eastern coast of Honsu, where he introduced Buddhism to Japan. Sagara had long since returned to the undersea ruins with his precious stone still in place.

Key elements in this Japanese myth are found among related tales often separated by many thousands of miles and cultures utterly unknown to each other: The Chintamani originated in a former kingdom, since sunk in the middle of the ocean. Sagara wears this Jewel That Grants All Desires at the center of his forehead, corresponding to Buddhist concepts of the brow chakra, or sixth wheel of psychic energy associated with spiritual perception in the Third Eye. Throughout Asia, dragons have always been symbols for Earth-energy, a revealing significance that will become more apparent as the crystal is traced to other parts of the world.

❧❦☙

Another pre-Buddhist myth upon which the story of Sagara was based related that his pearl arrived in Japan after all: Known as the Kaname-ishi, a facsimile of the original is still revered at Kashima-Jingu, perhaps the country's oldest shrine, just outside Tokyo on the Honsu coast, where the god Kashima Daimyojin is said to have landed with the "Keystone" (also referred to as the "Bellybutton Stone," or "Navel Stone") after a great flood annihilated his homeland in the sea. Kashima Daimyojin is portrayed in a wood-block print riding the back of an oversized catfish pressing the Kaname-ishi to its head, while around him a city is going up in flames. Although this illustration ostensibly commemorated a mid-19th century natural disaster that devastated Tokyo (then known as Edo), it was actually meant to compare 1855's terrible earthquake with the ancient destruction of a Pacific Ocean kingdom where the Keystone originated. It was pressed to the giant catfish's brow in Kashima Daimyojin's belated attempt, as

depicted by the wood-print, to stop the monster from moving.

In early Japanese myth, earthquakes and floods were caused by a dragon dwelling at the bottom of the ocean. Later versions first merged, and then replaced the dragon with a catfish. Indeed, traditional representations of the Japanese islands commonly portrayed them surrounded by a dragon, which was often identified in accompanying texts as a catfish (*namazu*). The Kaname-ishi was said to have the power to prevent earthquakes, although the replica displayed today is nothing more than a round, 2-foot-long stone with a 6-inch hole in the center. Even so, the one-time importance of its location is evident in Kashima's former status as the "Navel of Nippon [Japan]."

The Kaname-ishi, or "Navel Stone," at Nara, Japan.

That standing was later transferred to Japan's oldest city, when the original Keystone and a bronze mirror were sent from the Kashima-Jingu shrine. The relics were worshiped at Nara, once the capital of Japan, in the Todai-ji monastery, where a representation of pre-Buddhist cosmogony was observed by a visiting British antiquarian, J.S. Blackett, in the late 19th century. In the monastery's Daibutsu-den, or Great Buddha Hall's holy-of-holies, he was shown a nest-egg floating in a vat of seawater. "The entire world," it was explained to him, "at the time of Chaos, was shut up in this egg, which floated upon the surface of the waters."[14] According to the abbot, the egg was a symbol of the Kaname-ishi and its origins, as depicted on the back of the mirror, etched with an illustration of Mount Meru, a sacred mountain at the center of the world where religion was born and itself symbolic of the Sacred Center found in the practice of perfect meditation. The etching portrayed Mount Meru as an island in the middle of the ocean with the small figure of a man in a boat floating nearby. The abbot told Blackett that this image represented the *numen*, or spirit of Mount Meru, and was known as the "Fisherman of Light." The scene had been engraved on a mirror—the universal symbol of truth—to affirm its verity.

The British encyclopedist J.C. Cooper refers to Mount Meru as "the world axis," also known in India as Devaparvata, the "Mountain of the Gods." Among them was Agni, the divinity of fire, whose title is Nabhir Agnih prthivyah, the "Navel of the World."

The Kaname-ishi egg, Kashima Daimyojin's Pacific homeland overwhelmed by earthquake and flood, Mount Meru, its Fisherman of Light, and Kashima's ancient recognition as the Navel of Nippon are apparent Japanese reflections of Easter Island's Te-pito-te-henua, Te-pito-te-Kura, Mutu Nui egg-hunt, and watery destruction of Marae Renga. These otherwise uncanny similarities resulted from a common experience of Japanese and Easter Islanders; namely, the arrival of survivors bearing a "power stone" from their civilization after it was destroyed by some natural catastrophe. So many cogent correspondences make a mockery of so-called cultural coincidences.

The Treasure of the World

Although the sacred object was known in Japan as the Keystone or Chintamani, the latter name is actually Sanskrit for "magical stone of another world," and reappears in the oral traditions of India, China, Burma, and Tibet. It was here that one of the foremost personalities of the 20th century came in search of the legendary crystal. When he set out to find it in 1923, 49-year-old Nikolay Konstantinovich Roerich was already known around the world as the Russian Leonardo DaVinci, although he was of Scandinavian origins (his father moved with a Russian bride from Latvia to Saint Petersburg where Nikolay was born in 1874). Family roots could be traced as far back as Viking Sweden, and a 13th century ancestor was once leader of the Knights Templar.

In 1913, while assisting in the construction of Russia's first Buddhist temple, in Saint Petersburg, he found special favor with Agvan Dordgiev, the lama supervising the project. Dordgiev observed that the Russian artist, in addition to his elevated grasp of the esoteric core within all religions, emanated the same kind of calm sanctity otherwise found only among the most adept ascetics. He therefore confided a piece of occult knowledge never before revealed to any other European: the secret whereabouts of the Chintamani stone, last seen in the late 18th century by Abdul al-Hazred, an Arab scholar. In his manuscript, the *Kitab al-Azif*, al-Hazred described the Chintamani as "a key to all futures and everyone's destiny, capable of giving telepathic inner guidance, and effecting a transformation of consciousness to those in contact with it."[15]

With humanity on the verge of its first World War, the time had come, and Roerich was the man to bring the fabled crystal out of hiding and put its supposed powers at the disposal of a mankind committed to self-destruction. However, the lama was not even sure it actually existed, and explained that the object may have been only a Buddhist metaphor for spiritual perfection. Nor was he certain of its exact location. But if the Chintamani was real after all, the moment for its application could not be more appropriate. He said it was "in the King's Tower, at the center of Shambhala," an allegedly inaccessible realm somewhere high in the Himalayan Mountains.[16] The name in Sanskrit, "Place of Tranquility," describes its inhabitants' dedication to the Kalachakra, the highest and most esoteric branch of Tibetan mysticism.

No one since Abdul al-Hazred, more than 100 years before, had supposedly visited Shambhala, which most scholars considered to be entirely mythical. Roerich's contemporary, Polish scientist Ferdinand Ossendowski, spent years among the Himalayas during a fruitless search for the elusive Place of Tranquility. Although he never found the Chintamani, he heard many references to it throughout his extensive travels among native sherpas and Shamans as the "Shining Trapezohedron," a solid figure made up entirely of trapeziums, or planes with four sides, no two of which are parallel—in other words, a crystalline formation.

In Ossendowski's 1922 book *Beasts, Men and Gods*, he describes an encounter with Chultun Beyli, the Tibetan prince who claimed to have once visited the "Shining Trapezohedron," which allowed him a simultaneous glimpse of both past and future. He then spoke of a prophesy known to other initiates for countless generations: "Materialism will devastate the Earth, terrible battles will engulf the nations of the world, and at the climax of the bloodshed, in 2029, the people of Agharta will rise out of their cavern world."[17] As was Shambhala, Agharta was a quasi-mythical kingdom, half-believed to actually exist, but, as mentioned, more metaphorical for the underworld of the dead. As such, its appearance in the old prophesy repeated by Prince Beyli is allegorical for a return of the old wisdom. Ironically, the Mayan calendar's more famous prophesy likewise forecast the end of the "Fifth Sun," our present age, with the start of a global upheaval. Known as Four Ollin, literally, a "Rebellion of the Earth," it too is scheduled to occur during the early 21st century; more precisely, winter solstice, 2012.

In 1923, Nikolay Roerich finally set out for Shambhala and its Shining Trapezohedron. His quest had been postponed for 10 years due to the war and its revolutionary aftermath, which the

Chintamani was supposed to have prevented. During the next six years, he led his followers for 15,500 miles across the Gobi Desert, over Tibet and Xinjiang, and through 35 of the world's highest passes in the Altai mountain range. Beset by natural hazards at every turn, harassed by hostile tribes, his porters succumbing to avalanches and blizzards, the expedition would have been a physical ordeal for any man younger than his 49 years. The undertaking was attempted at a time when ground-positioning radar, medevac helicopters, mylar ropes, and kevlar jackets—much less portable radios—were unknown. Worse, Roerich had no idea where he was going, how long his search would take, or even if the place and object of his mission were real. Everywhere the mad Russian inquired about Shambhala and the Chintamani stone he was told neither existed, or that they could not be found, least of all by a heathen foreigner such as himself. Sometimes he was given directions, but they were invariably wrong and intended to mislead him.

Early in 1928, a tired Nikolay Roerich, now aged beyond his mid-50s, heard a traditional Tibetan story that at once enlightened and depressed him. It told of a man who, after crossing many mountains, found rest and shelter in the cave of an elderly hermit. "Where are you going across these wastes of snow?" the hermit asked his guest. "To find Shambhala," the younger man replied. "Ah, well then, you need not travel far," the hermit said. "The kingdom of Shambhala is in your own heart."[18]

With that, Roerich knew at once that utopian tales describing the Place of Tranquility referred only to the inner perfection achieved through constant meditation and practice of the Kalachakra. Rather than vent feelings of frustration and disappointment, however, he expressed his sincere gratitude to the many native people who had aided him, even to those who had hindered him, because they all helped to awaken the higher nature within himself. Overhearing his words, a simple monk told him he was now worthy of going to Shambhala, and gave him specific directions!

When Roerich arrived a few weeks later at the Trasilumpo lamasery, he was surprised to see a tall structure at its very center. Was this the "King's Tower" of Shambhala? His question was answered when the abbot, who knew all about Roerich, unceremoniously presented him with the Chintamani, as though he had been waiting all along for the opportunity. Repeating a version of the ancient Chinese account, the abbot stated that Mu Kung brought the sacred crystal with him long ago when he fled to Tibet after his golden palace at the island of Chien-Mu was overwhelmed in the Eastern Sea. The object was thereafter broken into pieces: One was sent from Tibet to Jerusalem, where King Solomon fashioned it into a ring. Centuries later, Mohammed received three other fragments, which he placed into the Ka'bah, Islam's most sacred shrine, at Mecca—both Jerusalem and Mecca have each been known as the Navel of the World for centuries.

Finally able to personally examine the Shining Trapezohedron, Roerich guessed it was a form of moldavite, a magnetic mineral said to be a spiritual accelerator. The name derives from the Moldau River Valley, in Moldavia (today's Czech Republic), where the gem is most commonly found. Iron content causes its moss-green color, reminiscent of the punamu, New Zealand's own green stone cited earlier. Composed mainly of silicon dioxide, it is, in fact, a kind of crystal with a five-to-six rating on the MOH scale of 10 (Friedrich Mohs' scale of hardness in precious and semiprecious stones), making it relatively easy to cut and shape. Traditionally, moldavite is associated with high vibrational energy, and generally regarded as a powerful "chakra opener," particularly of the fourth, or heart chakra, whose chief quality is compassion.

"Lapis Exilis, thus is named the stone," the abbot said, "which is mentioned by the old Meistersingers. One sees that the West and the East are working together on many principles."[19] Interestingly, Lapis Exilis, the "Stone of Exile," is how the 13th century German writer Wolfram von Eschenbach described the Holy Grail in his medieval epic, *Parzifal.* Indeed, Roerich noticed that the exterior of the Chintamani was etched with a faint inscription in Sanskrit that read, "I bring the chalice. Within it I bring a treasure." In fact, the stone was known as the "Treasure of the World," the Mongolian version of Navel of the World.[20]

The abbot went on to explain that it was charged with currents of an amoral psychic force known as *shugs,* which could be used for good or evil purposes, depending upon the intent of anyone coming into close contact with it. That was why this Shining Trapezohedron had been hidden for so long. It must only be entrusted to a selfless, compassionate person intent on establishing harmony in the world during a time of global crisis. In the wrong hands, the Chintamani would become the ultimate weapon, with catastrophic consequences for all mankind.

"Only know how to use it," the abbot admonished Roerich, "and how not to misuse it. Do you in the West know something about the Great Stone in which magic powers [shugs] are concentrated?"

To Roerich, it resembled "an electrical accumulator, and may give back, in one way or another, the energy stored within it. For instance, it will increase the spiritual vitality of anyone who touches it, infusing him with knowledge, or enhancing psychic abilities."[21] The 5-inch long oblate gem had been presented to him on a carrying pillow and concealed beneath a veil he was instructed never to remove under anything but important circumstances. His wife, Helena Ivanova, wrote that the Shining Trapezohedron possessed a somber luster, "like a dark heart." Both she and her husband observed that it was "all of one piece," although it appeared to have been somewhat carved or modified, and showed no sign of having been fragmented in any way, contradicting accounts of sections broken off some larger original to be parceled out to Solomon, Mohammed, and other historical worthies.[22]

With the Chintamani at last in his possession, Roerich returned to the west, where he immediately got to work. He was instrumental in transforming the League of Nations, originally established in 1919 as a post-World War I victors' club set up to preserve their imperialistic status quo by keeping Germany in perpetual servitude, while divvying up Asian, African, Pacific, Indian, Caribbean, and Central American colonies among the Allies. At his behest, its headquarters were transferred from one-sided Paris to nonbelligerent Geneva, where wartime neutrals and former enemies were no longer excluded, and the League's chief thrust was changed from institutionalized revenge and exploitation against a vanquished foe to international cooperation and "the self-determination of peoples."[23] Its more elevated purpose was referred to as a covenant between humanity and world leaders. A concrete step toward that accord, the Roerich Peace Pact obligated governments at war to respect museums, cathedrals, universities, libraries, and other cultural sites as they did hospitals, and was signed by President Franklin D. Roosevelt in 1935. Just 10 years later, the Pact was included in the United Nations' organizational charter.

But the influence of neither a Russian DaVinci nor an old stone from Tibet could ameliorate the animosity between governments. The U.S. Congress declared American participation in the League unconstitutional, while Britain refused to compromise its empire, and France rearmed against Germany. Mussolini, condemned for his invasion of Ethiopia, withdrew Italy from the League, which Hitler abhorred and Japan ignored in its conquest of China. The Soviet Union, because of its Communist regime, had been excluded altogether from the League. Roerich was forced to admit that his efforts on behalf of international harmony had failed.

As civilization split into contending Allied and Axis halves, Prince Chultun Beyli's prophesy of mutual destruction was about to be fulfilled. Roerich initially resolved to find the Shining Trapezohedron just before World War I. Now, on the eve of another global conflagration, he had it returned to the Trasilumpo lamasery. In gratitude for his noble, if futile attempt, the abbot gave Roerich another Chintamani, confirming Roerich's earlier conclusion that there were several such stones, not just fragments that had been broken off from a single, original object.

With Roerich's death just two years after the conclusion of the war he hoped to prevent, his personal Chintamani was donated to the Moscow Museum. There,

visitors may still admire this exceptionally clear quartz crystal, unlike the inscribed, moldavite trapezohedron it took him six years and 15,500 miles to find. Meanwhile, the 13th Dalai Lama decreed that all such stones must never again be allowed to leave Tibet, where they were hidden once more in separate, secret places for safekeeping, although one somehow escaped to the Museum of Natural History, in Manhattan.

The Motherland of the Stone

The remarkable consistency of evidence surrounding Chintamani-esque stones from Tibet to Bolivia, from New Zealand to the American Southwest, describes their origins in a great civilization that dominated the Pacific World before it was obliterated by a natural catastrophe during the remote past. As its physical remains are still being discovered in the waters off Japan and Taiwan, a timeframe for this destructive event is simultaneously beginning to emerge. According to oceanographic understanding of sea level rise, the ruins at Yonaguni's Iseki Point last stood on dry land some 12,000 years ago. At that time, a deluge caused by glacial melt-off inundated them during the global warming that drastically elevated sea levels and ended our planet's last ice age.

Although mainstream scholars refuse to consider any possibility for an early human civilization outside the narrow limits of the Near East in the early 4th millennium B.C., they are contradicted by a growing abundance of disaffirming physical and oral source materials. These proofs describe the lost civilization as the motherland, Mu, or Lemuria; less an actual continent, it would seem, than a people and culture spread across the central Pacific on numerous islands and archipelagoes, some of which were either drowned by rising sea levels, or swept clean of all human habitation by monstrous tsunamis, similar to the one that killed nearly a third of a million people throughout the Indian Ocean in December of 2004. Others survived; their high peaks still stand above sea level as the islands of Polynesia and Micronesia.

At some point in their cultural development, the Lemurians cut specific gems, most often crystals or crystalline minerals, as centerpieces for a spiritual discipline that much later melded with the religious views and practices of other peoples influ-

The Lemurian Motherland overwhelmed by a Great Flood, as depicted in this mural at Thailand's sacred ceremonial center, the Wat Phra Keo, Bangkok.

enced by survivors of the Deluge. It is largely through the flood accounts of such host races that the character and fate of these stones are described. Native sagas depict the objects as more than symbols: They are active components functioning in a cult of psychic empowerment, with emphasis on spiritual rebirth, as emphasized in stylistic concentration on the womb. These enduring traditions stress that certain crystals interacted with human consciousness to generate altered states of awareness, awakening innate but otherwise dormant psychic abilities for extraordinary paranormal empowerment.

In the beginning, the holy stones stood at the center of their homeland: Easter Island's Marae Renga; the Hawaiian Muri-wai-hou and Honua-mea; the Mohave Indians' Mount Avikome; the Incas' Pacaritambo; the Australian Aborigines' "Land of Perfection"; the sunken realm of Japan's dragon-king; China's Chien-Mu, and so on—all overwhelmed by a great flood. The lost motherland is invariably remembered as a place of high wisdom, where sorcerers, magicians, *kahuna*, or priests were skilled at applying spiritual forces on a scale never surpassed in our post-Deluge world. These powers arose when the adepts interfaced with an outstanding stone, most often a crystal or gem, usually green. Personifying the regeneration cult it also symbolized, their sacred stone was associated with, and sometimes assumed the physical attributes of the cosmic egg of eternal rebirth—as in the annual race from the shores of Easter Island to Mutu Nui, that offshore simulacrum of the lost motherland to retrieve the first egg of spring; Hawaii's Pohaku-o-Kane; the five eggs of the Andes' Mount Condorcoto; Tibet's ovoid Chintamani, and so on. Often it is described as luminous and radiating with power: Easter Island's Navel of Light and the Hawaiian Navel of Kane; the gleaming mirrors of Mexico's Tezcatlipoca; Peru's Pachacutec; Japan's Daibutsu-den with its Fisherman of Light; the Tibetan Shining Trapezohedron; and so on. The radiant *omphalos*, or "navel stone," was surrounded by a golden enclosure, such as Cuzco's Coricancha, or Mu Kung's gilt palace. Sometimes it is associated with geologic upheaval: the seismic destruction of Marae Renga from which the Te-pito-te-Kura was carried to Easter Island, the Incas' Transformer of the World, or the Japanese Bellybutton Stone used by Kashima Daimyojin to suppress earthquake-causing catfish.

The universality, to say nothing of the uniformity of these traditions, can only be explained by the existence of some cult-objects that long ago made indelible impressions on various cultures that came into contact with Navel-of-the-World missionaries or survivors from the

Recreation of tablets from the Pacific civilization of Lemuria displayed at the Mu Museum, Kagoshima prefecture, Japan.

Lemurian catastrophe. Nothing else can satisfactorily account for repetition of the same, fundamental story in so many common details shared by numerous peoples often separated or isolated by centuries or even millennia and many thousands of miles, far beyond the opposite ends of the broad Pacific—from the civilized Incas to New Zealand's primitive Maori; from the tribal natives of Arizona to Tibetan lamas. Taken all together, they form a portrait of the lost motherland and her sacred stones supported by impressive archaeological evidence.

The power-crystals of the Pima Indians and Incas vanished with the arrival of modern Europeans in the Americas. But Japan's Kaname-ishi has its shrines at Kashima-Jingu and Nara's Todai-ji monastery; Easter Island's Navel of Light is still part of its own ceremonial platform; and alleged variants of the Chintamani are owned by at least two public museums in the United States and Russia. Tibetan tradition states that others went to Mecca and, centuries before, Jerusalem. Much earlier, however, another sacred stone supposedly traveled halfway around the Earth to Lemuria's successor as the next Navel of the World.

Atlantis, Navel of
the World

The story is a strange one, but Solon, the wisest of the seven wise men, once vouched its truth.

—Plato, the *Timaeus*

The Chintamani stone Nicholay Roerich brought back from his five-year quest for Shambhala was, as he learned, one of several such mystical gems carried to the outside world from their place of origin. A cataclysmic event not unlike, but far more potent than 2004's Indonesian tsunami or Hurricane Katrina the following year, overwhelmed the Pacific motherland, scattering her survivors and their Shining Trapezohedrons far and wide. Among the distant places of refuge they found was Atlantis, according to the curator of New York City's Roerich Museum, Josephine Saint-Hilair, a scholar of ancient Asian chronicles. According to her research, a "power crystal" was presented by Lemurian refugees at the palace of Tazlavoo, an early Atlantean emperor, of whom nothing else is known. More, however, may be said for his empire, thanks to one of the most influential minds of all time, who left us a rich, credible description of Atlantis before she too succumbed to the violent temper of our planet: Plato.

While formulating those principles that would become the basis of Western thought, Plato composed a strange narrative of cultural splendor, imperial ambition, and international war brought to its climax on the waves of a post-Lemurian catastrophe. The account was not some atypical digression from his philosophical work, but rather designed to support it with historical allegory; namely, the stages of decadence and self-destruction even the most powerful society suffers when its citizens stray from the originally virtuous principles that created it and sustained its existence. Plato had not inexplicably discarded his philosopher's crown for a historian's cap, but intended to dramatize his ethics by way of a cogent comparison from the ancient past. Atlantis was not his ideal utopia, as skeptics insist, but quite the opposite—the example of a formerly healthy kingdom gone horribly wrong. As such, he attempted to demonstrate the cycle of birth, growth, maturity, decline, and death endemic to every people, and how his fellow Athenians might break this circumscribed pattern.

Plato's predecessor, Herodotus, stated that Atlantis lay near the southern slopes of Mount Atlas, from which the city derived its name: "Daughter of Atlas," located "beyond the Pillars of Heracles."[1] This was the Classical world's definition of the Strait of Gibraltar, separating the western Mediterranean Sea from the Atlantic Ocean, itself named after Atlantis.

Writing in the mid-4th century B.C., Plato did not provide its specific location. But the direct control he stated the Atlanteans exerted over Spain and Libya necessitated their relatively close proximity to Iberia and North Africa. This conclusion is seconded in the *Kritias*,[2] where the Atlantean cataclysm is cited as "the source of the impenetrable mud which prevents the free passage of those who sail out of the straits into the open sea." A geologic aftermath immense enough to close off the western Mediterranean could not have been too far "beyond the Pillars of Heracles." Current marine-floor surveys of the eastern Atlantic undertaken by Scripps Oceanographic scientists in La Jolla, California, have in fact located at least a dozen sunken, formerly dry-land mountains, any one of which may be the original Mt. Atlas, within a 250-mile range west of Gibraltar.

According to the *Timaeus*,[3] the island was "larger than Libya and Asia combined," leading some modern readers to conclude that Atlantis was an immense continent. After more than 50 years of sea-bottom profiling, however, oceanographers have found no trace of any "lost continent" at the bottom of the Atlantic Ocean, whose floor, in any case, is too weak to have ever supported such an extensive land mass. Moreover, a geologic event potent enough to sink an entire continent "in a day and a night," as Plato described, would have obliterated the entire planet. On the other hand, islands—some of considerable size—*have* been known to collapse into the sea, sometimes in the midst of terrific violence during very brief periods of time, such as the late 19th century eruption of Krakatoa in Indonesia, or Surtsey in the Atlantic, as recently as 1963.

More to the point, the Libya and Asia that Plato knew are not the same territories familiar to the modern world. In his day, 2,400 years ago, Libya was a thin strip of Mediterranean land along the North African coast stretching from Egypt in the east to the Numidian frontier with Mauretania (the Algerian–Moroccan border) in the west. During Classical times, Asia did not comprise China and Japan, but signified only the west coast of Asia Minor, today's Turkey. Combined, these areas do not constitute a continent, but very roughly define a sizeable island perhaps as great as Tenerife, largest of the Canary Islands, off the Atlantic coast of North Africa. Plato, in fact, describes Atlantis as a *nesos*, Greek for "island," and distinguished it from anything continental. In the *Timaeus*,[4] he stated that the Atlantean kings "ruled the whole island, and many other islands as well, and parts of the continent" on the other side of the ocean: America?

His succinct history of Atlantis was actually a Greek version of Egyptian documents preserved at Sais, a Nile Delta city ancient even by Egyptian standards. The sacred documents were read to Solon, the famous law-giver, who was visiting Sais while the social reforms and legal code he introduced back home were still being hotly debated by his fellow Athenians. Psonchis, the chief priest, translated the text inscribed in hieroglyphs from a pillar at the Temple of Neith. That sacred edifice was an appropriate repository for the account, because Neith was an early dynastic goddess who had caused the Great Flood.

Returning to Athens, Solon worked all the details of the narrative into an epic poem, *Atlantikos*, substituting Greek equivalents for Egyptian names and numerical values. The "Etelenty" described by Psonchis became "Atlantis," and Egyptian *aroura*s were converted into Greek *stadia*, but Solon was as true to the original text as possible. Unfortunately, he was distracted from completing the project by political problems prior to his death in 560 B.C. The unfinished manuscript was passed on to Plato, who reworked it into a pair of dialogues: the *Timaeus,* composed circa 365 B.C., and the *Kritias,* about 10 years later.

Plato's Atlantis

Exceptionally tall and beautiful mountains, he wrote, surrounded the island of Atlantis, which was thickly forested and populated with many kinds of animals, including elephants.

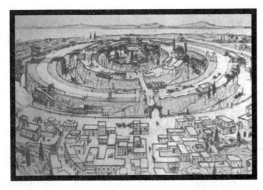

An artist's rendition of Atlantis strictly based on Plato's description of the imperial city. From Unser Ahnen und die Atlanten *(Our Ancestors and the Atlanteans), by Albert Herrmann, 1934.*

Mention of this creature was long used to fault the *Kritias* by skeptics, who pointed out that the existence of elephants on an Atlantic island was impossible. But in 1967, dredgers began hauling up enormous quantities of pachyderm bones from the ocean bottom at more than 40 different sites along the Azores–Gibraltar Ridge, between 200 and 300 miles off the Portuguese coast. Today, oceanographic evidence indicates that the now-underwater ridge was once a land bridge over which elephants migrated from North Africa into the near-Atlantic. Plato, of course, knew nothing of the Azores–Gibraltar Ridge, and could have only written about such animals in Atlantis from an original source—among the strongest arguments against his account became one of its most persuasive proofs.

Over successive generations, the city became a metropolis that outstripped in splendor anything comparable in the ancient world. It was also unlike contemporary urban or ceremonial centers anywhere else on Earth before or since. A god looking down from heaven on this "Daughter of Atlas" would have beheld it laid out beneath him similar to an immense target of concentric circles. These were alternating rings of land and water, artificial islands formed by surrounding moats, and interconnected by several 500-foot-wide bridges leading from the smallest, central island to three harbors constantly filled with warships, freighters, merchantmen, passenger vessels, and smaller craft of all kinds from three continents. A channel 300 feet wide, 100 feet deep and nearly 6 miles long joined the outermost land-ring to the shore, "thus making it accessible from the sea like a harbor." Its entrance was, as Plato put it, "large enough to admit the biggest ships."[5]

A 4th century Greek vase portrays the Daughter of Atlas between Poseidon, sea-god creator of Atlantis, and Hermes, divine patron of the Navel of the World mystery cult.

The great canal and its harbors were protected by a monumental wall fronting the sea somewhat less than 6 miles from the outermost land-ring, which it entirely surrounded. At its base, both sides were densely crowded with contiguous villages of small houses and shops, forming public areas where noisy commerce went on day and night. To dispel any impression of monotonous uniformity, all buildings were made with the kinds of construction materials most plentiful on any volcanic island; namely, red tufa, white pumice, and black lava, which the residents combined and recombined into imaginative designs. The defensive wall itself was interspersed with formidable watchtowers and gateways continuously manned by rotating companies of armed sentinels.

Visitors allowed to pass through would have crossed a bridge adorned on either side with colossal statuary, and spanning a 1,821-foot wide moat to the first land-ring. It too was protected by a high, stone wall sheeted in great panels of burnished bronze. The land-ring it guarded was open to members of the general public, who were invited to stroll among its numerous gardens, ogle the opulent mansions of the very wealthy, make offerings in the numerous temples, listen to poetry and musical competitions, applaud athletic contests at the gymnasia, and, most popular and ceremoniously exciting of all, cheer horses and their riders at the world's longest racetrack that went straight around the entire land-ring.

Access over the next moat was restricted. It surrounded the innermost of the ring-shaped islands fronted by its own high wall gleaming with sheets of a polished alloy Plato referred to as "tin" for lack of any comparable metal known to him. The area was given over entirely to the military, with headquarters for navy and army commanders, plus barracks, training fields, and parade grounds for elite guards. A wall encircling the central island blazed with orichalcum, exceptionally high-grade copper, an important contribution to the Atlanteans' wealth and on which they imposed a jealous monopoly. The 1.33-mile-wide "acropolis," as Plato referred to it, featured the royal residence with gardens (including vineyards and hot and cold running water), in addition to barracks for the imperial guard.

Nearby reared the magnificent Temple of Poseidon, the foremost structure in all Atlantis, 300 feet wide, 750 feet long, and 100 feet high, its silver exterior contrasting with the golden statues of gods gazing down from the pediment. Inside, a colossus of the sea-god bearing his emblematic trident stood inside a chariot ornate with oceanic motifs and drawn by six winged horses, personifying waves. At 80 feet in height, the statue's bearded head brushed the temple's ivory roof, "picked out with gold, silver and orichalcum." During the day, dim light filtered only though its clerestory, imparting a milieu of divine presence on the already imposing atmosphere hazy with burning incense, and making the orichalcum-coated walls, pillars, and floor radiate with an unearthly glow. Surrounding the base of the godly figure were a hundred Nereids—representations of boys riding dolphins—while along the walls were statues of the original 10 Atlantean kings with their queens. "There was an altar of a size and workmanship," Plato writes, "to match that of the building."

Despite the temple's supreme grandeur, its spiritual power was eclipsed by a much smaller, humbler shrine—although it too had been dedicated to Poseidon—located at the precise center of the acropolis, and therefore the focal point for the whole civilization. This was a low hill where the powerful sea-god himself was believed to have appeared before a mortal woman, Kleito, who bore him five sets of twins, thus inaugurating the island's royal family. Plato apparently considered her mother worthy of mention, although he wrote nothing more of Leukippe, the "White Mare." She nonetheless figures prominently in many post-Atlantean Navels of the World.

The Tree of Life

Non-Platonic myth adds that an ancient oak, a form Atlas himself assumed, grew in the middle of his garden, where its apples of eternal life were tended by a serpent-dragon, Ladon, coiling around its bough, and Atlas' seven daughters by Hesperis, the Hesperides. Their leader was Hespera, whose "perpetual flame," according to the encyclopedists Martha Ann and

Dorothy Myers Imel, "embraces the centricity of the universe."[6] That "centricity" was reaffirmed by the sacred tree she helped guard with her sisters, themselves mythic personifications of the seven chakras, or "wheels," of energy connecting the physical and psychological natures of individual human existence in Kundalini yoga. Sanskrit for "serpent power," Kundalini is understood in Indian metaphysics as an internal force coiled up at the base of the human spine. As this energy is made to rise through each of the major chakras, it ultimately reaches the crown of the head, where heightened consciousness is achieved, regeneration activated, spirituality reborn, and innate psychic potential realized.

The Ceibra Tree, revered by the ancient Maya as the Tree of Life and associated by them with the Great Flood.

The concept is more easily recognized in the West in the Caduceus, a wand entwined with serpents ascending to a winged sun-disc (in other words, enlightenment), internationally known as a medical insignia, and symbolic of the tree in the garden of the Hesperides. Its bough is the human spinal column, the real "Tree of Life," its "golden apples" the "fruit" of spiritual illumination, and Ladon the "serpent energy" of Kundalini associated with the seven major chakras. Their embodiment in the Hesperides, Daughters of Atlas (and therefore "Atlantises") demonstrates the Atlantean origin of this deeply ancient concept. In *De immenso et innumerabili*.[7] Giordano Bruno, regarded by some as the father of modern science, equated the Caduceus with the rays of life and enlightenment eternally entering into the womb of Mother Earth. His understanding of the Caduceus is a succinct definition of Atlantean spirituality. The Caduceus was the Navel of the World's badge, its symbol of healing and regeneration. Still in use today, it has endured the passing of millennia as a common token of civilization itself. Although the countless millions of people familiar with it do not begin to suspect its ancient origins and significance, the Caduceus is nevertheless the Tree of Life personified, the emblem of Atlantean mystery religion.

Roger Cook, a published expert in the interpretation of archetypes, points out that:

> the image of the Cosmic Tree or Tree of Life belongs to a coherent body of myths, rites, images, and symbols which together make up what the historian of religion, Mircea Eliade, has called the 'symbolism of the Centre'—In the symbolic language of mythical religion, it is often referred to as the "Navel of the World," "Divine Egg," "Hidden Seed," or "Root of Roots,"

and is also imagined as a vertical axis, the "cosmic axis," or "Axis of the World."[8]

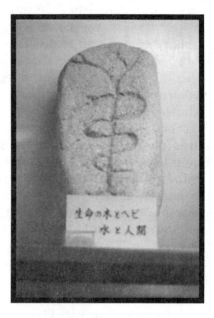

Representation of "serpent energy" (in other words, enhanced consciousness) ascending the Tree of Life, symbolic of the human spinal column, and epitomizing the Navel of the World mystery cult. Stone on display at the Mu Museum, Kagoshima prefecture, Japan.

The Tree of Life was not only a symbol for Atlantis itself and of its geopolitical position as the Navel of the World, but epitomized her mystery cult of the same name. This physical and metaphysical *axis mundi* is made clear in Plato's *Kritias*, which tells of offerings from all over the empire converging on the centrally located shrine where a mortal woman, Kleito, lay with Poseidon to produce five pairs of imperial twins. The hallowed ground was surrounded by a golden enclosure that forbade entry, save once every year, when a high priest administered to the holy-of-holies. Although Plato mentions no cultic stone, his description of Kleito's sacred precinct clearly defines it as a Navel of the World.

Homer was more specific. In the *Odyssey*,[9] he describes a sorceress living in a cave on an island in the Far West (the Atlantic Ocean), where she had the power to grant eternal life to mortal human beings. Her name, Calypso, derived from *kalybe*, the Greek word for cave. As a daughter of Atlas, she was an Atlantide, an identity underscored by her island, Ogygia, from Ogyges, a flood hero in Greek myth. Apparently, her island and Atlantis were one and the same. Ogyges, in fact, was regarded as the founder of the Eleusian Mysteries, a Greek version of the Navel of the World spirituality he carried to the Peloponnesus after the Deluge. The Atlantean connection is underscored by Homer's reference to Ogygia as the Umbilicus maris, or Omphalos thallasses, the "Navel of the Sea."

The oceanic location of Ogygia is reaffirmed by his fellow Greeks' designation of the North Atlantic as Kronios Pontus, the "Sea of Kronos," identically known to the Romans as Chronis Maris. Kronos was king of the titans, who ruled the world before the ascension of the Olympian gods. Forewarned that one of his 12 children would be his undoing, he devoured them all. His wife, Idaea, wrapped an oblate stone in swaddling clothes, and then presented it to her husband in the hope that he would mistake it for their infant son, Zeus. The deception succeeded, and Kronos quite literally swallowed the ruse. Zeus grew into a handsome youth, all the while concealing his true identity, and was eventually chosen as cup-bearer to his ignorant father. In this capacity, the lad was able to slip Kronos an emetic that made him regurgitate first Idaea's stone, followed by the remainder of his cannibalized progeny, who then made war on the titans,

overthrew them to establish the Olympian New Order, and Zeus himself set up the vomited stone, the Omphalos, at the center of the world, where it served as the foremost oracle.

Homer's allegorical tale of Kronos is a mythic rendering of Navel of the World origins in Atlantis, when it, as was Kronos' imprisonment at Ogyges, was a mountainous island in the Atlantic Ocean. The "golden cave" where he experiences altered states of conscious recalls Kleito's golden walled precinct at the center of Atlantis; the Incas' *Coricancha*, the "Golden Enclosure" at their own Navel of the World in Cuzco; the Chinese Mu Kung's golden wall surrounding his Lake of Gems, and so on.

After the Hesperides, Atlas sired another septuplate of daughters, the Hyades.

The Hyades correspond to the seven major energy-centers duplicated by their sisters, the Hesperides. Pytho is the psycho-spiritual "serpent power" coiled at the base of the human spine in the root chakra; Tyche, or "good fortune," exemplifies the pleasure principle of the sacral chakra; Plexaris, or the "solar plexus" of the navel chakra, signifies self-mastery; Coronis is the heart chakra of compassion; Endora is synonymous for self-expression in the throat chakra; Pasitheo is the "brilliance" of the Third Eye's inner vision located in the brow chakra; and Ambrosia is the "divine" or "immortal" experience of an awakened crown chakra.

In the Hyades' correspondence to the major chakras, they personify the Navel of the World cult, with its emphasis on altered states of consciousness, and comprise the name by which it was known (through their father, Atlas, the Atlantean identity): Hyde. Thus, the name may be traced in an almost straight-line progression from the mythic realm of lost Atlantis to the neighboring Canary Islands, across the Mediterranean to Asia Minor and India. Its reappearance at the spiritual center of cultures wholly unrelated to Greek legend suggests the migration of cult practitioners among survivors fleeing eastward from the destruction of Atlantis.

Descendants of Atlantis in the Canary Islands

The first step from traditional myth to archaeological reality took place in the Canary Islands, 56 miles off the Moroccan coast of North Africa. Mid-15th century Portuguese explorers found the islands inhabited by a native people, the Guanche (a contraction of Guanchinerfe, or "Child of Tenerife," largest of the islands). Tall, fair-haired and light-eyed, the Guanches were a white people some modern investigators believe were the last examples of Cro-Magnon man: Their well-preserved human remains at Tenerife's Mummy Museum, in the capital city of Las Palmas, show numerous curved spines, bone deformation, cranial irregularities, and many varieties of inheritable disease.

The Guanche built stone pyramids, massive walls, and lofty pillars of native volcanic red tufa, white pumice, and black lava stone, the same colors Plato mentioned adorned the oceanic capital. Located on the Canary Island of Las Palmas, the best preserved example of Guanche sacred arhitecture is identical in its concentric layout to Plato's description in the *Kritias*. There can be no question that the Las Palmas ruins and the first city of the Atlantic Empire were conceived in the same building style—Guanche monumental construction is tangible proof that an Atlantean mode actually existed, and in the exact area of the ocean where Plato said it did. According to Henry Myhill, in his study of Canary Island archaeology, "All the architectural finds made in recent years in the Canaries go to prove that these islands were the outposts of an earlier, higher culture, however provincial and barbarized. Large, city-like settlements have been discovered, [and] imposing grave layouts and finds of inscriptions keep coming."[10]

The Guanches' chief deity was Atlas, known to them as Ater, typically represented in rock art petroglyphs as a man, his arms upraised, as though supporting the sky. Referring to Ater/Atlas, they told their Portuguese discoverers in the early 15th century that the Canary Islands were anciently part of a larger homeland once engulfed by the sea in a cataclysm their forefathers survived by climbing to the top of Mount Teide, Tenerife's great volcano. The native account of this catastrophe concluded, "The powerful Father of the Fatherland died and left the natives orphans." The same oral tradition was heard some 1,300 years earlier by the Roman geographer Marcellus, who cited in his *Tois Aethiopikes*:

> *The inhabitants of the Atlantic island of Poseidon preserve a tradition handed down to them by their ancestors of the existence of an Atlantic island of immense size of not less than a thousand stadia [about 115 miles], which had really existed in those seas, and which, during a long period of time, governed all the islands of the Atlantic Ocean.*

The mid-1st-century Roman naturalist, Pliny the Elder, seconded Marcellus, writing that the Guanches were in fact the direct descendants of survivors of the disaster that sank Atlantis. Proclus, a Greek Neoplatonist philosopher, reported that they still told the story of Atlantis in his day, circa 410 A.D.

The Canary Islands received their name probably sometime in the mid-1st century B.C. from Roman visitors, who observed the inhabitants' worship of dogs (*canarii*) in association with mummification, and ritual ties to the Nile Valley, where dog-headed Anubis was a mortuary god. These and other cultural commonalities shared with pharaonic civilization had been independently inherited by Canary Islanders and Egyptians from the lost "fatherland" that sent its flood-survivors to both cultures.

According to the Guanches, their Atlantean ancestors sought refuge atop Mount Teide—at 12,198 feet, the highest mountain in Europe. Its fiery vent was believed to open into the subterranean kingdom of death presided over by Echeyde, "I, Heyde," or more usually, Heyde. Its philologic and mythic resemblance to the Greek Hades cross-references Tenerife's Mount Teide (a Spanish corruption of the Guanche Heyde), affirming origins in the Atlantean Hyade, and strongly suggesting the spread of the Navel of the World cult to the Canary Islands.

This supposition is attested by Guanche religious practices, as documented by early 16th century Spanish observers.[11] They reported that a Guanche high priest, the Fayracan, was alone permitted to attend the Fayra, "a round stone in a place of worship," known as the Zonfa, or "navel." These terms again demonstrate linguistic parallels far beyond the Canary Islands: *Veiha* is Gothic for "priest," while Zonfa is the "zone" used by the ancient Greeks to describe the sacred precinct at Delphi, where the Omphalos, or "navel stone," was enshrined. If, as seems probable, Fayra does in fact mean "fire," then it appears to characterize the same kind of radiant energy said to emanate from the Chintamani and other sacred stones. They and their attendants were invariably associated with healing, just as the Guanche Fayracan was a physician in addition to his duties as high priest on the sacred slopes of Mount Heide.

The Navel of the World in Greece

Mount Ida's sacred cave, the Idaeon Antron, Crete's Navel of the World, birthplace of Zeus, king of the Olympian gods.

The Hyade theme broke into the Mediterranean world with Idomeneus, son of Deucalion, a flood hero in Greek myth who escaped the Great Deluge that destroyed a former age. He fled to the eastern Mediterranean, where he became the first Minoan king with his son, Idomeneus. The post-disaster arrival of these two Deluge survivors at Crete signifies introduction of Navel of the World cultists in the Aegean following the Atlantean catastrophe. They installed themselves at 8,051-foot-high Mount Ida in a large cave sacred to Zeus. It was here that the king of the gods' umbilical birth-string—his inherited connection to the Olympian immortals—was enshrined and venerated as a sacred navel stone. Today, after unguessed millennia, the Idaeon antron, or Mount Ida cave, may still be entered by modern-day visitors to Crete.

The ruins of Ilios, the capital of Troy. Remains of the outer fortification with base of a watch-tower, one of many that ringed the city's defenses.

Another Mount Ida, this one the holy mountain of Troy, stands across the Aegean Sea in western Asia Minor at 5,381 feet high. Northeast from its foot, splendid and doomed Ilios, the Trojan capital, enshrined the Navel of the World in the form of the Palladium, a statue of the girl Pallas who had been accidentally killed by her playmate, Athena. The grieving goddess had the memorial wrought to represent young Pallas wearing the *aegis*, a protective device, about her shoulders, and fixed atop Mount Olympus in a place of special honor.

But it did not stay there long. In his amorous pursuit of Athena, Hephaestus, the misshapen technologist of the gods, accidentally brushed against the Palladium, defiling it. In disgust, Athena hurled it out of heaven toward the Earth, where it was caught by Electra. She, in turn, gave the image to her son, Dardanus, as a going-away present when he crossed the Mediterranean to found Troy and give his name to the Dardanelles, the strait joining the Aegean world with the Sea of Marmara. His founding voyage signified Navel of the World cultists arriving in Asia Minor from their Atlantean homeland, as personified by Electra, another daughter of Atlas from an additional set of seven sisters, the Pleiades, and consequently an "Atlantis." Singled out as "the lost Pleiade," she personified the sunken city. The relationship is underscored by Pallas herself, whose grandfather was Poseidon, the divine progenitor of Atlantean kings.

The Palladium was, in fact, a sacred stone venerated in the Temple of Apollo at the very center of Ilios. With the city's destruction, it was carried off by Aeneas when he led survivors of the Trojan holocaust to Italy. There, it was eventually set up as the Umbilicus Urbis Romae, the "Navel of Rome," at the Forum, in its own shrine behind the Temple of Saturn (the Roman Kronos). Built to hold the city treasury, it contained 13 tons of gold, 114 tons of silver, and 30 million silver *sestertii* coins during Julius Caesar's rule at the very beginning of the Empire. In later centuries, as the imperialism he set in motion spread to embrace the known world, the treasury multiplied many times over. Today, eight granite columns are all that remain of the immense and elegant structure.

After the passage of millennia, the words "Umbilicus Urbis Romae" are still legible on the ruins of ancient Rome's Navel of the World.

Site of the "Navel of Rome" beside the Temple of Saturn.

The Forum's inauguration in 497 B.C. took place over the remains of a prehistoric site dedicated to Satres, an Etruscan version of Kronos, from whom the Romans obviously derived their Saturn. According to Plato's account of Atlantis, the Atlanteans occupied western Italy's Etruria, a statement seconded by the Etruscans themselves, who believed Atlas was worshiped in the Italian peninsula before all other gods. The name "Italy" in fact derives from "Atlas," the eponymous king of Atlantis.

Near the Tempio di Saturno in Italy stood a building that housed the Umbilicus Urbis Romae, a circular structure of solid brickwork about 14 feet wide. The current ruins date to circa 200 A.D., when Emperor Lucius Septimius Severus reconstructed part of the earlier shrine, built four centuries before, to give space for an arch, in which fragments of the older monument were used in the new one. The 200 B.C. structure had itself been built atop a far more ancient, Etruscan Navel of the World, as confirmed by its original Latin name, Umbilicus Mundus. Tradition held that Romulus had a circular pit dug in the Forum when he founded the city, and all citizens had to throw in a handful of dirt from their various places of origin, together with the first fruits of the year, as sacrificial offerings. The pit was filled and then capped with a sacred stone, depicted in Constant Moyaux's meticulously detailed 1865 watercolor of the shrine as conical. The Umbilicus Urbis Romae was the external part of the Mundus, a subterranean chamber where the Omphalos was kept.

Only the high priest was permitted to enter this holy-of-holies three times each year, at the vernal equinox and summer and winter solstices.

The Roman Forum as it appeared in the 2nd century A.D. *The rectangular building with columns at the center was the Temple of Saturn, site of the "Navel of Rome." Model on display at Eur, Italy.*

Among the wealth of Bronze Age artifacts he dug out from the Turkish hill at Hissarlik, Heinrich Schliemann, the famous discoverer of Troy, unearthed a terra-cotta female figure illustrated with a "fire-altar" dedicated to Mount Ida.[12] The early 20th century historian Zelia Nuttall observed, "It is significant that the Trojan image exhibits a triangle surrounded by

seven discs containing the Swastika—'the holy fire.'"[13] The triangle represented Mount Ida, where Navel of the World practitioners activated the major chakras, or human energy-centers, as indicated by the seven Swastika-adorned discs.

Perhaps mankind's oldest icon, the leftward-oriented hooked cross symbolized Prometheus and the motion of his fire-drill stick. Brother of Atlas, Prometheus presented fire (in other words, technology) to mankind. Throughout the ancient world, the Swastika was associated with heavenly light and/or fire, and was likewise associated with Apollo, the sun god. Its reverse, the Sauvastika, was the emblem of lunar deities Artemis, Diana, and the moon goddess of Minoan Crete.

The Sacred Stone in India

Schliemann's Trojan "fire-altar" recalls the Canary Island Fayra, Tibetan Chintamani, and other "fire-stones" from the Pacific to the Atlantic and the Mediterranean. It also points to yet another Ida, this one in India. There, an officiating priest kindling the Agni jatavedas, or "holy flame" of his fire-altar declares in the *Rig Veda*: "We place Thee, O, Jatavedas, in the place of Ida, in the *nabha* ("navel") of the altar, to carry out offerings."[14] In Hindu myth, Ida was the "mountain daughter" of Manu, the flood-hero of Indus Valley tradition. His recognizably Atlantean character supports the continuity of the Ida-Mountain theme from Atlantis to the Subcontinent. In the

Matsyu Purana (among the most ancient texts in Indian literature), Manu is warned of the catastrophe to come by the god Vishnu in the guise of a fish: "The Earth shall become like ashes, the aether, too, shall be scorched with heat."[15] India is extraordinarily rich in traditions of the Great Flood.

A particularly Atlantean version is recounted in the most famous Indian epic of its kind, the *Mahabharata*. According to the *Encyclopaedia Britannica*, it was based on actual events that took place from the 15th to 11th centuries B.C., the same time parameter framing the zenith and fall of Atlantis. Beginning in the Drona Parva—Section XI of the *Mahabharata*—the destruction of the oceanic kingdom of Tripura is set forth. Tripura is described as a wealthy and powerful kingdom, whose eastern shore faced the coast of Africa. The *Mahabharata* calls it "the Triple City" after the trident presented to the residents by Shiva, the island's creator, as a national emblem. The city itself was designed by Maya, "of great intelligence." He built three artificial islands surrounded by circular moats, configuring each one on a massive, opulent scale, and "shaped like a wheel" (*chakrastham*, Sanskrit for "circular"). "And they consisted of houses and mansions and lofty walls and porches. And though teeming with lordly palaces close to each other, yet the streets were wide and spacious. And they were adorned with diverse mansions and gateways."[16]

Tripura's Bronze Age timeframe, location in the near Atlantic Ocean, circular design, luxury, and Poseidon-like trident could only describe Plato's Atlantis. In confirmation, the *Mahabharata* adds that this "principle city" was also known as Hiranyapura, a reference to its residents who "dwelt in the womb of the ocean," also known as the Navel of the World. The title

may actually be one of the few surviving Atlantean words, as indicated by its appearance on opposite sides of the globe. A late 19th century Mayanist, Augustus Le Plongeon, pointed out that "the name Hiranyapura means, in Maya, 'dragged to the middle of the water jar.'"[17]

Indian flood traditions are often centered on a sacred stone. The Hindu Shiva had a jewel fixed in his forehead—the Urna, a gem associated with his immortality. It allowed him to access the otherwise unsuspected wisdom that dwelt within himself, the brow chakra or famous Third Eye possessed by gods and men. Among the earliest Indian divinities, his image appears on a cylinder-seal from the Indus Valley city of Harappa, dating to around 2600 B.C., making it contemporary with Troy's model Navel of the World altar. The myth of Shiva abounds with Atlantean themes: Ash-colored, he was envisioned as a dangerous, volcanic mountain who whipped up the Great Flood by violently stirring the ocean with a monstrous serpent. He is commonly portrayed in temple art carrying a trident, Poseidon's own scepter.

The Hindu *Atharva Veda*[18] reads, "Time, like a shining steed with seven rays, full of fecundity, bears all things onward. Time, like a seven-chakra, seven-navel car moves on." The *Atharva Veda* goes on to describe a central concept in Kundalini yoga, the *nadi*, a twin nerve current coiling around the human spinal column—the real Tree of Life—through its respective channels: Pingala on the right, and Ida on the left. The former is male energy: acquisition, materialization, and consciousness; the latter, female energy: nurturing, instinct, and the subconscious mind. Referred to as the Chandra Nadi for its association with the pale-white moon, or lunar-female energies, Ida is regarded by yogis as "the great nourisher of the world." Their goal is to so harmonize Pingala with Ida that they meet at the *Brahma Garanthi,* where the balance of their contrary energies ensures enlightenment at the Navel of the World. Here is the Atlantean concept of the sacred center also preserved in Greek myth as the serpent entwining the Tree of Life; in other words, spiritual energy made to ascend the human vertebrae.

A linked progression of name and function follows the Navel of the World mystery cult from Atlantis to the Canary Islands, the Aegean, Asia Minor, and the Indian Subcontinent. It is discernable in the Atlantean Idaea and Hyades, Tenerife's Mount Heyde, the Greek Hades, Mount Ida in Crete, Troy's own Mount Ida, and India's "mountain daughter," Ida. These peaks are each associated with a sacred stone—Idaea's lithic substitute for infant Zeus, his navel stone enshrined in the Cretan Idaeon antron, the Guanche Fayra, the Trojan Palladium, and Shiva's Urna. These, in turn, were carried away from one mountainous sanctuary to the next on waves of immigration from a Great Flood— the destruction of Atlantis, the Guanches' drowned "fatherland," Deucalion's arrival in Crete after the Ogygean Deluge, the coming of Dardanus to Asia Minor following the loss of his Atlantean mother, and Manu's survival of the cataclysm in India. The cohesion of these interrelated themes traveling from west to east among otherwise diverse, unconnected cultures and peoples separated by formidable distances argues persuasively for Atlantean Navel of the World missionaries setting up cult-centers at various locations halfway around the globe.

But they traveled in the opposite direction, as well.

The Navel of the World in Southeast and Central America

Tribal peoples of the American southeast preserved a tribal memory of their ancestral origins on a large island in the Atlantic Ocean. After it was lost in a terrible deluge, survivors sailed across the Sunrise Sea, arriving on the shores of a new land. Among the few possessions they managed to salvage was a "power stone," which they enshrined in what is now the state of Virginia. The object was the focus of a ritual honoring the flood-heroes who brought it, and conducted at the summit of Mount Olaimy, one of the tallest peaks in the Appalachians. There, six caged birds were released at high noon on a commemorative feast day. Following their flight, honey was poured into a stone box, and pilgrims entered the small temple in a large grotto on the mountainside to bathe in a holy spring: The freed birds parallel those let loose by Deucalion, who escaped the Great Deluge in Greek myth and uncaged six birds, following their flight direction to a safe landfall. That accomplished, his first act was a sacrifice of honey to the gods for his salvation. According to British antiquarian W.S. Blackett, at the center of Virginia's Mount Olaimy shrine was a cube-shaped altar, upon which rested "a single crystal, three or four inches square."[19]

Something of the ancient reverence for crystal in what is now Virginia and Louisiana may have lingered in a venerable Cherokee legend, as recorded by Phyllis Galde, the publisher of *Fate* magazine:

> The chief of the mineral tribe, Quartz Crystal, was clear, like the light of Creation itself. Quartz put his arms around his brother, Tobacco, and said, "I will be the sacred mineral. I will heal the mind. I will help human beings see

the origin of disease. I will help to bring wisdom and clarity in dreams. And I will record their spiritual history, including our meeting today, so that in the future, if humans gaze into me, they may see their origin and the way of harmony."[20]

In the Valley of Mexico, pre-Columbian America's crystal theme was particularly linked with Feathered Serpent, the fair-haired "Man of Watery [sunken] Aztlan." From his title, Aztecatl, the Aztecs derived their very name. His better known variant, Quetzalcoatl, was often portrayed in temple-art wearing the Ehecailacacozcatl about his neck. This was the "Wind Jewel," stylized as a conch shell cut away to reveal its spiral interior, a metaphor for power. It was set up in his shrine at the very center of Tenochtitlan, the Aztec capital, site of today's Mexico City. He was venerated as the Lord of the Year, the Xiuhteuctli, a fire-deity, god of all primal energies, who originally dwelt in a circular, stone tower surrounded by the sea. Further showing his identification with Atlas, he could transform himself into a foursome of "atlantes" supporting the sky, indicated by the cross design adorning the coal brazier he wore. "This ultimate manifestation of the Earth's navel," as Aztec authority Henry Brundage referred to him, was additionally portrayed in sacred sculpture as an old man with a distended belly and wearing a coal brazier on his head.[21] It was in the Feathered Serpent's Xiuhteuctli temple that his Wind Jewel was preserved, and served as the centerpiece of Central America's own Navel of the World. Appropriately, Xiuhteuctli was a red, white, and black pyramid of circular steps, each one smaller than the next, rising in five levels at the very center of

Tenochtitlan, the Aztec capital. The very name, "Mexico," derives from *Metztli*, literally, the "Navel of the Moon."[22] The same tricolor arrangement and sacred numeral (five) Plato stated typified Atlantean construction occurred at this centrally important temple dedicated to the Mesoamerican flood hero from Aztlan. Comparison between Xiuhteuctli and Atlantis could hardly be more clear.

When Did Atlantis Fall?

"This ultimate manifestation of the Earth's navel," Xiuhteuctli, the Aztec Lord of the Year, possessed the "Wind Jewel."

Plato was far more ambiguous regarding a timeframe for that first Navel of the World than he was in his detailed description of its physical appearance. Both dialogues assert that the Atlantean Empire was on the march nine millennia before Solon was told about it in the mid-6th century B.C. at Egypt's Temple of the Goddess Neith. Plato's date makes for an internal contradiction between an identifiably Bronze Age civilization (attributed by the *Kritias* to Atlantis) and the late Stone Age when it was supposed to have flourished. The European Bronze Age began around the turn of the 4th millennium B.C., but only reached its zenith between roughly 1500 to 1200 B.C., when citadels similar to the one featured in Plato's account were being built at places such as Homeric Greece and Troy. The kind of imperial city he described, to say nothing of Athens or Dynastic Egypt, did not exist during the Upper Paleolithic.

As Desmond Lee points out in the appendix to his translation of the Dialogues:

The Greeks had a bad sense of time. That is what the Egyptian priest in Timaeus...means when he says, "you Greeks are all children"; Greek tradition and Greek memory are, he explains, comparatively short. And though the Greeks, both philosophers and others, were interested in origins, they seem to have been curiously lacking in their sense of the time-dimension....

Yet, 11,600 years ago was about the time Atlantis' Pacific predecessor was being engulfed in catastrophically rising sea levels spawned by a melting ice age that thrust its ruins, similar to those near the Japanese islands and Taiwan, to their present positions on the ocean floor. It was just then that Lemurian survivors of the Navel of the World cult may have conveyed its sacred principles and power stone to the Atlantean Emperor, as determined in research by Josephine Saint-Hilaire. If we take Plato's 9,550 B.C. date at face value, it appears to mark the beginning of Atlantean civilization, as suggested in his Dialogues, which show Poseidon transforming the originally primitive island society ("for there were still no ships or sailing in those days,"[23] into a high culture. Other Atlantologists, such as Florida investigator Kenneth Caroli, have long wondered if the sea-god's arrival signified the incoming of a foreign, more advanced people who began building the Atlantis that Plato described. The Greeks, untroubled by indefinite chronologies to begin with, simply never bothered updating Atlantis from its Lemurian origins in the 10th millennium B.C. to its evolution as a Bronze Age civilization, some 8,000 years later.

Atlantis, as Lemuria before it and Egypt after, flourished, not for centuries, but millennia, time enough for its history to have been punctuated by several natural catastrophes. As the Nile temple-priest told Solon:

There have been and will be many different calamities to destroy mankind, the greatest of them by fire and water, lesser ones by countless other means. Your own story of how Phaethon, child of the Sun, harnessed his father's chariot, but was unable to guide it along his father's course, and so burnt up the Earth's surface, and was himself destroyed by a thunderbolt, is a mythical variation of the truth that there is at long intervals a variation in the course of the heavenly bodies and a consequent widespread destruction by fire of things on Earth.[24]

It was, after all, the violent close of the last ice age that prompted Lemurian survivors to seek distant refuge on an Atlantic island, where they interbred with its indigenous population to produce the hybrid civilization of Atlantis. From its Paleolithic origins, it evolved over the next several thousand years into the epitome of a Bronze Age empire that suffered a terminating event in 1198 B.C. This date coincides with both the kind of culture Plato described in such rich detail, and also a global catastrophe geologists know took place 3,200 years ago.

For decades, scientists could not explain what could have caused such widespread devastation. But during the last decade of the 20th century, as they began putting together different pieces of the geologic puzzle, a coherent view into the violent destruction of the Bronze Age gradually appeared. W. Bruce Masse cited "a locally catastrophic terrestrial impact around 1000 B.C." that occurred in the badlands of northern Montana.[25] West of Broken Bow, Nebraska, lies a mile-wide impact crater created approximately 3,000 years ago by a meteor that exploded with the equivalent force of a 120-megaton nuclear blast. Meteor and asteroid falls in the Atlantic Ocean caused massive coastal flooding in the southeastern United States, as indicated by a long pattern of impact craters, or bays, in South Carolina. Ice-cores drilled at Camp Century, Greenland's outdoor geological laboratory, reveal that a global catastrophe threw several thousand cubic kilometers of ash into the atmosphere around 1170 B.C.

In 1997, Swedish geologists Lars Franzen and Thomas B. Larsson felt compelled by the evidence to "propose that cosmic activity could offer an explanation for the observed changes. We even suggest that relatively large asteroids or comets (around 0.5 km in diameter) hit somewhere in the eastern Atlantic."[26] They argued that "relatively large extraterrestrial bodies hit somewhere in the eastern North Atlantic, probably on the shelf of the Atlantic coast of North Africa or southern Europe around 1000 to 950 B.C., mainly affecting the Mediterranean parts of Africa and Europe, but also globally."[27] The destruction of Atlantis was part of this worldwide conflagration that incinerated most other cities from Shang Dynasty China to the Near East and Bronze Age Europe. The eastern North Atlantic Ocean site for several meteor impacts identified by Larsson and Franzen coincide with the location of Plato's island. Although he stated that it ultimately succumbed to seismic violence, he foreshadowed an extraterrestrial cause in his unfinished account when he mentioned "a variation in the course of the heavenly bodies and consequent widespread destruction by fire of things on Earth."[28]

The global catastrophe that consumed millions of human lives left in its wake a dark age, covering the ruins of civilization for the next five centuries. The former splendor of the Pre-Classical world faded into dim legend for another 3,000 years, until modern archaeologists began to dig out its ruins. Hattusas, the Hittite capital in Asia Minor; Trojan Ilios; the Minoan cities of Crete; and Shang Dynasty China, had long been dismissed as entirely mythical, until their excavation began in the late 19th century. Atlantis also fell victim to the same planetwide cataclysm that snuffed out *their* greatness. The priests among its survivors fled west to America and east to Europe and beyond, leaving their Ida-signature from the Canary Islands to India. Among their most valued possessions were special stones they believed could somehow induce a uniquely potent transformational experience. These stones, wherever they were set up and enshrined, became midpoints around which the Navel of the World cult revolved.

The most influential and enduring of these spiritual centers was established in Egypt. Greek myth explains that the country derived its appellation from Aegyptus, grandson of Poseidon, the same sea-god who sired the royal house of Atlantis. Aegyptus' son, who brought the mystery religion to the Nile Delta, was Idmon, whose name belongs to the line of descending "Idas" from Atlantis to India, and, as was Idomeneus at Crete, his father was a survivor of the Great Flood. And the temple in which Idmon enshrined his Atlantean "Stone of Destiny" still stands as the greatest building on Earth.

CHAPTER 4

The Great Pyramid: An Egyptian Home for the Power Stone

Whoever would know the secret of the Pyramid must know the secrets of the Earth.

—Hermes Trismegistus

The global disasters that obliterated the Stone of Destiny's homelands, first in the Pacific and then in the Atlantic, by no means signified its demise or loss. On the contrary, these catastrophic events set in motion its profound impact on the outside world over the following millennia, down to our present day. The story is as long, complex, and twisted by the vagaries of fate and human interaction as the history of civilization itself. The narrative makes more sense, however, the more clearly we understand the truly stupendous setting prepared for the Fire Stone in Egypt.

Crystal technology, evolving from Lemuria through Atlantis, had already reached high levels of applied development prior to the natural catastrophe still known around the world as the Great Flood. That global cataclysm may have been powerful enough to overturn early civilization, but it did not entirely extinguish the accumulated wisdom of previous ages. The long use of power stones to interface with human and geological input was not terminated, but spread by virtue of disaster far beyond its oceanic origins, as recounted in the enduring folk traditions of numerous peoples across our planet.

The Power Stone in Egypt

When the inhabitants of ancient Egypt spoke of their origins, they told of a "Primal Mound" surrounded by a vast ocean located in the distant west. It was here, they said, during the Tep Zepi, or "First Time," that early humanity and deities lived together in peace, creating a kind of paradise on Earth. But in successive generations, most men grew arrogant, thought of their divine mentors as no better than themselves, and began to quarrel over riches and power. In disgust, the gods selected a few virtuous mortals, then sailed away from the island, which sank beneath the waves with its ungrateful population. Passing into the Great Green, or Mediterranean Sea, the elite survivors then arrived at the Nile Delta, where they began life anew.

In their company was Thaut, the patron of wisdom. Known later to the Greeks as Hermes Trismegistus, he carried Emerald Tablets that contained all the high knowledge of the former Tep Zepi. With them, he educated dwellers of the Nile Valley in the arts of writing, irrigation, mathematics, mysticism, medicine, and large-scale construction. As testament to the cooperation between native Egyptian labor and the flood survivors' genius, they together raised a stylized monument to the Primal Mound that still stands on the Giza Plateau: the Great Pyramid.

The Great Pyramid by the Numbers

At an original height of 480.95 feet, the Great Pyramid was the tallest building in the world until New York's Flatiron Building was completed a little more than 100 years ago. With a perimeter of 3,023.13 feet, it covers 13.11 acres, a space equivalent to seven midtown blocks of New York City, and 30 Empire State Buildings could be built from all the stone in the Great Pyramid. It contains enough masonry to make not one, but two walls, each 3 feet high and 1 foot wide, spanning the United States from the Pacific to the Atlantic oceans. Sawed into blocks 1 foot on an edge and laid end to end, its stones, combined with those of its two companions, could build a wall extending two-thirds of the distance around the Earth at the equator. The Pyramid has more stone than all the combined cathedrals, churches, and chapels in England. And these are only some of the mind-boggling highlights of the world's greatest building. Flinders Petrie, the renowned British Egyptologist at the

turn of the 20th century, wrote that the Pyramid showed "the marks of such tools as we have only now reinvented."[1] Toward the end of the last century, pyramid researcher William Fix concluded that "the technology does not exist today either to build the Pyramid or even repair it to its original specifications," a conclusion seconded by most investigators.[2]

The Great Pyramid emerges from behind its Giza Plateau companion, Khafre's Pyramid.

The Pyramid sits on a stone platform that is still dead level to within .08 of an inch (21 millimeters) over a distance of 758 feet (231 meters) on a side, despite thousands of years of seismic activity. Its casing stones were placed with an accuracy of .005 of an inch, while gaps for mortar average .02 of an inch. The Pyramid contains nearly 2.5 million mostly limestone blocks, each one cut and fitted to .01 of an inch tolerance: the same precision used by modern gem cutters. Petrie found that the so-called Descending Passage, which begins at the Pyramid's north face to penetrate the solid bedrock beneath, runs a quarter-inch from perfection over its entire 350-foot length. Polished to a high degree of gloss, the 80 acres of casing stone that originally covered it made the Great Pyramid the only man-made object on Earth visible from outer space — when light reflected off a side facing the sun. (Popular misconception contends that the Great Wall of China may be seen from orbit, but only its shadow is sometimes visible.)

Some appreciation of the scope of the Great Pyramid is provided by the human figures standing on its lower courses.

The stones of the Great Pyramid weigh from 2 to more than 70 tons—an average locomotive weighs 68 tons. They are all fitted to .01 of an inch, an accuracy modern masons cannot approach even when handling bricks, which they can tap into place to only .1 of an inch between joints.

It almost goes without saying that a 70-ton block cannot be tapped into place. Moreover, these heavier blocks were not even used to create the lowest course of the base, but raised 100 feet and higher up the sloping face of the structure—a modern engineer's nightmare.

Limestone used to build the Great Pyramid was available locally, but the thousands of tons of granite that went into its construction were brought to the Giza Plateau from quarries 500 miles away— about the distance from Chicago, Illinois to Memphis, Tennessee. Just the human labor required to ferry such ponderous tonnage over vast and difficult stretches of the Nile, with its strong currents and sharp bends, seems incredibly harrowing, even by today's transportation standards. Delicately lifting and placing 70-ton stones on what must have been enormous barges, then lifting them again to shore— all without breaking or chipping a single block—necessitates a machine technology that, at least in some respects, surpasses our own.

The Great Pyramid Measures the Earth

Theorists are free to imagine any number of propositions to explain the Great Pyramid's method of construction, purpose, or age. But in its shadow, all conventional attempts at interpretation melt away. When confronting the enormity of its dimensions and the obvious perfection of its workmanship, individual considerations rapidly dwindle in the awestruck mind of the beholder. One conclusion survives such encounters, however, and suggests its true character: The Great Pyramid was designed as a geodetic structure—in other words, its interior and exterior dimensions measure the Earth itself.

Geodesy is the precise measurement of the Earth to determine the exact position of specific locations on its surface.

Myriad correspondences between the Pyramid and our planet are not the results of mere speculation, theorizing, or coincidence. The Great Pyramid was originally positioned as closely as possible to the absolute center of the world's land mass. This means that it sits at a unique location where the lines of latitude and longitude pass over more of the Earth's surface than at any other place. Its location and very form epitomize its identity as a geodetic symbol. As Alexander Braghine explained:

The summit of the pyramid is situated in 29⁰ 58' 51.22" of north latitude. This circumstance at first sight does not seem significant. The moment, however, we remember that the apparent position of the Polar Star is invariably 1' 8.78" out, owing to the phenomenon of atmospheric refraction, we see what was in the mind of the builder. If we add the value of the refraction, i.e. 1' 8.78" to 29⁰ 58' 51.22", we get exactly 30⁰, and we realize that the mysterious builder of the pyramid, guiding himself by the Polar Star (or by a corresponding point in the constellation of Draconis), wished to center the pyramid upon the 13th Parallel. This Parallel is remarkable for the fact that it separates a maximum of the land of our

planet from the maximum of the ocean surfaces. Apparently, the builder wished to record permanently the distribution of the continents and oceans of those days, and we can see that this distribution has remained almost the same until our own times.[3]

Physicist Michael Csuzdi seconded Braghine's explanation: "The six continents of the Earth markedly form a pentagonal pyramid. Africa is at the apex; lines drawn from its center to the centers of the other continents are evenly spaced at 72 degrees. The other five centers are nearly on a common plane to form the pyramid's base line." In the 2nd century B.C., long before extra-mortuary interpretations of the Great Pyramid were considered, the Greek geographer and historian Agatharchides of Cnidus concluded that it "incorporated fractions of geographical degrees."[4] In other words, the very configuration of the Great Pyramid is a reflecting microcosm of the Earth itself.

Incorporated in the dimensions of the Pyramid is a trio of key measurements that calculate the size and shape of our planet with uncanny accuracy. They correspond to the three most important planetary measurements defining circumference, polar radius, and equatorial bulge. From them may be precisely deduced the flattening at the poles and the irregularity of the equator, neither of which was rediscovered until the 18th century. The perimeter of the Great Pyramid, established by its "sockets" (shallow, squared holes, whose original purpose is unknown), equals a half-minute of equatorial longitude, or 1/43,200 of the Earth's circumference. Its total original height equaled 1/43,200 of the polar radius. Its original perimeter exactly equaled one half-minute of latitude at the equator, which means that its base-length represented the distance the Earth rotates in half a second.

If the perimeter of the Great Pyramid were reduced to inches, it would express 36,524.2; this figure equals exactly 100 times the number of days in a year—the number of days in a century. The baseline of the Great Pyramid is 500 cubits, or 750 Egyptian feet. This number corresponds precisely to the distance our planet travels in half a second of time at the Equator, because the Earth's circumference is 86,400 cubits, just as one 24-hour day is made up of 86,400 seconds. Until the advent of satellite surveys from outer space as recently as the mid-1970s, the ancient building's architectural measurement of our planet was not duplicated.

Even the weight of the Great Pyramid incorporates profound knowledge of the Earth. Its 6 million tons equals one-quintillionth the weight of our planet. If the Pyramid's volume of 88 million cubic feet is multiplied by the average density of its stone, the result, expressed in ancient Egyptian units of measurement (known as elbows), will be 552, which is the density of the Earth in its relation to water. Perhaps most incredible of all, multiplying the original height of the Great Pyramid by 1 billion produces 93 million—the average distance of our planet from the Sun, something only rediscovered in the 19th century.

U.S. physicist Joseph Farrell observed that:

> the mean density of the Earth is approximately 5.7 times that of water at 68 degrees Fahrenheit at a barometric pressure of 30 pounds per inch.[5] In the King's Chamber, all the stone courses have 23 or more stones, except the fifth course,

> which contains only seven. Thus, encoded in the fifth course of the King's Chamber is the mean density of the Earth.[5]

Moreover, the Great Pyramid's interior is a constant 68 degrees Fahrenheit—the average temperature of our planet. Farrell goes on to point out that the Pyramid's original height of 5,449 inches equals the average height of land on the Earth above sea level.

Each of the four faces of the Great Pyramid, with its almost imperceptible indentations, represents a curved quarter of the Northern Hemisphere, a perfect spherical quadrant of 90 degrees. A structural engineer from Leeds, Yorkshire, David Davidson, proved that slight indentations on each of the Pyramid's four sides calculated the solar year (the exact time between equinoxes), the anomalistic year (the time needed for the Earth to return to the point nearest the sun, the perihelion), and the sidereal year (the time it takes for a given star to reappear at the same spot in the sky).[6]

Each side of the base of the Great Pyramid measures 9,131.416 inches, a figure corresponding to the number of days contained in 25 years. This allots to each sidereal year of 365.25664 days, just a 30-second difference from the sidereal year ascertained by 20th century astronomers. Moreover, this same measurement virtually equals .0021 (1/480) of an equatorial degree. Braghine remarks:

> At this rate, the total length of the equator line would come to 24,903.86181 miles, which quantity is only 1.5 miles more than the measurement adopted by modern science. If we divide the length of the equator as given by the pyramid

by pi, we will get the diameter of our planet equal to 7,927.1 miles, which quantity is only 0.5 miles longer than the measurement calculated by the modern astronomer, Sir James Jeans [240].

But each of its four sides at the base is also 500 royal cubits, which, translated into nautical miles, results in the number 24,883.2, the exact measurement of the meridian of the Earth. The accuracy is so great that it has only been marginally surpassed in tenths of a degree by the U.S. Satellite Survey of the planet at the close of the 20th century. Using the same set of calculations, Dublin University mathematician Alan Mitchell proved that the Great Pyramid's base, sides, and "capstone" base correspond to the Earth's equatorial, mean, and polar radii.[7]

The Great Pyramid dimensions used here were ascertained during the 1950s by Livio Stecchini, Ph.D., a Harvard professor and scholar of ancient weights and measures and of the history of cartography in antiquity. After completing the most accurate survey of the monument ever undertaken, he determined that its original perimeter of 921.453 meters is precisely half a minute of latitude at the equator, or 1/43,200 of the Earth's circumference. This fraction is revealing, because, when multiplied by 147.14 meters—the original height of the Great Pyramid from its base—the result equals the distance from the Earth's center to the North Pole. The Great Pyramid's calculation of this Polar Radius is off by a mere 120 meters. But even this seeming error, however inconsequentially slight, appears to have been deliberately factored in by the pyramid builders, because 120 meters is equivalent to the same number of feet in 120 meters as there are days in a solar year:

365. Expressed in inches, the Great Pyramid's perimeter lies within 1 or 2 inches of 36,524.2: 100 times the number of days in a year, or the number of days in 100 years.

As long ago as 1805, French mathematician P.F.J. Gosselin deduced that the Pyramid represented the circumference of the Earth, a conclusion reworked and subsequently validated by American geographer A.E. Berriman nearly 150 years later. In fact, a standard unit of ancient Egyptian measurement, the *remen*, used throughout the structure, is precisely .0000001 (one ten-millionth) of Earth's mean polar radius. The Great Pyramid incorporates our planet's geometry more accurately, according to Berriman, "than anything that has ever yet entered into the mind of man to conceive."[8]

We know the geodetic coordinates incorporated in the Great Pyramid are not coincidental, because there is evidence that such measurements were ascertained elsewhere—and earlier—in Egypt: Sun-t, or "Allowing the Entrance," was a solar observatory that the Greeks knew as Syene, opposite Elephantine Isle (the largest rock formed by the Nile River near the first cataract). It was located near the Tropic of Cancer, and was the only place in Egypt from which an accurate observation could be made to establish the circumference of the Earth at the summer solstice. As such, observations obtained at the Sun-t observatory may have contributed to the storehouse of terrestrial data incorporated in the Giza Plateau complex.

This illustration from a 17th century scientific text shows its author understood the Pyramid's geodetic identity as the center of the Earth and of cosmic (that is, spiritual) harmony. From Mundus Subterraneus *(1665), by Athanasius Kircher.*

A 6,000-Year-Old Map of the World

Neither this observatory nor the Great Pyramid, however, provides the only evidence for ancient man's knowledge of the Earth. American professor Charles Hapgood (Berkeley, California) showed that someone mapped the world, even to the shores of Antarctica, about 1,000 years before the generally accepted beginning of the first Egyptian dynasty, around 3100 B.C. Dr. Hapgood published his astounding findings during the 1960s, and they have not been disproved since, despite academic unwillingness to acknowledge them. His years of research were based upon the 16th century map of a Turkish admiral: Piri Reis. Hapgood demonstrated that this map was actually a conglomeration of many earlier charts superimposed on each other, their sources dating back to the 1st century Great Library of Alexandria and much earlier. His masterful investigation of the Piri Reis map revealed that both the North and South

Atlantic were familiar to its creators 6,000 or more years ago—literally millennia before either ocean was officially explored during the European Renaissance.

He determined that the ancient Egyptians did not employ our system of latitude and longitude, but rather some form of spherical triangulation that Hapgood could not understand. The answer finally came from an unexpected source. In their magnetospheric investigation of our planet, Russian astronomers Nikolai Feodorovitch, Vyachesalv Moroz, and Valery Morkov documented magnetic lines encircling the Earth, making it a dodecahedron (12-sided figure) superimposed on a icosahedron (20-sided figure). This arrangement describes a hypothetical graph of triangles in series that, when superimposed on a representation of the globe perfectly matches a system of geographical measurement used by the makers of the Piri Reis map. The conclusion generated from this discovery is even more mind-boggling than the world knowledge it featured: Incredibly, a 5th millennium B.C. cartographer understood the magnetospheric configuration of the Earth (unknown to our civilization until the 1970s) and used it to construct a system of geographical measurement. Equipped with such knowledge, sailors could navigate the seas of the whole world—it seems they did.

Hapgood also revealed that several of Europe's leading mapmakers possessed confidential information about world geography from sources predating the contemporary explorations of Columbus and Magellan. Among the most famous of these Renaissance cartographers was the Flemish Gerardus Kremer, better remembered today as Mercator. He invented the technique of using curved lines on maps to designate lines of equal longitudinal degrees, an innovation still in use today and employed worldwide as "the Mercator projection." This projection is made from the absolute center of the Earth onto a hypothetical cylinder enveloping it and meeting at the equator, thereby allowing meridians to be equally spaced into parallel lines of latitude and longitude. Interestingly, Mercator announced his discovery after returning from Egypt in 1563, when he undertook a prolonged investigation of the Great Pyramid. Described as "indefatigable in searching out the learning of long ago," he appears to have cracked the building's geodetic secrets.[9]

In 1646, John Greaves published *Pyramidagraphica*, in which the Oxford mathematician and astronomer concluded that the Great Pyramid embodied the dimensions of our planet and established tables of measurement from which all Western geometrical systems ultimately derived. His more famous colleague, Sir Isaac Newton, used the figures in *Pyramidagraphica* for his paper, "A Dissertation upon the Sacred Cubit." Scholars such as Mercator, Greaves, and Newton, who ascertained the Giza monument's geodetic qualities, are derided as "pyramidiots" by today's mainstream scientists, including the Undersecretary of State at the Giza Plateau and Director of the Egyptian Supreme Council of Antiquities, Dr. Zahi Hawass. Yet these independent investigators conclude that the advanced mathematics responsible for its construction must have originated from outside the Nile Valley.

The ancient Greeks, such as Hesiod in the 8th century B.C., recorded a deeply prehistoric time when an *oicumene*, or worldwide civilization, created a golden age for early mankind. On the other side of the world, the Quiche Mayas of Yucatan wrote that "the first race of men were capable of all knowledge. They examined the four corners of the horizon, the four points of the firmament and the round surface of the Earth."[10]

It has been only recently rediscovered that the Great Pyramid's geodetic qualities were known to the Classical Greeks, who gave us the word we still use to identify the structure: *pyramid*. Its meaning is quite different, however, from the ancient Egyptian word for the same structure: *mr*. This refers to a unit of measurement, which, in view of the Great Pyramid's geodetic qualities, seems appropriate. One of the names the Egyptians gave to their country was To-mera, or "Land of the Pyramid," and the modern Arabic name for Egypt, al Misri, appears to be derived from *To-mera*. In Coptic Egyptian, a partial survivor of the otherwise dead Egyptian language, *piramit* likewise suggests the "measuring" qualities of the Great Pyramid: The word signifies "the tenth measure in numbers." So too, the standard unit of ancient Egyptian measurement, the *remen*, used throughout the structure is precisely .0000001 (one tenmillionth) of Earth's mean polar radius.

But the Greek word is more mysterious. It means, "fire within." Why, if they knew it embodies the dimensions of the Earth, should the ancient Greeks have chosen such a word to describe the largest stone building ever made? Does their name for it in any way allude to the real meaning of the Great Pyramid?

CHAPTER 5

Why Was the Pyramid Built?

Take back with thee the warning that when men forsake their Creator and look upon their fellows with hate, as with the princes of Atlantis, in whose time this Pyramid was built, they are destroyed by the weight of their own iniquity, even as the people of Atlantis were destroyed.

—A disembodied voice allegedly heard inside the
King's Chamber of the Great Pyramid
by British author Dr. Paul Brunton in 1935.

The Great Pyramid has two inescapable qualities: its incorporation of geodetic information, and the vastness of its material achievement. They comprise the only hard evidence we have about the structure, but from them we may determine *why* it was built. The persons responsible for its creation obviously knew the dimensions of our planet somehow, and attained levels of mathematics and architecture equal—and in some respects superior—to modern technology. More to the point, their achievement was far beyond anything else erected by the ancient Egyptians, for no other structure in the Nile Valley begins to compare with the Great Pyramid (save for its slightly smaller neighbor, the Khafre pyramid). It is, strangely, the most *un*-Egyptian monument in the land, because

it was never adorned with the usual profusion of hieroglyphs that bedecked all other public buildings, excepting its fellow pyramids, in pharaonic times: All the splendid structures raised by Ramses II, built many centuries after the Pyramid Age, are covered with hieroglyphs.

Most surviving traditions about the Great Pyramid were handed down by Islamic scholars. They preserved some of the philosophy, technology, and history of Classical and even pre-Classical civilization, while the Dark Ages shrouded Europe for 500 years. Around 870 A.D., the Arab historian Abou Balkh repeated a tradition that "wise men, previous to the Flood, foreseeing an impending judgment from heaven, which would destroy every living thing, built upon a plateau in Egypt pyramids of stone in order to have some refuge against calamity."[1] In the early 10th century, Masoudi was the historical author of *Fields of Gold-Mines of Gems*, in which he wrote:

> *Surid, one of the kings of Egypt before the Flood, built two great pyramids. The reason for building the pyramids was that the king, who lived 300 years before the Flood, once dreamt that the Earth was twisted around, the stars fell from the sky and clashed together with a great noise and all mankind took refuge in terror.*[2]

From the 7th to 14th centuries, other Arabic writers repeated this story with little variation: The Pyramid was built against the recurrence of a world-deluge brought about by some celestial impact with the Earth.

Predating even the Arabs was at least one surviving Roman source that underscores their reports. It is a fragment of a history by Marcellinus Ammianus, who wrote in 390 A.D., "Inscriptions which the ancients asserted were on the walls of certain underground galleries of the pyramids were intended to prevent the ancient wisdom from being lost in the Flood." Another Roman-era historian, Flavius Josephus, recorded the same tradition.[3]

The Islamic scholars seem universal in affirming that the architect of the Great Pyramid was Thaut, the god of science and hieroglyphic writing. In Egyptian mythology he was said to have survived a catastrophic deluge that destroyed his island home in the distant west, before arriving in the Nile Valley. Much earlier sources, such as Sanchunaithon, a Phoenician scholar in the 6th century B.C., recorded from temple inscriptions that Thaut was the first king and architect of Egypt. These traditions appear confirmed by the Egyptians' own ceremony that preceded the building of a pyramid: According to Kevin Jackson and Jonathan Stamp in their 2003 investigation for the British Broadcasting Corporation, when the king inaugurated its construction he was aided by "a priest personifying Thoth." Together, they "would mark out the base lines of the four outer walls."[4]

If we consider the various accounts of a pre-Flood architect building the Pyramid in preparation for an anticipated natural cataclysm, then the purpose of the structure must relate directly to that event. Both the Arabs and Marcellinus stated that the Great Pyramid was designed to preserve the knowledge of a great civilization for future generations, and some modern investigators agree with this time-capsule theory. But are we really to believe such an incredible building was made only to pass on geodetic information to posterity?

The answer is certainly no, if only because a structure with an internal capacity of 88 million cubic feet makes for a monstrously overdone repository. A smaller, scaled-down monument, even a tenth as large, would have served just as well. There simply was no *need* to create such a stupendously oversized structure for so relatively small a purpose, and at so incredibly high a cost. In short, everything we know about the building demonstrates that conventional, and even most *un*conventional theories posited to explain it can account for neither its dimensions nor geodetic measurements. From its very size and precision, we may logically deduce that the Pyramid's construction was considered the most vital undertaking by every member of the society that produced it. Nothing else could have won the cooperation of what must have been the entire national workforce focused on a single project. No observatory, time capsule, tomb, or temple is deserving of such a nationwide effort. The Great Pyramid was something else; something far more needful.

Contrary to academic dogma, the Great Pyramid was not a tomb: Its tiny entrance and cramped corridors would have rendered impossible the passage of a pharaonic sarcophagus and accompanying funeral cortege.

The Great Pyramid's Mysterious Light

A clue may be found at the very apex of the Pyramid itself. There, from ancient times to the present day, an irregularly occurring phenomenon has been seen by a few fortunate eyewitnesses and documented by trained observers: Visitors at the Giza Plateau sometimes see the summit of the Great Pyramid lit by a bluish haze, cloud, mist, or halo of varying luminosity.

Whatever we may think of Aleister Crowley, the notorious cabalist did spend a night inside the Pyramid's so-called King's Chamber in 1903. He was surprised to see that the entire compartment was suffused by a blue glow, the source of which he could not determine. Crowley reported that he could read by the light, although it was very dim.[5]

The Great Pyramid's blue light continues to be observed by modern visitors, who usually doubt the testimony of their own senses. One of the best and most recent sightings of the pyramid-light was witnessed by an American tourist, Robert Houseman, visiting Egypt in 1994. He was staying at the Mona House, close to and slightly lower than the Great Pyramid. On the night before he was scheduled to leave:

Everyone else had gone to bed, but I had to have one last look at the pyramid looming over the hotel. Around midnight, I went to see the incredible structure one more time. There was a mist or fog of some sort around the pyramid. I could just make out the triangular structure. Yet, as I gazed at it, a bluish light began to form all around it. As I stared at it with curiosity, wondering where this light was coming from, it grew brighter. I was a little taken aback, as I noticed this blue light forming a ball around the top of the pyramid. I stood there for at least 20 minutes, as the light grew brighter and more distinct. I remember wondering if I was hallucinating or actually seeing the pyramid's aura.[6]

Another American visitor, William Groff, was equally astounded to witness a blue light illuminating the summit of the Great Pyramid. As a prominent physicist, he was influential in bringing fellow scientists from the Institut Egyptien to the structure. Despite an exhaustive investigation of its internal passages, however, they were unable to find a cause for the phenomenon.[7]

The British Museum's leading Egyptologist around the turn of the 20th century, Sir E.A. Wallis Budge, whose translations of important dynastic source materials are still regarded as definitive, found what he believed was the oldest written allusion to the Great Pyramid. He experienced difficulty precisely interpreting the term, already archaic by the close of the Old Kingdom around 2155 B.C., because it occurs only once in the Egyptian *Book of the Dead*. Budge nevertheless concluded that *khahut* must have meant "the pyramid's luminous aspect," or "pyramid light," an apparent reference to the lingering phenomenon witnessed by Houseman, Groff, and others, but known from the beginning of Egyptian history.[8]

While early reports of the event were filled with superstitious dread, investigators today believe the Pyramid's blue light is generated by stress building within the Earth directly beneath the structure. It appears to be the same occurrence known as "earthquake lights"—usually dark blue clouds that sometimes appear just before seismic activity. Basically, as the forces that produce a quake squeeze subterranean minerals, electrical currents are generated to break down underground water molecules, thereby releasing charged ions of oxygen and hydrogen into the air. The process chemically separates electrons from their paths around atomic nuclei, transmuting their energy into light. Affected water molecules are thereby condensed into statically charged mists or clouds that appear glowing or incandescent. As a growing earthquake exerts stress on granite and/or other crystalline rock in the planet's crust, a visual charge is emitted. These earthquake lights were photographed

for the first time in 1966, immediately preceding an earthquake that struck the Japanese town of Matsushiro, when the horizon was ablaze with an eerie, azure glow.

The "blue aura" commonly witnessed at Pinnacles National Monument in southern California is generated by seismic energies interacting with the natural formation's crystal-granite matrix.

The same phenomenon takes place in the Alps and Andes Mountains, from whence the term "Andes Glow" originates. It is a brilliant discharge of electrical energy into the atmosphere, sometimes hundreds of miles long, generated by seismic activity. The event likewise occurs in the United States, notably at Pinnacles National Monument in the California Coast Ranges, south of Hollister. Here the blue light most often manifests itself along a 3-mile-long, .5-mile-high ridge of rock formations resembling pointed towers or conical pyramids. In 1973, David Kurbin, a British historian, photographed a massy but amorphous light-form hovering directly over the monument before it rotated and vanished in midair. Pinnacles National Monument sits on its own Pinnacles Fault, a closely connected spur of the notorious San Andreas Fault, which, in fact, gave birth to the volcanic structures a million years ago.

The Great Pyramid is also located within a seismically active zone, so the blue light sometimes seen flashing at its apex results from the same energies responsible for earthquake lights and the Andes Glow. Mr. Houseman observed the pyramid-light (the ancient *khahut*) on September 22, 1994, a few months after a 6.2-scale earthquake rocked Egypt, damaging massive, ancient structures at Kom Ombro, but leaving the Great Pyramid unscathed. Tremors were reported throughout Egypt for about half a year following its major shock, so the September sighting appears to have been the piezo-electric effect of ongoing seismic activity.

Piezo-electricity is the conversion of mechanical energy into electrical energy when stress is applied to crystalline minerals. The term derives from the Greek *piezein*, to "squeeze" or "press," and refers to an electrical charge resulting from certain crystals when they are subjected to physical pressure. To produce this effect, these crystals must be electrically neutral, with symmetrical striations separating negative from positive charges. This electrical neutrality is energized as their symmetry deforms under applied stress, generating voltage. As such, not all crystals feature piezo-electric qualities. Of the 32 classifications of crystal, 20 are conductive, although most

vary in quality. While not exactly rare, more or less perfectly symmetrical crystals—particularly rutilated specimens containing some iron for heightened conductivity—are less common, and noted for their exceptional clarity, the result of at least partially uniformly linear striations: A half-ton pressure exerted on a 0.4-inch crystal can produce 25,000 volts. In 1981, Dr. Brian Brady at the U.S. Bureau of Mines in Denver, Colorado, performed a controlled laboratory experiment that proved the electrical properties of the mineral. In subjecting a slab to extraordinarily high pressures, the granite specimen emitted an electrical discharge accompanied by a spark display that was photographed and measured.[9]

The phenomenon is not only luminous, but a real power, as Sir William Siemens demonstrated on April 14, 1859. Siemens, whose pioneering life achievements in electrical engineering won him a British knighthood and a commemorative window in Westminster Abbey, was one of the great inventive geniuses of the modern era. On a visit to Egypt, he climbed with local guides and a party of friends, fellow electrical engineers, to the top of the Great Pyramid, now a mostly flat platform 30 feet square. After reaching the summit, Siemens celebrated their ascent by drinking a toast from a wine bottle. As he did so, he tasted a faint electrical charge. Curious and wishing to pursue the effect further, he wrapped some dampened newspaper around the bottle, which had metal foil about the neck. When he held it above his head, the bottle quickly became so charged with static electricity that blue sparks began shooting from both ends. A native guide, terrified that Siemens and his colleagues were sorcerers, seized one of the scientists and threatened to throw him off the Pyramid. Siemens thrust the flickering wine bottle at the Arab, who was abruptly knocked off his feet and rendered unconscious by an electric shock that leapt from the glass to the stunned guide's nose.

Building a Charge

With Siemens' experience in mind, let us examine the interior of the Great Pyramid, setting aside all previous theories to explain it. Unlike what one might expect for a "Hall of Initiation," as the structure is sometimes called, the Pyramid's internal details are not meandering or complex. The vast majority of its cut blocks are calcium carbonate limestone, which combine to create a perfect insulator. Meanwhile, at the very bottom-center of the Pyramid is a 30-foot square hole cut into the bedrock and positioned directly beneath the apex—the same relationship between the "ground" (negative) and the discharge point (positive) of a battery.

That apex, as mentioned, is today a flat 30-by-30-foot square platform. Archaeologists believe it was originally surmounted by a *pyramidian*, or pyramid-shaped capstone, allegedly removed by Arabs in the 13th century. But such a capstone would have weighed more than 1,000 tons—so heavy that it would have deformed the entire upper portion of the Pyramid. According to Islamic tradition, the apex featured not a capstone, but a gold-sheeted chamber. Hieroglyphic symbols for the Pyramid as far back as those found on Old Kingdom mastabas (flat-roofed tombs from the late 4th millennium B.C.) usually depict the apex in yellow pigment, signifying gold. The precious metal is well known for its high conductivity and integral role in the electronics industry, especially as a finish to electrical connectors.

The King's Chamber

Moving back into the structure's interior, we direct our attention to the so-called King's Chamber. It is a descriptive name only, because no human remains, least of all those belonging to any king, were ever found in the compartment. The chamber is extraordinary, in that it is made entirely of granite, unlike the mountain of limestone blocks that conceal it. And even though it is buried deep within the bowels of the Pyramid, the chamber has a roof—although the roof cannot be seen, it must have been put in place for purposes other than keeping off rain! The King's Chamber is 17 feet wide, 19 feet high, and 34 feet long. Its mystery deepens with these dimensions, because they perfectly express the ratio of two Pythagorean triangles, as though this very room was defining the gigantic structure enclosing it. The Chamber is absolutely bare, save for a solid granite basin (referred to by tourist guides as the "sarcophagus") that was installed before its level of the Pyramid was completed: It is far too large to have been carried through the narrow passageway that leads to the King's Chamber.

Sections above it are divided into five additional chambers separated by several feet of airspace with alternating layers of nine and eight granite beams. Its gabled "roof" is pitched with a jeweler's precision, a feat made all the more astounding when we learn that the cut blocks in this elaborate internal arrangement weigh 70 tons each. Combined, they put 3,010 tons of pressure on the small King's Chamber below. Furthermore, Egyptian granite often comprises more than 55 percent silicon quartz, and is therefore a superb material for electrical purposes. Containing conductive mica and feldspar in addition to silicon dioxide, granite generates a piezo-electric field when submitted to intense pressure. The tonnage of microscopic quartz crystals lining this chamber is in the hundreds.

How much voltage could the 3,010 tons of pressure on the King's Chamber generate? According to Devereux, from 10,000 to 100,000 volts per square meter.[10] In fact, the King's Chamber is a highly charged field, in which the alternating layers of granite slabs and air spaces above it are nothing less than a capacitor, a device used for storing an electrical charge. Also, piezo-electricity is similar to the charge created by the subterranean pressures leading to an earthquake. The earthquake lights and Andes Glow described previously closely resemble the discharge of pressurized quartz, even to the bluish luminescence that accompanies both. These azure mists or clouds that suddenly appear as pressure builds up are aggregations of highly charged ion molecules.

The Queen's Chamber and the Grand Gallery

Although the King's Chamber is located near the center of the Great Pyramid, it is actually off-center. But beneath it, in a direct line between the apex above and the equally large square excavated into the bedrock, lies the smaller Queen's Chamber. Contrasting with the room's rough, unworked floor, its ceiling was constructed of gigantic, precisely cut limestone slabs pitched at a 30-degree, 26-minute slope, creating another gabled roof identical to that of the King's Chamber, down to the same degree and minute. The Queen's Chamber is almost square: Its north–south wall is 17 feet, 2 inches long, with an east–west wall of 18 feet. Into this wall was carved a cavity 16 feet high and 3 feet, 5 inches deep. If this niche originally held a vessel of liquid almost in proportion to

the cavity, the entire Queen's Chamber would have been similar to the altered wine bottle William Siemens experimented with atop the Pyramid—in other words, a kind of Leyden jar, or condenser of static electricity.

Also suggestive of a purposeful arrangement, the Great Pyramid's internal passageways do not meander in a ritual maze, but travel directly to its four compartments. They are more akin to service corridors, by which attendants could reach each chamber in the shortest possible time. The four air shafts leading from the bases of the King's and the Queen's Chambers outwardly direct the longitudinal or "shear" waves generated by a piezo-electric transducer. And that is the real identity of the Great Pyramid: It is a high-voltage generator, a device designed and constructed to convert physical energies into other energies. It is likewise a transducer for the conversion of mechanical energy into electrical energy and back again.

A transducer is the application of piezo-electricity, such as the ceramic phonograph needle that made long-playing records possible. The first radio receivers ("crystal sets"), television remote controls, some of today's high-end ink-jet printers, and most modern medical ultrasound scanners are piezo-electric transducers. Likewise, when the button of an electric cigarette lighter or a portable sparker used to light stoves is depressed, it trips a spring-loaded hammer to strike a tiny crystal that consequently generates enough voltage to ignite the stored butane.

The transducer identity of the Great Pyramid is yet again suggested by its so-called Grand Gallery, the building's largest internal feature. At 125 feet long and 26 feet high, it is an ascending corridor configured similar to a parallelogram, rising at a 45-degree angle from the end of the Queen's Chamber's horizontal passageway, and connected with a smaller anteroom abutting the King's Chamber. Today, tourists climb through the Grand Gallery to the King's Chamber, but the wooden stairway they use is a modern addition. Previously, the Grand Gallery never provided access between the Chambers, and defied the ability of mainstream scholars to adequately explain this persistent enigma until Christopher Dunn looked at it through different eyes. After all, the Great Pyramid had not been built by Egyptologists, but by construction engineers such as himself. Dunn instantly recognized the Grand Gallery as a "resonator hall," used to reflect sound and direct it into the King's Chamber with its crystal capacitor.

The "Gallery" inside the Great Pyramid.

The 27 pairs of slots (which have stumped conventional thinkers) in the side ramps of the Gallery contained a framework of wood (an efficient responder to vibration) to hold banks of Heimholtz resonators—spheres of varying sizes used to determine each one's specific, resonating frequency. Their purpose was to step up the vibrational energy from the Queen's Chamber, amplifying it into the King's Chamber, converting and concentrating the vibrations into airborne sound. This would explain the remarkable acoustics found in the Grand Gallery and King's Chamber.

For the series of different Heimholtz resonating spheres to function as intended, they would have required progressively smaller walled separations, thereby preventing any frequency from crossing or bleeding into one another, and eliminating distortion of individually generated resonance. As though to perfectly accommodate such an arrangement, the Grand Gallery's walls do indeed step inward from floor to ceiling in seven short, separate partitions. The magnified vibrations accumulating there would have created too much oscillation for such a confined cavity to contain: To prevent it from being broken apart, its 36 ceiling stones are, in fact, unattached and removable, allowing them to oscillate in vibrational sympathy, while avoiding any structural damage. As author Edward Malkowsky explains, "As a result, the maximization of resonance is achieved, and the entire granite complex becomes a vibrating mass of energy."[11]

While the Grand Gallery's otherwise inexplicably stepped walls and unattached ceiling stones are identifiable features of Dunn's "resonator hall," at least one of its Heimholtz resonators has been known since 1872.[12] In that year, a granite ball was discovered in the Queen's Chamber, where it may have rolled through the horizontal corridor from the base of the Grand Gallery.

Among the very few artifacts ever recovered from inside the Great Pyramid, the unadorned sphere weighs 1 pound, 3 ounces. Nothing like it has ever been found in any other ancient Egyptian context, yet this unique object appeared in the same structure that made use of the Heimholtz resonators.

Typically, transducers are cone-shaped or pyramidal in order to force the energy radiated from the core (the King's Chamber) into and through a narrowing area smaller than that of the core itself, thereby increasing its intensity as energy is forced upward. According to Illinois physicist Joseph Farrell:

> *Professor Nelson* [Dr. Charles Nelson, Physics Department, Concordia College, Maryland] *suggests that if the coffer in the King's Chamber was filled with an aqueous solution of natron (N_AHCO_3, N_ACI and $N_{A2}SO_4$), the salt water itself would act as an effective conductor of electricity for the piezo-electric induction from the matte-finished walls of the King's Chamber. This, Professor Nelson affirms, would make it unnecessary to line the coffer with metal— salt is an effective conductor of electricity. In fact, salt deposits have been found throughout the internal features of the Great Pyramid. Professor Nelson correctly points out that such a process would naturally produce poisonous chlorine gas, which, somehow, would have been vented from the Chamber.[13]*

It appears that, in addition to outwardly directing latitudinal shear waves of piezo-electrical discharges, the so-called air shafts simultaneously vented poisonous chlorine gasses resulting from the coffer's conductive solution.

A Crystal Conductor

Although a natron solution would have been effective, a large crystal would have been more efficient—stable and capable of simultaneously collecting and generating greater static discharge. The stone itself would have had to have been sufficiently large, approximately 3 feet long by 2 feet thick, to accommodate the massive energies focused in it; entirely possible, because crystals can grow to 20 feet and beyond, and a specimen displayed at the Chicago Museum of Natural History is some 5 feet long and weighs nearly 1,000 pounds. Crystals are important components in numerous electronic instruments because they magnify, resonate, refine, and direct electrical energy. Thus, the Great Pyramid's crystal would have been of exceptional clarity, a visible expression of its fine symmetry, and hence, high conductivity. It was not simply dumped into the granite coffer, but first placed inside a metallic container that enhanced the crystal's function as a capacitor.

This is not unfounded assumption: The renowned French mythologist, Rene Guenon, recounted an Arab narrative that described a Stone of Destiny maintained in its own chamber within the Great Pyramid. Indeed, its cross-section compares identically with a cut-away of a standard transducer, including the piezo-electric crystal. That the very configuration of the monumental structure was predetermined according to the Stone of Destiny it concealed is suggested by the termination of natural quartz crystals, which most often slant at 510 degrees, 51 minutes, the same angle of the Great Pyramid.[14]

Our modern transducer's exponential cone is also present in the Great Pyramid, at the very base of which, literally cut into the bedrock, is a "ground" that matched in area the gold pyramidian 481 feet directly above. Precisely in between is located the condenser (Queen's Chamber), which, from its pitched roof, threw the stored electrical charge to the off-center capacitor (King's Chamber). There, the energy was accelerated, and jumped to the crystal at the apex, surrounded in its chamber of highly conductive gold, from whence it was focused and directed outward with a massive spark-discharge into the atmosphere.

The 6 million tons of surrounding calcium carbonate limestone blocks acted as the insulation necessary to contain such dangerously high accumulations of energy. Focused current would have streamed from the pyramidian in a vertical column of light toward the sky, just as seismic pressures preceding an earthquake build beneath a conical mountain. The most memorable display of this kind was witnessed by hundreds of observers in 1878, when Mount Logelbach in Alsace shot a vertical, radiant pillar, akin to a gargantuan searchlight, from its summit toward the heavens.

But what was the power source for this colossal generator? For the answer, we must return to our earlier description of the Great Pyramid's unique position at the geographic center of the world's land mass and the geodetic fundamentals incorporated in its architecture. As we have seen, the Pyramid mathematically embodies the very Earth it represents, an embodiment underscored by its midpoint location on the Earth. As Dunn writes, "By incorporating

the same basic measurements in the pyramid that were found on the planet, the efficiency of the pyramid was improved and, in effect, it could be a harmonic integer of the planet."[15] New finds made inside the Great Pyramid seem to confirm his identification of it as a monumental electronic device. In 1995 and again in 2002, robotic investigation of so-called air shafts in the Queen's Chamber discovered two "doors," each with metal "handles." Dunn told *Atlantis Rising* magazine that "the so-called handles are actually electrodes of a circuit, or circuits, which would be closed if electrically conductive fluid were to rise up the shafts to the necessary level."[16]

Harnessing Earth Power

Among all their other achievements, the ancient builders created the most earthquake-proof structure in history. After unknown millennia of sometimes major seismic disturbances at the Giza Plateau, the Great Pyramid continues to stand intact. A few blocks have shifted from their original positions and others show cracks and fissures from causes other than seismic, but none have broken or fallen. As the authors of *Earth Facts*, Scarlett Hall and Cally O'Hara, point out, pyramid-shaped buildings are built to withstand the stresses of ground tremors, so there may be very good reasons for this earthquake-resistant design.[17]

The electro-mechanical energy produced by even a moderate earthquake is prodigious. Seismic upheavals are only sporadic concentrations of geologic intensity, but the Earth is constantly alive with various energy fields that are only partially understood by geophysicists. Even the easily demonstrable magnetosphere defies universally acceptable explanations for its origins and means of operation. The telluric forces ceaselessly at work within our planet are constantly generating levels of energy that escape the surface, and the Great Pyramid is strategically placed at the one position on the face of the globe where it can take maximum advantage of those telluric forces.

As a piezo-electric transducer, its function was to change geologic energy into electric energy. The entire structure had to work *with* seismic forces, not against them. If the very energies it was intended to harness could damage or destroy it, the Great Pyramid would have failed the purpose for which it was built. Except for the Temple of Artemis at Ephesus and the Statue of Zeus at Olympia (both destroyed by fire), earthquakes toppled the other Seven Wonders of the World, save only the Great Pyramid. It has successfully withstood the geologic violence it was meant to exploit, because it is, if not earthquake-proof, then earthquake-resistant.

For example, an almost imperceptible indentation in each of the four faces dampen structural oscillations that would otherwise shatter them. This subtle feature alone virtually proves its designers had earthquakes in mind when they built the Great Pyramid. Its Grand Gallery's roof slabs are separately jointed, thereby evenly distributing the tonnage along its whole length, while the King's Chamber's walls are only loosely attached to the surrounding interior. These features accommodate, rather than resist, the sharp movement associated with seismic activity. When Arab builders of Cairo's mosques stripped the Great Pyramid of its limestone casing, they revealed its alternating courses of larger and smaller blocks, a configuration that ameliorates the exponential accumulation of vibrational effects that can tear a structure to pieces. British investigator Ralph Ellis determined that the arrangement of stone courses in the Great Pyramid was identical to the kind of banding automotive engineers discovered for designing rubber tires, thereby preventing loud resonance when the car is in motion.[18]

Taken altogether, these internal features demonstrate that they were deliberately incorporated into the Great Pyramid as seismic safeguards to enable its survival by riding earthquakes or moving with them, instead of rigidly resisting and breaking apart. But why would the ancient inhabitants of the Nile Delta want to build such a monumental transducer? To provide electrical power for a civilization that we believe predated the electronic age by 5,000 or more years? Surely something even more compelling than a voltage generator, no matter how socially useful, would have been required to call forth the best effort of a whole culture.

The Pyramid's True Purpose

Arab commentators on the Great Pyramid repeat a centuries-old (at least) tradition of a king who learned of an imminent natural catastrophe, a terrible flood, brought about by the fall of some celestial object. He then had the Pyramid built as a "refuge" from the coming disaster. Now, "refuge" usually suggests a shelter. But the Great Pyramid is not hollow. Its narrow passages and chambers could accommodate no more than perhaps only 200 persons at a time, and very uncomfortably at that. But "refuge" also implies an action to escape difficulty. If we accept this interpretation of the word, the Pyramid begins to take on its ultimate, highly practical—and even urgent—significance. Its ultimate role begins to unfold in an electrically charged atom known as an ion.

An ion–pyramid connection was first demonstrated in July of 1969, by Dr. Luis Walter Alverez, Nobel prizewinner and professor of physics at Lawrence Radiation Laboratory, Berkeley, California, who helped develop the atomic bomb. He envisioned and then headed up a $1 million project involving leading scientists of the U.S. Atomic Energy Commission and the Smithsonian Institution to discover suspected secret chambers inside Khafre's pyramid, a near duplicate of the Great Pyramid. Dr. Alverez assembled within the Khafre structure "a cosmic-ray measuring instrument"—a computerized spark chamber, sensitive enough to record the fluctuations of neutrinos as they passed through the Pyramid.[19] These neutrinos, which penetrate virtually all matter, lose some of their energy as they infiltrate a mass proportionate to its density. The rays were supposed to pierce the solid masonry in straight lines, but move with greater intensity if they encountered a cavity. Computers and recorders monitored the spark chamber during its operation.

The results, according to Dr. Amr Goneid, director of Cairo's Ein Shams University computer, were "scientifically impossible." The equipment was checked, re-checked, and checked again. Instrumentation was in perfect operating order, yet showed that the cosmic rays that entered the Pyramid were bent at wildly erratic angles and in no steady pattern, but in an absolutely atypical shifting display, similar to bullets ricocheting off stone—as Goneid observed, "an impossibility." Exasperated, he concluded, "Either the geometry of the Pyramid is in substantial error, or there is a mystery that is beyond explanation."[20] Thus far, the Khafre's Pyramid is the only man-made object known to be able to affect the course of neutrinos.

Although it did not have the intended results, at the very least the spark chamber experiment showed that some incredibly strong energy was charging through the pyramid at Khafre. The cosmic rays affected by this unexpected and unknown force implied that only an energy connection with the ionosphere itself would be potent enough to affect cosmic rays so powerfully. The experiment likewise suggests that the Great Pyramid was not alone in its function as a tectonic transducer, but shared that function with its companion structure. In fact, as already pointed out, the 10th century Islamic scholar, Masoudi, claimed that at least the two larger Giza pyramids were constructed together by the same king.

Somewhat less than 100 pyramids, from Giza in the north down to the Nubian border in the south, stand on either side of the Nile River, and no original burial was ever discovered in any one of them. Moreover, most of them feature variations of essentially the same internal configuration found inside the Great Pyramid. Perhaps all are tectonic transducers deliberately positioned along the seismically active Nile Valley to diffuse the worst of the potentially destructive earthquakes that threatened the new civilization being built in early pharaonic Egypt.

The northeast region of Africa today appears geologically quiescent, but it has a long history of violent upheaval. On August 8, 1303, exceptionally powerful tremors destroyed most of the famous Pharos Lighthouse, after standing at the port of Alexandria for the previous 16 centuries. A leading expert on that structure, Larry Brian Radka, quotes *Les Seismes a Alexandrie et la Destruction du*

Phare: "The walls of the Great Mosque of Alexandria and a large part of the Pharos of Alexandria sunk" during a prolonged earthquake just 42 years earlier.[21] Previous earthquakes in 1258, 1211, 1202, 1196, 1191, 1186, and 365 left their enduring scars on strata throughout the Nile Delta. On December 28, 955, a "swarm," or series of catastrophic aftershocks rolled across Egypt and Syria for half an hour, according to the contemporary Arab historian, Masoudi.

An Ancient Energy Source

Giza's ancient geo-transducers might also have helped minimize earthquake activity in the seismically unstable Nile Valley by discharging seismic energy into electricity. As a small-scale example, many modern watches and small travelers' clocks feature a built-in quartz tuning fork that produces a regularly timed series of electrical pulses to accurately count hours, minutes and seconds. These quartz components, as do all piezo-electric crystals, have their own, precisely defined natural frequency determined by shape and size. They oscillate at a specific rate, thereby stabilizing the frequency of a periodic voltage applied to the crystal. Similarly, a sufficiently large, appropriately configured, and symmetrical piezo-electric quartz installed in the Giza transducer would have had an ameliorating effect on seismic energy by dampening it to the crystal's lower, stabilizing frequency. The bluish earthquake lights and Andes Glow that reappear at the Great Pyramid serve similar purposes. Some geologists believe these discharges not only warn of imminent tremors, but may tend to dissipate them,

at least to some degree. Indeed, early representations of pyramids, such as the mastaba temple art circa 2800 B.C. at Thebes, sometimes depicted the apex not in gold, but blue pigment, indicating that the electrostatic corona of the pyramidian was known to the ancients.

Skeptics may disagree, arguing that piezo-electricity was unknown until 1880. Before its discovery by the French brothers Pierre and Jacques Curie, the phenomenon was supposedly unfamiliar to all pre-industrial cultures. Yet some Native Americans have understood and applied its principle for countless years. Uncompahgre Ute Shamans are trained by their elder mentors to hunt for and collect only crystals of piezo-electric capabilities in the mountains of Utah and central Colorado. The specimens are then collected into ceremonial rattles made of translucent buffalo skin and revered as the holy man's most sacred objects. During nighttime rituals aimed at summoning the spirits of the dead, the shaken rattles blaze with bright flashes of light as their carefully selected crystals collide against each other, creating sufficient impact stress and mechanical pressure to generate artificial luminescence. If a preliterate, tribal people such as the Uncompahgre Ute have been able to apply at least a fundamental understanding of piezo-electricity for the last several thousand years, then ancient Egyptians building the high culture of Nile Civilization would certainly have been able to develop the same phenomenon far beyond a rawhide rattle.

The Ute tell of a bear-spirit that long ago threatened to destroy mankind. Extermination was prevented by an ancestral hero, Sunuwavi, when he found the beast's magic flame, and "doused it with water."[22] An earlier version of the same myth has Sunuwavi cause a great flood that sank the *qumu*, the bear-spirit's "fire medicine," the source of his spiritual power, to the bottom of the sea. The Lemurian elements of this rendition are apparent with the introduction of a deluge and the name of the bear-spirit's qumu, his fire medicine, as fire is associated in numerous cultures around the world with spiritual power. Moreover, the Navel of the World motif surfaces in the Ute's rather singular creation of magnificent quartz crystal blades used only in sacred ceremonies to sever a child's umbilical cord, which is stored in a special jar for the remainder of that person's life and then buried with him or her as part of the funeral—precisely the same practice was undertaken on the other side of the world at Te-Pito-te-Henua, Easter Island's Navel of the World.

Native American parallels are not so far afield from their related enigma at Egypt's Great Pyramid, and demonstrate a kindred appreciation for crystal technology rooted in the deep past. Farrell writes:

Celestial, solar, lunar, terrestrial alignments accurately reproduced over and over again. And we have touched on but a very few of a vast inventory. Strange, if not downright weird construction features. Accurate ratios of the thermal and mass gradients of the Earth, the astronomical unit, the precession of the equinoxes, the average height of land above sea-level. And all this to bury a pharaoh? Surely not, says Christopher Dunn. It was not a tomb. It was a machine.[23]

It was a very special machine, the like of which has not been built since, for all of modern man's vaunted technological accomplishments. All evidence suggests that the Great Pyramid was envisioned, designed, and constructed as an incredibly powerful geo-transducer for the transformation of telluric energies into electrical energies. It was primarily a device for diffusing seismic pressures to minimize the destructive capabilities of earthquakes.

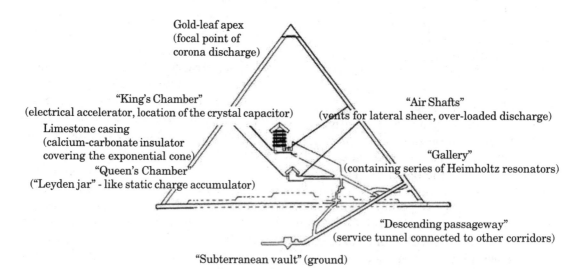

Gold-leaf apex
(focal point of
corona discharge)

"King's Chamber"
(electrical accelerator, location of the crystal capacitor)

Limestone casing
(calcium-carbonate insulator
covering the exponential cone)
"Queen's Chamber"
("Leyden jar" - like static charge accumulator)

"Air Shafts"
(vents for lateral sheer, over-loaded discharge)

"Gallery"
(containing series of Heimholtz resonators)

"Descending passageway"
(service tunnel connected to other corridors)

"Subterranean vault" (ground)

A cut-away of the Great Pyramid identifying its internal features as the components of a solid-state electrical device—a geo-transducer.

Remarkably, the same electrical components utilized in the Great Pyramid were independently discovered by Nikola Tesla, a humble Serbian who migrated to the United States with four cents in his pocket in 1884. Seven years later, he invented the Tesla impulse coil, still used in television sets and numerous other electronic instruments. Farrell was the first to notice a comparison with the Great Pyramid, which is "an electrical coil that is segmented—exactly in accordance with the principles discovered by Tesla—not only into separate 'windings' in the stone courses, but each of these 'windings' in turn is segmented into a discrete number of stones. The pyramidal form itself gives the distinctive geometry and properties of a Tesla impulse coil."[24] Fundamental resemblance of this early electrical device to the Giza structure helps confirm its ancient function as a geo-transducer.

The Power of the Destiny Stone

The most vital component of this Earth-powered device was a Stone of Destiny; according to 13th century Arab accounts, an exceptionally large, clear crystal that magnified and focused telluric energies channeled through the immense structure, and identified the Great Pyramid as the preeminent Navel of the World. Its geodetic orientation, cultural symbolism, and inclusion of a sacred stone clearly define the entire site as an axis mundi in keeping with fundamentally similar, though far less colossal, omphalos centers. It was part of a network stretching around the globe from the Pacific to Atlantic Oceans, and across the Mediterranean Sea to Asia Minor and India.

In the Judaic rendition, the Stone of Destiny was said to have been a great sapphire Adam received from God. It passed, after his expulsion from the Garden of Eden, to the patriarch after whom the Book of Enoch was entitled. Written by Hasidic compilers from the 2nd century B.C. to the 1st century A.D., substantial excerpts came to light in 1947 with the discovery of the Dead Sea Scrolls. They portrayed Enoch as the great-grandfather of Noah, to whom he entrusted the Stone of Destiny prior to the Deluge. The internationally acclaimed British researcher Andrew Collins tells of different Judaic sources that "speak of some kind of sacred stone being placed in hidden chambers beneath the Giza pyramids." Enoch was equated with their builder, Thaut, who "deposited a 'white oriental porphyry stone'" inside the Great Pyramid, which he appropriately describes as a "house excelling in splendor and magnificence and extent," built of crystals and encompassed by "tongues of fire." There the "white oriental porphyry stone" was known as the "sealed thing."[25]

The Destiny Stone was not really a sapphire, but its characterization as such was a poetic metaphor for the object's precious worth, just as Thaut's Emerald Tablets were not actually made of that gem, but intended by his myth to stress the especially valuable wisdom and piezo-electric properties they contained. More importantly, both Arab tradition and the Book of Enoch affirm the Stone of Destiny's Atlantean provenance in its antediluvian origins and survival of the Great Flood: The ability to subtly alter a natural crystal for electronic purposes, if not the crystal itself, survived with refugees of the Atlantean cataclysm seeking refuge at the Nile Delta. Their prehistoric arrival and the special object they carried is no modern fantasy, but authentic, dynastic traditions rooted in the Ben-Ben, ancient Egypt's supremely sacred item.

The Mansion of the Phoenix

Although sometimes described as conical, the Ben-Ben itself was smoothly, though irregularly, oblate and rounded. In any case, neither "conical" nor "roughly egg-shaped" describes a meteorite, as many Egyptologists speculate it may have been. Indeed, the crystal identification is suggested by the Hebrew word *ben-adamah*, which means that which is "hewn from or drawn out of the Earth"—not something fallen from the sky. The Ben-Ben was not only the Nile Civilization's most holy article, but also its oldest, even predating the Great Pyramid. Before that immense building project was completed, the stone rested atop a column at the very center of its own temple in Heliopolis, the "City of the Sun," the principal seat of solar worship, located 5 miles east of the Nile, north of the Delta's apex. According to the renowned author of *The Orion Mystery*, Robert Bauval, "the Ben-Ben stone was considered a relic of immense value by the pyramid builders, so valuable that it was placed in the holy-of-holies of Heliopolis, in the focal point of the 'Mansion of the Phoenix.'"[26]

The Ben-Ben was erected at the midpoint of a square court surrounded on all sides by contiguous buildings with numerous columns. Hence the city's original Egyptian name: A-wen, or "Place of the Pillars." Occupied since predynastic times, it may have been Egypt's first capital, or at least its premiere ceremonial center, where, millennia later, Pythagoras, Plato, and many Athenian scholars availed themselves

of its ancient wisdom. But by the 1st century B.C., the great Greek geographer Strabo found its streets deserted, and the town itself almost uninhabited, save for a few caretaker priests. After the fall of Classical civilization, the site was known as "the Well of the Sun," or 'Ayn S'ams to the Arabs, who used it as a quarry for building medieval Cairo. Today, virtually nothing of the once splendid City of the Sun remains.

The Ben-Ben is said to have come from the Celestial Waters—created by Atum, the chief diety of the City of the Sun—surrounding the Primal Mound. After his sacred stone was removed to the newly completed Great Pyramid, other, single pillars were set up in imitation of the original. These became obelisks, memorial columns topped with a pyramidal cap known as the *benbenet*, a word that demonstrated their exemplar at the Place of the Pillars.

"Ben-Ben" derived from "Bennu," the Egyptian phoenix that rose from its own ashes and epitomized the soul of Ra, the sun god. Its name is related to the verb *weben*, meaning "to rise brilliantly," or "to shine" like fire, and its title, "He Who Came Into Being by Himself," implies a function more essential than the gods themselves. The Egyptian *Book of the Dead*, a collection of mortuary prayers, exclaims, "I am the Bennu bird, the Heart-Soul of Ra, the Guide of the Gods to the Tuat [the Underworld]." Both the bird itself and its egg were synonymous with the Ben-Ben. The Bennu created itself from the Tree of Life when it caught fire in Ra's central precinct at the Primal Mound.

This Heliopolitan version of its myth seems to describe the rebirth of the Tree of Life mystery cult after the destruction of Atlantis. Indeed, the Bennu was also known as the "Soul of Atum," or the Soul of the Atlantic Ocean. The square surrounding the Ben-Ben's central pillar at A-wen defined its Navel of the World position at the midpoint of the four cardinal directions formed by the temple walls.

The Bennu was said to have perished in a fire from which it was reborn every 12,594 years. Florida Atlantologist Kenneth Caroli stated that the phoenix's recurring death and rebirth was "the precessional half-cycle or Great Season of Summer and Winter which were symbolically linked to worldwide conflagrations and floods. Each Great Season had six precessional months." Interestingly, this figure corresponds to a global climate cycle only recognized by modern geophysicists during the late 20th century: It demarcates the onset and closing of ice ages. Scholars are divided over their cause—sun-spot activity, perturbations in our planet's rotation relative in its angle to the Sun, or even meteoric bombardment aimed at the Earth from a regularly passing comet. But they concur that ice ages begin and end in transforming violence, during which the face of the world is reconfigured and whole species vanish. As the Egyptian priest remarks in Plato's story of Atlantis:

> *There have been and will be many different calamities to destroy mankind, the greatest of them by fire and water...There is at long intervals a variation in the course of the heavenly bodies and a consequent widespread destruction by fire of things upon the Earth.*[27]

If the Bennu's 12,594-year cycle was not coincidental, it is evidence of an inconceivably advanced science at work in Egypt from Old Kingdom times, if not before, as an heirloom brought by Thaut from the Primal Mound of Atlantis. In a variant of its myth, the Bennu dies, but its egg, the Ben-Ben, survives the flames to hatch out a new fire-bird. A 5th century B.C. mosaic

from Antioch now at the Louvre shows the Phoenix perched atop a mountainous island surrounded by 48 wild goats divided by 24 lotuses. The significance of this imagery is apparent: the ibex, a symbol of perpetual vitality, and the lotus flowers as the personification of rebirth, here represent the hours of the day—time revolving around the motionless center of eternity found in the Navel of the World's regenerative mystery cult, born on Mount Atlas.

Indeed, "Ben-Ben" derived from the root word *ben*, for the "seeding of the womb." The first translator of the Pyramid Texts, Kurt Sethe, referred to the Ben-Ben as "an omphalos." Egyptologist Rundle Clark concluded that the Bennu and Ben-Ben "are linked together."[28] His British colleague, Philip Gardiner, observes that the Bennu "represented the 'soul', the 'divine spark,' or 'life force' that is said to reside in every man and woman and inside the centre of the skull; hence, the placement of the Ben-Ben on top of the column, obelisk, or pyramid which represented the human spine and body."[29]

The Bennu bird's phoenix-quality renders its Ben-Ben egg a fire stone, not unlike the Guanche Fyra, Tibetan Chintamani or

Egyptian temple art (Memphis) depicts the Phoenix rising from its Ben-Ben Stone.

any of the other, radiant *omphalli* found around the globe wherever the Navel of the World mystery cult was headquartered. In fact, Spell 1080 of the Coffin Texts relates that the Ben-Ben had "a fire about it."[30] It lay surrounded by the sides of its golden box inside the granite "sarcophagus" of the King's Chamber to complete the Great Pyramid's function as a geo-transducer. There, the radiant energies this large crystal gave off were the "fires" that at once ameliorated seismic violence. Only thus understood do the Egyptian titles *khut* and *ikhet* for the Giza Plateau's foremost monument make sense: They mean, respectively, "Light," and "Glorious Light" or the "Shining One." As Farrell rightly concludes, "The sapphire 'destiny stone' is one of the most important components of the now-missing interior of the Great (Pyramid)."[31]

The Pyramid Texts are Ancient Egypt's oldest known religious spells, dating to the 5th and 6th Dynasties of the Old Kingdom, circa 2350 B.C., and mostly found in pyramids. The Coffin Texts are not as old, written from the late Old Kingdom to the Middle Kingdom on sarcophagi, but similarly deal with mystical incantations sometimes reflecting a belief in reincarnation, such as the "spell for not dying a second death."

The Sleeping Prophet

Remarkably, those scholars' conclusions, reached after years of often painstaking research, were foreshadowed by the greatest intuitive of the 20th century. Remembered as "the Sleeping Prophet," Edgar Cayce was an uneducated man born in 1877 in Kentucky, who later settled in Virginia Beach, Virginia. There, he devoted his life to providing surprisingly effective medical information obtained while in a dream state. Sometimes during these "life readings" he would mention events from the deep past, of which he knew nothing when awake. Some of his unconscious statements were later borne out by physical evidence; so many, in fact, that he was popularly regarded as the most credible psychic of his time, a reputation enhanced since his death in 1945 with numerous scientific discoveries tending to validate his utterances.

During one of his trance states, Cayce characterized the Great Pyramid as *"the earth's building"* [author's italics] that "kept the earth's record"—a singularly

Edgar Cayce, the "Sleeping Prophet," who inadvertently envisioned an Atlantean connection with Egypt's Great Pyramid through its "Fire Stone."

appropriate description, considering the geodetic qualities of the structure and its apparent basic purpose as a tectonic transformer.[32] Cayce generally referred to the Great Pyramid as "the House Initiate," wherein neophytes of a mystery cult experienced some profound religious activity that raised their spiritual consciousness and empowered them psychically.

Echoing Cayce's description are the religious beliefs of the Snohomish Indians, who for centuries have revered the blue light radiating at the summit of California's Mount Shasta as an open gateway to the Otherworld, through which spirits may come and go. The entire Cascade Range, of which Shasta is a part, is geologically unstable.

During his waking hours, Edgar Cayce knew nothing about these esoteric details. In altered states of consciousness, however, he depicted the Great Pyramid as a cooperative effort between native inhabitants of the Nile Valley (who provided most of the physical labor) and newcomers from Atlantis, its master planners and directors. He also spoke of the Tuaoi, a Fire Stone, characterized as "the terrible, mighty crystal."[33] It was located in a tall structure at the very midpoint of Atlantis, "centered in the middle of the 'power station,' or 'powerhouse,' that would be termed in the present."[34] It provided an unlimited stream of energy that allowed the Atlanteans to reach levels of technology unachieved until modern times and beyond. He said "it was set as a crystal...cut with facets in such a manner that the capstone on top of the same made for the centralizing of the

power or force that concentrated between the end of the cylinder and the capstone itself."[35]

Cayce's description of the Fire Stone coincides with the crystal element in the Great-Pyramid-as-Great-Transducer, the capacitor that transformed mechanical energy into electrical energy. He in fact stated that "the facets of the stones as crystallized from the heat from within the elements of the Earth itself...made for the connections with the internal influences of the Earth."[36] These earth-energies tapped into by the Tuaoi simultaneously produced power for cultural and spiritual development:

> *It was in the form of a six-sided figure, in which the light appeared as a means of communication between infinity and the finite, or the means whereby there were the communications with those forces from the outside...In the beginning, it was the source from which there was the spiritual and mental contact.*[37]

According to Cayce, the Tuaoi was at the center of a bitter controversy raging between the Followers of Belial, a kind of satanic cult, and the Children of the Law of One, another cult, this one monotheistic. During the course of their bitter religious struggle, the Followers of Belial seized control of the Fire Stone, and, through incompetence or abuse, caused it to malfunction. Instead of being vented and applied for progressive and enlightening purposes, the powers of the Earth were turned back upon themselves, resulting in catastrophic seismicity. In the midst of the mass evacuations that followed, the Tuaoi's handlers removed it from the "powerhouse," and carried it to Egypt, where most of the dispossessed Atlanteans resettled.

Cayce's version of these events explains why the technologically advanced Atlanteans of the late 4th millennium B.C. had declined into a typical Bronze Age people when they fought the Greeks and Egyptians with conventional weapons 18 centuries later. Atlantis suffered a brain-drain around 3100 B.C. when most of its scientific elite fled, taking their power crystal and its attendant technology with them into new lands. Those who remained behind and survived had to rebuild Atlantean society from its ruins, minus the secret technology carried away by a closed class of technicians—initiates of the Navel of the World mystery cult. Others sought refuge in the British Isles and beyond to the Continent, where their understanding of crystal's facility to tap earth-energies was manifested in the megalithic standing stones of western Europe.

But in Egypt, to protect their new society from the same kind of natural ravages that destroyed their oceanic homeland, they recreated their lost "power station" on the Giza Plateau. There, it operated successfully for 18 centuries, allowing dynastic civilization to flourish in the agriculturally rich but geologically unstable Nile Valley, while ameliorating the worst effects of seismic violence.

Cayce claimed that the name "Tuaoi" was an Atlantean word, and it does, in fact, find linguistic parallels in the languages of those peoples who preserved Atlantis-esque flood accounts. For example, the Mayan word *tuuk* means "fiery," just as Tuaoi meant "Fire Stone." Cayce said, "the records [describing the Tuaoi] were carried to what is now Yucatan, in America, where these stones [that they know so little about] are now."[38] The Mayas themselves claimed descent from the Halach, the "Lords" of Tutulxiu, a splendid kingdom of high wisdom sunk beneath the Atlantic. On the other side of that ocean, the Sumerians told in their oldest literature, *The Epic of Gilgamesh*, the story of a flood survivor, Utnapishtim, who possessed "the Stone that Burns." It was also referred to as "the Fire Stone," precisely the same term used by Cayce. In his *Les Vrayes Chroniques*, or "True Chronicles," the mid-14th century Flemish chronicler Jean Le Bel collected myths of Brittany, wherein the *Tua* was, literally, the "Son of the Giant (or "Great") Stone," the offspring of Belisama, Keltic goddess of the sacred, solar fire.[39]

Most remarkable of all, Islam's Holy Koran describes the Nile Valley as "the sacred valley of Tuwa." Not an Arabic word, Tuwa is Egyptian for "pillar," or a monumental structure, and close to "mountain" (*tjua*). According to author Ralph

The Great Pyramid as Telluric Transducer. Original pen-and-ink drawing by Kenneth Caroli used with permission.

Ellis, its plural is *tjui*, signifying "two mountains at sunrise and sunset," a descriptive term, he concludes, for the pyramids of Khufu and Khafre at the Giza Plateau.[40] In this, it appears that the Great Pyramid itself was known as the mountainous "tower" (tuwa), after the precious stone it encapsulated, the Tuaoi.

Widely disparate peoples separated by vast distances and many centuries nonetheless shared common renditions of a world-class flood associated with a fire stone described, despite the otherwise complete dissimilarity of their languages, by the same word-value: Tuuk, Napa-Tu, Tua, Tuwa, Tjua, and so on—cultural–linguistic variants of the Atlantean Tuaoi. The name is one of several recurring themes interweaving the worldwide drama of the Destiny Stone it describes, as in the Arab account of Surid (pronounced "shu-reed"), the pre-flood king who, forewarned of the coming cataclysm, commanded the Great Pyramid be built as a "refuge." Shu was the Egyptian counterpart of Atlas, likewise portrayed as a man supporting the sphere of the heavens at the center of the world, and the eponymous deity of Atlantis. He was also known as "the Keeper of the Pillars of the Sky," and portrayed in temple art surrounded by the four celestial columns.

Shu's "pillars" may be associated with the Pillars of Heracles Plato said separated continental Europe from Atlantis. Perhaps Surid's name was a variant of the Egyptian Shu, the most Atlantean of all Egyptian gods. Or he might have been Shu himself, his name slightly altered in the Arabic preservation. His and the other deluge stories associated with the Great Pyramid unquestionably bear more than a faint resemblance to the Atlantis disaster, even to the "fire from heaven" or "planet" they tell precipitated it—the same celestial impact the weight of our evidence has defined as the mechanism responsible for the final destruction. In the Coffin Texts, Atum, the primeval god who caused the Great Flood, declares, "First Shu emerged from me."

Contemporary with Dynastic Egypt, the Sumerians of Mesopotamia:

> *revered the sacred 'Shu' stone, the begetter of fire and life fostered by heat, designated as the precious stone, the strong stone, the snake stone, the mountain stone. The pregnant mountain of the Shu stone was to the Akkadians [the earliest writers in the Semitic language] the central point of the Earth. The people who are said in the Rig Veda to have first found fire by the help of Matarishoan, the 'fire-socket,' and to have brought it to man, are said to have placed it in the navel of the world, as the sacred Shu stone.*[41]

Matarishoan was the Sumerian Prometheus, who made the gift of fire to mankind. In short, the Sumerian omphalos has all the leading characteristics of the Atlantean Navel of the World stone. Richard Hewitt, the turn-of-the-20th century American Peabody Museum scholar, went so far as to argue that the Sumerians derived their very name from Shu: "These Shus were the Sumerian trading races of the Euphrates Delta and Western India who traced their descent to the Egyptians." The Sumerians, or Shus, would then mean, "the People of Shu, or Atlas"; in other words, "Atlanteans."[42]

The name also reached around the globe to Asia, in ancient China, where the oldest cosmogony taught that Sumeru was the cosmic mountain on an island in some distant sea at the center of the world inhabited by four kings. This royal quartet defines the Chinese Sumerus at the center of the world. Chapter 2 described Japan's omphalos at Nara's Todai-ji monastery and Daibutsu-den, or Great Buddha Hall's holy-of-holies. Underscoring the sacred city's Navel of the World identity, Nara also features a three-piece fountain representing Mount Sumeru.

Clearly, we are dealing with the worldwide tradition of precious stones that established sacred centers wherever they were set up. But what special quality did they possess that gave them such unique influence?

CHAPTER 6

True Pyramid Power

Egyptian initiation is characterized as a series of psychic transformations—a process of metamorphosis—that awakens latent spiritual powers already resident within the individual.

—Rosemary Clark, *The Sacred Tradition in Ancient Egypt*

Most modern archaeologists refuse to even consider the possibility that human beings of the ancient world were in possession of a scientific technology comparable to or more advanced than our own. Their refusal is understandable. To make such an admission would subvert accepted views of mankind's deep past, paradigms painstakingly pieced together with careful scholarship over the last several generations. But the Great Pyramid stands as the single most persuasive specimen of material proof for just such a supercivilization. We shall either have to deny the physical evidence, or radically revise our historical perspectives in accordance with it.

Megalith Earth Lights

Surprisingly, parallels for a prehistoric transducer, such as the Great Pyramid, are numerous and still in existence. Scattered throughout Britain are hundreds of stone circles and standing stones called *menhirs*, dolmens that were erected from 6,000 to about 3,200 years ago. These, of course, are the megaliths of Neolithic times, such as Stonehenge. The oldest known folk traditions describing the megalithic sites portray them as places of mystical power and "fairy lights." The same ghostly phenomenon is known as *das blaue Licht* in Germany, where it is still reportedly witnessed at Externsteine, a famous Neolithic site near the town of Horn, in Lippe. Scandinavian tradition refers to the phenomenon as *haug-eldir*, or "the lambent flame," sometimes seen dancing about megalithic structures.

Investigating these reports in 1982, geologist Paul McCartney discovered that virtually every British stone circle and menhir was located either within a seismic fault zone or positioned above an intrusion of mineral enhancement; in other words, the intense compression of various minerals, especially igneous granite, in a concentrated area to generate high levels of magnetism. When his map of all known megaliths was overlaid on a plat of the country's mineral enhancement and seismic zones, he discovered that the man-made and geologic regions correlated almost exactly.

The Chicago Field Museum of Natural History's restoration of Carnac as it appeared 5,000 years ago.

McCartney's conclusions were supported at another major megalithic complex on the other side of the English Channel, along the south coast of Brittany, beside the Gulf of Morbihan. Carnac, or Karnag, is Western Europe's most extensive arrangement of prehistoric uprights, comprising more than 3,000 stones hewn from local rock. While the formation's time-parameters are elusive because little datable material has been found beneath it, archaeologists tentatively date the site's main phase of activity to circa 3300 B.C., about two centuries before the birth of Egyptian civilization. Eyewitness accounts of strange lights at Carnac go back to time out of mind and are still reported by local residents and the occasional tourist. Following up on these sightings, geologists

from the University of Lyons discovered that the long rows of granite or other metamorphic, crystal-veined stones appeared to have been deliberately planted between once-powerful fault lines. How the megalith builders at Carnac could have suspected the presence, much less determined the exact subterranean distribution of these seismic areas with enough precision to insert the stones between the faults baffles scientists. Yet, the same relationship between monumental construction and geophysical forces reappears at the Giza Plateau.

The Great Pyramid's straight, uncomplex, and undecorated corridors do not define it as a temple of any kind. To be sure, structures a fraction of its size, such as the British megaliths, could serve mystical functions just as easily. As the British expert in megalithic mysteries, Paul Devereux, observes, "The known placing of certain types of megalithic sites in northwestern Europe in geological areas suitable for earth lights occurrence is quite possibly a result of the use of this environmental method of causing mind-change effects."[1]

Devereux knew whereof he spoke. A fellow Briton, Kenneth Shaw, demonstrated that quartz does indeed interface with human consciousness. During the summer of 1980, he participated in a controlled experiment that required him to position the palms of his hands 6inches above a crystal connected to a molecular resonance meter. It was designed to detect changes in the way molecules in minerals bond together. Digital read-outs indicated no change. But when Shaw was instructed to visualize healing energy streaming from his hands into the crystal, the meter registered a powerful reaction. As soon as he suspended his visualization, the readings immediately fell back to normal. The experiment was repeated many times, always with the same result.[2]

Britain's megalithic structures may have been precursors of the Great Pyramid, or later, less colossal versions of it. Perhaps Neolithic Britons and Ancient Egyptians were both recipients of an advanced technology from some X-culture (who else but Atlantis?). In any case, England's standing stones are identical to their Egyptian counterpart in that they were deliberately positioned over concentrated points of geologic energy, which they continue to manifest in similar displays of Earth lights and related altered states of consciousness.

Earth Lights

The relationship McCartney discovered among the British megaliths is complemented by early Germanic myth. Erda, the primeval earth-mother, occasionally manifested herself in a cave at the summit of a mountain. Her appearances were invariably accompanied by an eerie blue light that suffused the vicinity and usually preceded a disaster of some kind, just as earthquake lights warn of an impending geologic upheaval. Erda was most dramatically brought to life by Richard Wagner in *Das Rheingold*, when she rises in an azure-lit cave at a mountaintop facing Valhalla, the new home of the gods. She returns in *Siegfried* (Act III, Scene I), the third of the *Ring* musicals, again in a mountain cave aglow with bluish light. In both instances, Erda's appearances come at moments of heightened tension, just before some catastrophe takes place.

Myths describing a mystical blue radiance also appear to have evolved from actual altered states of consciousness experienced by Shamans. These were mostly men who fell into deep trances to achieve spiritual ecstasy. According to Norman Bancroft Hunt, in his comprehensive *Shamanism in North America*, "In Eskimo and Aleut belief, blue is thought of as representing a life-force that exists beyond the constraints of the physical body, and the penetrating gaze of shamans that enables them to see beyond the immediate and the obvious is often said to be accompanied by an intense aura of blue light."[3]

On China's southernmost mountain, Wu T'ai Shan, a dormant volcano, is the site of a 500-year-old temple built specifically for viewing the blue light that occasionally illuminates the summit. Known even in Malaysia as the *bilek hantu,* or "spirit room," the temple was regarded as a sacred site where individuals came for metaphysical development.

Second only in importance to the Ka'bah in Islam was a shrine over the tomb of Allah's prophet, Muhammad. For nearly 10 centuries after his death in 632, Muslims on a *hajj,* or holy pilgrimage, to Mecca in Saudi Arabia, passed the small structure, richly adorned with precious and semiprecious stones, including the finest crystals. They sometimes saw the shrine enveloped by a blue light, which they regarded as a saintly halo. Anyone who walked within the shrine while it was thus illuminated is said to have been blessed a thousandfold. Ludovico di Varthema, the first non-Muslim to make a *hajj* to Mecca incognito, in 1510, witnessed the shrine's blue light and described it in his memoirs. An earthquake the following century badly damaged the shrine, and although it was rebuilt, the blue light was never seen again.

A shrine over the tomb of Muhammad gives off a mystical blue light in this line drawing by Ludovico di Varthema, who witnessed the phenomenon in 1510.

As with Egypt's Pyramid, Britain's megaliths, China's *bilek hantu,* and Muhammad's original tomb, the blue light occurs at structures in zones of seismic unrest.

Effects on Human Consciousness

While the Great Pyramid's fundamental operation aimed at transforming geophysical energies into electrical energies for purposes of safeguarding civilization from natural disasters, a by-product of that energy transformation (whether it occurs at man-made or natural locations) is its profound effect on human behavior. These energies generate electromagnetic fields that can powerfully affect the bio-electric circuitry of the brain to induce altered states of consciousness. This electromagnetic interface with the human mind may

also explain the blue light's association with the trance-like inductions, and Edgar Cayce's description of the Great Pyramid as the "Hall of Initiation" for persons seeking spiritual empowerment. Directly translated, the Egyptian word for "pyramid," *mr,* is "the Place of Ascension," a literal term with obvious esoteric implications, suggesting the spiritual qualities spoken of by Cayce.

Appropriately, the spiritually evocative blue light of these many sacred sites allegedly corresponds to a level in the human aura known for its own lofty spirituality. Blue in the human aura is supposed to denote the inspirational, devotional, religious, and artistic qualities of an individual. The color also belongs to the pituitary and pineal glands of the brain most identified with the seat of the soul, psychic abilities, and our personal relationship with nature. If so, then the interior of the Great Pyramid might have been used as a focal point for potent geo-electrical energy that had some direct effect on the corresponding bio-electrical energy of the brain to produce altered states of consciousness.

Yoga Connections

Mystery-school preservation of the Pyramid's esoteric knowledge appears to have extended beyond Greece—not a particularly amazing possibility, because such information often spread to influence various spiritual belief systems separated from each other by great distances. In the chakra system of Kundalini yoga, the third "wheel" or level of the spine corresponding to the navel is known as *manipura.* It is the control chakra, the seat of our willpower and urge to master our environment. The navel chakra is signified by the Greek letter *delta*, at the center of which is the symbol for fire.

Surrounding Kundalini's navel-triangle are 10 lotus petals the color of smokey-purple. They are supposed to resemble storm clouds streaked with lightning, an electrical display that parallels the pyramid light phenomenon. Interestingly, a person assuming the famous lotus position for meditation conforms to the configuration of a pyramid, while the spine is the axis that the "serpent power" of spiritual transformation climbs from the base up through the seven major chakras toward enlightenment at the apex or crown of the head. The Earth's telluric energy is similarly characterized by many cultures as a dragon or serpent. A pre-Greek example is the Sanskrit *nwyvre*, meaning "wavy serpent-strength of the Earth." It rises from the Great Pyramid's subterranean "ground," through its internal transducer to escape at the apex as a coronal discharge. It occurs, as we have seen, in a mystical light; so too each of the lower chakras passes on accumulating energy into the *sahasrara*, which radiates with a splendid light from the top of the head when "the rapture" has been attained. Similar to the golden pyramidian, this Crown chakra is portrayed as golden in temple art. Such imagery exactly reproduces, therefore, the Great Pyramid as a form for channeling telluric power.

With Kundalini yoga, the Pyramid's mundane and spiritual qualities merge, suggesting that the earth-energies flowing upward through the structure are the same forces that generate man's spiritual development and enlightenment. If so, then the Great Pyramid did indeed serve dual functions as a geo-transducer and sacred center. The harnessed power of our planet was something not only directed to disperse and relieve tectonic stress, but used, perhaps as a beneficial side effect, in spiritual ways we are only just rediscovering. For example, it is now understood that granite in large volume produces relatively high levels of radiation that alter human consciousness by inducing drowsiness and psycho-spiritual experiences, such as a sense of traveling through time and astral projection. The King's Chamber in the Great Pyramid emits 36 percent higher levels of radon than the surrounding environment. Revealingly, the Egyptian word for granite, from which the Chamber is built, is "spirit stone."

The Science of Power Crystals

Somewhat better understood than such things as astral projection are the effects negative ions exert on the mind. As long ago as 1934, C.P. Yaglou, at the Harvard School of Public Health, published a series of papers demonstrating their physiological effects on human consciousness. Following 50 years of research, American medical pathologists L.W. Buckalew and A. Rizzuto asserted, "There does remain the possibility of a physiologic, psychological or performance response to higher concentrations of negative ions."[4] More definitive conclusions were reached just a year later, in 1985, when British endocrinologist L.H. Hawkins found that "evidence that ions do have biological effects is overwhelming," after his studies confirmed a significant beneficial effect of negative ions. Hawkins was seconded by England's K.T. Fornof and G.O. Gilbert, who reported that indoor negative ion levels increase conceptualization and attention span, coinciding with reduced stress. Autonomic nervous system stability was additionally improved.[5]

These studies in turn led Israeli medical researchers A.P. Kreuger and F.G. Sulman to discover serotonin as the interactive mechanism between negative ions and biological systems. Serotonin is a powerful neurohormone that produces neurovascular, endocrinal, and metabolic effects throughout the body, and plays a vital role in mood and sleep patterns. Experimental observation revealed lowered levels of serotonin in the respiratory systems of laboratory animals subjected to concentrated negative ions. Hawkins later verified their discovery. Serotonin is also responsible for migraine headaches, which can be cured by an increase in negative ions. Reducing serotonin levels with negative ions is used in the treatment of clinical depression as well as migraine headaches.

An 8th century B.C. Etruscan necklace. Its clear quartz crystal was meant to lay over the sternum, where it magnified the wearer's bio-electrical field, further amplified by the conductive, gold baubles. The same principle was applied in the Great Pyramid's golden-sheeted apex and encoffined crystal. Etruscan Archaeological Museum, Tarquinia, Italy.

According to Electrostatic Solutions, a British-based online static electricity consultancy center, "the consensus of the literature reviewed is that environmental air ion concentration levels and balance can affect a wide range of biological organisms, including humans."[6] We have an embedded layer of high ion content in our bones forming the walls of the sinuses, or the deep-seated sphenoid-ethmoid sinus complex in close proximity to the brain. It reacts to high doses of negative ions by connecting with the temporal lobe, itself sensitive to electromagnetic influences. Otherwise known as the hippocampus, its functions include dreaming and memory, conscious and subconscious awareness. Consequently, a person spending any time in the King's Chamber, especially when it was properly "charged" with a negative ion flow generated by tectonic action, could undergo mind-altering phenomena akin to a powerful spiritual experience.

The Chamber's ion cavity is an electrodynamic resonator at extra low frequency that directly centers on the brain's so-called Alpha frequency. When we are passively alert, awake but tending toward sleep and fully relaxed, we are said to be in an Alpha state. Medical researchers now realize that the brain generates an electrical field of its own in relation to the Earth's magnetic field. In fact, researcher Francis Ivanhoe demonstrated that the Ammon's horn of the brain actually "reads" the fluctuating field strength of the Earth's magnetosphere. As the hippocampus is stimulated with negative-ion discharge, the brain's Alpha frequency deepens to generate sensations of physical euphoria, while the mind may experience time-space alterations, apparitions, or other psychospiritual phenomena.[7]

Christopher Dusch, a Wisconsin materials engineer, found that "when a condition of meditation is achieved, human brain waves resonate at 7.8 Hz, the same frequency as the Earth's electromagnetic ionosphere."[8] This is, of course, the same frequency at which the Great Pyramid resonates. The relationship between that foremost structure in the world, the Earth it sits upon, and the human mind that conceived it seems clear.

These effects on human consciousness were by-products of the Great Pyramid's original purpose as a geologic transducer—they may have been discovered only after the colossal device began operation. Its tremendous fountain of negative ions discharged to relieve tectonic stress was observed to alter mental perceptions. As a secondary, religious purpose to the initially mundane intentions of its builders, the Pyramid could also be used as a place of spiritual transformation. If the Great Pyramid was used as a hall of initiation, it was probably as an inadvertent side-function or by-product of the originally practical mission for which it was built.

An interpretation of the Pyramid based solely on the physical evidence of its existence, not forcing that evidence to fit preconceived theories, identifies the colossal structure as a device, an instrument created to answer some great need on a scale with its own gargantuan construction. External and internal design features, materials, and placement match its identification as a tectonic transducer far closer than any other purpose later assumed for the structure. The pyramid builders noticed the effect of its electrical properties on human behavior and permitted select initiates to experience its internal energies for spiritual advancement. With this recognition, the colossal electrical instrument additionally became a temple for the transformation of human consciousness and spiritual enlightenment.

CHAPTER 7

How Old Is the Great Pyramid?

[The Great Pyramid] *stands for the planet Earth itself, in harmony with its cosmic environment.*

—Peter Lemesurier

We must conclude from the evidence of the Great Pyramid's unprecedented scale, perfection, and advanced instrumentality that some time in the deeply ancient past a super-civilization knew the whole planet and possessed an earth-energy technology different from, and in some respects superior to anything achieved since. And if the Pyramid is all that remains of such a vanished technology, then we have no conception of what other cultural feats—perhaps even greater—its makers may have accomplished. Because of the long-term developments in science that had to precede construction of the Great Pyramid, the society that produced it must have already been hoary. If so, then the origins of civilized mankind extend further back into prehistory than we have so far dared to imagine.

Neither a tomb for an obscure king nor an unnecessarily oversized time capsule,

the Great Pyramid is the oldest device in the world—and among the most advanced, built to be a "refuge" against an impending world calamity. The first of these global cataclysms prompted refugees from Atlantis to resettle at the Nile Delta, where they erected their monumental geo-transducer as a countermeasure against any recurrence of the natural catastrophe that devastated their civilization around 3100 B.C.

Many scholars have attempted to date the construction of the Great Pyramid by way of its stellar alignment, but their arguments are wildly interpretive and ultimately unconvincing, because many astronomical orientations can be made to fit virtually any structure from different vantage points. But hard evidence more credibly narrows dating scales. For example, during the fall of 1990, something apparently confirming the early dynastic or even pre-dynastic origins of all three

Giza pyramids was found in the desert west of the Nile, north of Thebes. The discovery was a large, perfectly preserved late Gerzean vessel dated to the end of the 4th millennium B.C.

Gerzean pottery is outstanding for its skillful manufacture, with stylistic but eminently recognizable scenes of contemporary life along the Nile painted in bold, black lines on bright orange surfaces. Typical are depictions of palm trees and animals along the banks, together with many-oared rafts or boats floating down the river.

The specimen in question, presently on display at the Luxor Museum, is not unlike dozens of similar examples, save that it portrays three delta-shaped figures—two side-by-side of relatively equal size, the other one much smaller—standing above the Nile. If they are not the pyramids of the Giza Plateau, it is difficult to imagine what else they were intended to represent. The Gerzean pot on which they were illustrated was dated from 3200 to 3000 B.C., a transitional period known as Naqada III-c, when Egypt was changing from a pastoral society into a high culture. If, in fact, the pottery drawing does depict the Giza pyramids, then they must have been observed by a Gerzean artist at the very dawn of Egyptian civilization, at least 500 years before textbook opinion posits their construction.

The most recent radio-carbon dates for the Great Pyramid were obtained by Dr. Mark Lehner from December 1995 to March 1996: "It is a safe assumption," he said, "that the material [collected from the exterior covered by decorative casing stones until their removal in the 13th century] is from the original construction." The calculation Dr. Lehner's team obtained was 1,244 years older than the officially accepted King Khufu timeframe, placing construction of the Great Pyramid around 3109 B.C. This scientifically ascertained date not only places the Pyramid's origins outside the 4th Dynasty, but beyond dynastic civilization altogether. It does, however, correspond with the Gerzean illustration, mentioned earlier, of the same era.

Dr. Lehner later distanced himself from any statements he may have made that aroused the ire of mainstream colleagues, who were emphatic in their insistence that any dating of the Great Pyramid previous to the 3rd millennium B.C. was inadmissable. "Despite claims that these dates were incorrect," Caroli points out, "the mortar from the Great Pyramid averaged to about 2988 B.C., once calibrated, but the boat dates to 3400 B.C.!"

The "boat" Caroli mentions is one of five others buried in their own rock-hewn chambers around the base of the Great Pyramid. The best-preserved was found complete, but in a disassembled condition in 1954. Today, the fully restored, 100-foot-long ship stands in its own modern museum. Was it, along with its companion craft, the vessel in which the pyramid builders arrived at the Nile Delta from overseas 5,400 years ago? Caroli continues:

A subsequent 1990s study produced a lower average for the Great Pyramid, yet did not lower the dating for the boat. While the C-14 dates may be distorted for one reason or another, they imply that the boat is notably older than the pyramid, if not its contemporary. Oddly enough, a celestial alignment for the descending passage, which was excavated down into the Giza Plateau itself, was carbon-dated to circa 3440 to 3330 B.C.[1]

But even Carbon-14's low estimate added almost 300 years to the conventional date, bringing construction up to near the beginning of pharaonic times. These test results suggest that the Pyramid was built at some point within the extremes of their date parameters; in other words, from the mid- to late-4th millennium B.C. "Conservatively, the Great Pyramid's calibrated date falls between 2850 and 3050 B.C.," according to Caroli, "and so is 300 to 500 years older than the date agreed upon by standard chronologies. 2950 B.C. might be treated as the absolute calibrated median." These earlier dates for its construction are important to understand pyramid origins, because they indicate that the foremost building of the ancient world was completed at the very start of Egypt's dynastic history. Consequently, the pharaonic identity of its builders becomes all the more uncertain, and we must look elsewhere for the master builders responsible. As Alexander Braghine concluded in 1940, "In the solution of the problem of the origin of the pyramid builders is hidden also the solution of the origin of Egyptian culture and of the Egyptians themselves."

Internal evidence also implies a date circa 3000 B.C. Caroli points out:

> *There are indications that data concerning cycles of time were also included in the Great Pyramid. Its four sides might relate to the Sothic cycle, that stellar calendar by which the Egyptians calculated time. In inches, the structure's basic measurements equate to one century. Its primary figures [height, apothegm and circumference] parallel a Sothic cycle known to have*
> *been employed by the Egyptians in chronicling their "mythic" past. That particular cycle ran from approximately 45,000 to 5,000 years ago. While a 45,000 year-date for the monument is certainly out of the question, its construction around the turn of the 4th millennium happens to coincide with the start of the First Dynasty, the very beginning of Pharaonic Civilization. If true, then it should be obvious that the Great Pyramid was engineered by foreign culture-bearers from some highly advanced society who arrived at the Nile Delta to build the structure.*[2]

Its very placement also suggests that the Great Pyramid was built before the 2500 B.C. date found in standard textbooks on the subject. Although oriented to the cardinal directions (thousands of years before the known invention of the compass), its base is nevertheless off a north–south line by just 1/12 of a degree. This apparently insignificant miscalculation made by its builders actually implicates their time period: Given the incremental movement of our planet on its axis over the millennia, the Great Pyramid's 1/12 of a degree error would not have been an error before 3000 B.C. If its architect did know how to orient his masterpiece to True North, he must have built it at the start of or before the beginning of Egyptian civilization—not 600 years later.

Conventional scholars have long taught that Khufu built the Great Pyramid. Its design was copied in the second-largest specimen by his son, Khafre, who, out of deference for his father refused to make it quite as high. The third and smallest of the pyramids was supposedly built many years later by Menkaure, almost as an afterthought. This official scenario for the Giza Plateau is absolutely without foundation, an utter fiction that has nonetheless become one of the tenets embraced by mainstream Egyptologists. Their skewed chronology and obsolete history are contradicted by current testing, wrongly neglected information, and geodetic facts incorporated in the Great Pyramid itself. This contrary evidence indicates that some unknown centuries or even millennia before the first Egyptian dynasty arose around 3100 B.C., Atlantis had already achieved incomparable levels of civilized greatness.

CHAPTER 8

Son of the Sun

Who shall call his dream fallacious
Who has searched or sought
All the unexplored and spacious
Universe of thought?

—Henry Wadsworth Longfellow,
Hermes Trismegistus

Events culminating in the deactivation of the Great Pyramid with the theft of its Stone of Destiny were set in motion 273 years before by the loudest noise in recorded history.

At Thera, known today as Santorini, a small island in the Aegean Sea 60 miles north of Crete, a volcanic eruption many times more powerful than any man-made nuclear detonation took place sometime during the autumn of 1628 B.C. Vibrations streamed forth through the Earth's atmosphere from Thera's epicenter to encircle the entire globe. People from Portugal to Afghanistan, from Norway to Zaire, heard the blast, and millions within that radius watched its cloud, filled with 60,000 miles of ash, rise 23 miles into the sky. It was the result of 7 cubic miles of rhyodacite magma ejected from a 30-cubic-mile hole, its crater nearly 50 square miles in area. Multi-ton boulders were ejected into the stratosphere, and some have been found as far as the Black Sea, 700 miles from the blast-center at Santorini. More than 70 miles to the east, in excess of a foot of ash fell on the islands of Kos, Rhodes, and Cyprus. Phaistos, Minoan Crete's second city, was carbonized in a flash.

The pall of dust and gas that enveloped the planet was so vast that a Chinese scribe reported during the contemporary reign of Emperor Qin:

> *In the 29th year of King Chieh* [the last ruler of Hsia, the earliest recorded Chinese dynasty], *the Sun was dimmed. The Sun was distressed. During the last years of Chieh, ice formed in* [summer] *mornings, and frosts in the sixth month* [Chinese July]. *Heavy rainfall toppled temples and buildings.*

The Sun and Moon were untimely. Hot and cold weather arrived in disorder. The five cereal crops withered and died.[1]

Thera had hoisted many megatons of ultrafine dust 50 miles into the stratosphere, where they shaded out solar radiation, absorbing its heat before it reached the ground.

Santorini's explosion was still recalled with horror by the great Athenian playwright, Euripides, 1,000 years later in *The Hippolytus*:

Strange fear fell on us. Where did the voice come from? To the sea-beaten shore we looked, and saw a monstrous wave that soared into the sky, so lofty that my eyes were robbed of seeing the Scironian cliffs. It hid the isthmus and Asclepius' rock. Then, seething up and bubbling all about with foaming flood and breath from the deep sea, shoreward it came.[2]

Euripides was referring to the horrifying wall of water Thera's eruption set in motion: Racing across the Aegean Sea at more than 300 miles per hour, it towered 800 feet high by the time it slammed into western Asia Minor. After crashing 30 miles inside Turkey, the tsunami receded, dislodging house-sized boulders and ricocheting them at high speed along the ground like 250,000-ton pebbles, obliterating everything in their erratic path.

In Lower Egypt, massive earthquake "swarms" rippled throughout the Nile Valley, toppling monumental structures and private domiciles alike. The assault came from both below and above, when a hail of volcanic stones rained down like a celestial barrage. At least a quarter-inch of ash from Thera's sulfur-rich dust-cloud fell as acid rain. So dense was this cloud that by the time it reached the Delta, sunlight was blocked out for the better part of a week.

What later became the land of Israel did not escape that eruption unscathed. Archaeologists found a layer of ash there identified with the geologic upheavals of 1628 B.C., and believe accompanying seismic activity, together with falling volcanic stone, devastated the entire region. The Old Testament writer of Psalm 46:1-8 seemed to describe the Theran eruption when he told how Yahweh protected his Chosen People: "Though the Earth give way, and the mountains fall into the heart of the sea, though its waters roar and foam, and the mountains quake with their surging. Nations are in uproar, kingdoms fall. The God of Jacob lifts his voice, the Earth melts. Come and see the works of the Lord, the desolations he has brought on the Earth."

Unwelcome Immigration

Driven away from their homes by these deteriorating conditions, Semitic refugees crossed the Egyptian frontier en masse at the eastern Delta. The self-styled rulers of the 14th Dynasty could not hold them back. The newcomers' chaotic arrival was further compounded by Sobekhotep IV's own inveterate weakness and the simultaneous devastation of his kingdom by the Thera cataclysm. He and his fellow countrymen referred to these unwelcome arrivals as the Heka Khasewet, or "Rulers of Foreign Lands," a motley conglomeration of various tribes forced from their eastern Mediterranean home by the power of natural events. Grouped loosely together under the better remembered Greek version of their Egyptian name, the "Hyksos" included Canaanites, Phoenicians, Hebrews, and other Semitic peoples now lost to history. Nonetheless, the Jewish historian Flavius

Josephus could write 1,500 years later that the Hyksos were "our ancestors."[3]

The momentum of their arrival carried them beyond the marshes of the Western Delta to overwhelm Memphis and even the capital at Itjtawy, and then most of Lower Egypt. Theirs was less a military invasion than conquest by immigration—unlike the Egyptians, they possessed the composite bow, metal helmets, and chain-mail armor, but these weapons were war-surplus from the Hittites and Mittani of Asia Minor and northern Syria. Historians long believed that horse-drawn chariots successfully spearheaded the incursion, because the Egyptians were allegedly ignorant of such military vehicles. But when archaeologists completed excavation of all Hyksos sites in the eastern Nile Delta, none yielded a single chariot, nor produced any inscribed or visual references to their supposedly characteristic battle-wagon. It would appear instead that the chariot was an entirely Egyptian innovation designed specifically by the Theban kings to roll over the hard, flat plains of the Nile Delta against occupation forces from the east. Hyksos daggers, swords, and shields, however, are identifiably Indo-European.

Despite the presence of this equipment, there is little real evidence of battles, much less a war, during Egypt's Second Intermediate Period. Instead, as the outsiders migrated across the northern part of Egypt, they encountered only a number of weak, feuding kings whose demands for tribute and obedience were ignored with impunity, and having no state-form of their own, the immigrants set up a crude copy of the Egyptian model. They installed their tribal leader, Salitis, as "Pharaoh," thus creating a nation divided in half between the Lower and Upper Nile Valley. The "Rulers of Foreign Lands" had become the predominant rulers of Egypt. Lacking sufficient numbers to take over the entire country, they were content with their northern occupation, imposing commercial conditions favoring themselves on the remnant native monarchy located at Thebes, which they surrounded by a military alliance with Nubia. They thereby checkmated any possible indigenous opposition by potential intervention from the south. Thus hemmed in by enemies on either side, the Egyptians lived under the constant threat of a two-front war they would be hard pressed to win.

As the Hyksos solidified their power, they founded their seat of government at Memphis, with Avaris as a summer residence, where they assumed the trappings of Egyptian culture and took the ass-headed god, Seth, as their tribal deity. Previously a beneficent mortuary divinity, now, because of his adoption by the enemy, he was forever regarded by Egyptians as the god of evil. Reflecting their perception of the Heka Khasewet and the geologic disaster that introduced these hated foreigners, "he was abominated by the people for his harsh and bloody ways," according to Egyptologist Anthony Mercatante, "and regarded as the personification of drought, darkness and perversity, and the natural opponent of all that was good and life-giving in the universe. Set [Seth] was the arch-enemy of the Sun," representing "the cosmic opposition of darkness and light."[4]

During the 100 years they were hemmed between hostile powers in the north and south, most Egyptians never lost their sense of national identity, and eventually replaced the royal mediocrities responsible for the downfall of their country with dynamic leaders focused on liberating it. Out of their victory not just another dynasty, but an entire New Kingdom arose to usher in a golden age of pharaonic civilization.

〜〜

The Semitic peoples who originally accompanied the Hyksos "invasion" had been at least outwardly Egyptianized, adopting the language and culture of their host, and so were allowed to remain unmolested if generally despised in the Eastern Delta, where they formed their own, reclusive communities. The Egyptians knew them as the Shahu or Habiru, the first recorded reference to the Hebrews, although Heka Khasewet endured as an anti-Jewish epithet for centuries thereafter. The name, Hebrew, deriving from *habiru*, or "desert foreigner," means "one from the other side of the river," referring to the Semitic residents on the eastern side of the Nile. Whenever "Hebrew" appears in the Bible, it is most often used by a Gentile to describe the Israelites, as in the First Book of Samuel: "Then said the princes of the Philistines, What do these Hebrews here?" Popular association of the Hebrews with the Hyksos was not altogether baseless, as their third ruler, Yaqob-her, was a form of Ya'iqob, or Jacob.

General animosity for Jacob's people incrementally faded in the glow of economic revival and concurrent cultural magnificence, as many Heka Khasewet grew rich as merchants, grain speculators, gem brokers, landowners, and importers of luxury goods. By the time Amenhotep III ascended the throne in 1417 B.C., many Shahu or Habiru were already holding positions of prominence in civil authority. Known even during his lifetime as Amenhotep the Great for his tremendous construction programs, his regime was characterized by general prosperity and international peace. He raised an immense

mortuary temple in western Thebes fronted by the famous Colossi of Memnon. On the other side of the Nile he was responsible for the main portions of the temple complex at Luxor, and set up a monumental pylon in the temple of Karnak.

Toward the close of an illustrious 38-year reign, Amenhotep III was no longer able to entirely shoulder the burden of government due to declining health, and began sharing co-regency with his wife, Tiye. His devotion was all the more remarkable, because Tiye was a commoner and only half Egyptian. While her mother, the noblewoman Tjuyu, was a descendant of Ahmose, the liberator of his country from Hyksos' occupation, her father was an Asiatic foreigner. Five years after his coronation, Amenhotep personally led a military expedition against insurgents in Nubia, where he raised a temple to his swift victory at the city of Soleb. Tiye accompanied her husband on the campaign, and had her own Nubian temple built beside his. Conscious of her Asiatic roots, she caused to be inscribed the name of the Israelite god, "Yahweh in the land of the Shahu," on one of the pillars. The name Shahu was not Hebrew, however, but derived from *s'sw*, Egyptian for "to wander," implying that the Jews were a rootless people, not an established nation. The half-Hebrew Tiye then rose to become queen and her son became Pharaoh Amenhotep IV, in 1349 B.C., when he was 30 years old.

Amenhotep IV's ascension had been vigorously opposed by the nobility, the Amun priesthood, and royal counselors, who already had cause to suspect the young man's obsession with the sun disc. They were overruled, however, by an insistent Amenhotep III, himself besotted with love for Tiye, the real power behind the throne after he grew too ill to rule save in name. "The bloodline of Abraham, Jacob, and Joseph had married into the pharaonic line," according to investigator Ralph Ellis.[5]

The Rise of Aton

Almost immediately after assuming the crown, the new king changed his name to Akhenaton, the "Potent Spirit of Aton," to personally flaunt his religious heresy. Hardly an innovation, Aton had been locally known as a primitive solar deity at Heliopolis since early dynastic times. But Akhenaton revived it from obscurity as the one and only image of his universalist creed—the world's first monotheism. Its central tenet was based on worship of a single creator and divine will personified in the Sun. All other religious beliefs were erroneous and therefore worthy of abolition. Moreover, Aton was not an exclusively Egyptian conception, but, as the bright disc that shines on every living thing, the supreme being of all mankind. An inscribed stele at Akhenaton's future capital confidently announced, "soon all the nations of the world would come here to bring Aton, giver of life, the tribute they owed to him."

With modern translations of his hymns, Akhenaton gained new fame as a humanitarian poet, the world's first religious reformer, preaching a precursor to Christianity, whose compassion for all mankind was ahead of its time, and therefore hated by his less enlightened contemporaries. But as more information came to light about "Atonism," his formerly exalted reputation began to sour. It was learned, for example, that he alone claimed access to the sun-god's attention. All other worshippers of the solar disc could not hope to have their prayers heard, save through their pharaonic intermediary. "Only he had the power to interpret the divine will,"

according to Ahmed Osman, author of *Moses and Akehnaton*.[6] One of the colossal stelae marking the boundaries of the king's city proclaimed that "Aten would unveil his plans to no one but him alone…he would listen to no one, not even the queen, should one try to persuade him to build Akhetaten elsewhere".[7]

The would-be reformer regarded his intolerant faith as the greatest power-phenomenon ever devised, wherein blind religious fanaticism was the dynamic that centralized all authority in himself. Canadian Egyptologist Donald B. Redford, professor of Classics and Ancient Mediterranean Studies at the Pennsylvania State University and director of the Akhenaton Temple Project, was put off by:

> *the rigid, coercive, rarefied monotheism of the Pharaoh. The historical Akhenaton is markedly different from the figure popularists have created for us. Humanist he was not, and certainly no humanitarian romantic. To make him a tragic 'Christ-like' figure is a sheer falsehood. If the king and his circle inspire me somewhat with contempt, it is apprehension I feel when I contemplate his 'religion.'*[8]

After Akhenaton publicly announced the formation of his religion, his subjects throughout the Nile Valley were stunned. Whoever happened to be pharaoh at the time was god, whose word was law. Yet, he was telling them that everything they and their ancestors worshipped from the foundation of their civilization was wrong, and merited substitution by a lone solar figure few even recognized. Confident in the superiority of his creed, Akhenaton was certain the broad masses would embrace it as their metaphysical liberation from centuries of oppressive priestcraft. When, however, they evidenced little enthusiasm for his unprecedented cult, he reacted angrily.

Henceforward, Aton was not just the supreme god, but the only god. All temples, save his—which numbered very few— were closed, their servants turned out into the streets, monumental statues overturned, artwork smashed, and hieroglyphic inscriptions effaced. Both public and private worship were restricted to the solar disc; all others were outlawed. Even traditional reverence for his supremely sacred position was not enough, Akhenaton felt, to guarantee the thoroughness of the reformation he was determined to carry out. "Each time a squad of workmen entered a temple or tomb to destroy the name of Amun," writes Osman, "it must have been supported by a squad of soldiers who came to see that the royal decree was carried out without opposition."[9]

Sun City

These measures could hardly have been expected to win converts from his already embittered fellow countrymen, who shrank from the heresy he persisted in foisting upon them. After just three years of countenancing their sullen, deepening rejection, Akhenaton left them in disgust, abandoning the Theban capital for the desert, swearing never to return. There, 250 miles away, near the east bank of the Nile on virgin ground, he built a new city that was his own world, in which he could play out his role as self-styled messiah to a captive audience composed of perhaps 50,000 admirers. These were mostly people from the Eastern Delta. Although now settled and even affluent, with influence in government, they were still a minority under suspicion, their role in the Hyksos "invasion" neither forgotten nor entirely forgiven, and mistrusted for their perceived undue prestige. Yet, the Habiru had been

enthusiastic supporters of Amenhotep for embracing their patriarch, the biblical Joseph, as his "Unique Friend," and allowing them to flourish in his prosperous kingdom. Their devotion to his son seemed even more well-deserved, thanks to Akhenaton's kinship with them through his mother. They flocked in large numbers to Akhetaton, "the Horizon of the Aton."

It had already been declared the new capital 24 months before the religious metropolis was completed following five years of hurried, unremitting labor. Stelae defined its boundaries in the four cardinal directions, some 8 miles in extent from north to south. These extremities were marked by 11 stelae carved into the limestone cliffs, including those cut into either river bank in a form of city planning found nowhere else in the Nile Valley. So-called Stele U, on a cliff near the entrance to the royal wadi, is 24 feet high. Statues of the royal family originally stood at its base, but all that survive of them are telltale outlines and adhered fragments, remnants of the frenzy of destruction that purged Akhetaton after its fall. Even so, these monumental stelae are virtually the only relatively intact physical evidence for the urban center's former existence. A 120-foot-wide "Royal Avenue" running southward from the palace was the central axis around which it had been laid out. On either side of this processional way were administrative offices, another palace, more temples, and shrines to the ubiquitous Aton. Beyond spread shops, markets, residential sections, and estates.

Akhenaton praised the new capital of the sun-god as "the seat of the First Occasion, which he had made for himself that he might rest in it."[10] His ceremonial hub differed as much materially from every other town as it did heretically—monumental colonnades, statuary, obelisks, temple art, and all the other architectural features for which

Egyptian construction is famous were missing from Akhetaton, which was built of mud-brick and plaster-coated walls. Its mostly undecorated, rectangular buildings were uniformly purist, less clean than sterile, lending the entire city a strikingly modern appearance. This design disparity was a material expression of fundamental theological differences. Although traditional Egyptian forms had striven to impart a sense of eternal truth and justice in the perennial principle of *ma'at*, or "right," "balance" (in other words, cosmic harmony, order), Akhenaton's alternative statement emphasized the mundane and transient in its sparse, smaller-scale construction and homely portrayals of everyday affairs.

The otherwise nondescript cityscape was occasionally relieved by spacious, open-air villas of the very rich, and the king's own "Window of Appearances," a kind of balcony on which he would often stand smiling with his gorgeous wife and little daughters to greet noisy crowds of enthusiastic or sycophantic well-wishers gathered below in the street. During these royal exhibitions, he often tossed golden trinkets, such as necklaces or bracelets, to the grasping mob below, as scraps of meat to a pack of dogs.

Akhenaton's Fire Stone

If art is a reflection of the spirit generating it, then the most monumental feature at the Horizon of the Aton was Akhenaton's ego. His many temples, all of them dedicated to the one god, were indistinguishably identical, with open courts surrounding colossal statues of the king and queen. Different from all the rest, however, was the Hwt-bnbn, or "Mansion of the Ben-Ben," the most important shrine. Set up in the eastern section of the sun disc's largest temple, the Great House of the Aton, at the midpoint of the mansion stood "a round-topped stelae of quartzite

mounted on a stone dais."[11] This was nothing less than the very same Ben-Ben crystal installed in the Great Pyramid 18 or more centuries before.

As part of each new pharaoh's ascension, the selected monarch was required to enter the King's Chamber, where he was supposed to have been infused with a special divinity believed to transfigure him from royal prince into living god. When he stepped before the Ben-Ben, he may have sung hymns or chanted formulaic prayers memorized as part of his preparatory education. These vocalizations were intended to set up a sympathetic resonance within the crystal, activating its harmonic frequencies. The Ben-Ben was additionally sensitive to constant, if unnoticeable fluctuations of telluric current, and was therefore sufficiently energized for initiation at almost any time. Radiated with concentrated negative ions emitted by the Fire Stone from its granite coffer, the new king underwent an altered state of consciousness resulting in catharsis—a psychological transformation. The spiritual euphoria he experienced was more than an epiphany; it was a theophany, the recognition and sensation of his own godhood that empowered him to absolute rule.

While still Amenhotep IV, he had to pass through the same process prior to his coronation, but its impact on him was more

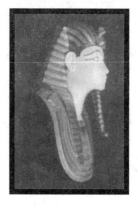

In the total darkness of the King's Chamber each new pharaoh underwent a spiritual catharsis that transformed him from a mortal prince into a living god.

profound than that made on any of his predecessors; he may not have been as physically or emotionally sound for the rigors of such a critical encounter as they were. Research undertaken in 1988 by British pathologists K.T. Fornof and G.O. Gilbert in 1988 confirmed that "people of different sympathetic nervous system reactivity respond differently to air ion levels."[12] Perhaps Akhenaton's ritual interaction with the Ben-Ben happened to take place during a surge of geologic instability, generating an abnormal degree of increased energy that detrimentally affected him in mind and body. In any case, historians are otherwise at a loss to explain why this man alone, of the many dozens of pharaohs before and since him, chose to abruptly replace the spiritual foundations of Egyptian civilization, rooted in the 4th millennium B.C., with a diametrically opposed monotheism. Something life-changing must have happened to him. Everything about the passionate, inspired, intolerant nature of his struggle bespeaks sudden conversion brought about through a soul-altering conversion of some kind.

Investigators Andrew Collins and Chris Ogilvie-Herald write of "Akhenaton's unique fascination with the Ben-Ben stone," a fascination which became an obsession that drove him steadily mad, and may have even killed him by undermining his physical health.[13] But the euphoria it generated in him became an addiction he could not live without, especially if he was leaving the outside world to reside forever in the city of his dreams.

In 1355 B.C., during the sixth year of his reign, the innovative pharaoh set yet another traumatic precedent by having the Fire Stone removed from the Great Pyramid, where it had been kept inside the granite box of the King's Chamber for almost 1,800 years. From the Giza Plateau, the sacred object was transferred under military guard to the new capital, and mounted atop a pillar in the Mansion of the Ben-Ben at the "Great House of the Aton."

Although regarded by virtually all Egyptians as supremely blasphemous, the relocation of their holy crystal to the Horizon of the Aton was nevertheless in keeping with the establishment of other stones such as theirs in places referred to as Navels of the World. So too the city of Akhetaton was deliberately built at the geodetic "navel" of Egypt, exactly halfway between the Nile Delta's northernmost coast on the Mediterranean Sea and the first cataract in the south. The Fire Stone itself was set up on a pillar in the middle of the Hwt-bnbn shrine, constructed at the very center of the city. Clearly, the king, for all his heretical obsession, was fully cognizant of the esoterica required for the crystal to perform as it was designed and intended.

Alone at the secluded shrine, Akhenaton spent most of his time in mesmerized contemplation of the radiant crystal. It inspired him to write florid poetry, such as his famous "Hymn to the Aton." However, excessive exposure to the potent aura of negative ions induced a form of addiction that disassociated him from reality, as reflected not only in his increasingly unorthodox behavior, but even his physical degeneration, as demonstrated in his renovation of the graphic arts. The king allowed himself to be depicted embracing family members or worshipping the Sun in domestic services—a tableau his admirers, then and now, find endearing. But in striving to capture the reality of his every-day life, these scenes provide a disturbing image of the ungainly pharaoh. He was shown with an unnaturally long face, lantern jaw, swollen lips, scrawny neck, spindly arms, pot-belly, broad hips, and fleshy thighs—the physical opposite of every other pharaoh before his time and after. Some researchers believe such a bizarre representation was the result of a new art style, and was not actual portraiture. But the realistic, contemporaneous bust of his wife, Nefertiti ("She Who Comes in Beauty"), challenges that theory. True, she was sometimes depicted with the same deformed features, as were her daughters, but their stylistic portrayals more flattered the king by emulation, just as Castilian Spanish began in fashionable imitation of a lisping monarch.

Some pathologists speculate Akhenaton suffered from Marfan Syndrome, as did Abraham Lincoln, judging from their common physical resemblance. Named after Antoine Marfan, the French pediatrician who first described it in 1896, Marfan Syndrome is a genetic disorder of the connective tissues typified by characteristics such as elongated fingers, arms, and legs—similar to those depicted in the 18th Dynasty wall art and statues at Akhetaton. Worse, it impairs the cardiovascular system, and may cause leakage of the mitral valves that control the flow of blood through the heart, resulting in an aortic aneurysm. Although details of the king's death are not known, scholars believe he died during his mid-40s of natural causes, stemming perhaps from Marfan Syndrome. In a Louvre statuette of Akhenaton holding hands with Nefertiti as young teenagers, he exhibits none of the extreme physical traits found in later representations, implying that the king suffered from a progressively degenerative condition. It is also possible that his already weakened constitution was fatally undermined by an influenza epidemic known to have swept the closely clustered neighborhoods of Akhetaton when he and his co-regent, Semenkhare, disappeared at the same moment in history. Or perhaps fanatic devotion to the radiant Ben-Ben Stone might have brought about his deterioration.

Eminent Scottish Egyptologist Cyril Aldred seems correct in stating that Akhenaton "wished to have himself represented with all those deformities that distinguished his appearance from the rest of humanity."[14] Their appearance was a sign from Aton that his royal namesake had been divinely chosen to serve as the sun disc's lone intermediary. As there was only one God in heaven, so he only needed one high priest on Earth.

His city is today known as el Amarna after the Beni Amrana, a nomadic tribal people who left the eastern desert 300 years ago to settle on the banks of the Nile over the sand-buried ruins of Akhetaton. The ruins were accidentally discovered in 1887 by a local woman grubbing for *sebakh*, deteriorated mud-brick often manufactured during dynastic times, and since used as an agricultural fertilizer or fuel for fires. The sebakh covered a cache of more than 300 cuneiform tablets recording official communications between Akhenaton and Egypt's allies. Mostly written in Akkadian, the lingua franca of diplomatic correspondence in the ancient Near East, the Amarna Letters, as they have come to be known, reveal a chaotic state of affairs. They are filled with ever more strident appeals from client rulers for immediate aid against raiding bedouin. Without the pharaoh's military intervention, desert tribesmen were emboldened to seriously threaten the existence of the Egyptian holdings in Syria his predecessors had pledged to protect.

Akhenaton answered few of their desperate appeals, tersely writing that he could not offer any help, and urged them to pray instead for guidance from Aton. It would have been a simple matter to order the Egyptian army against desert tribesmen, thereby regaining the confidence of his subjects, without compromising Atonism. But by then he was so lost in his own metaphysical musings, the outside world seemed insignificant.

Contrasting his apparent pacifism, the number of troops at Akhetaton would have been sufficient to quell any Syrian uprising. "The city was virtually an armed camp," according to American Egyptologist Alan Schulman. "Everywhere we see parades and processions of soldiers, infantry, and chariotry with their massed standards. There are soldiers under arms standing guard in front of the palaces, the temples, and in the watchtowers that bordered the city, scenes of troops, unarmed or equipped with staves, carrying out combat exercises in the presence of the king."[15] These forces could not be deployed to protect Egyptian holdings in Syria, so long as they were needed to carry out Akhenaton's religious reformation and defend the new capital against possible attack from his own, unconverted subjects.

In all of Akhenaton's endeavors, he was supported by his invaluable right-hand man, without whom even his divine status would have eventually proved insufficient: Ay. Earlier, Ay had become a relatively obscure official thanks to his sister, Amenhotep III's wife, Queen Tiye. Her father, Yuya, the biblical Joseph, was master of the horse, a coveted position he naturally handed down

to his son. As such, Ay was not only the brother-in-law of Amenhotep III, but the maternal uncle of Akhenaton himself. More importantly, he was the only high-ranking minister from the Theban government who went over to the iconoclastic pharaoh, openly declaring his sympathies for Atonism. Akhenaton immediately embraced the older man as "Bearer of the Fan on the Right Hand Side of the King," the title of his chief advisor, and supreme military commander, Overseer of All the King's Horses. Ay's sudden rise to prominence was additionally aided by his wife, Tey, who had been Nefertiti's wet nurse when Akhenaton's beloved queen was an infant. Thus well-connected, Ay boasted in his tomb text, "As his favorite, I am in front of the officials and the King's companions, the first of all his followers. He doubled for me my rewards in silver and gold."[16]

Ay certainly earned his royal patronage. His well-disciplined troops never mutinied, despite overwhelmingly polytheistic sentiment in the military, and under his iron orders, they unquestionably carried out Akhenaton's reformation, which never shrank from armed intervention. Temple treasures were seized, priests of the old gods arrested, potential dissent intimidated, and private persons spied on and punished for their proscribed worship. Ay was not unjustified in describing himself as "effective for his lord."[17]

The erosion of Egyptian foreign influence was symptomatic of the kingdom's social dislocation and economic decline. Akhenaton had decreed that only he, as God's personal ambassador to the world, could legally own gold, the sun-disc's earthly symbol. Accordingly, the treasuries of the anathematized gods were confiscated from their closed temples and transported under guard to Akhetaton. Domestically too his family was falling apart. Nefertiti left him, seeking refuge at the distant Karga oasis, for reasons never made clear, but his increasingly monomaniacal monotheism, deteriorating physical condition, and alleged homosexuality are speculated causes.

In any case, the devotion of his followers at Akhetaton seemed largely undiminished. Composed in large measure of Egyptianized Semites, they were, in a very real sense, his chosen people, who, mistrusted and often excluded at the Eastern Delta, found acceptance and belonging in Atonism. Foreshadowing Judaism, "Akhenaton did not permit any graven image to be made of the Aton. The true God, said the king, had no form; and he held to this opinion throughout his life," according to the early 20th century Egyptologist Arthur Weigall.[18] Meanwhile, the pharaoh's "Aton" became *Adon*, the Hebrew word for "lord."

The Heresy Dissolves

With Akhenaton's death in 1334 B.C., his monotheistic reformation utterly collapsed. A long 17 years of enforced silence contemporaneous with the country's wholesale desecration propelled a surge of popular contempt that swept away every vestige of the despised heresy. Akhetaton, his ideal city, was abandoned and forever after shunned as cursed ground, its former inhabitants skulking back to their relatives in the Eastern Delta. Akhenaton's name

and memory were expunged from the royal list of kings, his mummy shredded, as was his mother's (although a small fragment of her coffin is on display at the Cairo Museum). Archaeologists also identified a handful of small pieces from her son's sarcophagus lid, but every sign of burial was scoured from the crypts he built for his nobles.

Even the name of Akhenaton's young son, Tutankhaton, was changed to Tutankhamun, "the Living Image of Amun," after the restored king of the gods. The 9-year-old boy also became a king, if in name only, because as the most immediate descendant of Amenhotep the Great, he alone was eligible for the crown. Ay coveted it, but without any familial connections to royalty, he could never become pharaoh. Even his command of the army was not enough to set him on the throne at a time when every manifestation of the Amarna heresy was being purged from Egypt. His own words in reference to Akhenaton, "My lord instructed me just so that I might practice his teaching," came back to haunt him, so he began by emphasizing his now more politically correct prenomen, Kheperkheprure, "Everlasting are the Manifestations of Re," and switched religious loyalties with the same alacrity with which he earlier embraced Atonism when such a conversion seemed advantageous.

As a gesture of national restoration, Ay had the stolen Ben-Ben stone returned to its granite coffer in the King's Chamber of the Great Pyramid. At his command, the soldiers who had once vigorously implemented Akhenaton's reformation now persecuted his freshly disempowered followers, and he missed no opportunity to distance himself from the dead, discrediting Akhenaton by loud declarations of the old piety. Through Tutankhamun, he announced, "I found the temples fallen into ruin, with their holy places overthrown, and their courts overgrown with weeds. I reconstructed their sanctuaries, I re-endowed the temples, and made them gifts of all precious things. I cast statues of the gods in gold and electrum [a gold/copper alloy], decorated with lapis lazuli, and all fine stones."[19] Though the nominal king was still a child, he served as an obedient mouthpiece.

Shortly after coming into his majority, Tutankhamun died in a convenient accident that left his teenage widow free to wed Ay. Through his marriage to Ankhesenamun, a member of the royal house, the 70-year-old aspirant to the crown could become pharaoh. He began his reign with a puzzling act. In 1325 B.C., he surreptitiously built the largest, most ornate tomb at the abandoned site of Amarna, and inscribed on its walls the longer of two, surviving versions of Akhenaton's Hymn to the Aton. While laborers and craftsmen sweated in its covert construction, Ay was overtly pursuing the

Twenty-five-foot tall colossus of Tutankhamun at the Oriental Institute of the University of Chicago.

reconstruction of polytheistic society. As a diversion, he ordered work to start on another, more ostentatious mortuary temple in the traditional royal cemetery at Thebes' Valley of the Kings, near Medinet Habu. It seems that, as an ambitious politician, he catered to public passions but was privately still an Atonist.

The same appears to have applied to Nakhtmin, his *iry'pat* or "executive" from the day he became king. Nakhtmin was Ay's closest confidant and henchman, a high-ranking general under the late Tutankhamun, in whose tomb he had placed an *ushabti*—a funeral statuette—with the curious inscription, "the servant who makes his master's name live." But which name: Tutankh*amun* or Tutankh*aton*? Was the inscription a threat of resuscitating monotheism? In any case, Ay clearly intended Nakhtmin to be his successor and envisioned him as the pharaonic leader of an Atonist revival after an extended cooling-off period. The Egyptians were notorious for their occasional outbursts of xenophobia, followed inexorably by more extended epochs of cultural amnesia, when the pariahs of yesterday became the celebrities of today. The sun disc's time would come again.

After a reign of just four years and one month, Ay passed away during his middle or late 70s. While he had been grooming Nakhtmin to take his place, both men ignored or underestimated the groundswell of anti-Atonist sentiment growing in the army. Most military men had been content to watch the heresy melt away in the blaze of popularity enjoyed by the old gods following the downfall of Akhenaton. But even in death, he seemed to exert a revivifying effect on a few die-hard adherents obviously planning to stage a comeback when the opportunity allowed. While Ay lived, his iron grip on the armed forces could not be broken. But his demise offered a chance to purge the last of the Atonists and scotch their schemes for a return to the days of Amarna.

A veteran of Tutankhamun's brief regime, Horemheb and his fellow generals seized control of the army before Ay's body was cold. The coup struck with such abrupt thoroughness that Nakhtmin was fortunate to escape with his wife and children. They fled Thebes, sailing northward along the Nile into the Eastern Delta and Avaris. Here, the dispossessed couple found sheltering anonymity from both Horemheb and history. This was the same city the Hyksos had used as their capital, and specified in the Old Testament as Goshen, where the Israelites were supposed to have settled. According to the bible, they were employed as slaves to build Pi-Ramses, formerly known as Avaris, thereby identifying them with Akhenaton's followers.

The one-time adherents of Akhenaton's now forsaken religion were unmolested, but shunned as much for having been the unorthodox king's "Chosen People" as for a strange disease they carried away with them from his cursed city. The unprecedented epidemic was regarded as divine punishment for their participation in his hateful heresy. Even 1,000 years later, Manetho, the native chronicler for Ptolemy I, Egypt's earliest Greek ruler, mistakenly referred to the Jews as lepers, because, even in classical times, influenza was still a mystery.

Back in Upper Egypt, Horemheb and his compatriots engaged in the furious extirpation of everything and everyone tainted by association with Atonism. Today, only two large fragments survive of a once magnificent statue portraying Ay's intended successors. These include the head, shoulders, and upper torso of Nakhtmin, and the head of his wife—the eyes, nose, and mouth of both man and woman deliberately effaced. All stelae he dedicated were mutilated, including a pair of quartzite colossi of Tutankhamun. Ay's tombs near Medinet Habu and at Akhetaton were sought out, his name excised from all wall paintings and texts, and his sarcophagus smashed to pieces. In 1972, its lid was discovered buried under 35 centuries of debris by Dr. Otto J. Schaden. The American Egyptologist could only recognize it by a relatively untouched cartouche enclosing the monarch's name, because the figure depicting Ay had been entirely hacked out. All ushabti representing the dead pharaoh were destroyed. As Bob Brier writes in *The Murder of Tutankhamun*, "in Ay's tomb, the destruction was so thorough that not one [image] of him has ever been found."[20]

While Horemheb's comprehensive purge spread outward in all directions from Thebes to encompass the entire country, veneration for the proscribed sun-disc cult, expunged from every other corner of Egypt, lingered like a lambent flame flickering throughout the esoteric quarters of Avaris. Yet the long-suffering Habiru managed to hold on to their accumulated wealth and often high-level positions in regional government. By the turn of the 13th century B.C., still more were promoted to positions of prominence in the civil administration of the early Ramesside kings. The most powerful and famous ruler of this line, Ramses II, even adopted a Semitic name for one of his favorite daughters, calling her Bint Anath.

Egypt Invaded

The prosperity Ramses II passed on to his successor was seriously threatened in the early spring of 1227 B.C., when an armada of Meshwesh, or "Sea Peoples" struck the Nile Delta. Belonging to a confederation of various Eastern Mediterranean kingdoms dislocated by the Trojan War, they constituted the most serious attempt to take over Egypt in more than 400 years. Their coming, according to temple records, had been envisioned by Merenptah the night before the attack. At 60 years of age, the new pharaoh seemed at a distinct physical disadvantage. But his divine namesake, the god Ptah, appeared to him in a precognitive dream, offering a sword and commanding, "Defend my civilization!"

Unlike the Hyksos' incursion, which had been more of a mass migration, the Sea Peoples staged a full-fledged military operation aimed at overwhelming all resistance and subduing the entire Nile Valley in a lightning advance. Their thousand vessels not only outnumbered the Egyptian navy, but outclassed its biggest warships. Handily brushing aside these coastal defenses, tens of thousands of Meshwesh marines stormed ashore, their bronze swords, helmets, and plaited armor superior to Egyptian equipment. Slashing their way across the Delta, they took the strategic cities of Damietta, Busiris, and Sais in quick succession, while the main body of battle-cruisers supported them by sailing down the Nile, parallel to their advance. The early goal of their march inland was the leading administrative center. Once taken, the Egyptians would have had difficulty coordinating resistance.

In concert with the sea-borne assault, Libyan forces led by King Meryey rolled into the Delta from the west. As his 30,000 troops pushed the defenders behind their own border, he brought along his own royal family members and even personal luxuries, sure that he would be soon setting up his throne in Memphis. But Merenptah was more agile than his advanced age implied. Rising to the situation as an authoritative general and wily strategist, he ordered his soldiers, retreating before the Meshwesh onslaught into Prosopis, not to surrender the port town, but to fight to the death if necessary to hold the enemy at bay while the Egyptians brought up all their forces. Unaware of its refortified condition, the Sea People's marines advanced on Prosopis in a headlong attack, only to be cut down by thick volleys of bowfire. In the midst of their confusion, the main body of Egyptian infantry fell on them from the rear.

Before the noose around them could be drawn too tightly for escape, the invaders fought a desperate flight northward. In the *Odyssey*, Homer's hero said of Prosopis at this time:

> *The whole place was filled with infantry and chariots and the glint of arms. Zeus, the Thunderer, struck abject panic into my party. Not a man had fortitude to stand up to the enemy, for we were threatened on all sides. They ended by cutting down a large part of my force and carrying off the survivors to work for them as their slaves.*[21]

All along their retreat, they were mauled from the rear by the pharaoh's army, which pursued them to the mouth of the Nile.

Meanwhile, Merenptah had ordered a stiff defense of Perite, the last important strategic position against the invading Libyans. On the early morning of April 15, with the rising sun in their eyes, their foot-soldiers were slaughtered by massed salvoes of arrows while advancing on the fortress. Despite heavy losses, reinforcements pushed on against continuing fusillades, engaging the Egyptians in hand-to-hand combat under the walls of Perite for six hours. Speeding to the defenders' aid was a chariot squadron and a brigade of spearmen. At the sight of these reinforcements, Libyan resistance faltered, then collapsed. Meryey joined the rout, leaving behind 10,000 warriors fallen on the field of battle, among them his six sons. Of 9,111 prisoners of war, the pharaoh's men severed the hands of 2,362 officers, and captured 120,000 pieces of military equipment—numbers reflecting the vast scope of the invasion. Meryey returned to his palace alone, his family taken by the Egyptians.

Who Stole the Pyramid Stone

While Merenptah's forces grappled in a life-and-death struggle with a coalition of foreign enemies, his own chancellor, the most powerful man in Egypt outside himself, staged an uprising with his followers at the Nile Delta. Josephus reports that they tried to "raise a sedition, and bring innovations into Egypt."[22] Those "innovations" included a forced return of Atonism led by "someone called Irsa," according to an official history from the 20th Dynasty. The Harris Papyrus documents the actions of one of the most influential figures in late 19th Dynasty affairs, a Grand Vizier of "Syrian" (in other words, "foreign") origins, known as Irsa, Irsu, or Iarsu (related to the Hebrew Ira) Beja, sometimes called Beya, who changed his name to Ramose Khamenteru when he went to work as a scribe in Ramses II's administration.

Previously, he had been a priest at Heliopolis, Egypt's own City of the Sun, where Aton worship originated 18 centuries before Akhenaton's revival, and the only place where the Amarna heresy was still under discussion. Permitted to use the temple's cult facilities, Ramose must have made a significant impression on the priesthood there, because a small statue of him—his only known representation—was recovered from its ruins by archaeologists in the early 20th century. He was described as a self-made man who rose to the top of Egypt's bureaucracy despite his humble roots, approaching the apogee of his influence after he became vizier and secretary to Merenptah's preferred son, Baenre Merynetjeru. As some indication of the importance Ramose assumed, he was among the very few commoners, and certainly the only non-Egyptian, granted the privilege of building his own tomb in the Valley of the Kings, a sanctuary otherwise reserved for royal family members. Following his boundless ambition, he seduced Meryamun Tausret, the widow of his former ruler, Ramses II, and she gave him total control of the national treasury.

But Ramose only really came into his own with the arrival of the Sea Peoples. Their initially successful occupation of the Nile Delta suddenly deposed regional Egyptian governments, creating a gap in authority the self-made man was quick to fill. After pledging non-interference to and even support for the invaders, he set himself up as chief regent on a wave of popular hatred he helped instigate against the pharaoh for whom he was still nominally chancellor. To curry favor with the masses, he publicly castigated Merenptah for snubbing the petitions of nomads from Edom, fellow Semites who begged in vain for water in the "land of Goshen" (the area around Avaris) during the height of a terrible famine then devastating the Near East, as recorded in the Anastasi Papyrus.

In truth, the king had his hands full trying to stave off the foreign conquest of his country, and could not be bothered with livestock petitions at the moment. Having fired up the mob with revolutionary indignation, Ramose used it to implement his one-man tyranny by imposing massive taxation on the Delta's Egyptian residents, and "made this law for them, that they should neither worship the Egyptian gods, nor should abstain from any one of those sacred animals which they have in the highest esteem, but kill and destroy them all," according to the 3rd century historian Manetho.[24]3

His report was preceded by the author of the Harris Papyrus, who wrote that neo-Atonites "treated the gods like mere mortals. No offerings were offered up within the temples."[24] The 20th Dynasty scribe described Ramose-Iarsu Beja's anarchistic rule in the context of the Sea Peoples' incursion as:

the Syrian-Palestinian usurpation of Egypt. The land of Egypt was overthrown from without, and every man lost his rights. The land of Egypt was in the hands of chiefs and of rulers of towns. One slew his neighbor, great and small. Iarsu, a certain Syrian, was with them as chief. He set the whole land tributary before him together. He united his companions, and plundered their possessions.[25]

As in the days of Akhenaton, the temples were looted, and priests were abused and even murdered. They were often forced to butcher and cook the many cult animals—including bulls, dogs, cats, and falcons—cared for and venerated in the sanctuaries, as food for Ramose's followers.

Now in complete control of the Giza Plateau, they chased away the *rosthau*, or "watchers"—guards entrusted with protection of the pyramid precinct—then ransacked local tombs of the lesser nobility. Ramose participated in the looting, but his

was of a more ambitious kind. As a high-ranking priest of the Heliopolitan clergy, he knew all about the Ben-Ben reinstalled in the Great Pyramid after Akhenaton's downfall, 128 years before. While agitated crowds rampaged outside, he led his servants through a secret entrance. David Hatcher Childress, president of the World Explorers Club, writes:

Opening the main door from the inside, Moses [a.k.a. Ramose] and his companions removed the Holy of Holies from the King's Chamber of the Pyramid," where they lifted the golden box containing its crystal capacitor from the granite coffer, "and took it with them during their Exodus from Egypt to the Promised Land....Indeed, it is quite possible that for this very reason the Egyptian army decided to pursue the fleeing Israelites, even after they had given them permission to depart.[26]

Making their way from the King's Chamber with Egypt's national treasure, Ramose knew it was now his own "Stone of Destiny."

Who was Moses?

None of this information is new. Remembered as "a man of encyclopedic knowledge," Gnaeus Pompeius Trogus was a Roman historian who reported in the 1st Century B.C. that Moses "secretly took the sacred objects of the Egyptians," who pursued the thief and his gang into the wilderness.[27] Born at Egypt's Siwa Oasis and Gnaeus' contemporary, the renowned Greek grammarian and author of "Androclus and the Lion," Apion wrote that Moses was actually "an Asiatic, renegade priest" from Heliopolis, who preached

Akhenaton's defunct sun-cult to the Jews. But if Ramose/Moses depended on a lasting victory of the invaders to secure his power at the Nile Delta, he badly miscalculated. Fresh from Merenptah's crushing success at Perite, the indomitable pharaoh wielded his army around to the north, driving the Sea Peoples in crowded confusion onto the beaches at the mouth of the Nile. To avoid slaughter under the arrows of his amassed bowmen, they retreated to their ships, and escaped back across the Mediterranean Sea. Shocked by this unexpected turn of events, Beya-Iarsu-Ramose and his consort, Meryamun Tausret, fled Egypt for their lives, followed by virtually the entire non-Egyptian population of the Eastern Delta. Avaris was mostly evacuated, its panicked residents sure that an enraged Merenptah would revenge himself on them for the atrocities that occurred during his absence.

To be sure, after surveying the desecration of temples and the mistreatment of priests, he was in no mood for compassion. Something of his anger survives in a declaration he caused to be copied on the walls of his Theban mortuary temple and at Karnak. The 10-foot-high stele is the first known reference to Israel, not as a nation, but a people among his various enemies, including the Libyans and Meshwesh invaders. The so-called Victory Stele of Merenptah states tersely, "Israel is wasted, bare of seed. All who roamed [a pointed reference to the Israelites, often characterized as "wanderers"] have been subdued".[28] There follows a passing reference to his pursuit of the Jews into Palestine, although the few additional words about them were meant rather to emphasize his supposedly undiminished influence in the Levant, the eastern Aegean shores of what would much later become Israel, rather than an actual military campaign carried out there. Taken literally, his stele declares

that Merenptah faced a revolt that he crushed. Which was indeed what happened, as supported by the Harris Papyrus, the Anastasi Papyrus, Manetho, and other Egyptian source materials.

The historical events they document—a mass migration from Egypt of monotheist Hebrews pursued into the desert by a revengeful pharaoh—are unmistakably reminiscent of the story of the Exodus. In fact, as Hebrew University professor Abraham Malamat observes, "there are now a few scholars who boldly maintain that Beya/Irsu is in fact the biblical Moses."[29] Among them is a prominent authority on the Old Testament, Johannes C. De Moor, who concludes that the Exodus took place at the end of the 19th Dynasty, a period coinciding with biblical chronology. His research demonstrates that Beja and his followers fled to an area of Syria known as Bashan on the Yarmuk River, where the proto-Israelites were known to have originated.[30]

An important addition to these parallels between the Old Testament Exodus and late 19th Dynasty upheavals is a close resemblance of Beja's Egyptian name, Ramose, to the biblical Moses. Ramose's Egyptian lover, who accompanied him into Bashan, was Meryamun, not unlike the name of Moses' sister, Miriam. Both the Egyptian Meryamun and Hebrew Miriam were priestesses. As some verification of De Moor's comparisons, contemporaneous attestations of Meryamun's passage along the suspected route of Exodus to the Yarmuk have been identified. In a version of the Exodus garbled by the passage of 10 centuries, Manetho reported that a certain Egyptian priest from Heliopolis called Osarseph led leprous Asiatics out of Egypt into Syria, where they became Jews. While "Osarseph" is an apparent confusion with the Hebrew patriarch Joseph (the Egyptian vizier Yuya), Manetho's portrayal of the migrants as "leprous" refers to the influenza epidemic that struck Akhetaton in its last days.

The biblical Exodus was certainly an actual event additionally documented, although in not such detail, by Tacitus[31] and Justinus.[32] These Roman sources fundamentally agree with the so-called Second Book of Moses, except to add that the Egyptian pharaoh, far from refusing to liberate the Jews, expelled them. *Exodus* itself, in chapters VI and XII, 1 and 39, respectively, quotes Yahweh as saying, "with a strong hand shall he [the pharaoh] let them go, and by a mighty arm shall he drive them out of his land...the Egyptians drove them out."

Tacitus and Justinus reported that the pharaoh's army pursued the Hebrews after they had traveled some distance beyond the eastern border—not to bring them back, but to recover numerous valuables appropriated by the Children of Israel. Again, *Exodus* has God promise His Chosen People,[34] "And it shall come to pass that when you go, you shall not go empty-handed. But every woman shall borrow of her neighbor and of her that sojourns in her house, jewels of silver and jewels of gold, and clothes. And you shall put them on your sons and on your daughters, and you shall despoil the Egyptians."

A corroborative Elephantine stele attributed to the 19th Dynasty Stenakhte records the expulsion of "Asiatic rebels" on their flight from the Nile Delta. In their eagerness to escape the wrath of the pharaoh, the people of Avaris left behind vast quantities of gold, silver, and copper they had stolen from the Egyptians, and with which they had intended to hire reinforcements among the other foreigners in Syria.

The Old Testament author characterizes these appropriated treasures as "borrowed" by the Israelites, because they "found favor in the eyes of the Egyptians." But the language in *Exodus* ("You shall despoil the Egyptians...And thus they stripped the Egyptians")[34] makes it seem doubtful that the Egyptians voluntarily parted with their wealth because they wanted to help the anathematized Hebrews. Besides, one wonders what use jewels would serve in the desert. These baubles, however, were not the only nor the most important treasure with which the Israelites left Egypt "empty-handed."

CHAPTER 9

The Pyramid's Stolen Secret

Woe, even the secret that was in the Pyramid has been stolen away!

—The Ipuwer Papyrus, 1178 B.C.

Observant visitors to the King's Chamber of the Great Pyramid have often remarked on the scorched appearance of its walls, ceiling, and the "sarcophagus" itself. Conventional guides argue that the burn marks were made by torches in the hands of 19th century archaeologists. But this conjecture inadequately explains the vastness of the scorching, which extends into other internal features, including the so-called air shafts, which are too small to accommodate a man with an ignited torch. The widespread evidence of intense burning can only have been caused by exceptionally potent surges of seismicity overloading the transducing capabilities of the Great Pyramid. During such periods of unusually powerful activity, its internal cavities were blasted with monstrous bolts of electrical discharge, which seared the walls and ceilings.

Physical evidence left by such an event is still visible on the scorched ceiling of the King's Chamber and in cracks across its granite beams. Although mainstream Egyptologists speculate that they must have been caused by an earthquake, no trace of seismic damage appears in any lower chambers or passageways, which would have been more directly affected by such a powerful geologic incident. Moreover, visitors have long remarked on the peculiar bulge of the Chamber's walls and their separation from the floor, as though abruptly pushed outward by some extraordinary explosive force. Christopher Dunn pointed out that the rosy granite of the so-called sarcophagus appears to have been chemically altered into its atypically chocolate-brown color after subjection to intense heat.[1]

High-temperature blast-effects can only have been caused by exceptionally potent overloading beyond even the Great Pyramid's transducing capabilities. Energy outbursts backed up in the King's

Chamber; its walls, despite their prodigious tonnage, could not adequately contain it. Similar to a computer into which a cup of water was poured, the internal mechanism of the entire instrument was shorted out, and its constituent parts melted or shattered, rendering the Great Pyramid a ruin of its original greatness. But what could have caused such considerable destruction?

Transducers may self-destruct if they are subjected to more power than they can accommodate. A sudden burst of electrical energy can push components beyond material bounds and fry them. (Against the same eventuality, modern computers are plugged into surge protectors.) But an earthquake strong enough to have similarly overloaded the interior instrumentation of the Great Pyramid would have leveled every other man-made structure throughout the length of the Nile Valley, and left geologic scars still visible to this day. A nearby meteor impact similarly sufficient to short-circuit the Giza power plant would have also closed down Egyptian civilization, with even more obvious and enduring consequences for the natural environment.

However, the internal undoing of a transducer may also occur during the course of normal operations—if its most integral part goes missing. Remove its piezo-electric crystal, and the device's other conductive components will be overloaded beyond the capacity for which they were designed, supercharging the entire configuration with high temperatures beyond system tolerance. The only options for throwing off such an excessive amount of energy are meltdown and explosion. This is most likely what happened inside the Great Pyramid. If it was in fact engineered as a device to transmute the tremendous power of the Earth into diffused electrical energy, then removal of its component crystal would have effectively sabotaged the solid-state instrument in the event of any significant seismic upheavals. No earthquakes occurred from the Ben-Ben's theft in the mid-14th century B.C. and throughout the next 100 years, but around the turn of the 12th century B.C., a natural catastrophe struck with far more disastrous effect than the Theran eruption that had devastated the eastern Mediterranean 300 years earlier.

A Global Impact

Although researchers had suspected its impact since at least the late 1800s, this truly global cataclysm was not generally recognized by scholars until 1997. For three days during mid-July of that year, the Society for Interdisciplinary Studies at England's Fitzwilliam College in Cambridge hosted a symposium of world-class professionals in dendrochronology (tree-ring dating), astrophysics, astronomy, archaeoastronomy, archaeology, geology, paleobotany, climatology, and related academic fields. They came from a dozen countries to discuss "Natural Catastrophes During Bronze Age Civilizations, Archaeological, Geological, Astronomical, and Cultural Perspectives." The specific event under consideration was allegedly responsible for a 500-year dark age separating pre-Classical from Classical civilization, circa 1200 B.C. to 700 B.C. This crucial occurrence was suggested by annual growth rings at Irish bogs and oak forests, abrupt lake level changes from western Europe to South America, and small, glassy spherules resulting from cometary collisions that subjected rock to intense heat.

The symposium delegates had been particularly alarmed by ice-core samples taken from Greenland and Antarctica that showed a mounting ash layer beginning around the turn of the 13th century B.C., peaking over the next 40 years with the eruption of Iceland's Hekla volcano. These considerations and abundant supporting evidence helped the scientists to identify a comet, known since the late 18th century as Encke, after its Swiss discoverer, Johann Franz Encke, as the culprit. Although largely wasted, after millennia of orbiting around the Sun diffused most of its material, 3,200 years ago it was a far more dense apparition when it made too close a pass near the Earth. In so doing, Comet Encke showered down a barrage of meteoric debris that spread a 1,000-mile-wide swath of devastation around the entire northern hemisphere. China's Shang Dynasty collapsed under storms of corrosive ash-fall, as nitrogen and oxygen in the atmosphere combined with nitric acid released by the relentless impacts of celestial debris thousands of miles away. Chinese chroniclers at the time blamed "a great star whose flames devoured the sun" as the cause.[2]

On the other side of the world, Comet Encke spat an asteroid moving 100 times the velocity of a 9mm bullet into the Caribbean Sea. It plunged to the ocean bottom with an explosive force equal to 1,000,000 megatons of TNT, excavating a 900-foot-deep crater on the submarine floor. The resulting 1,000-foot wall of water swept inland as far as Alabama, and triggered volcanic eruptions from the Antilles to El Salvador. In the Eastern Pacific, among the Hawaiian Islands of Lanai, Maui, Molokai, and Oahu, deposits of unconsolidated coral were placed nearly 1,000 feet above the coast by an inconceivably monstrous wall of rushing water, many times greater than the tsunami that devastated Indonesia in December of 2004.

Some 13 centuries after the event, a Greek historian, Diodorus Siculus, recounted how the shores along Mauretania (modern Morocco) were deformed by an unprecedented series of prolonged earthquakes during the years after the fall of Troy, around 1230 B.C. Fully 2,000 years

later, his report was confirmed by geologists, who found that the rim of the Moroccan coast known as the Draa Depression collapsed abruptly "as a result of large faulting movements" near the close of the 13th Century B.C.[3]

Although 7,800 feet above sea level, the eastern Alps' Sphagam Bogs were entirely reduced to ashes. Bavaria's Black Forest went up in flames, the British Isles were virtually depopulated, and Asia Minor's Hittite capital, Hattusas, was incinerated. While their chief city burned, the Hittites were battling for control of northern Iraq with Assyria's Emperor Shalmaneser-I, whose description of an enormous comet illuminating the heavens still survives in a well-preserved clay tablet. The anonymous author of Ugarit's *Ras Shamra* inscription related that "the star Anat has fallen from heaven. She slew the people of the Syrian land and confused the two twilights and the seats of the constellations."[4] Shortly thereafter, Ugarit itself was burned to the ground. In nearby Babylon, Nebuchadnezzar-I's palace scribes documented the frightful appearance of a dangerous comet.

In the southern Levant, the great city of Lachish fell in flames, along with the entire stretch of territory known in later Roman times as the Via Maris, in Palestine, stretching from Syria to the Egyptian border. Of the 320 Greek cities and towns standing in 1200 B.C., perhaps 40 were still inhabited 10 years later. As many as 200 Greek centers of civilization were suddenly evacuated when the fabulous Palace of Nestor at Pylos was consumed by fire.

British anthropologist Richard Desborough stated that these dramatic changes brought about in the civilized world were:

> *little short of fantastic. The craftsmen and artists seem to have vanished almost without a trace:*

There is little new stone construction of any sort, far less any massive edifices; the metal workers' techniques revert to primitive, and the potter, except in the early stages, loses his purpose and inspiration; and the art of writing is forgotten. But the outstanding feature is that by the end of the 12th century B.C., the population appears to have dwindled to about 1/10 of what it had been little over a century before. This is no normal decline, and the circumstances and events obviously have a considerable bearing on the nature of the subsequent Dark Ages, and must be in part at least a cause of its existence.[5]

Renowned Austrian Egyptologist Franz Schachermeyr described Earth's late 13th century B.C. encounter with Comet Encke as "a catastrophe which was one of the worst in world history."[6]

Nor was Egypt spared. The contemporary *Ipuwer Papyrus* reported, "gates, columns, and walls are consumed by fire. The sky is in confusion."[7] The wall texts of Medinet Habu, a major temple complex in West Thebes, told how "the House of the Thirty [a huge, luxurious palace for the chief nobles] is destroyed. The Earth shakes. All the water is useless." The Medinet Habu inscription continues, "the Nile was dried up and the land fell victim to drought. Egypt was without shepherds."[8] The texts describe even worse conditions in Libya, which until then was considered a relatively fertile, prosperous country:

Libya has become a desert. A terrible torch hurled flame from heaven to destroy their souls and

lay waste their land. Their bones burn and roast within their limbs. The shooting-star was terrible in pursuit of them, a mighty torch hurling flame from the heavens to search out their souls, to devastate their root.[9]

Inscriptions dating to the reign of Seti-II—among the last pharaohs of the 19th Dynasty—depicted Sekhmet as "a circling star that spread out her fire in flames, a fire-flame in her storm," spewing forth heat that "burned the forests and meadows of the Nine Bows [in other words, the whole world."[10] A later Egyptian text seconded the extent of devastation by claiming "the fire was to the end of heaven and to the end of the Earth."[11] Found near the ruins of Medinet Habu, the Harris Papyrus reported on unusual conditions during the coronation of Ramses III in 1198 B.C.: "Men go about looking like ravens, because there are none whose clothes are white in these times. All are laid low by terror." The Sun paled, the skies lost their light, and the air was unusually chill because of "a great darkness" that overshadowed the entire country.[12]

Although Moses (a.k.a., Ramose, Iarsu Beja, or Beya) left the Nile Delta about 30 years before this event, its global nature meant he and his followers were likewise eyewitnesses to the catastrophe. In Chapter 9:23–25, the Old Testament *Exodus* describes a barrage of falling meteors:

The Lord sent thunder and hail, and lightning ran along the ground. And the Lord showered hail upon the land of Egypt. So there was hail and flaming fire mingled with the hail, very grievous, such as had never been in all the land of Egypt since it became a nation. And the hail smote throughout all the land of Egypt all that was in the field, both man and cattle. And the hail destroyed all the herbs of the field and broke every tree.

The conditions described in *Exodus* were seconded by a surviving text at the el-Arish shrine. Although inscribed during Ptolemaic times, about 1,000 years later, it is part of an Egyptian history referring specifically to the end of the 19th Dynasty when "the land was in great affliction. Evil fell on this Earth.... It was a great upheaval in the residence....Nobody left the palace during nine days, and, during these nine days of upheaval, there was such a tempest that neither the men nor the gods could see the faces of those next to them."[13] The language is similar to that of *Exodus*: "There was a thick darkness in all the land of Egypt three days. They did not see one another."[14]

These source materials describe a "dust veil event" caused by large-scale volcanic activity or extraterrestrial collisions with the Earth. Because no volcanos ever existed in the Nile Valley, the ash clouds drifted from outside sources, save those that may have arisen from celestial debris falling on Egypt. Plagues of animals are also known to be among the occasional consequences of major geologic upheaval, and the sudden appearance of thousands of snakes in China has long been used by seismologists there to anticipate imminent earthquake activity.

The Egyptian Harris Papyrus' contemporary report that "all the water is useless" echoes in Chapter 7: 20; 21 of *Exodus*: "All the waters that were in the river were turned to blood. And the fish that were in the river stank, and the Egyptians could not drink the water of the river. And there was blood throughout all the land of Egypt," just as massive volcanic out-gassing results in prodigious quantities of ash that is often blood-colored due to high levels of reddish, pulverized tufa. Sufficient volumes of ash falling into rivers and lakes would turn them a ruddy hue, not unlike the color of blood, and render them undrinkable.

It was this natural catastrophe, characterized by the noted scholar of Hellenic civilization, Myron Lesky, as "the most frightful in the history of the world" that finally caused the Great Pyramid's interior explosion.[15] Removal of its crystal capacitor 157 years before ensured that 1200 B.C.'s excessive geologic violence would overload the monumental structure's conductive configuration and overheat it into meltdown.

The Ben-Ben had been taken from its granite coffer in the King's Chamber by Amenhotep IV when he became Akhenaton during his 1355 B.C. relocation to Amarna, where it was set up in its own temple for his private worship. Following a reign of 17 years, his heresy collapsed, and the power crystal was restored by Akhenaton's chief advisor, Ay, to its previous place in the King's Chamber of the Great Pyramid. With military occupation of the Nile Delta by invading Sea Peoples around 1230 B.C., Pharaoh Merenptah's grand vizier took advantage of the resultant chaos to make himself the supreme regional authority. But when the King's forces returned, Ramose Iarsu Beja and his followers fled across the Syrian border into the wilderness, taking with them the Stone of Destiny.

Missing its vital crystal component, the Great Pyramid could not perform the geo-transducer functions for which it had been built, and once subjected to an extraordinary energy surge it could no longer direct, it overloaded and underwent an internal explosion.

The Dimensions of the Ark

By the time the Great Pyramid's transducing mechanism was fried by a late Bronze Age catastrophe, destroying its raison d'etre, the Israelites had been gone from Egypt for some 30 years. Three months after their departure, described in *Exodus* 19:1, they arrived at the foot of Mount Sinai, where Moses (the former Ramose) received the Ten Commandments inscribed on a pair of stone tablets. Yahweh then gave him detailed instructions concerning the creation of a special container for their storage. Carpenters and goldsmiths were to start work on it at once. Exodus 25: 10–22 begins:

And they shall make an Ark of acacia wood, two cubits and a half shall be the length thereof, and a cubit and a half the breadth thereof, and a cubit and a half the height thereof [62.5 inches long, 37.5 inches wide, 37.5 inches high]. And you shall overlay it with pure gold, within and without shall you overlay it, and shall

make upon it a crown of gold round about. And you shall cast four rings of gold for it, and put them in the four feet thereof. And two rings shall be on the one side of it, and two rings on the other side of it. And you shall make staves of acacia wood, and overlay them with gold. And you shall put the staves into the rings on the sides of the Ark, wherewith to bear the Ark. The staves shall be in the rings of the Ark. They shall not be taken from it. And you shall put into the Ark the testimony which I shall give you. And you shall make a mercy-seat of pure gold; two cubits and a half shall be the length thereof, and a cubit and a half the breadth thereof.

This "mercy-seat" continues to perplex readers after many centuries, but appears to have been a less than perfect English rendition of the original Hebrew *kapporet,* itself of possible Akkadian derivation, signifying "atonement." If so, the word kapporet is particularly meaningful, because the Jewish "Day of Atonement," or Yom Kippur, was the only day of the year that the Ark could be attended by a lone high priest. Literally, the kapporet was a detachable or hinged lid that allowed access to the coffer's interior. When in place, it acted as a kind of platform or altar on which Yahweh manifested in the form of a luminous cloud or haze; in other words, an electrical discharge formed between the positive and negative terminals depicted in *Exodus* as opposing metal figures:

And you shall make two cherubim of gold. Of beaten work shall you make them, at the two ends of the mercy-seat. And make one cherub at the one end, and one cherub at the other end. Of one piece with the mercy-seat shall you make the cherubim on the two ends thereof. And the cherubim shall spread out their wings on high, covering the mercy-seat with their wings, with their faces one to another. Towards the mercy-seat shall the faces of the cherubim be. And you shall put the mercy-seat above upon the ark. And in the Ark you shall put the testimony that I shall give you. And there I will meet with you, and I will commune with you from above the mercy-seat, from between the two cherubim which are upon the ark...

"Cherubim" derived from another Akkadian word, *kurubu*, a kind of divine intermediary between men and gods, which perfectly defines the esoteric function of the Ark to connect mortals with their higher spiritual nature.

Exodus describes how the Ark of the Covenant was made by Jewish craftsmen in the wilderness. "This seems unlikely," David Childress believes. "Rather, it is more likely that the Holy-of-Holies and the Ark were relics from an earlier time, and were being taken out of Egypt by the fleeing Israelites."[16] Indeed, the unquestionable physical resemblance of Yahweh's Ark to contemporary chests made in the Nile Valley has long been recognized. A famous specimen was found in Tutankhamun's tomb, but other, very similar examples from much earlier dynasties confirm a traditional Egyptian style. Twin "cherubim" with wings outstretched over the top of the Ark are indistinguishable from Shai and Renenet, double aspects of the goddess Isis

(Eset) as the divine guardians of sacred objects.

A relationship between the biblical Ark of the Covenant and Egyptian counterparts does not end with external correspondences, however. As many investigators have observed since the Great Pyramid was entered for the first time after the fall of Classical civilization in the 9th century, the explicit dimensions laid out for Moses define a container that perfectly matches the interior space of the erroneously named sarcophagus in the King's Chamber. Childress writes, "the Ark is said to have once been kept in the King's Chamber of the Great Pyramid. The famous 'lidless' coffin of Cheops was in actuality the receptacle for the Ark of the Covenant."[17] According to *Exodus*, the Ark of the Covenant measured 2.5 by 1.5 by 1.5 sacred cubits, for a cubic capacity of 71,282 cubic inches.[18] The measure of 71,290 cubic inches is also the cubic capacity of the stone vessel commonly referred to as "Pharaoh Cheops' sarcophagus," in the King's Chamber of the Great Pyramid. Childress goes on to explain:

During the Exodus, the Ark was housed in what the bible calls the Tabernacle of the Wilderness...the use of the Tabernacle seems to have been as follows: The visitor entered into the Outer Court through an opening on the eastern side of a fence. The opening was covered by three curtains which had symbolic meanings, though sources do not agree as to what these were. A portion of the Great Pyramid at Giza also has an entrance known as the Triple Veil.[19]

During a 1955 experiment undertaken by Dr. Alfred Rutherford from the Institute of Pyramidology in Illinois, an exact replica of the Ark made to the specifics given in *Exodus* (minus its gold overlay and stone tablets), and lowered into the granite container, fit with remarkably even precision. A roughly uniform, half-inch gap surrounded the installed facsimile on all four sides. This unexpectedly close fit between two (supposedly) radically different objects produced by deeply dissimilar peoples can only mean that Yahweh's Ark was formerly inside the stone coffer of the Great Pyramid. As the supreme Holy-of-Holies, its interior was the most inaccessible site in all of Egypt, open exclusively to high priests and the Pharaoh himself, so its sacred dimensions would not have been known outside a very small circle of privileged initiates, and impossible to reproduce by outsiders, most especially hated foreigners. No, the acacia wood chest in the possession of Moses and his fellow Israelites fleeing into the wilderness was the original container of the Ben-Ben, the Great Pyramid's Stone of Destiny.

The Ark was entirely gilded, less for adornment than the fact that gold is a primary conductor in electronics: The purpose of the King's Chamber crystal was to act as a capacitor for the discharge of energy. Childress believes the stolen pyramid-crystal's identity as such an electric device is made evident by the Ark itself: "The three boxes were a sandwiching of gold (a conducting metal) and acacia wood (a non-conductor). There were dangers in handling the Ark, which was generally done by the Levites who were said to have worn what could easily be described as protective clothing."[20] In effect, the Egyptian Stone of Destiny was quite literally lifted from its granite "sarcophagus" in the King's Chamber to become the Hebrew Ark of the Covenant.

Mount Sinai

Its pyramidal origin has been reconfirmed by Ralph Ellis through a cogent parallel conclusion presented in his 2000 book, *Tempest and Exodus*. No other investigator has more thoroughly researched Mount Sinai, where the Ark was supposedly built, nor devoted so much in-depth attention to its actual location, which is "completely unknown, either within the bible or later traditions."[21] To be sure, no attempt to fix the actual location of Mount Sinai was made until more than 1,500 years after Moses, when Egeria, an affluent nun who visited Saudi Arabia around 330 A.D., declared that Jebel Musa was Mount Sinai, although her choice was just one of a dozen or more possibilities suggested since then.

Ellis begins by closely scrutinizing the name, *Sinai*, which, according to the King James' concordance, derived from the Hebrew *cinay* for "sharp," "pointed," or "peaked." This characterization previously appeared in the works of Flavius Josephus, the 1st century Jewish historian, who wrote that Mount Sinai was "the highest of all the mountains that are in that country, and is not only difficult to climb, on account of its vast altitude, but because of the sharpness of its precipices."[22] *Exodus* also refers to Mount Sinai as Horeb, or "desert"; the two names combined signify a "desert peak." It is the largest of three mountains—Sinai-Horeb, Seir, and Paran—and all featured deeply recessed "caves," the most important located inside Mount Sinai.

Yahweh urged Moses to "come up to me *into* the mount."[23] He "went up *into* the mount."[24] "And Moses was *in* the mount..."[25] Ellis observes that *shini-t* is ancient Egyptian for a temple chamber, "a reference to the chambers inside the pyramids,"[26] and even bears a phonetic resemblance to Sinai. The Old Testament portrays Sinai as the tallest summit in the desert—sharply pointed, featuring a deep cave, steeply sided, and therefore not easily climbed, yet its base was small enough to be cordoned off. Such a description matches no mountain in the Near East, but *does* match Egypt's "Mountain of Ra" in every respect. "The conclusion is becoming inescapable," Ellis writes. "Mt. Sinai is the Great Pyramid of Giza."[27]

Biblical descriptions of Mt. Sinai match no peak in the Near East, but correspond in every particular to the Great Pyramid. The Egyptians themselves referred to it as the Mountain of Ra, the same Mountain of God cited in *Exodus*.[28]

After the Israelites' departure from the Nile Delta, Yahweh manifested Himself "in a flame of fire out of the midst of a bush."[29] Remarkably, even this detail connects to the Great Pyramid, where the god Anpu or Ap-uat (better remembered by his Greek name, Anubis) appeared in his own tree: The Egyptian *Book of the Dead* tells of "Ap-uat, who comes forth from the Asert Tree." The name literally refers to a burnt sacrifice, from *asher* for "a fire or flame."[30] Both the biblical and Egyptian "flame" associated with a burning bush or tree was actually the radiant energy generated by the original Fire Stone in the King's Chamber of the Great Pyramid. Anpu's association with the Great Pyramid was particularly meaningful, because he was the god of spiritual transformation, conveying the *ba*, or soul, from mundane existence into the blessed afterlife, just as the powerfully ionized aura of the Ben-Ben crystal engendered metaphysical catharsis.

The Fire Stone reflected in Yahweh's "burning bush" and Apuat's Asert Tree is also the "Tree of Life" often connected to the Navel of the World in so many omphalos traditions around the globe. With its position at the precise center of our planet's land masses, the Great Pyramid was the preeminent sacred center and Navel of the World. Hence, its Asert Tree, the biblical burning bush, was the Tree of Life—in its esoteric sense, the human spinal column—with serpentine *kundalini* energy poeticized as "holy fire."

Furthermore, in Book 11 of *The Golden Ass*, a tome from the Roman Era, Anubis/Apuat was portrayed as the "messenger between heaven and hell." And "messengers" was how the Rosthau, or "Watchers"—guardians of the Giza Plateau—were described in the Egyptian *Text of Unas*, which admonished them to "keep watch, O messengers of Qa."[31]

Yahweh ordered the Israelites to "take heed to yourselves, that you go not up into the mount, or touch the border of it: Whosoever touches the mount shall be surely put to death: No hand shall touch him, but he shall surely be stoned, or shot through; whether it be beast or man, he shall not live."[32]

As Egypt's most sacred structure, the Great Pyramid was perpetually guarded by the well-armed Rosthau, who were under orders to kill all unauthorized persons from violating the perimeter surrounding the base of the monument. Had they not been driven off by the invading Sea Peoples, leaving the Giza Plateau unprotected, Ramose/Beja could not have had gained access to the King's Chamber and robbed its crystal power stone.

Referring to the Rosthau "messengers of Qa," Ellis found that the word *qa* was used in various, related combinations to define the height of heaven (*qa-pet*), a high place on which stood the god of creation (*qa-qait*), a high hill (*qaa*), height (*qa-t*), and two very high mountains (*qa-qa*). Qa was hieroglyphically signified by the profile of an ibis, the emblem of Thaut, the god of wisdom said to have built the Great Pyramid. "So the clear inference is that the text is talking about the Sanctuary of Thoth," Ellis concludes, "the Great Pyramid."[33] As messengers of Qa, therefore, the Rosthau were its armed stewards.

The ancient Egyptian *Unas* provides supportive source material, writing of the Pyramid's "Great Terror, Sedjaa-ur, who comes forth from Hep."[34] Sedjaa-ur was, appropriately enough, the Egyptian god of earthquakes, the "Great Terror," that shook Hep, the mythic personification of the Nile Valley, which the Great Pyramid was built to protect from seismic violence. *Exodus* 19:16–18 and 24:17 recounted:

> *There were thunders and lightnings, and a thick cloud upon the mount...and all the people that were in the camp trembled. And Mount Sinai was altogether on a smoke, because the Lord descended upon it in fire; and the smoke thereof ascended as the smoke of a furnace, and the whole mount quaked greatly...and the appearance of the glory of Yahweh was like devouring fire on the top of the mount.*

Although investigators have long searched in vain for a comparable volcano in the Sinai Desert to match this description, it far more resembles effects produced by the Great Pyramid when it transformed geological stress into electrical discharge, even to the air shafts ventilating energy-shear in visible smoke.

The Parting of the Seas

Acting on divine command to "despoil the Egyptians,"[35] the Israelites eluded capture at the hands of Pharaoh thanks to a miraculous event when Yahweh "caused the sea to go back by a strong east wind all the night, and made the sea dry land, and the waters were divided. And the children of Israel went into the midst of the sea upon the dry ground." The Israelites escaped to the other side of the Red Sea, with the Egyptian king's soldiers in hot pursuit. "And the waters returned, and covered the chariots, and the horsemen, even all the host of Pharaoh that went in after them into the sea; there remained no so much as one of them."[36] This story sounds similar to an Old Testament spin on the 22nd century B.C. fate of Menenre II: An Old Kingdom pharaoh of the 6th Dynasty, he was said to have led a military expedition for the recovery of runaway slaves from Giza, site of the Great Pyramid complex. Led by a disgraced general of the previous king, they were trapped against the Sea of Reeds, but managed to escape somehow, while Menenre II, his horsemen, and his chariots mysteriously vanished. Whether or not the account is true, it dates to a remote period in Egyptian history, 1,000 years before the parting of the biblical Red Sea, which it resembles. To be sure, the name in *Exodus, yam suph*, commonly mistranslated as "the Red Sea," is actually the Sea of Reeds, a marshy region known to contemporary Egyptians as Papyrus Marsh, near the city of Per-Ramses, located in the same area of the eastern Delta from which the Israelites undertook their departure from Egypt.

"During unusual storm conditions, strong winds have been known to blow back waters and cleave a temporary passage," according to the late 20th century Marshall Cavendish in *Genesis and Exodus*. "At the north tip of the Suez Gulf, off the Red Sea, northwest gales occasionally still drive the waters back until it is possible to wade across. And sudden rainstorms can flood fords across the marches north of Suez."[37] It was here, based on these natural conditions, that the Israelites probably crossed out of Egypt, a conclusion seconded by a growing number of scientists, such as Mike Fillon. In his 1996 article for *Popular Mechanics*, he pointed out that the original yam suph as a Sea of Reeds "most aptly describes the lake region north of the Gulf of Suez, including the Bitter Lakes and Lake Timsah." He went on to cite computer calculations published by *The Bulletin of the American Meteorological Society* indicating that a moderate wind blowing constantly for about 10 hours could have caused the sea to recede about a mile, dropping water levels by 10 feet, due to Bitter Lakes' peculiar geography at their northern end, "leaving dry land for a period of time before crashing back when the winds died down."[38]

Contributing to the possibilities was the simultaneous approach of Comet Encke, which seems implied in *Exodus* 14:24, when Yahweh "looked forth upon the host of the Egyptians through the pillar of fire and of cloud, and discomfited the host of the Egyptians." The devastation brought to Earth by this celestial phenomenon around the turn of the 12th century B.C. had already entered its preliminary phase, with cataclysmic consequences the Israelites used to their advantage.

Further Evidence

The leader of the Israelites has been identified with Akhenaton himself by some important scholars, such as Sigmund Freud, and more recently, Egyptian historian Ahmed Osman. Although, as we have seen, Moses was probably King Merenptah's turncoat vizier, Ramose Iarsu Beja, the great law-giver appears to have shared something fundamentally significant in common with the heretical pharaoh after all: Both men experienced a life-changing catharsis in the presence of the same sacred object. Whether known as the Egyptian Ben-Ben or the Hebrew Aron ha-Berit (literally, the Ark of the Covenant), both men were similarly effected by it. As did Akhenaton, Moses enjoyed exclusive access to his God, who tells him in *Exodus* 25:22, "And there I will meet with you, and I will commune with you from above the mercy-seat, from between the two cherubim, which are upon the Ark of testimony, of all things which I will give you in commandment unto the children of Israel."

A modern recreation of the Aron ha-Berit.

Both Yahweh and Aton were the lone figures of a kindred monotheism. The former's admonition, "You shall have no other gods before me,"[39] was no less applicable in Akhenaton's heyday. Just as he never hesitated to call out the Egyptian military for the suppression of traditional worship, so Moses, when faced by a popular reversion to the old gods, ordered his Levite cadre to "put every man his sword upon his thigh, and go to and fro from gate to gate throughout the camp, and slay every man his brother, and every man his companion, and every man his neighbor...and there fell of the people that day about 3,000 men."[40]

Yahweh's appearance in "clouds of fire and smoke" atop the Ark was really an energy-field established between its two identical cherubim or Isis-images (electrical terminals), as clearly defined by the bible itself. The *Baraita*, or "Book of the Tabernacle," tells how the Israelites dropped serpents and scorpions between these twin angelic figures, which spat out sparks, killing the pests—strange behavior for a mere icon. The *Baraita* is an ancient collection of oral traditions, regarded as basic "proof-text" by Talmudic scholars in their analysis and interpretation of Jewish law. It goes on to state that the Ark was successful in "burning thorns and briars" out of the Israelites' way, as they passed through the wilderness. After dark, they often saw a strange "fire" burning within the tabernacle, where it was contained.

An authority on electronic technology in the ancient world, Larry Radka believes the electrical identity of the Ark's twin winged figures is self-evident:

> *Further evidence identifying the cherubim as carbon rods is the revelation that they were able to 'stretch their wings on high'—over the mercy-seat. The Hebrew word for 'stretch' is derived from paras, meaning 'to disperse,' and 'wing' is derived from kanaph, meaning 'edge' or 'extremity.' So, the pointed*

> *extremities of the cherubims or sharp edges of the carbon rods dispersed the electrical arc over the Electric Light God's mercy-seat.*[41]

A brilliantly powerful "arc light," or spark jumps between the points of two carbon "pencils," or rods, when electrically charged and aimed directly at each other, just as occurred between the twin figures facing each other over the mercy-seat.

Overhead view of the Ark of the Covenant reveals the "Mercy Seat" where Yahweh appeared as a static electrical charge.

Normally, the entire Ark was wrapped in a veil of badger skins and a blue cloth.[42] One person alone, the Cohen Gadol, a Levite high priest, could approach it with relative safety, but only if garbed in the *ephod*, a thick outer garment. His heavy coverall, plus the Ark's own alternating layers of cloth and leather, were nothing if not insulation against the lethal electromagnetic outbursts to which the Ark was all too prone outside its original component environment. These characterizations definitively identify it as a capacitor capable of discharging forceful electrical energy in a controlled application. Removing the electrically powerful Stone of Destiny from its proper setting had sabotaged the Great Pyramid's chief function as a geological transducer, but made possible its transformation into the Ark of the Covenant.

The Destiny Stone as a Tablet

According to *Kings*, "There was nothing in the Ark, save the two tablets of stone which Moses put there at Horeb [the Great Pyramid], when Yahweh made a covenant with the children of Israel, when they came out of the land of Egypt."[43] Similarly sacred stones in other widely separated cultures were likewise inscribed with divine wisdom, such as the Chintamani crystal obtained by Nikolay Roerich in Tibet. The Old Testament does not indicate the kind of stone on which the Ten Commandments were inscribed, and their familiar portrayal as plaques rounded at one end, beginning with Michelangelo, is entirely inferential. The word "tablet" itself refers only to "an inscribed stone," and does not define any particular configuration.

While *Exodus* mentions a pair of "tables" in the Ark, some Hebrew scholars believe the original meaning was "double stone": one stone inscribed on either side with the single Decalogue, because the word for "two" may be more properly understood as "twin" for a double-sided stone. When Israel's 6th century B.C. compilers began assembling and editing their collection of old oral traditions, they naturally experienced difficulty properly translating relative instances of archaic terminology, which they updated into the spoken language of their time. (Some appreciation for the difficulty of their task may be grasped via a comparable alteration of meaning in modern English. At the close of the 19th century, "immense" meant "great" or "wonderful." Just 50 years later, the same word was understood to only mean something very large.) A subtle change in emphasis appears to have transformed "double-inscribed stone" into the bible's "two tablets of stone."

Uncertainty about the Ark's contents stems from the Old Testament itself. *Kings'* assertion that nothing was in it "save the two tablets of stone which Moses put there" is contradicted by claims of the inclusion of "the golden pot that had manna, and Aaron's rod that budded," as described in *Exodus,*[44] *Numbers,*[45] and *Hebrews.*[46] Added to these items was the Cohen Gadol's richly embroidered outer garment, the ephod; the Philistines' peace offerings of golden mice and boils; pots of anointing oil and holy water; plus a dozen stones engraved by angels with the names of the tribes of Israel. According to Islamic tradition, there were also several scepters, a turban, and plates inscribed with the complete *Torah*. Clearly, the Ark was not large enough to contain all these items. But their mention suggests that religious scholars did not know what was inside the chest by the time they got around to writing about it. Independent researcher Graham Hancock expressed doubts about the "authenticity of the Tablets of the Law that Moses placed in the Ark."[47] He referred to the Priestly Code, wherein Moses is ordered specifically *not* to place the Ten Commandments inside the Ark, but beside it. The Priestly Code is a body of laws expressed in the Jewish *Torah*, as given orally to Moses by Yahweh while the Lord appeared in a cloud over the tabernacle housing the Ark of the Covenant, and according to an Ethiopian account, *The Glory of Kings*, the Ark contained a single tablet.

❧❧❧

As discussed in previous chapters, there was more than one Fire Stone, and at least several Ben-Bens were known to exist in Egypt as late as Akhenaton's time. Even so, he was fixated upon one outstanding monolith enshrined at the center of his desert city, the singular Tuaoi, engineered by the Atlanteans as a geotransducer. It was later returned to its rightful place in the Great Pyramid, then taken by Ramose/Moses, more than a century later. An Egyptian connection extends even farther back in time to the figure most associated with the Great Pyramid itself: Thaut, who arrived at the Nile Delta during the Zep Tepi, the "First Time," after the sinking of his Primal Mound in the distant west. He carried the Emerald Tablets inscribed with words of powerful wisdom responsible for creating the Giza complex, where they were entombed in its foremost monument. "Emerald" did not describe the gem from which Thaut's tablets were made, but indicated instead their priceless value. So too Moses' tablets were associated with his version of the Great Pyramid, Mount Sinai.

In view of all the foregoing considerations, the Ark likely contained a single, extraordinarily clear quartz crystal inscribed on either face with divine instructions, as suggested by the Jewish *Talmud*, a collection of ancient rabbinic writings. When Moses returned from the summit of Mount Sinai with a second edition of the Ten Commandments, they were described as having been "written on both sides," implying their appearance on a single "table." Although the *Talmud* cites a pair of tablets in the Ark, they were "made of a sapphire-like stone...not more than 6 hands in length and as much in width" (in other words, about 2 feet by 2 feet), and exceptionally heavy. "Sapphire," as mentioned, was not meant to be taken literally, but a term used in ancient times to describe any particularly outstanding jewel, not an ordinary mineral of the kind commonly associated with the Ten Commandments. Most revealingly, they are described as "transparent," a characterization less fitting granite-like tablets than quartz crystal.

The Ark as a Weapon

According to Ralph Ellis, the Ark "had become the Israelites' model substitute for the pyramid—a mobile Mt. Sinai and its secret chamber for god to inhabit during the exodus to Palestine."[48] Akin to the Egyptians before them, they used its Earth-sensitive Stone of Destiny to achieve altered states of consciousness whenever it generated negative ions. However, unlike its previous function as part of a geotransducer to mitigate seismic violence, the crystal capacitor was now made to perform military purposes.

If properly subjected to a high frequency tone, some modern manufactured electronic quartz crystals are able to modulate sonic input, magnifying it into exponentially powerful, vibratory waves that can shatter concrete. Current examples are acoustic drills based on the mechanical application of concentrated sound in numerous industrial projects. While the possession of such 21st century technology by a tribal people more than 3,000 years ago may seem incredible, a famous incident described in *Joshua* demonstrates that they were indeed familiar with the deployment of practical sonics[49]: When the Israelites arrived before the fortified city of Jericho, the former minister of the late Moses commanded, "Take up the Ark of the Covenant, and let seven priests bear seven trumpets of rams' horns before the Ark of

Yahweh...the priests blew the trumpets; and it came to pass when the people heard the sound of the trumpet, that the people shouted with a great shout, and the wall fell down flat..."

Joshua's method of attack, as described in the biblical book of his name, was a well-prepared, tactical offensive, the operation of which was thoroughly conceived far in advance of its execution, conforming as it did to a predetermined set of regulations: He had the enemy location surrounded ("you shall compass the city"), and pointedly ordered the Israelites, "You shall not shout, nor let your voice be heard, neither shall any word proceed out of your mouth, until the day I bid you shout; then you shall shout." There was a very specific order of battle: "And the armed men went before the priests that blew the trumpets, and the rearward went after the Ark, the priests blowing the trumpets as they went." Prolonged marching around Jericho, with no discernible effect on their opponents, apparently determined the optimum point of resonance between the Fire Stone inside its golden box and the city's outer fortifications, not unlike modern artillery spotters gauging the range of a target before their cannons commence firing.

After six days of using comparative sonics to ascertain a maximum field frequency between the Ark and Jericho's outer defenses, Joshua gave the order for all the trumpets to be blown and his people to shout simultaneously. Their combined output of sustained sound set up a resonance in the great crystal that exponentially multiplied the decibels, transducing them into reverberating waves of mechanical energy focused on the city. It was pulverized when rising frequency levels surpassed the target's material stress-point.

Today, resonant crystals are still employed as transducers to generate mechanical waves in solids. Although their modern application is used in the production of measuring instruments, such as sonar and ultrasonic cleansing devices, a much larger resonant crystal, similar to that contained in the Ark of the Covenant, would have subjected Jericho's fortifications to an intense frequency oscillation beyond their material tolerances, and pulverized them. In his eminently credible book, *The Giza Death-Star*, physicist Joseph Farrell lays out all the technical particulars for just such a military application of the Great Pyramid's industrial crystal, a potential fulfilled in the Israelite attack on Jericho.

Physical proof of the deployment of an advanced weapon was inadvertently unearthed in 1952 by Kathleen Kenyon, a British archaeologist excavating the remains of a Bronze Age site near the Dead Sea, at Tell-es-Sultan. Her digs revealed what was once a prosperous city. Unlike other such locations, its impressive walls had been leveled by some exceptionally powerful force. Kenyon determined that the destroyed city had been put to the torch soon after the collapse of its fortifications, an observation that conformed to the biblical report of Jericho's downfall: "And they burnt the city with fire, and all that was therein."[50] Its conflagration, however, helped establish the site's age. Just 44 years after Kenyon's initial work among the ruins near Tell-es-Sultan, half a dozen cereal grains were recovered from a burned layer there for radio-carbon dating by Groningen University researchers at

Holland's Center for Isotope Research. Their tests showed that the city had been burned circa 1320 B.C., plus or minus 100 years. Within these time parameters, the site perfectly matches Jericho's biblical description, and attests to the Ark of the Covenant's awesome power.

The Old Testament narrative of the city's sudden collapse demonstrated that the Israelites appreciated the Ark's extra-spiritual, geophysical potential long before taking to the field. Thus equipped with such radically sophisticated armament, they swept the more numerous, better-supplied Gentiles before them in their march toward the "promised land" of Jerusalem. Indeed, without the benefit of some major martial advantage, their unstoppable conquest seems incomprehensible. They were, after all, nomadic tent-dwellers, pastoralist sheep-herders, and merchants with no military background. Yet they challenged and mostly defeated professional standing armies long accustomed to desert warfare. Fortified citadels similar to Jericho had been built to withstand prolonged sieges. Yet each fell in a matter of days when confronted by forces bearing the Ark of the Covenant. Without some overwhelming trump, the Jews would have been made short work of by even bedouin tribesmen. In short, the Israeli juggernaut itself proves that the Ark had been converted into a biblical "weapon of mass-destruction," potent enough to melt away all opposition. After being repeatedly defeated by this invincible technology, against which they could offer no defense, the Philistines deplored its uniqueness, lamenting, "Woe unto us! For there has not been such a thing heretofore!"[51]

Potent as the Ark undoubtedly was, some powers were falsely attributed to it, such as its ability to clear a dry path through water. When the Israelites approached the Jordan River, they stopped before its banks at a place called Adam, known today as Damya, about 36 miles north of the Dead Sea, referred to here as the Salt Sea. For three days, they wondered how to proceed until:

It came to pass, when the people removed from their tents to pass over Jordan, and the priests bearing the Ark of the Covenant before the people, and as they that bore the Ark were come unto Jordan, and the feet of the priests that bore the Ark were dipped in the brine of the water (for Jordan overflows all his banks at the time of the harvest), that the waters that came down from above stood and rose up upon a heap very far at the city of Adam, that is beside Zaretan: And those that came down toward the sea of the plain, even the Salt Sea, failed, and were cut off; and the people passed over right against Jericho. And the priests that bore the Ark of the Covenant of the Lord stood firm on dry ground, until all the people were passed clean over Jordan ...And it came to pass, when the priests that bore the Ark of the Covenant of the Lord were come up out of the midst of Jordan and the soles of the priests' feet were lifted up unto dry land, that the waters of Jordan returned onto their place, and flowed all over his banks, as they did before.[52]

Although the oversized capacitor contained within their Ark was capable of effecting dramatic geological changes, parting rivers on command was not one of them. Sam Frydman, Professor of Geotechnical Engineering at the Technion Israel Institute of Technology in Haifa, wrote in 1997:

> This heap up of the Jordan's waters occurred at Damya, where the river crosses the major strike-slip fault. During an earthquake which occurred in 1546, the banks of the Jordan River caved in at Damya, and the waters of the river were cut off for two days, and it apparently also happened in 1267, 1906, and during the strongest earthquake, so far, of this century, which struck in 1927, when the banks of the river caved in at Damya, forming a barrier which caused the stretch of the Jordan downstream to run dry for several hours.[53]

The fortuitous earthquake that allowed the Israelites to cross the river may also have contributed to their success at Jericho, "the walls of which had already been weakened by the major tremor three days earlier."[54]

The Ark proved to be a dangerously erratic wonder-weapon, a double-edged sword quite capable of massacring friend or foe alike with impartiality. On occasion, it stubbornly refused to function, sometimes at a critical moment. Worse, it might inexplicably lash out at its handlers, killing them instantly and without warning, spewing great bursts of fire at anyone coming within its immediate vicinity. When an ox stumbled, threatening to spill the Ark from its cart, one of its caretakers, Uzzah, in a reflex action, reached out to steady it, and was instantly struck dead by a flash of energy. He was just one of reportedly thousands of the Ark's unwitting victims. Nadab and Abihu, Aaron's own sons, paid homage to it with incense, "and fire came forth from the presence of the Lord and devoured them, and they died before the Lord."[55] The Ark dealt similarly with a great many more officients who came too close: "And there came out a fire, and consumed the 250 men that offered incense." The Ark was no respecter of persons, high or low. When the 8th century B.C. king of Judah, Uzziah, an alleged linear ancestor of Jesus, attempted to worship in the Holy-of-Holies, "the tumors even rose up in his forehead before the priests in the house of the Lord, from beside the incense altar."[56]

As a precautionary measure, Joshua established an exclusionary zone of 2,000 cubits (more than half a mile) around the gold box whenever he deployed it against an enemy target. Eventually, the Ark became so treacherously unreliable, it had to be sequestered in the occupied Canaanite town of Shiloh, where just two attendants, Hophni and Phinehas, acted as caretakers. Without it, however, Yahweh's people were consistently beaten in the field. After the calamitous Battle of Eben-ezer, where they lost "about 4,000 men",[57] the temperamental Ark of the Covenant was sent for as a last-ditch effort to save themselves from annihilation. Although its reappearance was a boost to Jewish morale, the Aron ha-Berit let them down by failing to perform, "and there was a very great slaughter. For there fell of Israel 30,000 foot soldiers. And the Ark of God was taken. And the two sons of Eli, Hophni and Phinehas, were slain."[58] When word of the disaster reached their father, he fell over backwards out of his chair and broke his neck, "for he was an old man, and heavy."[59] His reaction expressed Israelite sentiments. Compounding a crippling defeat, the unthinkable had actually transpired: The Ark of the Covenant was in enemy hands.

By sharp contrast, the victorious Philistines exulted in their unparalleled war trophy, the ultimate weapon they would gleefully turn against its previous owners. But it would do them no good, either. Returning with the Ark in triumph to the coastal city of Ashdod, they installed it before their temple-god. But the next morning, they found his statue toppled over. "And they took Dagon, and set him in his place again. And when they rose early on the morrow morning, behold, Dagon was fallen upon his face to the ground before the Ark of Yahweh; and the head of Dagon and both the palms of his hands lay cut off upon the threshold; only the stump of Dagon was left to him."[60] As the Philistines' divine patron of agriculture, his humiliation was an especially evil omen. The statue had no sooner crashed to pieces, than their crops were suddenly beset by hordes of ravenous mice.

This disaster was accompanied by an epidemic of tumors, some lethal, that broke out among the Philistines themselves. They demanded its removal from Ashdod, so the Ark was taken from one city to another, always with the same, hideous results. But at Ekron, the Philistines decided they had suffered long enough from the troublesome box. Together with a "trespass-offering"—five golden representations of tumors and mice, "according to the number of the lords of the Philistines"—the Ark was put on a cart drawn by a pair of oxen, and left at the Israeli border near Beth-shemesh.[61] Astounded by the sight of its unexpected return, the Jews' elation was short-lived. God "smote of the men of Beth-shemesh, because they had looked into the Ark of Yahweh; he smote of the people 70 men, and 50,000 men; and the

people mourned, because Yahweh had smitten the people with a great slaughter."[62]

As their Philistine enemies were, they were now anxious to get rid of it as soon as possible, so they sent for help from the tribal authorities. "And the men of Kiriath-jearim came, and fetched up the Ark of Yahweh," which killed one of them (Uzzah, as mentioned previously) for trying to prevent its fall from the cart driven by his brother, Ahio.[63] The place where this act of divine ingratitude took place was henceforward commemorated as Perez-uzzah.[64] Eventually, Ahio "brought it into the house of Abinadab in the hill, and sanctified Eleazar, his son, to keep the Ark of Yahweh. And it came to pass, from the day that the Ark abode in Kiriath-jearim, that the time was long; for it was 20 years. And all the house of Israel lamented after Yahweh."[65]

The Capriciousness of the Ark

This rather dismal end to the early history of the glorious Ark was a consequence of its extended abuse. As the Ben-Ben stone, it had performed successfully according to its designed function for approximately 18 centuries, effectively transmuting potentially destructive earth-energy into harmless, even beneficial electricity. Removed from its purpose-built setting, however, the Ark became a loose cannon. During its irregular travels, while passing over seismically active ground, its crystal matrix resonated with tectonic stress, venting it in uncontrolled discharges. These were the outbursts of "fire" from God's box that indiscriminately killed so many of his own people. At other times, when they happened to set it up in geologically inert areas, it refused to operate for lack of telluric input.

The indifferent degree of success it demonstrated while in Israelite hands resulted from an incomplete understanding of the technology involved. When Ramose lifted the gold case from its granite coffer in the King's Chamber of the Great Pyramid, he knew enough about the Ben-Ben for its military deployment. He had been, after all, a high priest at Heliopolis, where the Stone of Destiny was originally enshrined. What he failed to appreciate, however, was the ability of all capacitors to accumulate and store energy: When their storage limitations are overreached, they randomly discharge. As the Ark of the Covenant was dragged across Palestine, it continued to soak up various energy forms—mechanical, seismic, sonic, and static. If someone strayed within its field of attraction, that person unknowingly created polarity (accumulated energy discharged as high-voltage bolts) and the victim fell dead, exactly as described in the Old Testament. The same process takes place when we sometimes reach for a metal doorknob, and receive a tiny spark. Prior motion across a thickly carpeted floor built up enough static energy in our own bodies to discharge electrically, as soon as we come into contact with something conductive.

So too an inanimate object placed within the immediate vicinity of an overloading capacitor creates an identical polarity. When the Philistines brought the Ark into their temple of Dagon, it destroyed the statue of their god. Later, it plagued them with an epidemic of tumors. An exceptionally powerful capacitor charged almost beyond its limits, but still unable to vent itself, would oscillate at a frequency high enough to induce effects similar to radioactivity, just as those reported in the Book of Samuel. It would also excite the behavior of certain animals, such as that of the mice that ravaged the Philistines while they were being afflicted by tumors. The familiar children's tale of medieval Hamlin, where the city's rat population

was extirpated through the agency of music, is not all that far from reality: Modern research shows that many species of mammals, especially vermin, are indeed affected by high-frequency sound. It's called "the Pied Piper Effect," and animal behaviorists find that a wide range of creatures—mice as well as humans—respond to electromagnetic impulses. Depending on the level of frequency to which they are exposed, mice can be agitated into abnormally aggressive behavior.

In 1993, Finnish cancer researchers at the University of Kuopio's Department of Pathology and Forensic Medicine repeated controlled laboratory studies to determine the effect of electromagnetic frequencies on living organisms. Their findings show:

> *EMF could be a promoter, but not an initiator of carcinogenic effects....Some animal studies suggest that RF [radio frequency] fields accelerate the development of sarcoma colonies in the lung, mammary tumors, skin tumors, hepatomas, and sarcomas. A substantial RF-induced increase in lymphoma incidence in transgenic mice exposed for up to 18 months has also been reported.*[66]

A related Swedish study of "occupational exposure to electromagnetic fields in relation to leukemia and brain tumors" took place 10 years earlier: Birgitta Floderus, research team spokeswoman, writes:

> *On the basis of the job held longest during the 10-year period before diagnosis, we found an association between the average, daily, mean level of EMF and chronic lymphocytic leukemia. The*

risk increased with increasing level of exposure. For brain tumors, a prolonged high level [high median values] *showed the strongest association. Our conclusion is that the study supports the hypothesis that occupational EMF exposure is a hazard in the development of certain cancers.*

Exposure to electromagnetic fields was also found to "accelerate skin tumor development. The results indicate that acute exposure to 50 Hz MF does exert distinctive biological effects on epidermal polyamine synthesis."[67]

Similar results were reported in the *Journal of Cellular Biochemistry*, by Sharmila Rao and Ann S. Henderson after their experiments at the Institute for Biomolecular Structure and Function, Department of Biological Sciences, Hunter College of the City University of New York. "The goal of the present study," they wrote, "was to determine if regulatory regions of the c-fos gene were responsive to electromagnetic field exposure. Cells were exposed to an environmentally relevant EMF of 60 Hz at 60 mGrms. CAT expression above control levels in transfected cells was observed following five-minute exposure to the electromagnetic field, with a peak at twenty minutes."[68]

Persons irradiated by prolonged contact with electromagnetic energy develop malignant swelling, both internally as brain tumors and also on the skin, which can lead to terminal leukemia and lymphomas. The Old Testament description of Philistines suffering from lethal boils after their exposure to the Ark of the Covenant shows that it contained an energy source resonating with intense electromagnetism. According to the Old Testament account, the Ark was present among the Philistines for seven months, sufficient time for its deleterious effects to have become noticeable. Thus, it perfectly matches the profile of an exceptionally powerful capacitor.

Quieting the Ark

Sequestering the Ark in a cave ("the house of Abinadab in the hill") was not unlike returning it to the King's Chamber of the Great Pyramid. Hence, the "Testimony of God" refrained from indiscriminate massacre. None too soon, as the Israeli takeover of Canaan was already virtually complete, aided in part by the Ark's more recent evil reputation among the Philistines as a biological wonder-weapon, even if it was no longer seen on the battlefield (*Chronicles* 13:3 states that it was never used, nor even consulted during the days of Saul leading up to the final seizure of Jerusalem).

As with their successful attack on Jericho, the Israelites seem to have taken advantage of the celestial cataclysm that persisted into the early 12th century B.C. When the Canaanite defenders rallied in a superior coalition, "the Lord hurled huge stones on them from the sky," then made the Sun stand still. *Joshua* 10:11 really describes a devastating barrage of meteors, in which the sudden overcast of an ash-cloud rising from their impacts would filter the light of the Sun in such a way as to make it appear motionless in the sky.

When David became king, he sought out the Ark, still in storage at Kiriath-jearim, for its removal to Zion, the Canaanites'

name for their stronghold defending Mount Moriah. Old Abinadab looked none the worse for his 20 years as its sole company, because the formerly overenergized capacitor had been dampened by the stabilizing environment of his King's Chamber-esque, subterranean home. It was then transported to another private residence, this one belonging to Obed-edom, enlisted as a guinea pig.[69] He was only an expendable Gentile, one of 600 volunteers from Gath, among the Philistine cities devastated by tumors and vermin. As such, his possible demise would be of no consequence. But if he survived the next three months alone with the Ark of the Covenant, the Israelites would know it was probably safe for installment in Jerusalem.[70] After passage of the allotted time, Obed-edom was still alive and unhurt, and David summoned the Levites to pick it up.

As members of an elite priesthood alone responsible for the Ark's maintenance, the Levites recalled Edgar Cayce's statement concerning the special caretakers assigned to the great crystal power stone of Atlantis. "The preparation of the Tuaoi," he said, "was in the hands only of the initiates at the time."[71] The Levites may have been similarly acting in the manner of their Atlantean precursors when they brought their potent charge into the new capital of Israel. Intriguingly, Jerusalem was known to the Greeks as "The Temple Robber of the Sacred Thing," an apparent reference to Moses (the temple robber) and the Ben-Ben Stone (the sacred thing) stolen from the Nile Delta, only to be set up in an occupied, Canaanite city. Indeed, when Jerusalem's temple was finally built, its shrine-room containing the Ark of the Covenant had been constructed in the same, internal, cubic dimensions (30 by 30 by 30 feet) as the King's Chamber of the Great Pyramid, and physically resembled its Giza counterpart down to the sparse, windowless interior.

Upon the Ark's arrival, the foundation of a permanent structure for it was sited atop Mount Moriah, still owned by Araunah (or Ornan), former king of the defeated Jebusites, a Canaanite subgroup. He was paid "600 shekels' worth of gold,"[72] and a temporary shelter was erected on the spot that had been his threshing-floor,[73] at the highest point of what would come to be known as the Temple Mount. Its selection had little to do with its panoramic vista—Mount Moriah was already a place profoundly steeped in related, mystical tradition: It was the cultic center of El Elyon, the "God Most High," administered by one of the Old Testament's most enigmatic characters, Melchizedek.[74] He was a Gentile, the priest-king of Canaan, many centuries before his country was occupied by the Israelites. But his association with them went back to their earliest patriarch, to whom he presented the "communion emblems" of El Elyon's mystery religion. The Old Testament story explains how Abraham's son was saved in the nick of time when an angel appeared, actually a metaphor for Melchizedek, whose delivery of the "communion emblems" supplanted human sacrifice. This was a transference of spiritual authority from Atlantis, as evidenced by the fact that *melchizedek* was actually a title—"King of Righteousness"—that Noah bestowed on his adopted son, the Gentile Canaanite Shem, when the young man was baptized and dressed by his father in the robes of high priest after the Great Deluge. As such, Melchizedek/Shem was the first royal leader of a spiritual lineage extending from Atlantean times to the House of David and, ultimately, Jesus.[75]

Noah chose Shem because he was conceived by his mother Sopanim without a man.[76] Virgin births also appear in the earliest traditions of numerous other cultures (such as the Hindu story of Krishna), invariably to indicate exceptional purity.

But Melchizedek's founding of Noachian religion at Mount Moriah actually signifies the arrival of survivors from Atlantis, who re-established their mystery cult there. Early Jewish tradition explains that Noah himself built the first altar in the Temple following the Deluge.

After Araunah sold his stone threshing floor to David, it became the *tabbur ha-arez*, literally, the "Navel of the World,"[77] "the Omphalos of Jerusalem."[78] It was also known as the *kibleh*, or "point of adoration," believed to cap not only Melchizedek's original cult headquarters, but also the waters of the *Genesis* Deluge. "If so," concluded biblical scholar Henry Halley, "it is a hint that this early, right after the Flood, God chose Jerusalem to be the scene of human redemption."[79]

The Cause of the Flood

Stripped of its religious metaphors, the Old Testament and its ancillary sources recount how Atlantean culture-bearers, personified in Noah, escaped the natural catastrophe that ravaged their oceanic homeland by sailing through the Mediterranean Sea to the shores of Palestine. There, they converted certain Canaanites, embodied in the figure of Melchizedek, to preserve their Navel-of-the-World mystery religion atop Mount Moriah. Some time later, the native converts shared its tenets with early Hebrews, as signified by the biblical Abraham, intermarrying with them to establish a bloodline of elect high priests extending into the house of David and far beyond.

In fact, the *Genesis* account and geological history meet in Atlantis. As the authoritative Professor of Old Testament and Biblical Theology at Michigan's Andrews University, Gerhard F. Hasel, calculates:

A reckoning of the date of the flood depends on the year of the birth of Abraham...if one takes the figures of either 1072 or 1172 of the Septuagint manuscripts for the span of time between Abraham's birth in ca. 2170 B.C. and the flood, the date of the flood would be reckoned accordingly to have taken place either in c. 3242 B.C. or 3342 B.C. The Samaritan Pentateuch and Josephus have slightly shorter time spans for the same periods, namely 942 years for the former and 983 years for the latter. These figures would lead to a date for the flood in either ca. 3112 B.C. for the Samaritan Pentateuch and ca. 3153 B.C. for Josephus.[80]

Remarkably, the date assigned to the Great Deluge by the Old Testament, particularly by the Samaritan Pentateuch and the Jewish historian Flavius Josephus, coincides with a major global catastrophe geologists know took place around 3100 B.C.: It was then that Encke, in the company of three other comets, made its first close pass to Earth's orbit. On its way, it collided with the asteroid belt between Mars and Jupiter, resulting in the Stohl Meteor Streams. According to archaeoastronomer Duncan Steel, a series of four comets spaced one month apart made "terrestrial orbit intersections" with the Earth in 3100 B.C.[81]; one lingering effect of their appearance is the 500-foot-wide Henbury crater in north-central Australia.

Greenland's Camp Century ice core registers an acidity spike at the same time, indicating a sudden, dense increase of ash-fall worldwide. Likewise in Antarctica, a distinct peak in sedimentation was demonstrated at Midge Lake, Beyers Peninsula, Livingstone Island, culminating around 2900 B.C. A "dust veil event," indicating the abrupt appearance of massive ash in the atmosphere, left its impression in Irish and English tree-rings, and the entire western hemisphere was covered with a thick strata of cosmic dust coincident with the widespread burning of bogs in northern Europe. Worldwide, erosion values of 20 to 30 tons per kilometer before the turn of the 4th millennium B.C. jumped to 140 tons.

In *Uriel's Machine*, authors Christopher Knight and Robert Lomas show that the direction of the Earth's magnetic field was abruptly changed around 3150 B.C., when a comet struck the Mediterranean Sea. Writing of the pre-Atlantis "Dardanian Flood" in the *Statesman*, Plato stated that the Sun turned back on its course at midday, during which time there was an immense mortality of men and animals. Massive flooding forced ancestral Austronesians belonging to an archaeological culture known as the Dawenkou in southern Shandong and Jiangsu to migrate from Taiwan to the Philippines. Both the Tigris-Euphrates and the Nile Rivers catastrophically overflowed their banks, as did Brazil's Amazon Basin, resulting in Lago Amazonicas, a low-lying lake that has since been absorbed by the Amazon River. At the same time, the Dead Sea abruptly rose 300 feet. In Mexico's Tehuacan Valley, the Abejas Phase of communal village life, when animal domestication was first cultivated and expanded, came to a sudden end after 13 centuries of existence.

To commemorate the beginning of a new era after the cataclysmic destruction of a former epoch, the Maya inaugurated their calendar on August 12, 3113 B.C. This was the precise date for what the Mayas called the "Greater Arrival" of culture-bearers on the shores of Yucatan from the *Hun yecil*, "The Drowning of the Trees," a world-class deluge. So too on the other side of the world, Persian tradition recounted that the Great Flood took place in 3103 B.C.

Atlantic Ocean vulcanism reached a peak around the turn of the 4th millennium B.C., particularly in Iceland at Mount Heimay, and in the Azores—the general vicinity of Atlantis. Severe earthquakes and intense volcanism triggered by meteoric material striking the geologically unstable mid-ocean overwhelmed large areas of the island. Some territories broke off and collapsed into the sea, but most of the Atlantean land mass endured. Its coastal regions were further devastated by 300-foot-high waves traveling at 500 miles per hour, and loss of life ran into the tens of thousands. But most inhabitants survived to rebuild their city, which would last another 900 years, until the return of Comet Encke at the beginning of the 12th century B.C. would trigger another global catastrophe that obliterated a number of late Bronze Age civilizations such as Troy, Mycenaean Greece, the Hittite Empire, and Shang Dynasty China, as well as Atlantis. Many Atlanteans emigrated to start life over in other, less devastated parts of the world. Among the survivors were flood-heroes personified by the biblical Noah. The pre-Deluge spirituality he brought to the Near East was re-established at the same hill later known as Mount Moriah, or Temple Mount. In choosing this site as Jerusalem's Navel of the World, Melchizedek initiated a continuity from the antediluvian mystery religion he inherited as Noah's adopted son to the installment of the Ark of the Covenant in the First Temple more than 2,000 years later. At the center of both the overseas cult Melchizedek took up around the turn of the 4th millennium B.C. and the gold box King Solomon enshrined in the 10th century B.C. was a sacred stone revered for its transformational power. It was by way of this holy object that the Ark of the Covenant traced its lineage back to Atlantis, through the Old Testament flood-hero and his chosen son, Melchizedek.

Melchizedek and a New Temple

The arrival of Noah's son in Jerusalem is no mere conjecture, but supported by physical evidence uncovered during the 1980s, when Yigal Shiloh excavated the lowest—and hence oldest—layer of human habitation at the Temple Mount. Among them, the Hebrew University archaeologist found remains of a small structure first thought to be a house. Later testing of its broken pottery suggested it was more likely a shrine or sacred enclosure of some kind. The same shards confirmed a reliable radio-carbon date circa 3000 B.C. (give or take 100 years), coinciding with both the biblical and geological period of the Great Flood, and Melchizedek's appearance at Mount Moriah.

Even 1,200 years later, when a 6-foot-thick wall surrounded its summit, the settlement was only about 10 or 11 acres, rendering it less a city than a cult-center, just as Melchizedek was supposed to have established there. Archaeological recreation of the 18th century B.C. wall revealed that it stood about 25 feet high and was interspersed at regular intervals with squarish watchtowers higher by another 10 feet, a pair of which stood close on either side of a main entrance. Jerusalem's first monumental enclosure was thus remarkably similar to Plato's description in the *Kritias* of the fortified wall that encompassed Atlantis, which approached the zenith of its far-flung, stylistic influence during the middle Bronze Age.

Melchizedek had offered Abraham bread and wine, not out of ordinary hospitality, but because this food and drink comprised a kind of Eucharist, part of the Patriarch's initiation into the sacred mysteries of Atlantis, and through him the Israelites, who thus became the Chosen People—chosen by Melchizedek as the trustees of the ancient Atlantean religion, which raised them above the tribal superstitions of their Semitic neighbors. This sacred relationship was doubtless the original motive driving the Exodus, the impetus behind migrating to the "Promised Land." It was this secret awareness that nurtured the Hebrews through centuries of misfortune in foreign lands, particularly in Egypt, sustaining them in their ancestral hope of someday returning to Zion to be with their "God Most High." Indeed, as early as their association with crazy Akhenaton, back at his sun-cult capital more than 200 years before, Palestine's "Urusalim" was repeatedly cited as a "great city" in Amarna's cuneiform archive. Its original Gentile name was Yerushalayim, or the "Foundation of Salem," the Jesubite god of prosperity.[82]

Melchizedek's presence at Mount Moriah is integral to the Ark's identity as the container of a geo-capacitor powered by seismic energy. Israel itself sits astride the Jordan Rift Valley, the boundary between the Arabian and African tectonic plates, where their grinding interaction causes major earthquakes of category seven or higher about once every century. According to Professor Frydman, "catastrophic earthquakes have continued to occur through the ages in Israel....Appreciation of the seismicity of the region has resulted in the establishment of seismic building codes."[83] Mount Moriah has been at the epicenter of numerous tectonic events in the past, as attested by archaeological evidence for several layers of geological destruction brought to light in excavated strata at the ancient Jewish temple. Between 715 and 780 A.D., the al Aqsa mosque, an

Islamic addition to the complex, was twice destroyed by earthquakes.

The seismic activity on Mount Moriah energized the Ark of the Covenant, enabling it to perform as intended, and the Mount was therefore an optimum location for this earth-powered device. *Kings* suggests as much, when Elijah exclaims, "Go forth, and stand upon the mount before Yahweh, and behold Yahweh passed by, and great and strong wind rent the mountains, and broke in pieces the rocks before Yahweh; but Yahweh was not in the wind; and after the wind an earthquake."[84] Long before, Jacob dreamt of "the gateway to heaven" atop Mount Moriah, just as various American-Indian tribes of the American Southwest still sleep atop Pinnacles National Monument, in the hope that its crystalline granite matrix, glowing with the ion-laden, mind-altering blue halo of geophysical energies rising from the San Andreas Fault immediately below, will likewise grant them heavenly dreams in their nightly vision quest under the stars of southern California. As such, the meaning of Moriah's name—the Chosen of Yahweh—is particularly appropriate.

King David died before the Temple could be more than founded, so its completion was inherited by his son, who succeeded him in 966 B.C. Construction was delayed for four years by more pressing business, such as the execution of Solomon's own usurping brother, until work finally began on an intended final resting place for the Ark of the Covenant. Building was to go on without further interruption for the next 12 years, but its end result was one of the most remarkable architectural feats of the ancient world. Although the Israelites were jealous of its profanation at the hands of unclean Gentiles, the temple was nevertheless raised entirely by Phoenician labor. "Unfortunately," writes author Maitland Edey, "his people lacked the necessary skills, so Solomon contracted

with King Hiram of Tyre for a team of architects, masons, carpenters and smiths...."[85] They were, in any case, under the direction and scrutiny of the Levite priests directly responsible for the Ark.

As described in the Old Testament *Book of Kings*, everything about the sacred edifice was monumental. It was built on the crest of Mount Moriah, just north of the city, over the threshing floor David purchased from Araunah—the *tabbur ha-arez* Navel of the World; Melchizedek's "point of adoration" capping the waters of the Great Flood that brought Noah's Atlantean mystery cult to this very spot. The summit on which the Temple stood was a relatively small area sloping off steeply to the west, south, and east, but more gradually to the north. To accommodate all the inhabitants of Jerusalem, together with pilgrims expected from across the country, a broad, level esplanade was laid out around the structure by filling in the slopes surrounding the top of Mount Moriah, and supporting the fill with the construction of retaining walls grounded in rock. The area enclosed by these ramparts was subsequently known as the Temple Mount.

Solomon's sacred structure had 10-foot-thick walls running 135 feet long and 35 feet wide to form a rectangular structure 50 feet high. Nearby, on the surrounding plaza paved with flat blocks of smoothed stone, stood a courtyard altar upon a larger platform that resembled a step-pyramid, its 15-foot summit reached by a flight of stone steps on the south. Between its base and the front of the Temple was a 30-ton, bronze basin, referred to as the *yam*, filled with several thousand gallons of holy water, resting on the representations of a dozen bulls. Workers transferred the precious liquid from the yam to two rows of smaller basins, known as *kiy-yorot*, wheeled about on mobile stands (*mechonot*) for the convenience of visitors who were required to ritually purify themselves before they could enter the temple.

A flight of stone steps rose to the Temple's eastern and only entrance flanked by a pair of 27-foot-tall bronze pillars between which visitors passed into the *ulam*. Leaving this small anteroom, they entered the *hekal*, or main hall, the building's largest open space and its most ornate. Just below the ceiling of cedar cross-beams, some 40 feet overhead, were recessed, celestory windows that allowed light to enter, as it were, from above. Shafts of sunlight angling into the hall were hazy with clouds of frankincense billowing from bronze burners and the smoke of daily burnt offerings, once at dawn and again after sundown, sacrificed upon an altar near the far end of the hekal. Some distance behind the altar, in the center of the hall, were a dozen small loaves of bread, symbolizing the 12 tribes of Israel, placed atop a low table. For after-dark ceremonies, lamps hanging from tall tripods stood against the cedar wood-paneled walls decorated on either side with the images of cherubim and lotuses.

Beyond the sacrificial altar, another flight of stairs rose to a very tall set of cedar doors set with gold. No one, not even Solomon, except on rare occasions, was permitted to pass through them, save the Cohen Gadol, the chief Levite priest, and he could do so only once each year, at sunset of October 1st, on Yom Kippur, the "Day of Atonement." Its purpose was to re-establish the special bond—the "covenant"—between Yahweh and his Chosen People, because they had alienated him by idolizing a golden calf while Moses was off getting the Ten Commandments. Today, nearly 3,000 years after Yom Kippur was celebrated for the first time, it still references the Ark of the Covenant. During the hour-long Ne'ilah ("Opening of the Gates") concluding the service, the entire congregation

stands when a cabinet, or ark, in which the scrolls of the Torah are kept, is only now allowed to remain open for this ceremony. The law inscribed in precious stone and its golden container were behind the tall doors in the next room, the cube-shaped Holy-of-Holies, known as the *debir*, or shrine. In the center of its floor rested the awesome Ark, guarded on either side by an identical pair of gilded, olivewood cherubim 17 feet tall.

The Cohen Gadol, or high priest of Solomon's Temple, prostrates himself before the Ark of the Covenant.

Although supposed to have been a purely Hebrew affair, the Temple was rife with spiritual elements from earlier cultures. As mentioned, dimensions for the Holy-of-Holies' room matched those of the King's Chamber in the Great Pyramid, and was likewise windowless. The two free-standing cherubim were colossal versions of the twin Isis-figures atop the Ark, and repeated as a design motif along the walls of the Hekal. The main hall was also decorated with a lotus pattern, honoring a flower symbolizing the Upper Nile Valley. There, it was sacred to Nefertum, the divine lord of perfumes, and signified rebirth: The Egyptian *Book of the Dead* tells how creation began when "a great lotus came out of the primordial waters."[86]

Outside, the tall, bronze columns on either side of the Temple's front entrance were named Boaz and Jachin, representing "stability and strength in the two lands [Judea and Israel, respectively] conjoined," according to historical author Francine Bernier. "Similarly, in ancient Egypt, pillars [obelisks] in pairs symbolized the union of Upper and Lower Egypt."[87] In fact, the Temple's entire entrance, known as the Migdol Gateway, strongly resembles the same east-oriented twin-pillar portico to Medinet Habu, a "Victory Temple" completed around 1190 B.C., in the Upper Nile Valley, West Thebes. Today the best-preserved of all major ancient Egyptian ceremonial complexes, Medinet Habu was built by Ramses III to memorialize his success against the Sea People's final invasion of the Delta, which occurred just 30 years after the Israelites left his kingdom. The repetition of dynastic sacred architecture in Jerusalem was in keeping with the Egyptian origins of the Ark itself.

The Hebrew Temple plaza's 30-ton holy water basin, the yam, was supported by a dozen cast-bronze bulls. While obviously standing for Israel's 12 tribes, the choice of animal was nevertheless the personification of Apis, the sacred bull of Memphis, where his movements were said to foretell the future. As such, he was associated with astrology and its 12 houses of the Zodiac. To indicate the god's fertility, Egyptian priests affixed a silver triangle to his forehead, the same emblem later modified into the Jewish *magan david*, popularly if erroneously known as the "Star of David"—the magan david does not represent a star, but twin, intersecting triangles signifying the sacred center created by a union of heavenly and earthly energies. The Egyptians believed Apis had been born of a virgin impregnated by Ptah, the god of creation, as had Melchizedek, Mount Moriah's first high

priest. His baptism by Noah was reflected at Jerusalem's great basin of holy water, just as the the loaves of bread placed at the center of the Hekal simulated the sacred eucharist he brought to Abraham after the Great Flood.

The Atlantean mystery-cult Melchizedek introduced to Palestine after the late 4th millennium B.C. cataclysm was likewise symbolized throughout the Temple. In his dialogue, the *Kritias*, Plato stated that five was the mystical numeral of Atlantis, where it was incorporated in sacred architecture and myth. Atlantis itself comprised five alternating rings of artificial islands and moats, and Poseidon, the sea-god creator of Atlantis, sired five sets of twins to rule the oceanic world. So too at Jerusalem, doubles of five were featured in all three staircases, each one comprising 10 steps, leading to the top of the courtyard altar, the Temple entrance, and the debir. The Hekal had 10 celestory windows and 10 tripods. Outside, 10 kiy-yorot lined up before the larger water basin. That this enormous receptacle was indeed meant to symbolize the yam, or sea of Atlantis was established by Israelite belief in the nearby Gihon spring as the cleft through which the tide of the Great Flood swirled into the bowels of the Earth.[88] Holy water that filled the yam and dispensed into the wheeled tubs for visitors to purify themselves before entering the Temple was drawn from the Gihon spring, where the Deluge waters were said to still reside. In the construction of a holy place as sensitive to every symbolic nuance as was Solomon's Temple, the appearance of its various spiritual roots in these numbers and objects was eminently appropriate.

Ensconced at last in a proper setting, the Ark of the Covenant no longer blasted thousands of innocent bystanders with great sheets of fiery energy. On the contrary, for the next 364 years, it blessed

Israel with a golden age, during which a mosaic of influences, beliefs, and experiences coalesced in the minds of its scholars. By the light of the Ark, they would compose the Old Testament and create the basis of Judaism, a new, unprecedentedly resilient religion able to survive the coming millennia of recurring disaster and persecution.

Solomon himself had special access to the Aron ha-Berit under the careful auspices of the Levite priests. As reported in *Kings*, "And God gave Solomon wisdom and understanding exceeding much, and largeness of heart, even as the sand that is on the sea shore. And Solomon's wisdom excelled the wisdom of all the children of the east country, and all the wisdom of Egypt. For he was wiser than all men."[89] The Ark's inspirational puissance seemed to irradiate the entire kingdom. The Israelites' expansion from the Euphrates River to the Egyptian border was an incredible political achievement for a people of tent-dwelling nomads. Solomon's proverbial wisdom spread throughout the civilized world, as did his reputation for untold wealth, which made construction of the Temple possible. He also sponsored trading expeditions to Ophir, his fleet of ships returning from South Africa's mines and markets with vast cargoes of gold and luxury goods.

Even in a temple purpose-built for its safest operation, the Ark was a potent phenomenon. Survival meant keeping a proper distance. When the Levites' Cohen Gadol approached it on the annual "Day of Atonement," his right ankle was shackled as a precautionary measure with a long chain held at the other end by assistants hiding behind the Hekal's high doors. In the event he was felled by a bolt from inside the gold chest, they pulled on the chain to haul his body from the unapproachable Holy-of-Holies back into the main hall. For all of Solomon's elaborate efforts to contain the power of the Ark, it still resonated with the Earth's tectonic pulse.

The Destruction of the Temple and Disappearance of the Ark

Almost immediately after Solomon died around 915 B.C., the tribal unity his reign cemented began to crumble. Generations of widening political dissension precipitated gradual military decline over the next three centuries, until the kingdom was reduced to a tributary of the Babylonians. In 597 B.C., they placed a 21-year-old puppet on the throne of Judah, who then changed his name from Matanyáhu, "Gift of the Lord," to Zedekiah, "Righteous of the Lord." Notwithstanding his client status and sworn loyalty to his foreign masters, he plotted revolt against them by forming an alliance with Egypt's Pharaoh Hophra (the historical and contemporary Apries). Learning of Zedekiah's betrayal, King Nebuchadnezzar II besieged Jerusalem "with all his host,"[90] beginning in early July of 589 B.C. During the 18 months that followed, "every worst woe befell the devoted city, which drank the cup of God's fury to the dregs."[91] After the capital's fall, General Nebuzaraddan was dispatched to complete its methodical destruction. He permitted a small number of vintners and husbandmen to remain behind and work the land,[92] while his lieutenant, Gedaliah, was posted with a Chaldean guard at Mizpah to rule over Judah.[93]

In Jerusalem, the Babylonians removed everything of value from the temple, then razed it to the ground. The Old Testament's *Second Book of Kings* documents a meticulous list of booty seized by Nebuchadnezzar's troops before they obliterated the "House of the Lord," an inventory repeated at the close of *Jeremiah*. Both record how the bronze pillars, great and small holy water basins, incense burners, all precious or useful things—even shovels, candle snuffers, pots, and pans— were taken away by the victors. In other words, the site was utterly purged of all materials prior to its demolition. Among the long catalog of items seized, however, the Ark of the Covenant was conspicuous for its absence. As the Temple's single greatest treasure, the Babylonians would hardly have overlooked a large, gold casket. And although it was the most valuable object the Israelites possessed for more than four centuries, it vanished from the Old Testament without further comment.

Fully 150 years after the fall of Jerusalem, they returned from their Babylonian captivity, along with virtually every stick of Temple property taken by the invaders. The *Book of Daniel* lists 10,938 seized artifacts handed over by the Persian treasurer, Methradath, to Shesh-bazzar, the prince of Judah. These included basins, censers, bowls, and vessels of many kinds, all of gold or silver. When describing the rebuilt Temple, however, the Talmud noted an important discrepancy: "In five things, the First Sanctuary differed from the Second—in the Ark, the Ark-cover, the Cherubim, the Fire, and the Urim-and-Thummim."[94] Whatever became of the Aron ha-Berit, at least it had evaded Nebuchadnezzar's clutches.

Further mention of the Ark was limited to a few unsatisfying remarks. A prophesy that the Ark could, in any case, be dispensed with when eventually the people became too righteous for its further use, smacks of sour grapes, written as it was long after the incomparable treasure's disappearance.[95] *Revelation*'s curt dismissal that the Ark simply went up to heaven is just an admission that it was lost forever.[96] Contrary to both evasions, a single passage in the deuterocanonical *Maccabees*[97] tells how the prophet Jeremiah, "being warned of God," took the Ark, along with other Temple goods, and buried them in a cave at Mount Nebo. He then declared that its location must remain secret "until the time that God should gather his people again together, and receive them unto his mercy."[98] Mount Nebo has been identified with Jabal Ni⁻bu, more of an elevated ridge than an actual mountain, about 2,680 feet above sea level, in western Jordan. Its only ancient ruins belong to a small Christian church going back no earlier than the late 3rd century A.D. Persistent attempts since at least that time to discover any trace of the Ark have come to nothing. Either Jabal Ni⁻bu is not the real Mount Nebo, or Jeremiah was the most skilled covert operations artist in history.

His story is repeated in the *Mishnayot* introduction to ancient records deleted from the *Mishnah*, the first section of the Talmud, among the *Massakhet Keilim*, a collection of 12 chapters describing the hidden treasure. The *Mishnayot* differs from *Deuteronomy*'s rendition by having the Prophet bury the Ark at an undisclosed location seven years before Solomon's temple was destroyed. Jeremiah is replaced by a quartet of angels in the *Syriac Apocalypse of Baruch* (in the Apocrypha), which tells of the temple treasures, "And the earth opened its mouth and swallowed them up."[99] The lack of specifics in any of these meager explanations means that their authors knew only that the Ark vanished after King Nebuchadnezzar's early

6th century B.C. invasion, escaped his troops, and was buried somewhere in the region.

After the Israelites' return from Babylon, they began to rebuild the Temple from its meager ruins, completing the construction on March 12, 515 B.C. It was demolished some 400 years later during King Herod I's massive expansion program to provide space for a far more colossal, square platform that covered the entire Temple Mount. But it, similar to its late 6th century B.C. predecessor, lacked the Ark of the Covenant. For all his imperial power, not even Herod the Great could determine its whereabouts. "When he finally penetrated the tomb where the coffins of Solomon and David reposed," writes Templar expert Steven Sora, "legend has it that one of his bodyguards was struck by a flame that incinerated him."[100] It would seem that even after five centuries of interment, the unpredictable "Testimony of God" still resonated with telluric harmonics.

Built to last for eternity, Herod's gargantuan structure was totally destroyed in 70 A.D., just five years after its completion, by General Titus and his Roman legions. They carried home many spoils of war, as depicted on their famous victory monument at the imperial capital. But the Ark of the Covenant was not among them.

CHAPTER 10

Crusades for and Against
the Ark

*For they had crafts beyond our ken, and sciences that lesser
men lack wit to grasp. With dextrous hand to rich invention
wed, they planned fair idols men might be forgiven for
worshiping in hope of heaven.*

—Hafiz Ibrahim, 14th century Islamic poet

After Titus destroyed the Temple, he went on to become one of his country's noblest (if shortest lived) Emperors. He was succeeded by a long series of mostly competent, even brilliant leaders, culminating 100 years later in the glorious reigns of men such as Hadrian and Marcus Aurelius. Exemplifying the Caesarean ideal, they stood securely atop the Classical world of art, architecture, public works, philosophy, literature, law, education, social well-being, military defense, and above all, the Roman ethic of wrenching order from chaos. The *Pax Romanum* became the meaning of life.

But immemorial hatred arose like a lethal vapor from the smoldering ruins of Herod's Temple. It was a deep-seated malice not dispelled and forgotten over time, but nurtured by generations of dispossessed Jews, for whom hatred of Rome became a religious duty—they vented their

rancor early as followers of the crucified Jesus. The first Christians were an even mix of Jews and Gentiles, and as such, lumped together by the Roman authority. In demonizing all other forms of spirituality to excercise their vengeance, these early monotheists defied the law guaranteeing religious freedom, and were expelled from the capital as militant atheists. Their forcible removal scattered them throughout the farthest reaches of the Empire, but in time they formed, according to famed 18th century historian Edward Gibbon, the power that would "bore out the inner life of Rome, leaving it nothing more than a thin shell easily blown away by the winds of change."[1]

There were other decisive causes, outgrowths of the broader religious crisis that brought into question the spiritual foundations supporting not only imperial esteem, but the entire Classical world. By the late

5th century A.D., the Empire's borders were dangerously under-defended, because Christianized Romans were loathe to hazard their immortal souls by becoming soldiers, thus violating God's Commandment, "Thou shalt not kill." Less encumbered by moral reservations, Germanic hordes crashed through the northern defenses that had held them back for 700 years, unleashing a pillaging flood-tide to sweep unopposed down the length of the Italian peninsula. On September 4, 476, Imperial Rome died when its young Caesar personally abdicated the throne to Odoacer. The barbarian chief dismissed his frightened captive as beneath contempt, pensioning him off to live the rest of his life in obscurity. Ironically, the last emperor had been named after the mythical founder of his enemy-occupied city—Romulus.

A Dark Age for the Ark

Romulus' humiliation did not merely signify a transition of power, however. Nor did Odoacer and his fellow tribesmen carry on in the best traditions of Classical culture. The final collapse of civilization is not a pretty sight, and the chaos ignited by invasion was hardly more than a foreshadowing of far worse to come. The material lifestyle to which Romans had so long been accustomed was no longer at hand. Absence of all the usual goods and services—from law enforcement and farming to medicine and education—translated into an ever-deepening abyss of hunger, lawlessness, and ignorance. With no central authority, society unraveled. Not for nothing were the difficult centuries following Romulus' surrender remembered as the Dark Ages. General hygiene was condemned and avoided, because the sinful Romans had loved their baths. Hence, disease and pestilence joined illiteracy, famine, superstition, poverty, and servitude in characterizing the former empire, its innumerable pieces picked up by militaristic landlords for their own feifdoms. Beneath them were a few wealthy families served by artisans and peasants, all of them surrounded by masses of human squalor.

The single most powerful component to arise out of this new world order was a monolithic church. Its leaders had already liquidated countless opponents in their zeal to suppress an apparently endless stream of heresies, thereby establishing God's earthly representatives as the sole, unquestioned authorities in this life and the next. For more than 500 years, they emotionally engineered European society—king and commoner alike—to embrace the Roman Church as the physical expression of divine will. Thus supernaturally empowered, every public and private aspect of existence fell within their spiritual and temporal domain. The breadth of human experience and activity—from birth to death and beyond—was subjugated by Christian dogmatists. They alone told their unwashed, benighted parishioners what to believe and how to behave, while exorcizing any perceived political incorrectness with every conceivable form of punishment, from fines to burnings at the stake.

Judgment Day

The leading motif of early medieval theology that sustained institutionalized Christianity was "Judgment Day." Century after century, priests all over Europe drilled into the consciousness of each generation the terrible consequences of sin and the promise of salvation when Jesus would appear enthroned on a golden cloud to gather a few pure souls to his side, send the majority of mankind to Hell, and destroy the world to celebrate the beginning of His millennium in the year 1000 A.D. It was His return, universally regarded with absolute certainty, that became the focal point of religious conviction and the dread inevitability that bonded the frightened masses to the Church, their only hope for salvation.

After the turn of the 10th century, popular anticipation of Judgment Day began to intensify, an acceleration of fervor stoked by churchmen holding out a last chance for redemption from perpetual torment. Europeans were so keyed up by the late 900s, they began donating their material possessions in exchange for plenary indulgences (mortal pardoning of sins) sold by bishops and cardinals. Poor people gave away their sons and daughters to seminaries and nunneries, while noble families deeded ancestral lands to the Church. As the new year brought another century, and with it the millennium, all Christendom held its breath. But minutes turned into hours, and days of anticipation grew to weeks, while no sign of an apocalyptic Christ appeared in the sky. Requests for the return of donated land or personal possessions were ignored by bishops, who offered paltry explanations for the millennial non-event. God's ways were a mystery no one should have the impudence to question. After all, the penitents had not really wasted their contributions, but "laid up treasures in heaven," in priestly safekeeping until the Day of Salvation.

Meanwhile, corruption was rife throughout every level of Christian society. Although widespread squalor was the norm and peasants struggled to survive, many clergymen could afford the double luxury of rich estates *and* holy piety. In a sense, this controlling world of rank hypocrisy did come to an end on New Year's Day, 1000 A.D. Until that moment, Christian prelates commanded devout obedience at every level of European society. But when the Day of Judgment failed to cast sinful humanity into the pit of Hell, simultaneously elevating the virtuous elect into everlasting bliss, a resentment began to set in that, for the depth of its hatred and the breadth of its impact, threatened to destroy the church root and branch. Previous centuries of pious corruption, undue influence, sanctioned immorality, and propaganda lies ignited violent reaction against any and all forms of organized religion across the continent. Looting and desecration struck hundreds of churches, their symbolic paraphernalia collected for waste disposal. Bishops could no longer travel in safety through their own diocese, while many priests no longer dared venture forth to visit local congregations. Papal authority disintegrated under this popular onslaught, and secular rulers pointedly ignored all admonitions from Rome, fighting among themselves for snatches of territory. With their moral compass gone, many ordinary people refused to further endure their lot as penitents, turning instead to highway robbery. Roaming bands of brigands proliferated, pillaging cities and farms alike, uncontested by any law enforcement. Crime waves contended with escalating warfare to ravage all of Europe, and Western civilization again tottered toward catastrophe.

Pope Urban's Plan

Efforts on the part of churchmen to avert their doom failed, their appeals to conscience falling on the deaf ears of former parishioners entirely disaffected by clergy of all kinds. So much so, that by the second half of the 11th century, prognostications for not only the collapse of the Church, but the extirpation of Christianity itself—or at least its Roman version—were voiced from the British Isles to the Balkans. Even Pope Gregory VII's strong-willed determination, beginning in 1073, to reverse Europe's precipitous decline and restore his office's central authority made no headway against the disintegrating spirit of the times. Faced with such apparently irrepressible dissolution, his desperate successor, Pope Urban II, hit upon an idea that would transform imminent disaster into a new lease on life for his troubled religion.

Beginning in July of 1095, Urban II set out from Rome on a high-profile expedition through southern France. It was the first time in more years than anyone could remember that a pope had been seen in this part of the world, and huge crowds turned out to see him. Despite the disrepute into which his Church had fallen, reverence for the pontificate experienced an upsurge at the sight of the famous man in person. Heretical animosities were at least temporarily put in the shade by greater pomp and circumstance than any king could muster.

But Urban II was interested in more than a public relations tour to bolster Rome's faltering papacy. On November 27, he appeared before an audience of mostly French aristocracy, nobles, warlords, and knights, known by their Latin name as *milites*. For nearly 100 years after the Last Judgment fiasco, they had grown steadily into a disrespectful, ungovernable force, a power unto themselves, plundering and fighting their way back and forth across Europe. Their interminable pillaging, feuds, and vendettas had made life increasingly impossible for everyone else. Something had to be done to get rid of them, or at the very least thin their ranks. And that was the real purpose driving Urban II's presentation just outside the city limits of Clermont. A dynamic speaker in command of real oratorical skill, he did not flaunt his personal religious authority, but appealed to his troublesome listeners, even flattering them as glorious, fellow Christians in a new, common cause. As very few single speeches have ever done, his words on that crisp autumn afternoon would alter the course of history, and set in motion an event still impacting the Western world's involvement in the Near East:

> *A race absolutely alien to God has invaded the land of Christians, has reduced the people with sword, rapine, and flame. These men have destroyed the altars polluted by their foul practices. They have circumsized the Christians, either spreading the blood from the circumcisions on the altars, or pouring it into the baptismal fonts. And they cut open the navels of those whom they chose to torment with loathsome death, tear out their most vital organs, and tie them to a stake, drag them around, and flog them, before killing them as they lie prone on the ground with all their entrails out. Nonexistent money is extracted from them by intolerable tortures, the hard skin of their heels being cut open and pealed back to investigate whether perhaps they have inserted something under it. What shall I say of the appalling violation of women, of which it is more evil to speak than to keep silent?[2]*

Listening to the vehement pontiff, one would have imagined that the sainted city of God had just been overwhelmed by demonic heathens. In point of fact, Jerusalem had been continuously occupied by Islamic conquerors for the previous 458 years. During virtually all that time, "the privileges and the security of the Christian population were provided for" by the magnanimous Arabs, who insisted upon total religious freedom for all its residents.[3] As recently as 1064, some 7,000 Christian pilgrims, led by the Archbishop of Mentz, together with the Bishops of Utrecht, Bamberg, and Ratisbon, were given free reign to celebrate at the city's Holy Sepulcher. The next year, Jerusalem was taken over by bands of pastoral tribesmen, the Turcomans, who violently deposed the benign Islamic authorities, then indiscriminantly massacred 3,000 citizens—Christian and Muslim alike. Even so, these events preceded Urban's outburst by 30 years. And even though his gory depiction of events was a nothing more than a colorful fabrication, it nonetheless provided the stuff of atrocity propaganda every warmonger needs for the fulfillment of ulterior agendas.

The Pope finally came to the real point of his speech:

> *On whom, therefore, does the task lie in avenging this, of redeeming the situation, if not on you, upon whom, above all nations, God has bestowed outstanding glory in arms, magnitude of heart, litheness of body, and strength to humble anyone who resists you? Let those who, in the past, have been accustomed to spread private war so vilely among the faithful, advance against the infidels! Let those who were formerly brigands now become soldiers of Christ; those who once waged war against their brothers and blood-relatives fight lawfully against barbarians; those who until now have been mercenaries for a few coins achieve eternal rewards!*[4]

He was calling for nothing less than a military invasion of the Holy Land and the "liberation" of Jerusalem from its Islamic conquerors. Any man who participated in such an endeavor would not only be absolved of all crimes he committed, no matter how violent, but assured his place in heaven. Whatever booty in terms of treasure, slaves, or land he might find among the enemies of the Church were his for the taking. By adding that the Day of Judgment could not take place so long as Jerusalem was occupied by God's enemies, the Pope indirectly explained why the world failed to come to its long-predicted end at the turn of the millennium. His clarion call ignited popular passions far beyond all expectations. Urban II's impassioned oration instigated the largest mobilization since the days of ancient Rome, a mass phenomenon without precedent in medieval times. Within months of his Clermont appeal to arms, 100,000 men and women from all walks of life were marching toward Jerusalem. Rich and poor suddenly uprooted themselves to join Christendom's greatest undertaking: The first Crusade.

The promise of abundant rewards in this life as well as the hereafter electrified millions of Europeans. But they were also profoundly inspired by the highest

Crusaders on the march to the Holy Land.

ideal ever offered to any generation: namely, to fight for God's own city, where the Savior Himself had been crucified and was buried at the Tomb of the Holy Sepulcher. Freeing it from desecrating Muslim hands was the noblest duty ever imposed on any generation.

As in many other wars, long before and especially since, masses of gullible people have been emotionally engineered to voluntarily sacrifice themselves for hidden objectives they neither understood nor suspected. The Pope was delighted. Not only would he be rid of those destructive milites, but also the numerous heresies that sprouted over the previous 95 years would be scoured away by the wave of mass hysteria he had loosed across Europe. The papacy could stage a comeback in their absence, and go on to expand its power, which had been until then seriously threatened.

Two Impious Princes

The campaign was chiefly organized and led by five princes renowned as Europe's foremost military men: While Bohemond of Taranto, Raymond of Toulouse, and Tancred of Hauteville ideally represented their class and times, Godfroi de Bouillon was different. Both he and his younger brother, Baudoin de Boulogne, were stirred by another, personal cause that bore nothing in common with the Pope's real intentions, and separate from the religious fervor fused with unrestrained greed that stirred their fellow Crusaders. In fact, the papacy had an aversion to Godfroi, which was understandable. He had long and openly despised the Church, excoriating its endemic corruption and hypocritical immorality, even going so far as to actually lay siege to Rome itself just a few years earlier. Although Vatican authorities regarded him as an implacable enemy, an impious despoiler of their lands, they reasoned that de Bouillon was, after all, just the kind of reprobate they wanted *out* of Europe. The political vacuum left in his absence, or hopefully, death in the Near East would be naturally filled by themselves.

For his part, Godfroi saw the Crusades as a unique opportunity to fulfill an old

family dream kept alive by previous generations, including his own. Around 35 years old when Urban II made his incen-

Godfroi de Bouillon, creator of the secret society for the Ark's excavation and protection.

diary speech outside Clermont, the handsome Flemish Duke of northern France grew even more self-conscious than usual of his suspicious ancestry with the onset of Christian mobilization: While he traced his lineage to Charlemagne, it really went back much further, to the very people supplanted by the Holy Roman Emperor. These were the Merovingians, a tribal people better remembered as the Franks, who formed Europe's first dynasty after the fall of Classical civilization, in the late 5th century. Their kingdom dominated most of France and some areas of Germany, but was not the crude culture commonly associated with barbarian society, as proved by the 37 beautifully minted Merovingian gold coins found at Suffolk, in England's Sutton Hoo treasure ship.

The Merovingians' Origins

The Merovingians were literate statesmen who sought to meld their Germanic ways with Roman forms. They derived their name from Merovee, a metaphorical ancestor who personified their multiple, singularly strange origins. His story relates that before he was born, his royal mother was wading one day in the ocean, where a *bestea Neptuni Quinotaur similis* impregnated her. Translated as "Neptune's beast, similar to a five-legged bull," the name alludes to the animal's sexual arousal. When thereafter the queen gave birth to Merovee, a twin heritage flowed through his veins: part mortal, part mythic. The story seems similar to a Frankish retelling of Europa and the Bull, an ancient Greek tale that described the abduction of a Phoenician princess by the king of the Olympian gods, Zeus, in the guise of a white bull. As such, he crossed the Aegean Sea with her on his back to Greece, where he sired on her a family of half-divine kings who created civilization on the continent named after her: Europe.

Atlantean Origins

Both legends imply the prehistoric arrival of overseas' culture-bearers who intermarried with native populations to engender the first royal families. This suggestion seems especially apparent in the Merovingians' supreme reverence for Noah, the flood-survivor in *Genesis*, above all other biblical heroes. Claiming descent from a bestea Neptuni Quinotaur similis seems inexplicable for a people separated by radically disparate cultural levels, time, and geography from the Tigris and Euphrates Rivers, where the mythic figure was known 4,000 years before the Franks coalesced into a 5th century kingdom—unless they and their ancestors preserved it from an actual Mesopotamian connection. A similar image was known to the Sumerians as Ea, the Lord of the Waters, a sea-god who presented the secrets of a lost, high civilization to early inhabitants of the Near East following a great deluge. A 5,000-year-old cylinder-seal from Nappur depicts Ea bidding farewell to an Atlas-like figure supporting the sky, just prior to the Deluge.

The Merovingians crafted egg-shaped quartz balls for scrying—the Shamanic practice of meditating on clear quartz to achieve an altered state of consciousness—and valued them so highly that the objects were buried with their kings, as evidenced in the tomb of Childeric I. Special emphasis on Noah and Merovee's half-oceanic lineage combine with the manufacture of crystal balls to suggest that Merovingian roots went back to Atlantis. Such a conclusion was reinforced by other symbolic artifacts buried with Childeric I, including a mummified horse's head and the representation of a bull's head in solid gold. Plato states in his dialogues, the *Timaeus* and *Kritias*, that the city of Atlantis was created by the sea-god Poseidon (the Roman Neptune), whose personal animal was the horse. Plato also describes the Atlantean kings' most important ceremony, which demanded the sacrifice of a sacred bull, whereby they consecrated their royal lineage. Grail expert Mark A. Pinkham suspects that the Merovingian emblem, the fleur-de-lies, may have been "a version of Neptune's trident."[5] Indeed, the name "Merovee" itself means the egg (*ovee*) from the sea (*mer*), suggesting the Atlantean omphalos. Other versions of his name—Merovech, "Born of the Bull," and Merovie, "Sea or Water of Life"—likewise imply Poseidon's Atlantis.

Biblical Origins

Merovee's people boasted a multiple lineage that flowed from a no less extraordinary source: Merovingian royals believed their ancestry lay in the House of David and Jesus Christ himself. A French folktale still repeated today recounts that Jesus escaped the crucifixion, thanks to the efforts of his uncle, the wealthy merchant Joseph of Arimathea, who arranged for him to be taken to an area on the south coast of France at a place known appropriately today as Saintes-Marie-de-la-Mer. There, he lived with his wife, Mary Magdalene, and raised a family from which the Merovingians claimed direct, lineal descent. While this story has been popularized in modern times by best-sellers such as *Holy Blood, Holy Grail* and *The Da Vinci Code*, it is hardly new. King Louis XI declared more than 500 years ago that French royalty began with Mary Magdalene, and the *Koran* stated some 8 1/2 centuries before, that Jesus, although a great prophet, did not die on the cross. No less a Church authority than Epiphanius Scholasticus, compiler of the *Historiae Ecclesiasticae Tripartitae Epitome* (or *Historia Tripartita*, the Tripartite History, a standard manual of church history completed around 510) cited a gnostic gospel contemporary with the life of Christ. Entitled the *Great Questions of Mary*, it described the Tantric sexual activity that took place between Jesus and Mary. The first historical Merovingian monarchs insisted that their ancestral mother was Magdalene, the sister of Lazarus, wife of Jesus, and the progenitor of their lineage.

Even today, a procession celebrating Mary's role in French history takes place through the streets of St. Maximin each year. On parade are her imagined relics otherwise preserved at the Abbey Church of Saint Marie-Madeleine in the nearby village of Vezalay. They were supposedly discovered by a nephew of King Louis IX in 1279, after being missing for the previous 569 years, when invading Saracens forced local monks to remove her remains from the ornate white-marble coffin that had contained them since the 3rd century. The Magdalene is said to have spent the last 40 years of her life secluded in a cave high up on a cliff face in Sainte Baume, where she was renowned as a teacher and healer before her death around 75 A.D.

Mary's persistent legend in the south of France is undoubtedly a remnant of the Merovingians' lineage myth, which they lived out by never cutting their hair; a precedent established by their first historical monarch, Clodion le Chevelu, "Clodion the Long-Haired," king of the Franks from 428 to 448 A.D. After marrying one of Mary's descendants, he set a stylistic precedent for his heirs by imitating the biblical Nazorites, who went unshorn. The Nazorites believed they could know God through their own personal experience without recourse to priestly intermediaries, not unlike the gnostic Arianism adopted by the Merovingians themselves until one of their kings, Clovis I, converted to Catholicism. Underscoring their connection to this important Hebrew sect, the title, "Jesus of Nazareth," was an obvious corruption of the original "Jesus the Nazorite," because the town of Nazareth did not exist in his time.[6] His brother, Saint James, was in fact a Nazorite. Appropriately, the Nazorites were themselves forerunners of Arianism, as revealed in their

Kerygmata Petrou, a doctrinal text that characterized Paul of Tarsus, the founder of the Roman Church, as "the hostile man who falsified the true ideas of Jesus."[7] It would appear that the Frankish Merovingians and Jewish Nazorites had more in common than untrimmed tresses, even though both believed their hair possessed spiritual power. Moreover, Old Testament names, such as Bera and Solomon, were used by the Merovingians: Miron le Levite was the Merovingian count of Besalou.

But the Merovingians' pedigree, imagined or otherwise, could not save them from the strife of their times. Distracted by decades of incessant warfare with feuding neighbors, they steadily relinquished political power to "mayors of the palace," high civil officials, until one of them, Pepin the Short, overthrew their house. In 754, he replaced it with the Carolingian Dynasty, named after Charles Martel, the renowned "Hammer," who saved Europe from the Muslims by defeating them at Tours 22 years before. His grandson, another Charles, became Charlemagne, to head The Holy Roman Empire in 800 A.D. That it was not holy, Roman, nor an empire meant nothing to its early rulers who, in an obvious attempt at legitimacy via continuity, took Merovingian women as brides. Thus, the Carolingian bloodline intertwined with the superceded Merovingian stem, from which Godfroi de Bouillon traced his lineage through a 10th century great-grandfather, Hughes de Plantard, himself directly descended from the Merovingians' most prominent king.

The last Merovingian King, Dagobert II died under mysterious circumstances in which Roman authorities, who hated him for his alliance through marriage with the Vatican-hating Visigoths, were suspected. But regional reverence for the murdered monarch was so enduring, a church was built for his locally canonized remains. Michael Baigent, Richard Leigh, and Henry Lincoln, authors of *Holy Blood, Holy Grail*, point out, "Godfroi was of Merovingian blood, directly descended from Dagobert II."[8] That he was conscious of this descent was made abundantly clear in his military expedition for the protection of his ancestor's memorial at Stenay, more than 400 years after the assassination. By then, a secretive cult had grown up around the memory of the sainted Dagobert, in which were preserved the gnostic ideals of his subverted dynasty. Godfroi therefore regarded the Crusades as a means to achieve a long-dreamt-of end. As a royal descendant of the House of David, he might claim the Holy Land as his inheritance for the restoration of the Merovingian state—not in France, but Jerusalem.

Godfroi's Crusade

More certainly, Godfroi had difficulty raising financial support, from whatever sources, for the costly expedition. He deeded his estates to the Church until his return, pawned virtually everything he owned—save his unassailable Castle Bouillon in the Ardennes—to the Bishops of Liege and Verdun, thereby underwriting his participation in the first Crusade, which set out with him in the lead during August of 1096. He was preceded by a kind of proto-expedition, the so-called People's Crusade, an immense, unruly mob of idealists and thieves, sincere penitents and common criminals, saints and sinners, driven by a poisonous mix of religious fervor and insatiable greed. Having pillaged, murdered, and raped their way across half of Europe to the Bosphorus, heedless of their victims' spiritual beliefs, the participants of this ungovernable rabble descended en masse on the heathen enemy at a place called Civetos. There, they were ruthlessly slaughtered by outnumbered but professionally led and superbly equipped Muslim warriors. Before the sun went down on October 21, the People's Crusade was annihilated, its pitiful survivors—mostly women and children—made slaves by the Fatimid Dynasts then ruling much of the Near East.

The People's Crusade's failure had not been in vain, however. The ease with which the Muslims defeated this first invasion attempt made them overconfident. Sure that his forces were no less inept than those so handily rounded up at Civetos, a Seljuq Turkish sultan in command of the area, Kilij Arslan, dismissed the arrival of Godfroi's army as insignificant. (At that time, in February of 1097, his army was straggling across the Bosphoros Strait to the northern shores of the Gulf of Nicomedia.) Instead, Arslan rode off to deal with a relatively trivial territorial dispute far away to the east. Had he chosen to mount a vigorous attack at this vulnerable moment, Arslan could have knocked the Crusaders off balance, very likely aborting their intentions. Instead, more than 40,000 knights and infantry under the golden Banner of Christ were able to deploy unopposed and in good order.

Consequences were soon in coming. By May, Nicaea, which had helped spark the Crusades when Seljuq Turks took it 20 years earlier, was besieged, falling to the Crusaders after less than two months. While full-scale engagements raged across the region, Genoese ships arrived at St. Simeon with abundant supplies for the Christians. More men and material were off-loaded at the same, vital port-city by an English fleet the next year, in early March. With these reinforcements in men, equipment, and food, the Crusade rolled victoriously across the Holy Land, while its Muslim defenders fought with great skill, tenacity, courage, and intelligence, often inflicting terrible losses on their enemy. But by May, the tide turned against them with the fall of Arqa, an ancient city just 13 miles northeast of Tripoli, where the Crusaders could now control the entire northern coast of Lebanon with its vital supply harbors, and from which the march to Jerusalem could begin.

On June 7, Godfroi, at the head of an advance army numbering some 1,300 knights and 12,000 foot-soldiers, stood awestruck before its gargantuan defenses. The invaders seemed to dwindle beside an urban area of more than 200 acres surrounded by 9-foot-thick walls 2.5 miles long and 45 feet high. Along these towering ramparts were ranked tens of thousands of Muslim troops armed with an abundance of superior weapons and sworn to defend their Holy City to the death. Clearly, brute strength alone could never hope to breach such prodigious fortifications, as proved less than a week later, when the Crusaders were beaten back with heavy losses. It seemed that they had traveled 1,800 miles, most of them on foot, fighting a desperate struggle across the Near East for nearly three years, only to be deprived of victory in the last battle by an impregnable fortress.

For nearly a month after their failed assault, Godfroi and his engineers had been conspicuously busy building an immense siege-tower before the enemy's quadrangular gate, their apparent target. The Muslims consequently went to great lengths refortifying their defenses here, devoting most of their preparations and attention to opposing the monstrous weapon of war growing taller and more terrifying each day. On the night before the battle, however, Godfroi's men quickly dismantled the siege-tower, then transferred its working parts without a word exchanged between them, under the cover of darkness, about half a mile to within striking distance of the under-defended St. Stephen's Gate. In the morning, the city's defenders were appalled to see the fully reconstructed behemoth standing ready to move against their weakest position. The ruse was a total success, and helped bring about the fall of Jerusalem on July 15, 1099.

A week later, because of his instrumental role in the victory, and his obvious leadership qualities, Godfroi de Bouillon was elected King of the Holy City by his fellow Crusaders. Finally, a royal scion from the

The Crusaders conquer Jerusalem.

House of David had returned to rule the biblical Navel of the World after an absence of more than 1,000 years. Reaction from the papacy was predictably contrary: Under no circumstances would this "despoiler of church lands" be allowed to set up his throne over the place where Jesus Christ had been crucified. To avoid the inevitable strife that would undermine their sacrifices, triumph, and hopes, Godfroi declined the crown offered by his comrades-in-arms. The wily Flemish Duke was at least as skilled in diplomacy as he had been in war, and used his popularity among his fellow nobles and position as the most influential man in the Near East

to incrementally build a power base, just as he built the mobile siege-tower.

Godfroi's Holy Order

The fires of conquered Jerusalem were still smoldering when he established the Order of the Holy Sepulcher. Ostensibly, its purpose was to protect pilgrim routes to the Holy Land and stand guard at the Basilica of the Resurrection, which housed the tomb where Jesus was said to have been buried. Godfroi found the sacred site in a deplorable condition. Byzantine Emperor Constantine Monomaces' half-hearted efforts undertaken more than half a century before failed to repair damage caused by the Fatimid Caliph al-Hakim in 1009 and nearly four centuries earlier by invading Persians. The original sepulcher dated back to Roman Emperor Constantine the Great, who ordered its construction some 300 years after Christ's miraculous ascent.

The Order of the Holy Sepulcher's vigorous restoration of the tomb provided public cover for Godfroi's ulterior intentions. Denied the crown of Jerusalem, he gave out that it was too great an honor for him to accept, and assumed the less offensive title of Advocatus Sancti Sepulchri, the Advocate or Defender of the Holy Sepulcher, thereby asserting his new role as Jerusalem's protector, though officially subservient to the pope. Meanwhile, membership in the order was restricted to a handful of his own family members, none of whom protected pilgrim routes or personally stood watch at the tomb of Jesus, assigning these menial duties instead to Crusader underlings. Theirs was precisely the same smokescreen used by their organizational descendants, the Knights Templar, less than 20 years later: Covertly, the crafty Advocate, in the company of his brothers and cousins, pursued a separate agenda to someday reclaim their lost heritage by creating a powerful, neo-Merovingian state in the Holy Land as a spiritual-political alterntative to Catholic Rome.

In doing so, the Order became an undercurrent of influence that survived far into the future. It not only appointed Jerusalem's kings for generations to come and set the tone for the city's almost gnostic resonance, but also created the Crusades' first religious military that would eventually combine both a public and covert power-phenomenon without precedent. Visual affirmation of the forces at work here occurred in the Order of the Holy Sepulcher's emblem, one Templar cross in each of the four quadrants formed by a larger *croix pattée*, precisely the same symbol for the Latin Kingdom of Jerusalem. As Bernier concludes, "In other words, the Templar cross is truly and originally the cross of the Order of the Holy Sepulcher."[9]

Such a long-lived, secret society has been erroneously described as the Priory of Sion in numerous books spawned since Michael Baigent, Richard Leigh, and Henry Lincoln authored *Holy Blood, Holy Grail*, in 1982. The authors were deceived by a convicted criminal and his confederates, who forged *Dossiers Secrets d'Henri Lobineau*, or "Secret Dossiers of Henri Lobineau." They tell that Godfroi de Bouillon established the conspiratorial Priory of Sion to overturn institutionalized Christianity with subversive documents proving that Jesus sired a bloodline whose descendants are the rightful heirs to the French throne. The Priory was supposed to have exerted its behind-the-scenes power for the last 1,000 years, and is today poised to set up a Holy European Empire that will create international peace and prosperity. A messianic mystery cult will replace all other forms of religion superceded by a Rex Deus, a linear descendant of Jesus Christ, enthroned over the world, known forever after as Greater Israel.

Despite a lethal wound dealt to *Holy Blood, Holy Grail*'s main argument by the exposure of faked documents, the book continues to serve as an invaluable source of otherwise legitimate information and credible interpretation concerning the often enigmatic events permeating the Middle Ages. Perhaps no other popular title of its kind has so much to offer about the sorely neglected Merovingians, for example. But following the long, twisted tale of how the *Dossiers Secrets* came to be debunked would lose the story of the Ark in an unnecessary diversion. And while the Priory of Sion never existed, save in the criminal consciousness of a few, late 20th century conmen, a genuine, covert organization founded by Godfroi de Bouillon to promote his secret agenda did operate behind the scenes to shape the destiny of Europe for centuries to come. Unlike the Priory, however, existence of the Order of the Holy Sepulcher was firmly recorded in authentic documentation.

The Holy Sepulcher

In consideration of what was to come, Godfroi's choice for his own sacred site was amazingly prescient. Local belief identified the Holy Sepulcher as the Earth's center point. From it, the resurrected Jesus descended into Hell, where he rescued the righteous souls of Adam, Abraham, Noah, and Moses, before ascending with them into Heaven, according to the apocryphal *Gospel of Nicodemus*. As such, the Holy Sepulcher was regarded as the New Testament Navel of the World, where a divine spirit was able to transcend the depths of perdition into the heights of redemption. All this seems like a Christian gloss on the long-vanished Fire Stone in its numerous cultural inflections as the Ark of the Covenant, the Ben-Ben stone, Fyra,

Tuaoi, and so on, and the various Navels of the World established wherever it was enshrined.

The singular propriety of Godfroi's choice in claiming the Holy Sepulcher for himself perhaps indicates that he was already aware of the close, albeit undiscovered proximity of the sacred object, and anticipated its recovery by making himself the Advocatus Sancti Sepulchri. Indeed, more than one researcher into these matters concludes that freeing the Holy Land was only propaganda to mask the real motive behind the First Crusade: namely, seizing Jerusalem to discover and retrieve the greatest spiritual object ever known to man—the lost Ark of the Covenant. In any case, the 11th century would not witness the last time in history that armed agression "liberated" a foreign people to ignorantly fulfill the hidden agenda of a remote power-elite.

Godfroi outfitted his elite corps of blood-related guardians with long white robes and distinctive insignia. The former were deliberately adopted after Constantine, the Sepulcher's imperial builder, who, in his last illness, was reputed to have put off his royal purple toga for a white gown of spiritual purity. His motto, *In hoc signo vinces*, "In this sign, conquer," was likewise borrowed by the new Order. Both the words and a cross were said to have appeared in the morning sky just before the emperor was about to confront the superior forces of his enemy; inspired by the celestial apparition, Godfroi won the battle of Saxa Rubra. This story, as with everything about the Order, was double-sided: On the surface, it celebrated the triumph of Christianity, but to Godfroi and his extended family it was a battle-cry for reviving his ancestors' true claim to the throne of the Holy Land.

An inherited blemish appearing on the chest in the shape of a red cross typified generations of Merovingian royalty, and it was this singular birthmark that Godfroi chose for the new uniform. It became famous when it was worn 30 years later by the Templars, whose roots grew from the Order of the Holy Sepulcher. Members of both wore the red cross "on their habits and mantels on the left side of the breast over the heart, whence they came afterwards to be known by the name of the Red Friars and the Red Cross Knights."[10] By deliberately choosing this design, the initiates of either group consciously celebrated— at least among themselves—their Merovingian roots.

The creation of a neo-Merovingian state in the Holy Land was plagued from the outset, however, with constant upheavals at home and abroad. Just a month after the fall of Jerusalem, Godfroi was fighting Egyptian Fatimids at Ascalon, where Islamic forces again went down in defeat, while a papal agent in the Holy City, Dagobert of Pisa, strove to turn it into the pope's own fiefdom. Exhausted by relentless Vatican intrigues and too many local battles, Godfroi contracted an illness while campaigning in Caesarea during June of 1100, and died on July 18. The Order of the Holy Sepulcher convened to appoint his younger brother, Baudoin de Boulogne, again over the strenuous objections of Rome.

Unlike Godfroi, however, Baudoin brushed aside Church sensitives, and exerted his considerable influence, backed up by the Crusader armies under his command. As a visible affirmation of his (and the Order's) authority, the trouble-making Dagobert was forced to crown Baudoin king on December 25, 1100. As a concession to somewhat mollify the Patriarch's revulsion at fulfilling the ceremony at Jerusalem, the coronation was allowed to take place in the village where Jesus was born, Bethlehem. But Dagobert continued to scheme behind the scenes until the king finally succeeded in deposing him two years later.

Rumors of the Ark

Baudoin I was always on the lookout for authentic religious relics. This was, after all, the Holy Land, so who knows what its sands might conceal? During the Crusade itself, the original lance that allegedly pierced the side of Jesus during his crucifixion came to light on June 14, 1098. An entire cult grew up around the True Cross allegedly found about the same time by Crusader Arnulf de Choques, before it passed on to Baudoin, who used it as a dramatic propaganda tool in his ascent to the throne. While both of these supposedly sacred objects, and thousands similar to them, turned out to be transparent fakes cashing in on the religious hysteria of the times, their "discovery" or manufacture continued to enjoy brisk business, if only because they were often the sole items Crusaders returning to Europe had to show for their service overseas, having impoverished themselves in the cause of liberating Palestine.

If Godfroi had been distracted by his duties as Advocatus, Baudoin I at least enjoyed occasional respite from the demands of his new kingdom by following up on leads to lost relics. A few questionable artifacts had surfaced, but virtually all of them were obvious frauds. Sometime within the first three years of his reign, however, a credible, though unverified report reached him regarding the general location of a very particular object that certainly merited special consideration. While too good to be true, the merest possibility of its existence could nevertheless have explosive political and religious ramifications for not only Jerusalem, but the worlds of Christianity and Islam as well.

Jerusalem was honeycombed with spies, not all of them from the Vatican, so the King was unable to take action on his own without being observed by his enemies, both foreign and domestic. As such, he confided the critical information to a high-ranking noble, swore the man to secrecy, and then dispatched him to northern France. Arriving at Troyes in 1104, he sought out Hughes de Champagne. Among the wealthiest lords in all of Europe, the 38-year-old count welcomed Baudoin's noble to a covert conclave of fellow aristocrats, all from some of the country's most prestigious families. They undoubtedly discussed Baudoin's message, but its contents and how they reacted to it can only be surmised.

Almost immediately after the meeting at Troyes, Hughes rode off to Palestine, where he resided at the King's palace for the next four years, although his purpose there was never disclosed. Returning to France, the count was full of enthusiastic, if unspecified preparations for a second trip to the Holy Land, whence he returned in 1114. Before the count departed, less than a year later, he almost certainly joined his royal friend on an expedition into the Oultrejourdain, French for "Beyond the Jordan," an extensive, ill-defined, inhospitable region east of the Jordan River extending southward through the Negev Desert to the Gulf of Aqaba, and north of the Dead Sea. It was in this remote, desolate area that Baudoin I ordered the construction of a small but strongly fortified castle, ostensibly to control the nearby Muslim caravan routes, which provided revenues for his kingdom.

His well-prepared construction engineers got to work at once, raising the stronghold in record time. It was never used, however, and stood vacant for the next three years; a curious fate for the castle, especially in view of the name he chose for it: Montreal, the "Royal Mountain." At about 40 feet high, the structure was hardly mountainous, nor was it situated atop a mountain. Yet its name was one that had been reserved in the past for only the most sacred places, most commonly associated in Christian thought with Golgotha, the high hill where Jesus was crucified. As such, Montreal was an especially odd choice for an obscure, rather insignificant, ultimately uninhabited fortification.

With the completion of its unused battlements, Hughes returned to France, and began at once to underwrite a group of monks known as the Cistercians for no apparent reason. Since its founding 16 years before, this Catholic order of monks had not amounted to much, but it did have an earned reputation for the fanatic loyalty of its adherents to Bernard de Fontaine—famous in life as Bernard de Clairvaux, canonized after his death as Saint Bernard—the most dynamic spiritual organizer in an era of potent churchmen. Thanks to the count's inexplicable generosity and the inspired leadership of Bernard, the Cistercians were pulled back from the abyss of dissolution to find themselves in the possession of their own lands and a new abbey.

The Knights Templar

Three years later, in 1118, Baudoin, the Crusader King of Jerusalem, died at the small Egyptian village of Al-Arish on April 2 following a bad meal of undercooked fish. His cousin succeeded him to become Baudoin II, and was soon after visited by nine anonymous Frenchmen. They asked his permission to protect pilgrim routes in and out of the Holy Land, wanting nothing for themselves but a place to stay. Impressed by the strangers' piety, he gave them free run of his own palace precinct atop Mount Moriah, site of the first Israelite temple, headquartering

in what they believed were the remains of Solomon's stables, "where they at once became the object of singular benevolence on the part of the King."[11]

That, at any rate, was the official explanation of how the Templars came to be. But it was, in truth, more fable than fact. Baudoin II would hardly have turned over the most sensitive residence in Jerusalem to a few unknown, impoverished volunteers, much less allowed them to camp indefinitely among the city's sacred ruins. Templar expert Karen Ralls asks, "why would the first nine knights have been given a wing of the King's palace, of all places, as their home base? We know the Templars kept their horses in the spacious stables under Solomon's Temple—which had room for thousands—so some speculate that this provided an ideal 'cover' for other activities, such as digging in the tunnels."[12]

Moreover, the beggars would more likely have been dismissed as either impudent or ignorant, because a large, fully developed law enforcement organization had already been in charge of protecting pilgrim routes for the previous five years. Nine unknown petitioners would have, in any case, never been allowed a personal audience with the king, and hardly on such a trivial matter. Their request for the creation of a new order would have been disregarded as redundant, and they themselves directed to enlist in the guardsmen looking for volunteers such as themselves. "Logic, as well as sound organization," Charpentier points out, "would have required that these nine knights, who wished to defend the pilgrims, should have addressed themselves to the Order of Hospitallers. They did nothing of the kind."[13]

The Templars' true origins began earlier, shortly after Baudoin I became the Holy Land's first Latin monarch. Sometime within the first three years of his reign, a trustworthy, forever confidential source whose identity is lost to history, told him he was quite literally sitting on the greatest treasure known to man. But the potential for danger was so enormous that even rumor of its possible whereabouts could destroy the world as he and his contemporaries knew it. Despite the high risks involved in the object's retrieval, falling into the wrong hands—Muslim or Christian—would be an unparalled calamity worth every effort to prevent. The information, though credible, was unverified, and before Baudoin I or anyone else could proceed further, its authenticity needed to be confirmed or debunked. At a moment like this, only members of his own family in the Order of the Holy Sepulcher were to be trusted, and one man among them, his cousin Hughes de Champagne, was alone capable, through his cultural connections in Troyes, of determining the fantastic claim's validity or lack thereof.

The King therefore summoned a high-ranking nobleman in the Order (unfortunately his identity is unknown), and entrusted him with a letter to Hughes explaining the allegation of "treasure" at the Temple Mount. Whether or not the messenger was aware of the information carried among his dispatches, he arrived with it at Troyes in early 1104, when the secret was revealed to the Count de Champagne and his closed circle of blood-related aristocrats. They at once sought out the world's foremost authority in matters of this kind, Solomon ben Isaac. Known throughout France's intellectual community as Rabbi Rashi, he was among the most brilliant Jewish scholars in European history, the doyen of Hebrew studies, and founder, in 1070, of a cabalistic school. There, the hidden legacy of ancient Israel, as preserved in secret commentaries on the Torah, was studied and debated. More importantly,

this arcane body of hidden tradition amended the Old Testament version of events surrounding the last days of Solomon's temple, as told in *Maccabees*.[14]

Before the Tabernacle's destruction by the Babylonians, the prophet Jeremiah was supposed to have saved the Ark of the Covenant by concealing it in a cave at Mount Nebo, insisting thereafter that its whereabouts must remain secret "until the time that God should gather his people again together, and receive them unto his mercy."[15] According to the cabala, however, Mount Nebo was not a different mountain altogether, but another name for Mount Moriah itself. Consequently, *Maccabees* states, in effect, that the Ark was hidden in the Temple Mount, which was and is honeycombed with hundreds of caves.[16] From the moment of its conception, Rabbi Rashi added, the Temple incorporated a design feature to conceal its sacred object from harm as an effective contingency against possible occupation by enemy forces—a trapdoor.

A secret trapdoor in the Holy-of-Holies itself, toward the southeast corner of the building, would allow the Levite high-priest to lower the Aron ha-Berit down a deep, man-made shaft connecting to a large, natural cave far beneath the Temple. Prior to its fall in 587 B.C., the Ark was stored in this prearranged hiding place, thereby escaping confiscation. Its subterranean concealment was not an exceptional piece of engineering, but entirely in keeping with excavations that had already been going on far beneath the Temple for centuries. Nearly 130 years before Nebuchadnezzar's invasion, King Hezeliah had expanded a previously excavated complex tunnel network. Earlier still, "underground hydraulic works were employed," according to Steven Sora, "because David's conquest of the city taught him just what a high price could be paid for making well water accessible."[17]

When the Israelites returned to Mount Moriah from the Babylonian Captivity 150 years later, however, they were distressed to observe that virtually all traces of the Temple had been obliterated, masking the precise position of the trapdoor through which the sacred object had vanished underground. Prone as Mount Moriah was, and still is, to outbursts of seismic violence, the secret shaft may have been further compromised or even effaced by one or more earthquake tremblers.

While the Ark could not be retrieved, at least its general location was known. Entombed forever, it defined Jerusalem as the Holy City. In the more than 15 centuries since then, pious Jews customarily bowed toward the southeast when entering their synagogues, thereby preserving the living, communal memory of the Ark's location for the time when they or their descendants would return to Zion. As that day appeared to be dawning with the coronation of a Merovingian monarch whose palace was already installed on the very grounds of the Temple itself, the moment had arrived to share this cabalistic tradition with those who could use it to their best advantage.

Almost immediately after the meeting at Troyes, Hughes de Champagne rode off to the Holy Land, where he imparted Rabbi Rashi's exciting disclosure to Baudoin I. Together, over the next four years, they carefully crafted a comprehensive strategy for excavating and then protecting the Ark of the Covenant. Planning its retrieval was on par with today's most top-secret military operations, and therefore required meticulous, long-term preparations. They began when the count returned to France in 1108 to line up a support apparatus necessary for not only unearthing the world's most sacred object,

but also to keep it forever beyond the papacy's long reach.

With Hughes' second trip to Jerusalem six years later, the scheme's preliminary phase came to an end. Hughes told Baudoin he would soon be sending a hand-picked team of investigators who needed to be fed and housed at the Temple mount, where their work must be allowed to proceed indefinitely, screened from the scrutiny of all outsiders by an impenetrable royal cover. Once found, the Ark needed to be immediately evacuated from spy-ridden Jerusalem to a secure holding place. To this end, they envisioned a purpose-built fortress constructed in a remote, mostly inaccessible, unsuspected location, far from the Holy City in the Negev Desert, manned by an elite corps of guards answerable only to the king. In 1115, he completed his Oultrejourdain castle, which waited in vain for the arrival of the singular treasure it had been designed to protect. Baudoin's only hint that the structure was something more than it seemed lay in the name he gave it: Montreal, the Royal Mount.

Meanwhile, Hughes de Champagne was back in France, underwriting the Cistercians as the elite corps he needed to make his operation possible. From its ranks, their charismatic leader, Bernard, selected nine of his brightest, most deeply pious, militarily skilled, and fanatically loyal monks. He suspended all their vows, and told them of the high mission for which they had been chosen. Henceforward, they were answerable only to himself, and their lives belonged exclusively to the performance of new duties in the Holy Land. They were given white robes to wear, as part now of Godfroi de Bouillon's Order of the Holy Sepulcher, whose members still sought the restoration of Merovingian greatness, which would be well-served by discovery of the world's most renowned religious relic. After three years of specialized training, indoctrination, and physical conditioning, during which the nine men were secluded from the outside world—even from their fellow monks—they set out for Palestine as the Milice du Christ, the Order of the Poor Knights of Christ, on account of their monastic vows to embrace poverty, chastity, and obedience. In their lead was one Hughes de Payns, said to have been of humble origins.

Virtually nothing is known about de Payns, save that he would eventually become the first Grand Master of the Templars, in contrast to the other eight warrior-monks, all of them well-connected and affluent. But his identity and mere existence have been seriously called into question by the disturbing fact that the area of Payns from which he hailed did not exist at the time he took charge of his fellow ex-Cistercians. His homeland was then, as it had been for the previous 23 years, part of Lorraine, and would remain so for the next seven years. In other words, there was no Payns when Hughes was on his way to Palestine. Who was he, then? Scholars have tried to connect him with Hugh de Pagens, Hughes de Puiset, Hugh Peccator, Hugh the Sinner, and any number of aristocratic nonentities, all without success. In any case, Bernard would never have jeopardized the whole enterprise by placing an impoverished nobody with a nonexistent background in command of elite, pedigreed knights on a delicate expedition into foreign lands. Regarding the very necessary secrecy that surrounded the Templars from their inception, a solution to the mystery seems obvious: Hughes de Payns was really Hughes de Champagne—even the names hardly differed from each other. The mission entrusted to the Poor Knights of Christ was far too sensitive for anyone less in authority than the count himself, who could ensure stable relations with the authorities at Jerusalem. Unlike his comrades, who had never before ventured outside France, he had visited the Holy Land twice and traveled it extensively in the company of its first king, whose cooperation was crucial to the success of their efforts.

Given Hughes de Champagne's deep, obsessive involvement in the undertaking over the previous 14 years, it seems unlikely that he could have restrained himself from personally participating in the fulfillment of his all-consuming quest. He had been, after all, its chief financier, researcher, and organizer, but his appearance at the head of eight aristocratic knights in the Holy Land would have focused attention on their covert task, making it impossible to undertake, and ruining all chances for any future attempt. Hence, he would travel under the alias of "Hughes de Payns," disguised as just one of the Poor Knights of Christ, come to make safe the pilgrim's way to the Holy Land. A few years later, the Count openly declared his membership in the Templars, and the façade of their official mission became transparent. As Louis Charpentier exclaimed, "A sovereign ruler of France come to police roads and communications!"[18] Moreover, as one of the eight subordinate Templars, the count would have been obliged to take orders from their leader, who was his own vassal—hardly likely for a medieval nobleman, especially one of Hughes de Champagne's prestige.

As for the other knights, most of them were Flemish, largely from the same Lower Lorraine homeland of Godfroi de Bouillon and the Baudoin kings, to whom they were at least distantly related. When they arrived in Palestine, Hughes was shocked to learn that his friend and coconspirator was dead. The king's elder brother, Eustace III, had been selected to rule by the majority of Crusader nobles, but the Order of the

Holy Sepulcher overrode their choice in favor of Baudoin de Bourcq, who became Baudoin II on April 14, Easter Sunday, 1118. As one of several possible heirs to the throne, the Order had earlier alerted him to his predecessor's secret scheme for exploring the Temple Mount, and he therefore expected the nine guests for several months before they arrived in midsummer. Indeed, he already knew Hughes de Champagne from previous visits, and understood at once the count's need for deception.

During all their years of residency, the warrior-monks never guarded a single road, nor attempted to recruit any new members outside their original, closed circle of nine men. Yet, the King of Jerusalem granted them, in the words of author Karen Ralls, "exclusive accommodation in his palace on the south side of the 'Lord's Temple,'"[19] and allowed them to camp without charge at the al Aqsa mosque, directly above the suspected location of Solomon's Temple. Henceforward, they called themselves la milice du Christ, the Pauperes Commilitones Christi Templique Salomonici, "the Knighthood of Christ, Christ's poor Fellow Soldiers of Solomon's Temple," or simply, Templars. In actuality, their numerically insignificant organization had already been operating for at least four years. Baigent, Leigh, and Lincoln quote a letter written by the bishop of Chartres, who learned that Hughes de Champagne had taken a vow to join la milice du Christ in 1114.[20] Earlier still, during the previous year, Saint Bernard founded a monastery in the obscure northern Italian principality of Seborga in anticipation of providing a secure hiding place for "a great secret" brought back from the Holy Land. Four years later, Bernard arrived at the Seborga monastery to personally release two Cistercian monks, Gondemar and Rosal, from their vows for the purpose of accompanying the other seven future Templars on their way to Jerusalem.

As knights, they were a strange lot, uninterested in recruitment and refraining from public duties of any kind. They wore no uniforms, but dressed in modest, civilian clothes. Their famous white robes and red crosses, inherited from Godfroi de Bouillon's Order of the Holy Sepulcher, would come years later, after they left the Near East. As such, they maintained a very low profile, largely unknown and unsuspected by the outside world. Baudoin II's court historian, Fulk de Chartres, was instructed to omit all mention of the Templars, even to the king's founding of their organization, from the royal record.

The Templars Dig for the Ark

Thus under cover of planned anonymity and sovereign protection, they began excavating a vertical shaft at what they assumed was the southeast corner of the first Temple, just as Rabbi Rashi had specified back at Troyes. As with most treasure-hunters, the Templars began with high expectations that gradually declined into disappointment, as months of digging yielded no trace of the priceless object. The Count de Champagne needed all his diplomatic skills and persuasive authority to prevent the low morale of his fellow Templars from aborting the great work at hand. Limited to just nine men, the work was painstaking and slow, because "only members of the Order or those closely affiliated lived or were allowed to live in these quarters."[21] According to a contemporary historian of the Crusades, Guillaume de Tyr, "throughout nine years, they refused all company, all recruitment."[22] As time passed, they carved out a deep network of corridors beneath the surface of Mount Moriah, but found very little encouragement for all their onerous labors.

In 1867, after the Temple Mount was scientifically surveyed for the first time, Captain Charles Wilson of the British Royal Engineers and his chief excavator, Colonel Charles Warren, discovered the Templars' subterranean complex. Any doubts concerning the identity of its 12th century excavators were laid to rest with discovery of a sword, spur, lance fragment, and metal cross, all obviously Templar artifacts. In 1912, the items were conveyed to the grandfather of Robert Brydon, Anthony Mayhew Brydon, an expert on the history of the Templars in Scotland. While these were the only finds of their kind made for some time, many more Templar tunnels were found the year before by Montague Parker, son of the Earl of Morley, and in 1968 by Israeli archaeologist Meir Ben-Dov, leading his team of university-trained investigators. As some indication of the magnitude of the digging performed by Hughes de Champagne's medieval engineers, Ben-Dov discovered a vertical shaft they sank 150 feet into solid rock.

More recently, a small Templar medallion came to light when Gabriel Barkai, another Israeli scientist and a specialist in biblical archaeology, together with his assistant Tzachi Zweig, was working one of the very few unrestricted zones at the Temple Mount. In January of 2006, Barkai stated that "the pendent is evidence of either Templar or later Free Masonic activity in the area. A square centimeter in size, the artifact was once gold-plated on one side bearing the symbols of a hammer, pincers, and nail. On the flip-side is what looks like a sun, as well as an altar and the Grail on a crown of thorns."[23] The widespread dispersal of these finds demonstrate the profuse excavations undertaken by the Templars during their stay at the al Aqsa mosque, and testifies to the promise of some incomparably rich treasure that alone could have sustained such a labor-intensive project.

After six years of relentless toil, the Templars still had nothing to show for the tons of dirt and rock removed from the Temple Mount. Trusting in their unbroken determination, Hughes de Champagne, still as Hughes de Payns, returned alone to France to settle affairs with his family and report to Bernard de Clairvaux. The finding of the Ark would necessitate a different strategy, which the two brains behind the quest had to devise. Palestine, they knew now, was no longer a politically stable region pacified by the first Crusaders. Relations with the former enemy had grown so cordial that just three years after the Christian capture of Jerusalem, the Grand Master of the Muslim Assassins sent his personal ambassador to Baudoin I.

The times had changed. No sooner had the crown been placed on Baudoin II's head than his realm was simultaneously invaded by Syrian Seljuks and Egyptian Fatimids. While trying to save the principality of Antioch from invasion, his army was annihilated in a battle the Crusaders came to call Ager Sanguinis, the Field of Blood. While the Templars were busily engaged digging up the Temple Mount, the king himself was taken captive by the enemy while patrolling Edessa's borderlands, where he was then held for ransom. Clearly, the Holy Land was no longer a proper refuge for the discovery Bernard and the Count hoped to make. Immediately after its excavation, the sacred object, if found, was to have been sent under cover to the new castle Baudoin I built for just such a purpose in the Oultrejourdain. But even near the close of his reign, he realized his hold on the area was becoming increasingly untenable, and sold Montreal, unused, before he died in 1118. Indeed, the mounting military challenges facing his successor rendered the entire Near East too hazardous for a resuscitated Ark of the Covenant.

A New Hiding Place

Risky as the attempt would be, covert arrangements were made for the Ark's removal from Jerusalem to Europe, where a suitable hiding place or places needed to be secured in advance of its arrival. St. Bernard's secret refuge at the Seborga monastery, in northern Italy, had already been chosen years before in anticipation of just such a contingency. But smuggling the Ark out of Palestine without arousing suspicion and under the noses of Muslim spies represented only the beginning of the operation, which included a perilous sea voyage, possible attacks by bandits, and skirting ecclesiastical authorities. If the Templars could successfully negotiate these formidable obstacles with their charge, their final duty would be delivering the Ark to a prearranged safe haven outside the pope's scrutiny and protected as much by its obscurity as its stone walls.

Less than a year after his departure, Hughes de Champagne returned, as himself this time, to his comrades still laboring at Mount Moriah. His appearance was not a gross lapse of security, but calculated to hide their mission in plain sight. King Baudoin II had just been liberated from the Ortoqid Turks by Armenian commandos, and the ecstatic, popular acclaim showered on his reentrance to Jerusalem put all excavations around the al Aqsa mosque in the shade. During the mid-summer of 1127, the persevering Templars broke into a small cave, one among hundreds they found beneath the king's palace since he welcomed them nine years before. Their latest find was different from the others, however. In its ceiling was the mouth of a very old vertical shaft mostly filled in with debris that prevented it from opening to the surface. Torches illuminating the natural chamber revealed it was bare, save for a single, large item standing in the middle of the floor. Hughes was summoned, and he arrived at once with the remaining knights.

Discovery of the Ark

They held back at the rough-hewn entrance, as Hughes stepped in alone like the Levite high-priest of old, and withdrew a moldering cloth, ragged and torn with the passage of many centuries, draped over the object. The cover disintegrated into a momentarily obscuring cloud of dust, from the center of which emerged the perfectly preserved Ark of the Covenant. The emotionally overcome discoverers fell to their knees before the golden vessel, heartily thanking God for having blessed their years of hard labor. Secretly notified, the king rushed to the excavations, where he was lowered into one of the Templars' deep work tunnels. At its bottom, they escorted him a few paces into the small cave sheltering their precious find.

As were Akhenaton and Moses before him, Baudoin II appears to have been profoundly affected by close proximity to the sacred object. Although a beloved and successful monarch, he voluntarily abdicated, despite the absence of a male heir. He resigned from one of the most powerful kingdoms on Earth: Jerusalem, the Navel of the World, vacating the throne to his daughter, Melisende, on the condition that she wed Fulk V of Anjou, in France.

Baudoin II, once again Baudoin de Bourcq, divested himself of his kingly wealth and all but the humblest personal possessions to live monastically for the rest of his life, in prayer and meditation, secluded among a few monks at the Tomb of the Holy Sepulcher. His transformation was not unlike, fundamentally at least, Amenhotep IV's metamorphosis to Akhenaton when he came into contact with the Ben-Ben stone, or Moses' transformation upon his descent from Mount Sinai with Yahweh's "tablets." Never particularly given to piety before, Baudoin appears to have been similarly affected by exposure to the Ark of the Covenant's profuse radiance of negative ions. They engendered in him a catharsis or altered state of consciousness equivalent to a Kundalini experience, the opening of his crown chakra to a previously unrecognized spiritual dimension.

The sacred object of the Templars' long search was discovered under strict secrecy.

As soon as the Templars made their discovery, time began working against them. Any outside inkling of what they had really been up to since 1118 could spark a cultural conflagration beyond the command of all earthly authority to extinguish. The longer they lingered in Jerusalem, with its tens of thousands of eyes, the greater their probability of being found out. Hughes sent a special courier to Bernard de Clairvaux with coded word of their find. "Your mission is completed," the Cistercian leader answered in a response filled with high praise, and begged them to return home at once. The Count booked accommodations on the next available ship to Europe, and sailed from the Holy Land with his fellow knights in early autumn. No one else on board could have dreamed that among their crated baggage was the world's supreme religious treasure.

The voyage passed without incident, as did their long trek across Italy, where the Ark and its Templars paused at the Seborga monastery before moving on into France in late 1127 or early 1128. At the Council of Troyes, in January of 1129, a beaming Bernard de Clairvaux succeeded in winning papal recognition of the Knights, who could now don the white robes, signifying purity of belief, for which they became famous. Their emblematic red cross would not come for another 20 years, until Pope Eugenius III allowed them to wear it for the first time "as a symbol of Christian martyrdom."[24]

A far more pressing problem than winning papal approval of official insignia was finding optimum security for their secret discovery. Its first, temporary hiding place was the Cistercian abbey Hughes de Champagne had made possible four years prior to the official founding of the Templars. Bernard de Clairvaux was devoted to its safekeeping, but could not resist making some obvious hints that imperiled his vulnerable charge. For example, when a student monk asked him for his own definition of God, he shocked the young novice by declaring, "I have seen Him! He is height, width, length, and depth."[25] Bernard's obvious reference to the Ark of the Covenant was underscored by his frequent characterization of the abbey in which it had been secluded as the entrance to "the heavenly Jerusalem." Even the Count of Champagne remarked that "the Abbot of Clairvaux became the oracle of Europe,"[26] meaning perhaps he told more than he should.

Worse, after Bernard received word from the Templars of their discovery under Mount Moriah, he announced to his fellow Cistercians:

> *Well has Damedieu [the Mother of God] wrought with us and our Saviour Jesus Christ, who has set his friends of the Holy Land of Jerusalem on march through France and Burgundy....The work has been accomplished with our help. And the knights have been sent on the journey through France and Burgundy, that is to say, Champagne, under the protection, as we shall see, of the Count of Champagne, where all precautions can be taken against all interference by public or ecclesiastical authority; where at this time one can best make sure of a secret, a watch, a hiding-place.*[27]

That "hiding-place" for their priceless charge was the Red Cross Knights' most urgent concern, which was far too often imperiled by St. Bernard's inability to "best make sure of a secret" from either "public or ecclesiastical authority." By then, the Templars were no longer the same nine humble functionaries blindly obedient to his will. Papal recognition had transfigured them with growing wealth and burgeoning membership from the nobility, opening up new spheres of interest in power politics. Despite their increasing involvement in earthly affairs, however, concern for the sacred charge placed in their hands remained paramount. They overrode the command of the indiscreet St. Bernard, removing the Ark from his abbey at Citeaux to Lower Lorraine, the duchy of Godfroi de Bouillon before he helped lead the First Crusade to the Holy Land, from which he never returned. But his formidable castle still stood, and had been deeded back to his family after his death. That the discovery he set in motion should find its permanent home in his fortress was not only fitting, but sensible: The massive structure was, in fact, eminently defensible, among Europe's foremost military emplacements any besieging attacker would find daunting.

Moreover, its location not far from Troyes allowed the Templars, members of the Order of the Holy Sepulcher, and a privileged few, access to the sacred object and its golden aura. It had been responsible for the deaths of thousands when misused as a wonder weapon and dragged across the Sinai Peninsula, but 15 centuries of burial deep in the Earth had dampened the Ark's static accumulation, making it safe to approach and positively responsive to low-frequency input, such as meditation, prayer, or hymns. The crafted mineral it contained was, after all, only able to transduce the kind of energy directed at it. Blasts of martial fanfares concentrated on the crystal matrix were once magnified into a sonic artillery barrage that knocked down the walls of Jericho, but now, vibrating with the piety of a surrounding religious order, the output would be altogether different: Troyes suddenly became the most remarkable urban center in Europe. While the rest of Christendom wallowed in bigotry, superstition, illiteracy, and ignorance, its citizens enjoyed an intellectual freedom and cultural florescence absent from the outside world. Here the first Grail romance was composed, and Hebrew scholarship blossomed. History and the arts were not conditioned by papal dogma, while Muslim science—particularly medicine—was studied without prejudice. Most remarkable of all, airy Gothic design suddenly arose in sharp contrast to the heavy Romanesque churches that dominated the early Middle Ages. No two patterns of religious architecture could have been more different from each other. The older paradigm was gloomy, deep, and oppressive, compared to the new style's soaring sense of the infinite. One embraced the dark; the other opened to the light; the cavern contrasted with the forest—the material results of two diametrically opposed points of view and spirit.

Historians have long wondered how and why the Gothic Revolution took place when and where it did. The fine medievalist, Louis Charpentier observed:

It appears suddenly, without preamble, towards 1130. In a few years, it reaches its apogee, born whole and entire without experiment or miscarriage. And the extraordinary thing is that all at once it has at its disposal mastercraftsmen, artisans, builders, enough of them to undertake the construction of 80, huge monuments in less than a hundred years....The Gothic does not follow the Romanesque. They existed together. The Romanesque builders carried on with their Romanesque, while the Gothic builders erected their Gothic. And the two "schools" did not mix. When the Romanesque school tried its hand at the Gothic,

there only resulted, most of the time, a somewhat bastard style which was named, later, and with courtesy, "transitional." The Gothic builders themselves did not grope....If the Romanesque only comes to its fullness from the day of the Roman and Byzantine after many "improvements," the Gothic appears at one blow, complete, whole, and throughout the West.[28]

Some investigators speculate that lost construction principles were found in the Holy Land by returning Crusaders who brought them to Europe, resulting in the abrupt Gothic florescence; similarly ancient plans were supposedly unearthed at Mount Moriah; a Sufi brotherhood shared their secret building techniques with European initiates, and so on. But nothing remotely similar to Gothic architecture ever appeared in the Near East or the ancient world. Instead, its beginnings coincide with the Templars' arrival in France. "I hold that the Temple was responsible for the building of the great Gothic cathedrals," Charpentier affirmed, "for the good reason that no other organization could possibly have enabled bishops and chaplains to raise such projects."[29] The sacred object carried away from the Temple Mount cast its aura over the vicinity of its location—first at northern Italy's Cistercian Seborga monastery, later in France at Citeaux abbey, then in Flanders' Castle de Bouillon—affecting the French of Champagne, just as it had long before energized the Israelites at Jerusalem and the Egyptians at Akhetaton. It spiritualized them, activating their highest potential for creativity, resulting in the proto-Renaissance city of Troyes and Chartres Cathedral.

A New Temple for the Ark

It was at this foremost religious edifice that the Templars apparently planned to permanently install their matchless treasure. From its temporary residences in Champagne and Lower Lorraine, the Ark of the Covenant was spreading an ionic resonance across northern France, imbuing its inhabitants with a spiritual euphoria, causing many of them to believe the established Church and the European world it dominated were about to fade away, naturally replaced by the elevated guidance of a new era. Chartres was to be the home of this vitalizing power center, from which its divine energies would radiate to transform all mankind from its base savagery into golden godhood. Here was the real meaning of alchemy, nothing less than the greatest transcendent leap in human evolution, expressed in the Gothic movement.

The beginning of construction at Chartres shortly after the Templars' return with their discovery from Jerusalem and the official recognition of their Order at the Council of Troyes in 1129 was no accident. Nor was the site selected for the cathedral coincidental. It was the special focus of ritual activities going back to the stone ages. The medieval building arose over a large, man-made mound, remembered as the Place of the Strong, probably referring to a locus for cultic initiation. Gathered around were numerous dolmens, menhirs, cairns (known in France as *mergers*), and other standing stones, all oriented to the great earthwork, as though paying homage to or spiraling from the single monolith mounted atop it. Thus, the mound simulated the Earth's swollen belly or womb with its navel-stone at the center.

Some of the megalithic structures dated from the 5th millennium B.C., but the spiritual practices associated with them carried forward over the centuries, well into the early Christian era by Druid priests known as Carnutes. They gave their title to the Paleolithic precinct, Carnutes-Ys, or Sacred Place of the Carnutes, from which the name Chartres derived. Ys, the Sacred Place, is the island-kingdom in northern French myth ruled by Gradlon Meur, or Gradlon the Great. He alone escaped its inundation, and brought the mystical traditions of his sunken civilization to Brittany, as evidenced in its profusion of megalithic ruins. Parallels with lost Atlantis are obvious enough, and Charpentier's characterization of old Carnutes-Ys as "the center of Druidism" with its womb-like navel and umbilical stone underscores its Atlantean Navel-of-the-World identity.

That description was reaffirmed by the discovery of the so-called Black Virgin in the Druids' subterranean grotto at the Place of the Strong, where Chartres Cathedral would be built. The stone figure was a representation of the Earth Mother, her feet on the head of a snake symbol, according to Charpentier, of those sinuous energies the Kelts knew as *nwyvre*, the "wavy serpent-strength of the Earth," which they accessed with their crystalline standing-stones. "The currents in old Earth," he wrote, "are numerous and various; but here, at Chartres, we are concerned with one that is especially sacred, capable of awakening a man to the spiritual life"[30]—precisely the cause for selecting Carnutes-Ys as the site of a purpose-built structure that would enshrine the Ark of the Covenant. These were just the concentrated telluric forces the crystal it contained required to function as intended. Using the towering cathedral as an immense antenna, it would transmit grace throughout the world, transforming mankind's baser instincts into godliness.

Discarded forever was the old religion of fear and suffering, as indicated by the Crucifixion, which appears in none of the 38 religious scenes found at Chartres. Its Door of the Initiates opens on the Cathedral's north side, where a pair of small columns depict the Ark of the Covenant carved in relief. On one, the Latin words *Archa cederis*—"You are to work through the Ark"—are inscribed near a representation of it in a cart drawn by two oxen. The other column depicts an unidentified man in the process of removing a veil from the Ark beside a mound of corpses. On a coat of chainmail worn by one of the dead men appears the statement, *Hic Amititur, archa cederis*: "Here things take their course; you are to work through the Ark."

The first scene shows the Ark's biblical return in an ox-cart, when the Philistines gave it up as too dangerous, signifying that the Ark, after its removal to France, is once again in good hands. The second portrayal was meant to be an admonition against misusing the Ark, which was quite capable of creating mayhem if its power was deployed for destructive purposes. Archa cederis, "You are to work through the Ark," is nothing less than a mission statement, a public declaration that the Ark still existed and was to be used, obviously for purposes other than those dramatized on the second column. That, in fact, was precisely what the Templars had in mind: to install it permanently at Chartres as the centerpiece of the New Jerusalem, the coming Heaven on Earth. The ancient fire stone that had engendered King Solomon's glory, Akhenaton's revolution, and Atlantis' technology now inspired the highest, otherwise dormant and untapped resources of the human spirit, giving birth to the sudden Gothic florescence epitomized at Chartres.

The Templars were committed to living the words inscribed at Chartres Cathedral, as some of them, similar to the Levite priests of old, began to surrender their lives entirely to serving the Ark. From these obsessive devotees those Knights who had not been so profoundly influenced drew a cadre of special guardians whose sole function was protection of their beloved charge from the outside world of royal and papal power-freaks. Its capture by any one of Europe's constantly feuding kings or some corrupt pope would be an unthinkable disaster. As soon as either the monarchy or the Vatican so much as suspected that the Ark of the Covenant was located at Chartres, they would tear down every stone to get at it.

The initial, overly idealistic hope for the cathedral as the new Temple, from which a transforming energy would irradiate civilization, changing the Dark Ages of ignorance and cruelty into a golden age of spiritual and cultural enlightenment, proved an unlikely alchemy in the real world of medieval politics. Any structure raised by the hand of man, no matter how powerfully fortified, could be destroyed by that same hand. The very times in which the Templars lived repeatedly demonstrated the failure of the strongest, most ingeniously built castles to ultimately withstand siege warfare. None were able to hold out indefinitely against outside enemies with access to unlimited supplies, while even the best provisioned defenders eventually succumbed for want of food and water. Instead of risking the Ark to the vulnerability of any permanent establishment, an elite guard of fanatical protectors willing to die for the sacred object, yet mobile enough to move it from one secret location to another as necessity demanded, was far better insurance against its seizure by enemies.

Cathar Custodianship

As the cathedral was no longer deemed a secure home for the sacred object, work at Chartres gradually wound down around 1206, leaving construction on the north face unfinished and the Ark without a final home. About 50 years before, the Templars had entrusted the Ark's safe-keeping to the Cathars, an elect brotherhood officially disassociated from la milice du Christ, although actually taking direction from the same covert society that commanded the Knights: the Order of the Holy Sepulcher. Originally, the Cathars formed one of many heresies that swept Europe around the turn of the millennium, and had little different to offer after 1012, when they first appeared with a handful of followers in southwestern France. About 10 years later, they were considered sufficiently irregular by the Church to merit several of them being burnt at the stake in Toulouse, but their numbers were still insignificant when some journeyed northward more than 100 years later, circa 1140.

The precise nature of the Cathars' relationship with the Templars at this time was shrouded in necessary secrecy, but many of them were known to have taken up arms in the Templars' defense well into the next century. It was in Champagne, the Order's headquarters, that Catharism first became a mass movement. Templars and Albigensians—another name for Cathars, after their early headquarters in the city of Albi—were, after all, contemporaries from the birth to the death of Catharism. Indeed, resemblances between the two groups eventually grew so close, one seemed to have become an adjunct of the other. Some Cathars themselves enlisted in the Templars, rising rapidly through the ranks to the highest levels of trust. Membership did not conflict with their vows against killing, because they performed non-military service as *frères casaliers*, "rural brothers," *frères de métiers*, "serving brothers," and chaplains, undertaking menial tasks and trades, or seeing to the spiritual needs of the Order.

Admitted into the mind-altering presence of the Ark, prolonged exposure predictably expanded their already heretical consciousness with religious zeal. According to William F. Mann, a modern authority on the subject, "The Templars, for all intents and purposes, probably assumed that they were, in fact, the substitute guardians of an 'ark' of the Cathars, which allowed for direct communication with God."[31]

"Cathar" derived from the Greek words *kaqaro,* "pure ones," or *katharsis,* purifying the emotions through inspiration, and actually referred only to the leaders of the movement. Known as the Perfecti, they alone were Cathars, and initiated into the unconventional doctrine, unlike the majority of supporters—the "believers," Credentes, who were not expected to adopt the ascetic lifestyles practiced by the "Perfects." More generally, both were regarded by sympathizers as simply *bons hommes* or *bonnes femmes,* the "good men" and "good women." To their enemies, they were mistakenly called the Albigenses, or Albigensians, after Albi, just one of many towns (but certainly not the most important) in the south of France where the Cathars held sway.

Their belief-system marked a radical departure from mainstream Christianity, which they condemned as satanic. The Old Testament Yahweh was not the God of creation, but a revenge-crazed monster who made Hell on Earth. Accordingly, the Trinity and Virgin Birth were rejected as unnatural nonsense, and the sacrament of the Eucharist discarded. They did not believe St. Peter was ever in Rome to found a church, whose popes were less likely the successors of the apostles than they were of Roman emperors. Christ supposedly owned nothing and was impoverished, but the pope lived in a palace. Jesus may or may not have existed, but was, in either case, significant only so far as he embodied the spirit of redemption from a world made for suffering. His image writhing on the cross might have been an appropriate emblem for the Catholic Church, which had killed God in the hearts of men, but the Cathars despised the crucifix as a repulsive emblem of deicide.

Their symbol too was a cross, but it predated Christianity by three or four millennia. An encircled, four-square crosshairs, or a cross with flared ends and a circle at its center, the oldest known examples of the so-called Keltic Cross occur in stone age caves at the Pyrenees, where the Cathars originated. Its solar symbolism had been appropriated during the early 6th century by missionaries as transitional imagery for Christianity in the British Isles. But throughout Keltic times, the circle-cross was associated with the Old Irish sun-god, Grannus, the same meaning embraced by the Cathars, who revered light as the visible manifestation of the holy spirit they likewise envisioned as a pure, white dove.

Throughout Ireland, the emblem is still familiar as the Ionic Cross, because it was most particularly identified with the Hebridean isle of Iona. It was here, according to the medieval *Annals of Clonmacnoise*, that a "sea people," the Tuatha da Danaan, or "Magicians of the Almoners (in other words, those who dispense sacred wisdom), arrived on the south coast of Ireland in 1202 B.C.; the final Atlantis catastrophe occurred in 1198 B.C. Their Atlantean identity is further emphasized by the philological resemblance of their name to the Tuaoi, the sacred crystal of Atlantis. They may have represented the class of initiates responsible for its care or operation, as implied by their title, *almoners*. The *Annals of Clonmacnoise* do, in fact, state that the Tuatha da Danaan brought a Stone of Destiny, the Lia Fáil, to Iona, which was known even as late as the 18th century as the Navel of the World.

The Cathars believed that the human soul was a spark of divine light caught within the material dimension like a butterfly in a spider's web. This was their understanding of the fall of man. Attracted by the sensory delusion of the physical world, man was ensnared by the Devil, a metaphor for cruelty personified in Yahweh with his mundane representatives in the Church, that "Synagogue of Satan" ruled by a real Prince of Darkness, the pope. The vital essence of humanity, its original grace (as opposed to Christianity's original sin), was being sucked out by these demons to indefinitely perpetuate their victimizing scheme disguised as a religion of love. Liberation could never come from some bogus Jesus in the service of this same pious fraud, but through individual marginalization and ultimate rejection of the material world.

Because Earth was Hell, no such place existed in the afterlife, including Heaven (at least in the conventional sense), Purgatory, or Limbo. Death was nothing more than a door through which one returns to life. The Cathars therefore believed in reincarnation, and even metapsychosis, the transmigration of souls, wherein consciousness survives death, reentering physical survival in a new body, human or otherwise. This cycle continues, so long as we are unable to resist the temptations of sensual being. Redemption from the apparently endless loop of birth, suffering, transient happiness, death, and rebirth could only be achieved by renouncing all illusory pleasures, and regarding the ego as adversary. Those who successfully undertook a regimen of strict asceticism freed themselves at death from the pattern of earthly sorrows, so they could return at last to the godly light, their source of eternal happiness from before the Fall. Others unable to embrace self-denial must restart their mortal existence. For the Cathars, reincarnation was neither good nor bad—nor predetermined—but resulted from a person's failure to escape the bonds of carnal existence through abstinence.

To achieve personal salvation, the Perfecti dedicated themselves to total spiritual renewal. Upon acceptance, they surrendered all their worldly goods to the Order, and wore simple, black robes with cord belts. The aim of their lives was purification in thought, word, and deed, which they achieved through simplicity, frugality, and modesty, depending entirely on alms for sustenance. No meat or dairy goods were permitted, as eating them was deemed a form of cannibalism—they still possessed something of the souls that once animated them, and killing in any form was strictly prohibited. Additionally, these foods were by-products of sexual reproduction, which the Perfecti personally foreswore and discouraged in others, because copulation tempted them to remain in the material world. Consuming fish was allowed, because it was generally believed in the Middle Ages that this animal alone did not sexually reproduce itself.

Perfecti observed complete celibacy, never performed wedding ceremonies for others, and on the contrary, urged the abolition of matrimony. In its place, concubinage—the gratification of sexual desire without producing offspring, thereby preventing the perpetuation and spread of human bondage—was considered preferable, although the very indulgence of physical passion enslaved men and women to another round of reincarnation. The Perfecti spent much of their lives in meditation, prayer, and charitable work. But their chief obligations and activity were winning converts to Catharism, as the means by which their fellow humans could free themselves from the world of the flesh and the Devil. Warfare, capital punishment, and swearing of oaths—three leading characteristics of the times in which they lived—were utterly rejected, and female Perfecti gained virtual equality with their male coreligionists.

While these ascetics never numbered more than a few thousand elect, the vast majority of supporters were Credentes. They followed the same dietary restrictions and adhered to the fundamental principles of nonviolence and charity, but married and led otherwise normal lives, and were not obligated to adopt austere disciplines. Those "believers" desirous of joining the Perfecti submitted to the *consolamentum*, in which they formally abjured the outside world, devoting themselves entirely to spiritual purification. A simple ceremony involved the laying-on of hands and ritual kiss of brotherhood, climaxing with a "baptism of fire" to celebrate the initiate's quest for God's primal light. More commonly, Credentes took the consolamentum on their deathbeds, because it assured their release, even as the final moment approached, from the cycle of reincarnation. To ensure the efficacy of the *endura*, as the process was known, they refused food or drink, thereby quickening their demise. Suicide was not otherwise condoned, although some of the last Perfecti did take their own lives by climbing high into the mountains, where they perished from exposure to freezing temperatures.

For the last 150 years, historians have argued that the Cathars were influenced by, or in fact *were* Pagan gnostics, heathen sun-worshippers, neo-Druids, proto-Freemasons, resurgent Mithraists, Sufi mystics, Bulgarian Bogomils, Tibetan Buddhists, Hebrew cabalists, Persian Zervanists, Zoroasterans, Rosicrucians, Jansenists, and any number or combination of famous and obscure cults and various faiths. As Markale remarks, "It is not at all certain that Catharism can be objectively viewed as a Christian religion."[32] While it did indeed resemble, at least in part, all these metaphysical notions and others besides, direct contact with any one of them is virtually absent. Any commonalities resulted more from the fundamental beliefs held by all dualists, who regarded the universe in terms of pairs of opposites.

That said, it seems nonetheless true that the Cathars were at least partially influenced by one outside doctrine: Manichaeism. Although documented proof of their affinity for Manichaeism is lacking, inferential evidence suggests it. Founded in mid-3rd century Babylon, the new faith was the inspiration of Mani, a Persian mystic, who preached a return to Ohrmazd Bay, the Original Man, associated with the Zoroastrian Ahura Mazda, the god of light, who was himself locked in immemorial struggle with the forces of darkness. Mani incorporated gnostic and Christian teachings with Buddhist ideas and imagery, apparently taking his religious name from the Hindu word for the sacred jewel of inner illumination. In Manichaeist texts throughout Asia he was, after all, described as "buddha."

As one of their Roman era competitors, Manichaeism was condemned by Christian leaders, although it lingered long after the fall of the Classical world into medieval times, when some 11th century heretics used it to deliberately provoke narrow-minded churchmen. Manichaeism was less seriously embraced by spiritual rebels than it was generally regarded as a symbol of opposition to mainstream religion. As such, a few Manichaean references were used as descriptive titles by the Cathars, most notably their supremely arcane ceremony, the Manisola, and the new name for the Ark of the Covenant: The Mani Stone. It had been known by different names before, passing from one culture to another, as the Atlantean Tuaoi, the Guanche Fyra, and the Egyptian Ben-Ben. To the Templars, who rescued it from 1,600 years of oblivion, it was the Desire for Paradise. Now, in the hands of Western European mystics, it was called the Mani Stone after the famous Buddhist symbol of spiritual purity and enlightenment, *om mani padme um*, "the Jewel in the lotus." Although it seems a far stretch, geographically and culturally, there nonetheless appears more than a philological commonality between the Cathars' Mani and the Tibetan Chintamani described in Chapter 2.

To Jean Markale, "it is obvious that the Cathars were heirs of the Manichaeans. This also means that Catharism appears more like an *entirely separate* religion than a Christian heresy."[33] In truth, no one will ever know to what extent, if any, the Cathars were directly influenced by any external doctrine, because none of their original source materials exist, so thorough were the politically correct despots of the Inquisition, who consigned every Albigensian document to the Christian "memory-hole." While opponents charged them with Manichaeism, the Perfecti never adopted its cosmology, and their employment of its terminology was primarily for purposes of description.

The bons hommes did, however, personally symbolize their leadership position in the Order of the Holy Sepulcher by growing their hair long in the Merovingian fashion. But all indications reaffirm that they primarily represented an indigenous western European spiritual phenomenon with some outward similarities to parallel religious movements that were for the most part coincidental. In the Cathars' case, the only real outside stimulus occurred when they were brought into prolonged contact with the mind-expanding negative ions radiating from their Mani Stone. As its constant guardians, the Ark of the Covenant's psycho-spiritual impact on them intensified over time, just as it affected the Templars, ancient Israelites, Egyptians, and Atlanteans before them. And as they did, the Cathars embarked on grandiose construction projects. Instead of a single city such as Atlantis or Akhetaton, a temple similar to the holy place built by Solomon, or a cathedral such as Chartres to enshrine their sacred charge, they built a whole series of mountaintop citadels across the south of France into the Pyrenees. Because, despite their superb defensive engineering and exceptionally daunting locations designed to withstand the most extended siege, any one of them might still fall in time to a well-supplied, determined campaign—but not all of them at once. In the event a protecting structure was in danger of capture, provision was made for safely removing the Ark to a different fortification, from one to another, on and on, making the entire circuit of keeps, if need be, always at least one step ahead of the enemy.

Appropriately, the first citadel to which the Cathars brought their precious item was Montreal-de-Sos, after the Crusader King Baudoin I's purpose-built castle in the Holy Land, intended as the Ark's original storage place. The French Grail historian, André Douzet writes of its placement at Montreal-de-Sos, "The old accounts add that the royal necropolis is eternally illuminated by this stone. It is said to be only visible to 'a handful of very noble warriors,'" in other words, the Knights Templar.[34] The Ark must have been installed in Montreal-de-Sos before 1147, when Pope Eugene III, alarmed by the Cathars' spreading popularity, ordered his most articulate priests and bishops to debate and debunk the heretics on their own ground, in the south of France. Among these leading Church propagandists was none other than Bernard de Clairvaux, one of the early founders of the Templars. He had since been distanced from the very organization he helped create, due as much to his indiscreet tongue as for his determination to reform Christianity from within, rather than the external overhaul most Knights preferred.

No longer in the physical presence of the Ark, his dynamic personality deteriorated. The encyclopedist of Medievalism, John Fines, writes that St. Bernard became "a mystical conservative, single-minded to the point of narrowness, puritanical, opposing all forms of radical scholarship, combative and vehement to a degree."[35] Two years before being sent to confront the Cathars, he had been the driving force behind an ill-advised Second Crusade. With its inevitable failure, "many lost faith in Bernard, and turned on him."[36] His effort to dissuade the Albigenses of their heresy was likewise unsuccessful. Not only had he lost much of his old evangelical fire, but he also openly sympathized, at least in part, with the bons hommes. "No one," he declared, "is more sincerely pious in their prayers than they."[37] Perhaps too he envied their custody of the sacred secret he once kept, however poorly, a loss that diffused his combativeness with melancholy for the lost Ark.

The Cathars were mostly concentrated in Languedoc, a loosely defined region encompassing approximately 16,490 square miles in the central part of southern France, roughly the region between the Rhône River on the border with Provence, and the Garonne River at Gascony, extending northward to the Cévennes and the Massif Central bordering Auvergne. The name "Languedoc" is relatively new, first mentioned only during the early 19th century, and means "the language of Oc," an ancient, Latin-based Romance tongue spoken in Occitania, itself an ill-defined area larger than the modern province of Languedoc, which it overlaps to abut the Pyrenees. To this day, the region is still known as *le pays des Cathares*, the land of the Cathars. The inhabitants of this rather nebulous realm never thought of themselves as Frankish, much the less "French," as much for their ethnic and cultural differences as for their different language. Contributing to their sense of separate identity now were the Cathars, regarded by the average Occitanian as indigenous "good men," while actual Perfecti membership never counted more than perhaps 10,000 adherents.

The Church vs. The Cathars

It was not their relatively few members, however, but their hundreds of thousands of sympathizers that frightened the Church. All other heresies had been little more than reactionary outbursts against excessive corruption and despotic theology, and therefore easily crushed. But the Cathars represented a counter-spirituality that dissolved the deep social ruts between rich and poor into class collaboration, thereby forming a very broad base of support. Nobles donated lands for castles, while peasants contributed their labor and food.

The entire Cathar outlook was regarded with horror by conventional Christians, but what most upset them was the women's role throughout the Albigensian hierarchy. Woman as responsible for the fall of man, born an unclean thing ever since, the inventor of sin, the Devil's handmaiden, had been an integral view of Christian doctrine for the previous 1,000 years. Mary Magdalene herself was regarded as nothing more than a prostitute. Women's participation in religious matters, according to such reasoning, was part of Satan's plan to infiltrate the Cathars. Their Perfectae scandalized Catholic clergy by discussing theology in public—unheard-of behavior for women. When one of Pope Innocent's churchmen found himself unable to convincingly answer her arguments, he exploded at Esclarmonde de Foix, "Go to your distaff, madam! It is not proper that you should speak at such a gathering!"[38]

Meanwhile, Pope Innocent III stormed to his Languedoc archbishop in Auch, "We give you a direct command that, by whatever means you can, you destroy all these heresies, and repel from your diocese all who are polluted by them. If necessary, you may cause the princes and people to suppress them with the sword."[39] In answer to these papal fulminations, the archbishop ignored his orders, and half a dozen noble ladies, led by Esclarmonde herself, flaunting their disdain, converted to Catharism during a public ceremony applauded by attending members of the nobility. Outraged, Innocent ordered Philip Augustus to punish the heretics without delay, but the count defied his Holiness by refusing to wage war on his own family. Clearly, the Church was losing its grip on European leaders.

The Cathars at the center of this controversy were utterly disinterested in political squabbles and wanted nothing more than to liberate their souls from an otherwise endless round of reincarnation, while helping others to achieve the same spiritual freedom. Inadvertently, however, their refreshing ideology—and especially the growing sympathy they attracted—amounted to nothing less than the most serious revolutionary challenge ever faced by the Christian Church. Pope Innocent III was forced to defrock several of his bishops in Languedoc, where they were increasingly unresponsive to his authority. The scandal prompted fears that the Occitanian heresy might eventually push the very organization founded by Christ himself into oblivion, thereby fulfilling Lucifer's dream of annexing the Earth. Such a catastrophe had to be avoided at all costs, and as tensions mounted, Innocent hoped for some provocation that would justify that usual solution to which tyrants typically resort.

In January of 1208, Innocent dispatched his personal legate to the Languedoc city of Toulouse, there to caution the powerful Raymond VI against complicity with the Cathars. The count had already been excommunicated once before for destroying the churches in his city. But that was under another pope, and Raymond had since been reinstated because the Vatican could not afford to lose any more influence in the region. But Innocent hardly lived up to his name by sending Pierre de Castelnau, an intolerant hothead, on such a delicate mission. Castelnau was already infamous for excommunicating noblemen he suspected of heresy, usually without trial, and often because the victim displayed insufficient reverence for the suspicious inquisitor. His meeting to patch up relations with an influential Occitanian leader predictably degenerated into vociferous charges against Raymond VI as "an abettor of heresy," for which the Count was summarily excommunicated yet again.[40]

The next day, on the road out of Toulouse near Saint Gilles Abbey, Pierre de Castelnau was fatally assaulted by unknown persons, possibly Cathar sympathizers—certainly not by Perfecti or Credentes, to whom killing of any kind, even of pompous windbags, was anathema. A knight operating under the personal command of Raymond was immediately accused by Church officials, but the count would hardly have been so transparent as to order an assassination of the man who excommunicated him just 24 hours before. More likely, Castelnau was an expedient victim of Vatican assassins operating on behalf of his own pope, who needed some dramatic outrage to galvanize French Christendom.

A New Crusade

To be sure, the papal legate's murder, and especially its presentation to the outside world as a bloody act against God's own representative on Earth, ignited the degree of emotional response sufficient for another Crusade. The difference this time, however, was that it was aimed, not at some distant foreigners, but against fellow Europeans in the continental homeland. Launching a major military campaign, instead of following ordinary procedure by the arrest of a single man—the excommunicated Raymond—to be arraigned for homicide, Innocent III revealed his real motives. "Forward, brave soldiers of Jesus Christ," he declared, "Fight the agents of the anti-Christ! Any person, as great a sinner as any, can escape the torments of Hell, if he fights against the heretics!"[41]

His Holiness whetted still more the Christian aristocracy's thirst for vengeance by decreeing that they could confiscate at will all land owned by the Cathars or their accomplices. As the population of Languedoc was predominantly sympathetic to the bons hommes, south-central France, until now an autonomous region, became open season for the nobility. The Languedoc was not just land, but *rich* land. Its fields were among the most productive on the Continent, and Occitania's agricultural economy was flourishing at a time when the rest of France tottered on insolvency. Languedoc was Western civilization's cultural bright spot, whose courts were far more splendid than anywhere else, arts and letters flourished, and literacy rates were highest. These extra-spiritual considerations combined in large measure to inspire the nobles of northern France against the heretics, whose lands they dreamed of plundering with the pope's blessing. Heady with an unhealthy brew of religious fervor and private greed, aristocrats across middle Europe flocked to punish the unbelieving enemies of the Church.

They were joined by many thousands of sincere Frenchmen, their patriotism and piety aroused by a perceived threat to their country and faith. On June 24, 1209, 20,000 knights supported by more than 200,000 peasants set out from Lyon along the Rhône River toward Languedoc. Gathering under the banner "Kill for Christ!" they were joined by recruits from as far afield as Burgundy, the Rhineland, Austria, Germany, Hungary, the Netherlands, and the Balkans—all of them convinced the greatest threat to Christendom must be uprooted from European soil.

As the Muslims had in Palestine, the Occitanians regarded the Crusade marching against them as nothing less than a full-scale invasion designed to conquer and dissolve their sovereign country. Unlike the Cathars, however, they were quite willing to fight for it, and marshalled powerful forces the enemy would find more formidable than imagined. Orthodox Christians unsympathetic to alternative theologies nonetheless fought against

aggression from the north for their country's existence.

From start to finish, the First Crusade to take Jerusalem lasted less than three years. The Albigensian Crusade would go on for more than *four decades*, interrupted by the death of Innocent III, but resumed with the rise of his successor, Honorious. It eventually swallowed the whole of northern French nobility, which suffered heavy losses under the command of another papal legate, Arnaud Amaury. In their first significant engagement against the Occitanians, his forces took the town of Béziers on July 22, 1209 through the sheer weight of numbers. Casualties on both sides were appalling, and he added to the carnage by ordering the immediate execution of all captured heretics. When one of his commanders asked how to distinguish them from fellow Catholics, Amaury replied, "*Caedite eos! Novit enim Dominus qui sunt eis.*" His words have been translated and used by other mass-murderers since his time as "Kill them all! Let God sort them out!"—which is closer to the genuine spirit of his order than the original Latin, "Kill them all! The Lord will recognize His own."[42]

Accordingly, his men broke through the great solid-oak doors of the Church of St. Mary Magdalene, where 7,000 Cathars and ordinary Christians, all of them non-combatants and many of them wounded or elderly, cowered in fear for their lives. They succumbed to a slaughter of truly biblical proportions—every last man, woman, and child. Outside, throughout Béziers, the victorious troops expanded their horrifying rampage in the name of Jesus. The usual methods of killing grew tiresome with overuse, so the occupying troops amused themselves by blinding people, dragging them behind horses, and using them as living targets for archery practice. To finish off anyone who might have escaped the victors by hiding in the town, it was burned to the ground, and survivors who ran from its flames were cut down as they fled. Amaury boasted in a written report to Pope Innocent, "Today, your Holiness, 20,000 citizens were put to the sword, regardless of rank, age, or sex."[43]

Consequences for the Ark

The Crusade put the Knights Templar in a serious bind. Although responsible directly to papal authority, they had obeyed the command of their actual leaders in the semi-secret society, the Order of the Holy Sepulcher, by handing over the Ark of the Covenant to the pope's worst enemies. The Templars had, in fact, *formed* the despised Cathars from their own ranks, and continued to fight as their ferocious, if mostly anonymous, protectors. In the Sabarthez region of the Pyrenees, the 20th century German scholar, Otto Rahn, found previously unexplored chambers, their walls covered with the croix pattée and similar emblems of the Knights Templar, side by side with the Cathars' dove and other symbols. His discovery demonstrated the intertwined relationship between both groups, actually wings of the same order. Mas-Deu, a fortress in the Roussillion connected to the Templar house of Le Bezu, near the more famous Rennes-le-Chateau, was a place of refuge for Cathar survivors. In the Razes area of Occitania, according to Markale, "their collusion was fully operational."[44]

Nowhere was this collusion more significant than at Montreal-de-Sos, where the Ark of the Covenant had been brought from Lower Lorraine's Castle de Bouillon prior to the outbreak of hostilities. It was guarded by the commandery of Capoulet-Junac, established in 1136 by the Templar Guillaume d'Arnave. Local legend recounted that Montreal itself had been built over the tomb of the Greek demigod

Heracles. Interred with his sarcophagus was a sun-stone that gave off so bright a radiance that it illuminated the entire ancient necropolis, and was visible only to "a handful of very noble warriors" similar, Douzet points out, to the knights of the Round Table.[45] The myth describes the Cathars' "Mani" before it was moved on ahead of the advancing enemy to safer keeping in a more inaccessible, mountaintop location.

As a revealing indication of the unique power the Templars had assumed by the time the Albigensian War broke out, they refused to officially participate in it with impunity, although their thinly veiled allegiance to the Cathars did not escape Vatican notice. One wonders if the decline in their fortunes that would bring them to disaster 60 years later had its origin in the Templars' double standard during Europe's fratricidal Crusade. Their identifying image was, after all, the representation of two knights on horseback, another link with the Cathars, who traveled in pairs. Ostensibly, this image was meant to symbolize the *pauperes commilitones Christ templique Solomonici*, the Order of the Poor Knights of Christ Solomon's temple; symbolizing that either knightly figure was too poverty-stricken to afford his own horse. In reality, however, the Templars had burgeoned into an economic power unto themselves. What would eventually come to be regarded as their duplicity was likewise their affinity for Cathar dualism, an insight into the ideological commonality shared by both groups, which were actually respective military and theological wings of the same movement.

Despite fierce resistance, and the covert participation of select Knights Templar, the Occitanians could match neither the numbers nor savagery of their enemies at places such as Béziers, and a slow, fighting retreat across south-central France began. Ever mindful of their sacred charge, the Cathars kept the Ark of the Covenant behind the front, moving it from Montreal-de-Sos to a series of other fortresses, as one castle after another fell to the Crusaders. Perfecti strictures against killing any living creature under all circumstances prevented them from deploying it as a weapon, as had the biblical Israelites (with calamitous repercussions for themselves).

The Albigensians' dedicated pacifism did not prevent them, however, from performing practical service during the war. They were the most renowned healers of the age, far superior to the superstitious quacks that passed as physicians in the rest of Dark Age Europe. As corpsmen, medevac personnel, and field nurses, Cathar courage was repeatedly demonstrated during and after each battle.

They were also tireless weavers, spinning soldiers' uniforms from sheep's wool, which were colored with their own mineral and vegetable dyes. The Perfecti manufactured numerous surgical instruments, belt buckles, rings, pendants, and religious items, particularly lead doves and badges in the shape of a pentagram, the Seal of Solomon, the Cathars' symbolic connection to him through their possession of the Ark of the Covenant.

They also cultivated groves of laurel for its solar symbolism, thereby exposing the pre-Christian roots of their faith. At least as long ago as the Bronze Age, laurel was the emblem of Apollo, the ancient Greek sun-god, whose temples were surrounded by the tree, because it

was believed to purify the souls of visitors seeking oracular advice from the Pythia. She was a virgin priestess who fell into an altered state of consciousness after chewing laurel leaves. Nearby was the omphalos, the "navel stone," through which the sun-god communicated with the virgin. The "heathen" themes of purity, light, a sacred stone, and intimate contact with the divine were likewise the leading motifs of Catharism.

By the beginning of 1243, the Royal French invaders occupied most of Languedoc, forcing the surviving good men and good women into their last stronghold: Montségur. Very likely the most impregnable citadel of the Middle Ages, Montségur derived its name from the *Castrum montis securi*, the "Secure Mount," as it was known to the Romans 12 centuries before. They were preceded by Iberian defenders and much earlier stone age mystics, who venerated its precipitous summit as a sacred site. Over the ruins of these ancient occupations, the medieval bulwark perched atop an immense, limestone needle known as a *pog*, rising 3,300 feet against the backdrop of the Pyrenees. Commanding views for many miles in all directions looked out on the Cathar heartland to forestall sneak attacks, and its sheer rock ledges were more formidable than any man-made castle walls. The fortress was accessible only on its east face via a ridge just a few yards wide, and therefore easily protected from adjacent cliffs towering 300 feet overhead. The battlements followed along the contours of the pog's uppermost ridge, and melding into it, formed an unassailable defense-work.

Anticipating persecution, the Cathars envisioned Montségur as their ultimate hope of survival five years before the war against them was launched. In 1204, they had engaged Ramon de Pereille to transform their retreat into a state-of-the-art military installation. Although neither a Perfect nor Credente, he was one of their protectors and probably a former or current Templar who covertly served by aiding the Cathars. Five years later, a Royal French general, Guy de Montfort, learned of Cathar intentions for Montségur, and planned to take it on his own initiative. But when he personally visited the base of the lofty citadel, he gave up the attempt as impossible.

De Pereille continued to fortify the isolated eyre until May of 1243, as Pope Innocent III's 10,000 troops surrounded the base of the mountain at an area still known locally as *el campis*. They craned their necks upward to squint in astonishment at the vertical spire of rock rising high into the sky, where a mere 200 Perfecti, together with slightly fewer Credenti, other sympathizers, women, and children sought refuge. Defending them against the enemy masses far below were just 98 men-at-arms—but they possessed the most valuable object on Earth.

The Seige of Montségur

Before he rode about Languedoc, trying desperately to raise an army strong enough to lift the Royal French Army siege, Ramon de Pereille left the garrison in the capable hands of his younger kinsman, Peter Roger de Mirepoix. His opposite in charge of Catholic forces was Hugh de Arcis, King Louis's own seneschal in the city of Carcassonne, and among his most determined, yet coolly calculating field commanders. De Arcis wasted no time. As his men set up camp, he dispatched numerous reconnaissance patrols through-

out the lower slopes of the mountain to bring back an abundance of accurate intelligence. His scouts reported several obscure goat paths that, if taken in a lightning attack, would lead directly to the summit. Perhaps the capture of Montségur would not be as daunting as it appeared after all.

When elite French assault troops undertook their first attack, however, they were virtually annihilated by unexpectedly intense and accurate crossbow and catapult fire. Throughout the summer and into autumn, de Arcis probed one goat path after another, sometimes sending only a few commandoes to slither passed the guards, other times throwing in whole detachments aimed at overwhelming the enemy through sheer weight of numbers. In every attempt, his troops were slaughtered by skilled warriors concealed among the rocky terrain.

With the weather turning colder, supplies diminishing, and facing the prospect of suffering through a winter siege, de Arcis decided on new tactics that might force a capitulation before the first snowfall. He knew Montségur was protected by less than 100 men, and therefore decided on a war of attrition. His sharp-shooters climbed within arrow-range of their human targets to kill one at a time. The lone bowmen suffered high losses, but inflicted growing casualties on the defenders, who, unlike the French, could not afford such losses. Although only 11 heretics fell to sniper-fire, that number represented more than 1/10 of the castle's men-at-arms.

But de Arcis could not wait for them to be felled one by one. His own army was becoming quickly demoralized by a combination of complaints, foremost among them a lack of proper supplies against falling temperatures. Adding to their physical discomfort, many soldiers huddling for warmth around their campfires condemned the pope's massive campaign against a handful of politically incorrect mystics (who had nevertheless bested the King's finest troops)—as dishonorable and absurd. Additionally, some of the besiegers were themselves infected by Catharism, and swore to do the bons hommes no harm, even under orders, if surrender came.

De Arcis was aware that time was working less for him than for the enemy, and resolved on an extremely bold commando raid that, if successful, could turn the struggle decisively in his favor. As the fighting temporarily mellowed, with Christmas celebrations beginning on both sides, he called a secret meeting of Gascon volunteers from an elite mountain unit. Their assignment: Take the Roc de la Tour, a natural columnar formation rising hundreds of feet parallel to the eastern summit and connected to the citadel by an easy incline less than 1,000 feet long. Any attack via the western approaches was foredoomed by the enemy's defense-in-depth. Surmounting the Roc seemed unassailable, but its capture held the key to Montségur. As if the operation were not suicidal enough, it could only be carried out during the dead of night to achieve surprise.

In pitch darkness, with their unsuspecting comrades singing Yuletide carols far below, the mountain troops scrambled up the vertiginous cliff face amid swirling snowflakes. The ascent was made yet more onerous and perilous by the heavy steel weapons they carried, all of them soundproofed in wraps of muslin. Incredibly, the attackers completed their climb without incident, took the bastion by storm, and tossed its surprised defenders to their deaths from the top of the Roc. At dawn, the victorious commandos peered over the walls they had scaled during the night, and almost fainted at the declivity. Had they known in advance the precipitous

extremes required for their attack, the hardy Gascons swore they would never have volunteered.

But it was their seizure of the Roc de la Tour that turned the tide for de Arcis. With the smooth, relatively flat, eastern approach to the castle no longer forbidden to him, he ordered his artillery into position. Trebuchets, "tall cats," mangonels, and various siege engines were dismantled at base camp, then hauled 3,300 feet up the mountainside piece by piece, and painstakingly reassembled outside the captured bastion, too far from the defenders to interfere, but close enough for them to watch the fearsome array of stone-throwing monstrosities being readied for their first barrage. It came in late January, when a hailstorm of 80-pound boulders thundered against the outer barbican of the citadel. While the walls still held, Templar-led sorties killed many attackers, slowing their progress, which seemed nevertheless inexorable. Howling winter storms sometimes ground the Royal French advance to a halt, simultaneously providing cover for crossbowmen, who picked off more of the invaders.

Despite continued, stiff resistance, defeat loomed larger with every bloody, incremental advance made by their enemies, and castle commandant de Mirepoix decided to send away Montségur's treasury as a precautionary measure.

It might seem strange that individual Cathars and Templars, who owned no personal possessions and were equally sworn to private poverty, should have been in possession of monetary wealth, but aristocrats and nobility from all over Europe richly funded both orders; donations the Perfecti and Knights distributed directly to the poor, contributed to charitable institutions, hospitals, selected seminaries, and monasteries.

In early January of 1244, shortly after the seizure of the Roc de la Tour, de Mirepoix entrusted "gold, money, and a great quantity of currency" with Pierre Bonnet and Matheus, according to a deposition later given before the Inquisition by Imbert de Salles, a knight at the citadel.[46] The two noncombatants successfully infiltrated the siege lines, perhaps through bribery of some Royal Army sentinels, many of whom were, in any case, suffering from acute war-weariness. Moreover, accumulating losses inflicted by Montségur's persistent snipers contributed to prevent de Arcis from adequately sealing off the 11-mile base perimeter of the mountain, enabling the embattled defenders to maintain more or less constant contact with the outside world via military couriers.

Bonnet and Matheus quickly made their way through the upper Ariege Valley to Donnezan, where, at the castle of Usson, they tried to find volunteers or hire mercenaries for a bold relief mission. Taking advantage of general disarray following a surprise attack on the Crusaders, commandos were to break through the confused ranks, then race up the mountain to the occupied Roc de la Tour, where they would either destroy the enemy's largest trebuchet, or turn it against its royal owners. As some measure of the Cathars' desperation, the leader they engaged for this last-ditch operation was a Catalan highwayman with the romantic name of Corbario, whose fellow robbers were the only recruits willing, for a price, to attempt such a hazardous sortie. It predictably came to nothing, as the motley band got hopelessly lost in a gorge during the night—fortunately for the participants. Had they actually tried to engage the professional soldiers of the French crown, Corbario and his followers would have been cut to pieces without having achieved much of anything.

Messengers easily slipped in and out of the besieged mountaintop castle, bringing news of the treasure's safe relocation, and its failure to purchase victory. Other envoys inaccurately reported that Ramon de Pereille had succeeded in raising an entire army already on the march to their rescue. The son of Peire Vidal, a well-known troubadour, carried word from the sympathetic Count of Toulouse, urging the defenders to "resist just another week," because Emperor Frederick II was mobilizing to break the siege at Montségur. But with the last courier to reach the mountaintop fortress in late February, its residents realized the reports were too good to be true. By then, the enemy had battered his way to within hailing distance of the citadel, which was crumbling beneath relentless fusillades of catapulted stone day and night. Further resistance grew steadily more difficult, though the few remaining knights fought on against impossible odds.

Finally, on March 2, to spare the crumbling castle's women and children from certain doom, Peter Roger de Mirepoix walked alone through its open gates carrying a white flag. In his negotiations with the besiegers, he asked for a fortnight to settle the residents' affairs, a condition de Arcis, who had been personally moved by his enemy's heroic fight, readily allowed. Enraged by the commander's generosity of spirit, the French Army chaplain, the archbishop of Narbonne, demanded that the rebels against God turn themselves over at once. None deserved clemency, unless they renounced their Albigensian heresy and submitted to the rigors of Church inquisitors. But they would be allowed the two-week truce after all, de Arcis insisted, and Montségur's laypeople were free to go on their mere promise to visit the Inquisition for interrogation. But not even he could save the Perfecti, unless they recanted their subversive beliefs.

As they prepared themselves for the worst, 21 Credentes requested the consolamentum, demonstrating, as nothing else, its ideological power. The following day, with just 48 hours left before the surrender, the new Cathars and their mentors participated in the Manisola, their most sacred ceremony. Shrouded in deep secrecy, and shared only with initiates, it somehow celebrated (activated?) the Ark of the Covenant, in keeping with very ancient traditions of the object's sacred light: the Stone (mani) of the Sun (sola).

A trusted Credente, Escot de Belcaire lit a signal-fire from the snowy peak of Mount Bidorta, virtually equal in elevation to the doomed fortress he left behind on the opposite side of the valley. Its distant flickering told his fellow Cathars celebrating a last Ritual of the Sun-Stone that their comrades entrusted with Montségur's great secret prize had successfully infiltrated Royal French lines, and escaped with the Mani Stone beyond the enemy's reach. De Belcaire was joined by one Amiel Aicart and two other assistants remembered only by their first names, Poitevin and Hugo—four men, which would have been required to carry the Ark of the Covenant by its two long poles.

Templar historians Lionel and Patricia Fanthorpe posed the same questions investigators have been asking ever since: "What was the secret of secrets which the Cathars would rather die than reveal? Did the Albigensians know where the Ark was hidden?"[47] That they did not carry a monetary hoard away from Montségur on the night of March 15 is clear, because two other couriers, Pierre Bonnet and Matheus, had already fled with the citadel's "gold, money, and a great quantity of currency" three months before. No, Aicart, Poitevin, Hugo, and their anonymous companion (probably de Belcaire himself) had charge of the Ark of the Covenant, which required four porters to lift by its pair of long poles; the Cathars' Manisola immediately prior to its departure was undoubtedly a ceremonial send-off to their beloved Mani Stone. With its safe relocation, they could at last fulfill their common fate in good conscience. The enemy might take their lives, but not their escaped Desire for Paradise.

True to his word, de Arcis allowed the surrendered laypeople to leave unmolested, and went further by having his surgeons attend the enemy wounded. Alone for two days in the now strangely quiet citadel, the Cathars wordlessly filed out the front gate on the early morning of March 16, 1244, to a clearing near the foot of the castle still known as the *prat des cramats*. Among them was Ramon de Pereille's wife, Corba, and daughter, Esclarmonde. The 205 men and women, barefoot and dressed only in coarse, dark blue robes, unhesitatingly approached a large, crude construction of logs. With the Royal Catholic Army looking on, the heretics climbed ladders to the top of the rough palisade. There, the Albigenses were tied together in random groups, their backs against stakes rising high overhead. As soon as the French soldiers jumped from the wooden pilings, the Archbishop ordered torches flung into the hastily built cribwork. Prayers murmured by the condemned were soon obscured by the mounting roar of the rapidly rising flames, which were so intense, they forced the armored witnesses to retreat several paces, their arms thrown across their faces.

Occitanians far and wide saw the rising black smoke, and understood what it meant. But no one, save the last four survivors of Montségur, knew what had become of the Cathars' Mani Stone, the Ark of the Covenant.

CHAPTER 11

The Perfection of Paradise

That was a thing called the Grail, which surpasses all earthly perfection.

—Wolfram von Eschenbach,
Parzifal, Book V, 235

The decision made by Hugh de Arcis to risk his elite mountaineer troops on a suicidal mission up the sheer slopes of the Roc de la Tour was motivated in part by an incident that occurred in mid-December of 1243. By then, the 10,000 Royal French Army soldiers laying siege to Montségur had been stalemated by its 500 defenders for the previous seven months. Hence, morale among the king's warriors was already low when several hundred of them marched up one of the goat paths to attack an enemy position. They were not met, however, by the usual archers.

Standing motionless on an exposed precipice not very high above them was a single man awaiting their charge. Wearing a full suit of gleaming, white armor, the immense figure bore a huge, unmarked shield on his left arm, while his right gauntlet grasped a gigantic, unsheathed broadsword. The French stopped in their tracks at the first sight of this formidable apparition, then fled back down the goat path toward camp without offering battle. They reported that their lone opponent was "a Grail knight," against which no mortal could prevail. As the Cathars must therefore have God on their side, the siege was as blasphemous as it was doomed. The men tore off their uniforms and went home.

Their experience was soon known throughout the French camp, where new doubts about the siege spread like a contagion. Commander de Arcis was therefore anxious to establish that the enemy was neither invulnerable nor divinely protected, which his Gascon volunteers proved a few nights later when they took the Roc de la Tour. The mysterious "Grail knight" was never seen again, and fate overtook the residents of Montségur.

What Is the Grail?

But why did the French eyewitnesses to his unexpected appearance immediately recognize him as a representative of Europe's most elusive image? What, precisely, *was* the so-called "Holy Grail," and what, if anything, had it to do with the Ark of the Covenant?

The Grail is most familiar today as the cup that caught the blood of Jesus during his Crucifixion. But this is a twist of the original story introduced by the Burgundian poet Robert de Boron around 1212. His *Joseph d'Arimathie* was itself preceded by several other accounts, in none of which did Christ appear, beginning with the earliest written version by Chretien de Troyes, circa 1190. Both his birthplace (where the Knights Templar were first envisioned) and period (just before the First Crusade set out to conquer Jerusalem) coincide with the location and time crucial to the Ark's restoration in Europe. Chretien's *Perceval, le Conte du Graal*, "Perceval, the Story of the Grail," portrays it as a shining, sacred object borne in procession by a noble-looking woman: "When she entered with the Grail, such a great light spread through the room that the tapers paled like the stars or moon when the sun rises. The Grail was of the purest gold...no gem can compare to those of the Grail."[1]

In this account, the holy article was carried, not by a Catholic priest, but in the arms of a secular woman. While women were firmly excluded from any participation in church affairs, save to a limited degree as nuns, they rose freely throughout the Cathar hierarchy to become Perfectae and share equally in administration of the consolamentum, endura, Manisola, and other sacraments. The Grail's extraordinary luminosity here is descended from previous traditions going back to the Old Testament, Egypt, Atlantis, and Lemuria for its fiery brilliance. Combined with Chretien's stress on the object's "purest gold," it suggests the Grail's identification as the Ark of the Covenant, here described as a cup or serving dish—a play on the Occitanian word for "platter," *grazala*; the Old French *gradal*, "cup"; or the Medieval Latin *gradils* for "plate." Actually, the term antedated Chretien's Grail story by unguessed centuries, if not millennia: It derived from *gral*, used by the ancient Gauls for "power," but closer in significance to *mana*, a word universally known, from Tibet and India through Polynesia to the Americas, indicating the spiritual energy animating all things, especially stones, yet independent from them.

Perceval, le Conte du Graal was the first in a spate of some eight different, obviously allegorical works, mostly written by leading French, British, or German authors, which suddenly appeared in public, minus any literary precedents, from the late 12th to the middle 13th centuries. They achieved broad popularity among educated Europeans—students, scholars, and aristocrats with at least a tinge of heresy—titillated by obvious double meanings and subtle hints of things more whispered than spoken. Isolated from the context of the era in which these "Grail books" were composed, such unheralded proliferation seems inexplicable. But given their production and wide reception bracketed precisely by that period that witnessed the First Crusade, the discovery of the Ark of the Covenant, its custody with the Cathars, and the papal war waged against them, the combined causes of their abrupt existence and instant vogue stand revealed. So too the ulterior meanings behind the courtly story and knightly quest for the elusive object of desire become clear.

In other words, *Perceval* and all the rest were occasioned by the relocation of the Ark from Jerusalem to France, and the subsequent secrecy surrounding its new role and fate. It was something no one was supposed to know about, but many people suspected, thereby forming the ingredients for an engaging controversy. Spiced liberally with political incorrectness and heretical propaganda, these books were premade best-sellers among the educated classes already predisposed against the establishment, whose authorities imposed a smothering despotism on society in the name of God.

Building upon Chretien's unfinished work, a Bavarian knight composed the most complete and authoritative source for the Grail: *Parzifal*. Very popular fiction in its own time, it is still regarded as the masterpiece of medieval German literature. Although Wolfram von Eschenbach's *Parzifal* is a chivalric "romance" of the Middle Ages, scholars agree its narrative is told against a recognizable, if somewhat deliberately blurred, backdrop of actual locations populated by historical figures. It is a somewhat obscured allegory of the author's own time and of the heretical revolution then threatening to overturn Christian society with a new order in Europe. As such, reading between the lines reveals clues to the real persons and events that form an important part of our investigation.

Elaborating on the Cathar theme introduced by de Troyes, Wolfram characterizes the Grail as the "Perfection of Paradise,"[2] just as the "Desire for Paradise" was how the Perfecti described their Mani Stone. He might just as well have been referring to a Perfectae, when he states in the same section, "Such was the nature of the Grail that she who watched over it had to preserve her purity and renounce falsehood." Throughout *Parzifal*, in fact, there is a Cathar-like emphasis on purity. According to the original Grail knight,

Titurel, Parzifal's predecessor, "The Lord of the Grail must be chaste and pure"—the arch prerequisites of every Perfectus. And in words that might have come from a Cathar catechism, Parzifal is warned, "Any man who has pledged himself to serve the Grail must renounce the love of woman."[3] Indeed, Parzifal at first fails in the quest, until his struggle purifies him. His colleague, Galahad, more easily succeeds, because he is a virgin who will have nothing to do with women. But when he at last enters the presence of the Grail, his mind and body cannot contain its grace, and Galahad blissfully expires of rapture.

At King Arthur's Round Table, surrounding the Holy Grail, was the Throne of the Invisible, or the Perilous Seat. Merlin forbade anyone from sitting in it under pain of death (just as close proximity to the Ark of the Covenant meant annihilation), until Perceval (Parzifal) was able to do so with impunity, because his Cathar-like "purity" had pleased the Grail. The Grail itself is "always pure,"[4] and is attended only by "virgin-pure" maidens,[5] whose messenger was Kundry, who wore a black mantle adorned with "many, small turtledoves, the emblem of the Grail."[6] As she did, the Perfecti wore mostly black cloaks (only Cathar bishops were robed in dark blue mantles), and their distinctive badge was the white dove, which decorated the saddles and shields of the Grail Knights.[7] Every Good Friday, associated not only with Christ's resurrection, but also the return of spring and light around the Vernal Equinox, a white dove descended from Heaven to leave a small white wafer on the Grail.[8] According to Markale, "The Cathar baptism is that received when one touches the light that emanates from the Grail,"[9] just as British scholar John Matthews points out that the consolamentum was "a means of transmitting light from one to another."[10] He goes on to observe that the

Cathars' Manisola "seems to have been the same kind of event as when the Grail passed among the knights who served it, and provided them with both literal and spiritual food."[11]

Concern for purifiation predates both the Cathars and Grail romances by thousands of years, back to Ancient Egypt: Before the Egyptian priests could administer to the Ben-Ben Stone in the Great Pyramid, they undertook a ritual cleansing in water brought from Lake Moeris, 72 miles away. Persons entering Solomon's Temple were required to first purify themselves with holy water from a gigantic basin, the yam, outside the entrance. But "purity" also meant "pure blood," as Egyptian priests mostly took over the office from their fathers. Likewise, the men who founded and operated the Order of the Holy Sepulcher became the Latin kings of Jerusalem, and instituted the Templars, who all claimed a royal blood-connection through the Merovingians to Jesus and earlier.

Before he died of advanced old age, Parzifal's father gave the Grail to his son, admonishing him to forever keep it within the family as the holiest heirloom. The sacred object as a Merovingian legacy appears in the old man's desire to pass it on from father to son. "All the Grail's company are chosen ones," Titurel tells Parzifal, "the same seed, which was sown forth from Munsalvaesche into the world."[12] His Grail family seems remarkably similar to the Levites, a tribe of Israelites who alone inherited privileged access to the Ark of the Covenant as its sole priests. "The 'holy' Grail is in the exclusive possession of a sacred lineage going back far in time, very far," Markale observes, "all the way back to King David."[13]

When Parzifal is early expelled from the Grail castle for failing to engage properly in the quest, a disembodied voice calls after him, "May the hatred of the Sun fall on you, you silly goose!" Even during the Middle Ages, this was a bizarre curse, but would have made sense to a Perfectus, to whom light was sacred and the Sun itself the representation of God Almighty. Later, Parzifal learns of the Grail Knights' Cathar class collaboration when he is told, "Poor and rich alike rejoice if their child is summoned to join this company."[14] His mentor was an old hermit, Trevrizent, who never ate "bloody foods"; as renowned Grail scholar Otto Rahn pointed out, "In the 12th and 13th centuries, any Christian who abstained from eating meat was instantly suspected of Cathar heresy. Quite frequently, the pontifical legates who were entrusted with exterminating heresy and the heretics gave anyone suspected of Catharism the choice of eating meat or being thrown into the fire."[15]

In a prequel to *Parzifal* written sometime after 1217, the Grail, which no one was allowed to touch, "hovers" in midair,[16] just as the Old Testament relates that Yahweh floated above the Ark of the Covenant, from which mortals were forbidden all personal contact. The Ark's "mercy-seat" where God made his will known in a fiery cloud is remarkably similar to God's written instructions appearing before the Grail Knights on the "Seat Perilous." A Merovingian connection to the Grail is additionally supported when the Perilous Seat announces in Robert de Boron's *Didot-Perceval*, "454 years after the passion of Jesus Christ this seat will find its master on the day of Pentecost."[17] As it so happened, Pentecost Sunday in the year 481 A.D., 454 years after Jesus's crucifixion at 27 years (considered his age at the time of death by 13th century scholars), coincided with the coronation of Clovis I, the earliest Merovingian king of a united France.

Left unfinished at Wolfram's death around 1220, the *Der Jüngere Titurel*, "The Younger Titurel," was completed some 40 years later by Albrecht von Scharfenberg, another Bavarian poet. It states that the last of Titurel's line, the fifth and final Grail king, would be Parzifal's son, Lohengrin, long regarded as the mythic ancestor of Godfroi de Boullion, and not without cause. Origins of the name are not only pre-Christian, but positively Neolithic. Its pedigree evolved from Ogyrvan or Ogryfran, Loherangrain, and Lorrain Garin, themselves Gaelic spinoffs of the yet older *grian*, the Keltic word for "sun," which paleolinguists believe Germanic occupiers of Ireland during the 7th century B.C. picked up from their stone-age hosts. Its significance is appropriate: The ancient Greek sun-god crossed the sea in a golden skiff drawn by a team of white swans (his animal totem), when Apollo traveled to visit the Hyperborean Maidens, keepers of his solar temple on an island in the far north. In the Lohengrin myth, he is the Swan Knight, because his golden bark is drawn by just one of the birds, who is actually the rightful heir to Brabant in Flanders, in animal guise, who had been cursed by a usurper to the throne. As Lohengrin leaves for the Grail castle, he lifts the young man's curse, thereby freeing Godfroi to rule over his realm.

The story is remarkably reminiscent of Merovingian claims to sovereignty, as expressed in the career of the real-life 11th century Flemish duke. Today, Godfroi's land is referred to as Lorraine, but in his time and long before, he and his people called it Lotharingia, loosely, "the Land of Lohengrin." In the *Chansons de Geste*, from a collection of medieval tales, the *Doon de Mainz*, he is known as the Garin de Lorraine, "the Light of Lorraine," demonstrating the enduring power of a holy word over the last five or more thousand years from megalithic times. It was such millennial continuity that provided everyone involved with the Ark/Grail a simultaneous sense of profound rootedness and potent destiny.

Various interrelated elements surface in Lohengrin's myth: the ancient cult of light, the Holy Grail, stolen royalty, and the Crusader himself as a proto-Grail Knight, all of which led Markale to conclude, "Lohengrin was the ancestor of the kings of Jerusalem, as well as the dukes of Lorraine....What a handsome family tree for Godfroi de Bouillon, himself a hero of the Crusades, and in his own way, a quester for the Grail!"[18] He, after all, initiated the quest that would bring the Perfection of Paradise to France, where it was eventually placed in the care of its Albigensian guardians. In Gerbert de Montreuil's *Roman de la Violette*, composed about 1225, a prophesy announces that the descendants of the Grail King Perceval after his son, the Grail Knight Lohengrin, will liberate the Holy Land by conquering Jerusalem.

In section H-5964 of *The Younger Titurel*, Albrecht seems to be describing the escape of the Cathars with their Mani Stone in Montségur, when he relates that the keepers of the Grail were surrounded by "evil enemies," from whom they sought refuge in the inaccessible mountain-fortress of Muntsalvatch—both Montségur and Muntsalvatch mean Secure or Safe Mountain. *Der Jüngere Titurel* differs most significantly from *Parzifal*, however, in its ambiguous conclusion, which has all of Europe fallen into dark defeat, an apparent allusion to the surrender of Montségur, which took place about 16 years before von Scharfenberg's composition.

Wolfram's spelling of the Grail castle is slightly different, but its meaning is identical. "A noble brotherhood dwells there," he writes in obvious reference to the Cathars defending themselves against Crusaders from across the Continent, "who, with valiant strength, have warded off the people of all lands, so that the Grail is unknown, save to those who have been called by name to Munsalvaesche and the Grail's company."[19] That Munsalvaesche was a poetization of Montségur is made obvious in their simultaneous growth: Wolfram began his epic in 1204, the same year Ramon de Pereille undertook the reconstruction of Montségur into a Cathar stronghold. *Parzifal*, in fact, features "Parilla" as the Grail King. At the time of its composition, the Albigensian Crusade was still five years away, but gathering stormclouds were already apparent; so much so, the military renovation of Montségur was deemed necessary.

Wolfram clearly portrays some Grail Knights as Credentes receiving the consolamentum through the endura to become Perfecti: "When life dies for them *here*, they are given perfection *there*."[20] He mentions "the consolation of the Grail's power,"[21] a transparent reference to the same Cathar initiation ceremony, and repeats their vow of chastity in Book IX: "Any man who has pledged himself to serve the Grail must renounce the love of woman."[22] Its guardians are, in fact, described as "these Templars."[23]

None of this had anything whatsoever to do with institutionalized Christianity. Not an ordained priest, but a secular woman carries the Grail, which is preserved in a castle, not a cathedral, commanded by a king instead of a bishop. "Nor did the Church ever recognize the Holy Grail as a valid Christian relic," according to Helen Mustard and Charles Passage in the introduction to their translation of *Parzifal*,[24] The cause is obvious: the Grail symbolized Cathar heresy. Among the most important researchers of the subject, Otto Rahn, accurately characterized Pope Innocent III's military campaign to exterminate them as "the Crusade against the Grail."

The Exiles' Stone

Wolfram is unequivocal in his definition of that sacred object: "The stone is also called the Grail."[25] He refers to it as an emerald, the origins of which were described by a contemporary poem, *Der Wartburgkrieg*. "The Wartburg War" was a song contest of contending troubadours, one of whom relates how, at the beginning of Creation, Saint Michael the Archangel took Lucifer's "crown from his head in such a way that a stone jumped out of it, which on Earth became Parsifal's stone".[26] Hence, Wolfram called it the *lapsit exillis*. Critics claim he bungled the original, *lapsit ex caelis*, "a stone fallen from heaven," to produce a nonsensical term. But Arnold of Villanova, perhaps the foremost alchemist of his times, used the same Latin term in his *Rosarium Philosophorum*, composed a few years after *Parzifal* appeared.

The early 20th Century British scholar, Arthur Edward Waite, rendered lapsit exillis as the "Exiles' Stone."[27] As such, it epitomizes the sacred object's long migration over the millennia from Lemuria to

Atlantis, Egypt, Jerusalem, and France. It recalls the *lapis exulis*, "the Stone of Exile," used by contemporary cabalists for *Shekhinah*, the materialization of spiritual energy in the physical world. That, in fact, is what the Grail, in all its cultural guises, was to its various owners throughout a long, checkered career. Shekhinah, as the Tabernacle of the Heart, itself suggests the Ark of the Covenant. Lapsit exillis is also a wordplay on *lapis elixir*, the Philosopher's Stone, sought by medieval alchemists as the means by which the base matter of mortality may be transmuted into the shining spirit of godhood. In view of its capacity to transform human consciousness, the Grail or Ark could have been the fulfillment of their highest hopes.

Its jeweled identity recalls the Emerald Tablets carried by Thaut to the Nile Delta, away from the Primal Mound sinking in the distant west. With these, he was said to have founded Pharaonic civilization and built the Great Pyramid, in which he placed the wisdom-inscribed stones after its completion. Here, ancient Egyptian myth and medieval German epic merge in the symbolic emerald to show the Fire Stone's survival from the distant past. The Egyptian Ben-Ben, installed as the Great Pyramid's electrical component and later removed by King Akhenaton to his desert city, derived its name from the Bennu, or phoenix, reborn continuously out of its own ashes, to signify the crystal's eternal energies. So too Wolfram writes of the Grail, "by its power, the phoenix kindles its death-flame from which that bird rises into new life."[28]

The Grail's "emerald" (supremely precious) quality is underscored in *The Younger Titurel*, where it reappears as *jaspis et silix*, from the Latin *iaspis*, understood by the vulgate Bible to be "green."[29] Silix— literally, "flint"—was added to stress the Grail's crystal reality. A 14th century manuscript, the *Speculum Humanae Salvationis*, at the Bibliotheque Nationale in Paris, features an illustration of the Grail castle, at the center of which a large emerald hovers above a six-sided pool of water.

Further hints surface in Titurel himself, its first guardian and the grandson of Barillus, whose name derived from *beryllos*, the sea-green gem or beryl deemed sacred by the ancient Greeks. To them, it was an attribute of Apollo, the divine personification of enlightenment, who inspired their cultural achievements. He was revered by some Cathars under his ancient title, the Son of Morning, or Lucifer, an adoration that won them the charge of "Satanists" from their conventional Christian opponents. The Perfecti conception of Lucifer, from whose crown, or forehead, the emerald Mani Stone came, was not the Devil, but the bringer of light against Yahweh's Old Testament darkness.

Ruins of Apollo's Temple at Delphi, Greece.

Lucifer has a remarkable counterpart in Hindu myth: Shiva, the Vedic god of creative destruction, who is sometimes similarly worshiped as a sun-god at places in India such as Srivilliputhur and the Vaidhyanathaar Temple, 60 miles from Madurai. He is more generally recognized as The Pure One, a title with which the Cathars could have easily identified, and perhaps did, because Shiva too had a precious stone at the center of his forehead. This Pearl of Great Price was the Urna, his godly brow chakra with which he beheld inner wisdom and the soul's perfection. Clearly, some Hindu connection—or at least an Indo-European source common to both—linked Lucifer to Shiva, whose lithic Third Eye signified the sacred stone's power to engender spiritual reality, or bring about the direct experience of God.

Markale points out that Wolfram's Grail is identical to the magical Chwarna stone,[30] which appears in the *Avesta*, a collection of sacred texts belonging to Mazdaism, the religion of light, better known in the West as the Zoroastrian faith. (Although "Avesta" was used beginning in the 2nd century A.D., the term's etymological roots in the old Persian *upastavaka*, "praise (of God)," date it to 1,400 years earlier, when Zoroaster himself wrote many of its hymns.)

Interestingly, this period, circa 1200 B.C., and Zoroaster's retelling of the Chwarna origins in an antediluvian golden age, hark back to numerous other traditions from around the world associating a magical jewel with a lost civilization Plato knew as Atlantis. In the *Avesta*, the Chwarna is a magical stone that radiated truly cosmic powers of regeneration, causing waters to gush from springs, plants to grow, winds to blow, men to be born, or stars and the moon to follow their orbits through the heavens. So too the Grail healed lingering wounds and restored the Waste Land, a formerly beautiful realm despoiled by sinful humanity. The *Avesta* tells how a dove descended from heaven to place a grain of wheat atop the Chwarna, just as Wolfram has a dove (the Cathar symbol) alight on the Grail with a wafer. These Near Eastern parallels with the western European Grail do not constitute, as Markale notes, fabulous theories, but precise facts.[31]

That this "Grail" was the European name for the Ark of the Covenant is made clear by the simultaneous florescence of Grail stories, the Templar discovery in Jerusalem, and the Cathar experience at Languedoc. Comparisons between them reveal they were one and the same object: Both emitted bright light; were surmounted by winged figures (the Grail's doves and the Ark's cherubim); covered in gold; killed, and healed on occasion; held the spirit of God hovering over them in a radiant cloud; could not be approached nor touched on pain of death; inscribed with divine messages; provided food; were associated with sacred food (a white dove left a wafer on the Grail, while the Ark produced manna); had an elite family of hereditary attendants (Levites for the Ark, Templars for the Grail) administer to it; were unpredictable, had a will of their own, dominated human affairs, and demanded purification; shared a common "seat" (the Ark featured a "mercy-seat" where God communicated with mortals, while a "seat perilous" served the Grail for the same purpose); contained a precious stone, which had the power to transform human consciousness. Even the name of the hero who wins the quest and sees the Grail revealed is evocative of attaining the Ark of the Covenant: Parzifal, or "Pierce the Veil"—both Israelite and European versions of the same sacred object portray it veiled from common sight.

As Frank Tribbe pointed out, "it is clearly true that the Grail is claimed to have attributes comparable to the

Ark...something most spectacular had to have happened in the 11th and 12th centuries that excited a few visionaries and intellectuals in northern France and southern Germany."[32]

Ancestors of the Grail

There certainly existed precursors to the Holy Grail. The most famous specimen in the ancient world was the Greek Omphalos, or umbilical stone enshrined at Delphi atop lofty Mount Parnassus overlooking the Gulf of Corinth. The very presence of this sacred object caused the city to be known throughout Classical times as the Navel of the World. The Omphalos was a large, egg-shaped stone that disappeared during the late 4th century, when Christian authorities proscribed its use. An artifact displayed today at the Delphi Museum is a Late Roman era copy in white marble, about 3 feet high—contrary to the quartz crystal original, which was perhaps 2/3 as large. The recreation is nonetheless revealing, as it was sculpted in relief to portray an *agrenon*, or snake charmer's basket. Exoterically, the theme

The Delphic Omphalos.

illustrates Delphi's pythonic myth, described in proceeding paragraphs. But its esoteric significance alludes to the Kundalini, or spiritual "serpent power" deliberately conjured by the Pythia, the site's Shamanic trance-medium, who achieved a heightened state of awareness when her consciousness eresonated with earth-energies transduced through the sacred stone, the Omphalos.

The Pythia

For more than 1,000 years before it was closed, the most important room in the temple at Delphi was the *adyton*, or *zonais*, the "sacred zone," the "navel," regarded by the Greeks as the absolute center of the Earth, where the Greco-Roman world's most respected seer functioned. The white-robed priestess with golden headdress, a virgin selected for her superior psychic abilities, drank once from a sacred spring, then poured some of the holy water on the ground as a libation to Mother Earth. While serving in this office, the young woman was known as a Pythia, from Python, the subterranean serpent of Delphi slain by Apollo in his conquest of the site, where the beast is perpetually "rotting" (*pythein*). He cast the monster's corpse into a cleft on the side of Mount Parnassus, where, forever putrescent, it emits fumes that assist the oracle to function. Apollo's myth signified the sun-god's victory of enlightenment and rebirth over the dark force of ignorance and death.

After chewing a laurel leaf, the Pythia seated herself on a tall bronze tripod in front of the Omphalos, where she fell into a trance while breathing the potent vapors. Shortly thereafter, she was seized by a divine frenzy, during which her utterances were regarded as oracular responses to questions from visiting clients. Likewise, in Wolfram von Eschenbach's story, the Grail was attended by a young virgin,

Repanse de Schoye, similar to the Pythia, and an "Answerer." But the Grail's spokeswoman was Kundry, a wild female, who went into ecstatic frenzies and talked in parables, similar to the divine rages that seized the Delphic priestess when she spoke for Apollo.

Modern historians attribute the renowned accuracy of her pronouncements to temple priests, who cleverly interpreted her often disjointed statements. But

Roman statue (early Imperial Period) of Apollo. Glyptotek Museum, Copenhagen, Denmark.

French geologists investigating the archaeological precinct at Delphi in the late 1990s found that a fissure at the base of the ruined adyton expended unusually high levels of ethylene dioxide, a gas used today by anesthesiologists as a noninvasive sedative. The scientists concluded that anyone confined in a small chamber over the rising gas would be almost overwhelmed with euphoria. And long before their discovery, the narcotic properties of laurel leaves were widely known. Together with the natural sensitivity for which the

Pythia had been chosen, these external influences undoubtedly engendered an altered state of consciousness that may very well have allowed her to envision some higher awareness. This phenomenon would have been substantially magnified by the quartz crystal before her, because Mount Parnassus has always been seismically active. As did the Ben-Ben inside the King's Chamber of the Great Pyramid, or the "stone tablets" in the Ark of the Covenant, the Omphalos resonated with enough tectonic energy to generate a spume of mind-affecting negative ions.

Wolfram von Eschenbach's Pythia-like attendant was Repanse de Schoye, literally Answerer of the Womb, while "Delphi" is a pre-Greek word for womb synonymous with cave.[33] The original oracle was located 7 miles from Mount Parnassus in a cave on the steep side of a hill (modern Sarandauli), known as Korykian, after Kore, the maiden, Persephone. She was the springtime goddess who disappeared into the bowels of the Earth, but reappeared once each year for six months. Her cyclical departure and return mythologized the Earth as the womb-and-tomb principle of eternal life associated with the Navel of the World cult. Cathar troubadours actually addressed the Virgin Mary's womb in their songs as "the Grail of the World."[34] Yet more specifically, the *Litany of Loretto*, contemporary with *Parzifal*, refers to Mary as *foederis arca*, the "Ark of the Covenant."[35]

Delos

The view over Delos, one-time Navel of the World, from inside Apollo's shrine on Mount Kynthos. The circular receptacle for his Omphalos is in the foreground.

According to alternative myth, Deucalion, the son of Prometheus, fled Zeus's Deluge into the Aegean Sea previous to the sacred stone's installment atop Mount Parnassus. He set up the Omphalos near the summit of its highest mountain on Delos, where all the Apollonian rituals later instituted at Delphi were identically practiced for the first time since the Great Flood. The holy object certainly appears to have cast its aura over the small island, because it became the cultural and spiritual mecca of early Classical civilization from before 900 B.C. until sometime in the 6th century B.C., when the growing threat of piracy necessitated the Navel Stone's relocation. Before it was taken to Greece, Delos became the world's foremost artistic treasure-house and religious sanctuary. Wealthy citizens and potentates from all around the eastern Mediterranean vied with one another, filling the islet to overflowing with superb statues, shrines, temples, and all manner of gifts to the Olympian deities, especially Apollo. One rich contributor donated the likeness of a full-grown palm tree—with which the sun-god most identified—realistically reproduced in solid gold: trunk, leaves, and all.

Leading architects, sculptors, musicians, philosophers, poets, playwrights, performers, painters, and craftsmen of all kinds lent their greatness to the otherwise insignificant, barren island. Just as all sacred centers with a Stone of Destiny, Delos was called the Navel of the World, so long as its omphalos was still in Apollo's primeval-looking shrine at Mount Kynthos. The title was particularly appropriate, because Delos lies at the very center of the Dodencanese Island group.

How much, if anything, of ancient Delos or Delphi contributed to events in 13th century Languedoc is impossible to precisely determine, but comparisons are unavoidable. The Cathars too were dualist worshippers of Light over Darkness; the Mani Stone was their own Omphalos; Montségur, their Parnassus; and the Christians shut both places down. Moreover, the Pythia is strangely reminiscent of Wolfram von Eschenbach's virgin Grail-bearer in *Parzifal*.

The archaic shrine of Delian Apollo resembles the vaulted roof-slabs in the King's Chamber of the Great Pyramid.

Ireland's Navel of the World

Ancient Greece did not, however, possess the only omphalos. The late 19th century historian, Terrence O'Neal, told of "the great idol or *castrum* [a "strong structure"] of Kilair, which was surrounded by 12 small ones, and called the 'Stone' or 'Umbilicus of Hibernia' [Keltic Ireland], and, as if placed in the midst and the middle of the land—*medio et meditullio*—Meath itself, wherein this Kilair navel stood, was anciently the central one of the five divisions of Ireland, and is called *Media* by Giraldus Cambrensis," a 12th century chronicler, who cited the same stone at Uisnech as "the Navel of Ireland."[36] O'Neal's folk tradition refers to the dozen monoliths surrounding the oldest building in the world, a Neolithic tomb, today an archaeological park located at Newgrange, in County Meath, overlooking the Boyne Valley north of Dublin.

At 30 feet in height, the circular mound was constructed of granite in 3200 B.C., a century before Egypt's Great Pyramid, its eastern face covered with thousands of white quartz gleaming in the light of dawn. A corridor penetrates the wall to 1/3 of the structure's 180-foot diameter, terminating under a 20-foot high ceiling-vault. On its far wall appears a triple-linked spiral illuminated once each year when the rising sun sends its first rays into the tunnel on the Winter Solstice. This seasonal orientation connects Newgrange with Delphi's shared light-versus-darkness drama, when the serpentine spiral deep in its otherwise black tomb is annually stabbed by an illuminated dagger on a solstice marking the rebirth of longer days. Accordingly, the Neolithic site was, as O'Neal observed, the "Umbilicus of Hibernia."

The Irish Omphalos

Another contender for that title is the Turoe Stone. During the 1850s, it was moved from its original location at the center of the Rath of Feerwore, a megalithic circle close to Kiltullagh, County Galway, in the west of Ireland. Today, the gray-white stone may be found on the front lawn of Turoe House in the town of Loughrea, where it is set in a concrete base surrounded by metal grillework to prevent grazing cattle from using it as a scratching post. At 4 feet high and 2.5 feet across, it is decorated with intricate spirals, circles, curves, whorls, and other swirling forms skillfully picked back in relief from the hard surface. Although typical of a Keltic art style known as La Tène that flourished about 23 centuries ago, some archaeologists suspect Iron Age artists carved these designs on a Neolithic standing stone already venerated for at least 1,000 years. In any case, the symbols, similar to those at Newgrange, were obviously meant to represent energies associated with the monolith, forces produced by the quartzite granite when activated by telluric stress.

Ireland's Omphalos, the Turoe Stone.

Perhaps the Turoe House artifact is Ireland's original omphalos. In Old Irish myth, the Lia Fáil was not a native stone, but carried to Ireland by the Tuatha da Danann, the Atlantean Sea Peoples described in the last chapter. Their mythology has them place the Lia Fáil atop Rath na Riogh, the Fortress of Kings, a 507-foot-high hill at Tara, in County Meath, which also encompasses Newgrange. It does not seem by chance that the Tuatha da Danann's Lia Fáil and ancient Egypt's Ben-Ben should both have been known as the Stone of Destiny. Other Irish omphalli are located at Castlestrange (County Roscommon), Killycluggin (County Cavan), Mullaghmast (County Kildare), and Derrykeighan (County Antrim). Physical resemblances to their Delphic counterpart are likewise apparent, suggesting that Navel-of-the-World cultists operated in both ancient Ireland and Greece.

The Slavic Navel Stone

As much may be said of Eastern Europe, where the Ala-Tuir appears in pre-Christian myth as a sacred gemstone. It was the source of ultimate power at the very center of Bouyan, the sunken island-kingdom from which Slavic ancestors migrated to the Continent across the western ocean. Atlantean parallels are here marvelously supported by obvious affinity with Edgar Cayce's Fire Stone. His Tuaoi and the Ala-Tuir certainly refer to the "mighty, terrible crystal," just as Bouyan and lost Atlantis were obviously the same place described by Plato. Both the Ala-Tuir and Bouyan belong to an enduring folk memory uninfluenced by either an American psychic or a Greek philosopher, which affirms its authenticity and validity.

The Mayas' Sacred Crystal

The Quiche Mayas similarly remembered a Bouyan-esque kingdom on "the other part of the ocean, from where the sun rises, a place called Patulan-Pa-Civan." Their cosmological book, the *Popol Vuh*, or *Book of Counsel*, tells of Balam-Qitze, leader of the U Mamae, or Old Men, Patulan-Pa-Civan's intellectual class, in their evacuation of the doomed homeland. Before he disembarked with them for Yucatan, the "Great Father," King Nacxit, entrusted him with the realm's most sacred object, the crystal Giron-Gagal, which was a "symbol of power and majesty to make the peoples fear and respect the Quiches." Another Mayan text, the *Chilam Balam*, reported:

> The wise men, the Nahuales, the chiefs and leaders, called U Mamae, extending their sight over the four parts of the world and over all that is beneath the sky, and, finding no obstacle, came from the other part of the ocean, from where the sun rises, a place called Patulan. Together, these tribes came from the other part of the sea, from the east, from Patulan.[37]

They landed on the island of Cozumel, just off the coast of Yucatan, where Balam-Qitze safely enshrined the Giron-Gagal in a new temple.

Links to Atlantis

"These stones," concluded William Blackett, the mid-19th century British antiquarian, "must have been brought into Europe and Asia from across the Atlantic Ocean in those great migrations and warlike expeditions of which Plato spoke in the *Timaeus*."[38] Judging from Mayan accounts, he might have included America. While the holy objects in ancient Greek, Irish, Slavic, and Maya traditions appear to have been carried by Atlantean survivors to various parts of the world, none of the stones, clearly, could have been the Grail/ Ark of the Covenant. Rather, all these supremely sacred items originated, as the written and oral records suggest, in Atlantis, where the technology to manufacture them had been passed down from still earlier Lemurian times. "Tuaoi," "Ben-Ben," "Aron ha-Berit," and "Grail" were merely different names a particular power-crystal, one among an unknown number distributed throughout the world, was given by its various owners, as it passed, respectively, from the Atlanteans to the Egyptians, Hebrews, and Western Europeans. As early as *Perceval, le Conte du Graal*, the first account of its kind, Chretien de Troyes wrote of *a* grail, just as the ancient Greek travel-author Pausanias described the Delphic Navel of the World as "one of these stones."[39]

Paralleling Blackett's belief in Atlantean migrations, encyclopedist Robert Hastings believes "the Omphalos [at Delphi] represents the incoming of a new race with different and, on the whole, higher ideas of religion."[40] His observation is underscored by supporting details at the site itself. Parnassus, after whom the oracle's mountain is known, was the inventor of augury and brother to Atlas, who gave his name to and was the first king of Atlantis. Mount Parnassus itself was regarded as the place where Deucalion and Pyrrha, the Greek husband-and-wife deluge heroes, landed after surviving the Great Flood. To celebrate their escape, a commemorative ceremony, the Aigle, was held each spring at Delphi. The Delphic oracle was originally administered by a *hosioi*, or college of five men who could claim direct descent from Deucalion. Why their specific number was chosen perplexed scholars, but Plato states in his dialogue, the *Kritias*, that Atlantean adepts regarded five as a sacred number they incorporated in their rituals. These facts confirm that the Delphic Navel of the World was established by culture-bearers

from Atlantis, who perpetuated their spirituality on the heights of Mount Parnassus.

The sunken city seems to reappear even as late as the Middle Ages. In describing the area surrounding the Grail castle, von Eschenbach wrote "it was rounded, as from a lathe,"[41] which compares with Plato's description of the Atlantean realm, which appeared "turned as with a lathe out of the center of the island."[42] The Grail too was located atop a great mountain on an island far out at sea. And the comparison goes even further: The city of the Grail comprised "clusters of towers, and numerous palaces stood there, marvelously embattled";[43] "The island [of Atlantis] in which the palace was situated—they surrounded by a stone wall, on either side placing towers. This they continued to ornament in successive generations, every king surpassing the one who came before him to the utmost of his power, until they made the building a marvel to behold for size and beauty. And there were many temples."[44] Otto Rahn observed, "Invariably, a vast expanse of water and an enchanted mountain appear in all these legends and myths."[45]

The most detailed description of the Grail metropolis is found in *The Younger Titurel*. Here, the city's concentric arrangement, golden wall adornment, and bronze columns combine with the castle's sacred hill, high altar, and side shrines to resemble Plato's portrayal of his lost capital with its great temple. The medieval German and ancient Greek accounts both emphasize the rich timberland surrounding their cities, but von Scharfenberg alone stressed that in the woods about the Grail castle grew the incombustible *aspinde*, from which Noah built his ark, yet another link between the Great Flood and the Perfection of Paradise. It would appear, then, that von Eschenbach's Grail city and Plato's Atlantis were one and the same place, a conclusion bolstered by more internal evidence or hints in *Parzifal*.

Book IX[46] cites Flegetanis, a "heathen" scholar, as the original source for the account. "He wrote the adventure of the Grail" in 1200 B.C., the same date for the final destruction of Atlantis. As a survivor of the cataclysm, did Flegetanis introduce the story to Bronze Age Europe? Markale points out that the name derived from Falak-Thani, Arabic for Mercury-Hermes, the Romano-Greek version of Thaut.[47] This was the Egyptian deluge hero, bearer of the Emerald Tablets to the Nile Delta from the Primal Mound sinking in the distant west. A credible Atlantean motif seems operative here, and is reaffirmed by the Grail's characterization as the Navel of the World.

CHAPTER 12

Where Is the Ark of the Covenant?

Now, if anyone could really understand the nature of these things, it seems to me that he would be possessed by the most divinely formed beauty, and would be able to renounce every other thing that is desired.

—Philo Judaeus on the
Ark of the Covenant, circa 40 A.D.

Mount Moriah

Some scholars, mostly Israeli, believe the Ark of the Covenant still lies where it was originally hidden before the First Temple fell to Nebuchadnezzar more than 2,500 years ago, in one of the innumerable caves that honeycomb Mount Moriah. Its discovery is made impossible, they state, because Jerusalem is the most contentious site on Earth, where the religious intolerance and mutual animosity of three faiths collide to render the merest archaeological attempt blasphemous. An excavation anywhere at the Temple Mount would ignite yet another holy war.

Rome

Other researchers conclude that Emperor Titus succeeded where King Herod failed in 70 A.D., when, with Roman thoroughness, he found the buried Ark of the Covenant and brought it back to the Eternal City (Rome) along with all the other spoils of war. There, it was under lock and key in the imperial treasury at the Temple of Saturn for the next 341 years, until Visigoths under their tribal leader, Alaric, sacked Rome. In the midst of barbarian pillaging, the Ark disappeared, broken up or melted down for its gold.

England

During the late 12th century, as popular interest in the Holy Grail was beginning to flourish, monks at Glastonbury in southwest England claimed that Joseph of Arimathea arrived there 30 years after the Crucifixion bearing the chalice of the Last Supper. Through this vessel, God commanded the construction of an abbey to house the sacred object. Centuries later, the building was destroyed during the

Reformation, when all Church lands were forfeited to the Crown. Prior to these troubles, the Grail was supposedly buried somewhere beneath the Abbey ruins, or tossed into a nearby stream that still runs red with holy blood. That is what famous authors Michael Baigent, Richard Leigh, and Henry Lincoln believe is the real meaning of the Grail, the *sang real*, or "royal blood" of Jesus, as it survived in descendants through his lover or wife, Mary Magdalene. His heirs included the Merovingians, the rightful kings of France, whose power was usurped in 800 A.D. by Carolingian intrigues; their, and consequently Christ's, living legacy is alleged to still exist in the members of a secret society, the Priory of Sion.

Again in England, a small stone cup, possibly a Roman era scent container, was found at Hawkstone Park. Investigator Graham Phillips wonders if the humble artifact is "the ointment jar of Mary Magdalene and the historical Holy Grail" that caught drops of Jesus's blood, and was brought by Joseph of Arimathea to Britain during the mid-1st century. Since its discovery in 1920, the artifact has been "returned to the Grail Chapel at Whittington Castle," in Shropshire.[1] "But in the texts of the Vulgate," according to another Grail specialist, Jean Markale:

> There is...certainly no mention of some kind of container in which he [Joseph of Arimathea] would have collected the blood of Christ...but that hasn't prevented certain authors of apocryphal books—or those judged as such—from stating this....It is important, however, to know that the name Arimathea means 'the tombs,' which casts a shadow of doubt on the authenticity of this character.[2]

Ethiopia

Tales describing the Ark of the Covenant's arrival in distant Ethiopia even before the First Temple was destroyed have circulated for centuries. The story goes that the country was known as Sheba nearly 3,000 years ago, when its queen paid her famous visit to Solomon in Jerusalem. Following her return home, she bore his child, Menelik I. When the boy came of age, he went to Israel, where he met his father for the first time. The old king was overjoyed to see his son, and promised him whatever his heart desired. But when Prince Menelik asked for the Ark of the Covenant, Solomon refused, offering anything else in its place. The young prince promised to think it over and make a new request the next morning. But during the night, he and some servants broke into the Temple and tore the Ark from its shrine-room in the Holy-of-Holies. When the priests arose at dawn to find the *debir* looted, they sounded the alarm. By then, the Ethiopians had a long head start on the Israeli authorities, and disappeared over the African border. Solomon lamented the theft, but declared that the Jews no longer needed the Aron ha-Berit anyway, and were still God's Chosen People. Welcomed home with his stolen goods, Menelik set up the Ark in the capital at Axum, where it supposedly reposes to this day in a church under constant guard, because no one, save only a single man chosen as its attendant, is allowed to see it.

The source for this story is the *Kebra Nagast*, a collection of various manuscripts known as *The Book of the Glory of Kings*. None of the manuscripts provide any indication concerning the identity of its compilers, nor when the papers were written. Although speculation dates the *Kebra Nagast* to the late 13th century, Prince Lalibela told crusaders of the Ark's location in Axum 100 years before, when he fled his Ethiopian homeland around 1160 to reside in Jerusalem for the next 25 years. Earlier still, a much-traveled Christian monk, Cosmos Indicopleustes, visited Ethiopia during the 6th century and testified to the existence of a small building where the Ark was said to have been enshrined. Its first known reference in Axum was made by Rufinius, a Byzantine theologian writing at the end of the 4th century of Ethiopia's premiere bishop, Frumentius. However, even this mention of the Ark in East Africa occurs some 1,200 years after Menelik supposedly made off with it.

That nothing in any pre-Christian source, including the Old Testament, so much as alludes to his story suggests it was fabricated to win over Ethiopians for the new religion. Additionally, the Queen of Sheba was not Ethiopian, but a South Arabian monarch from the historic kingdom of Saba, in what is now Yemen, as archaeologists have recognized since the 1960s. Additionally, the Ark of the Covenant was Israel's greatest treasure, locked in its own shrine within the Temple, where it was perpetually guarded by Levite tribesmen who killed anyone foolish enough to approach it, save only the high priest, and on occasion, the king. Moreover, in the highly unlikely event the Ark was stolen, they would have relentlessly pursued the thief to the ends of the Earth, not given up the chase half-heartedly, as the *Kebra Nagast* describes.

Childress writes of Menelik's Israeli adventure: "Assuming the story of this visit is true, it is most likely that the real Ark did in fact remain at the temple in Jerusalem, and that a duplicate Ark was taken to Axum."[3] Charpentier found it equally implausible that "Solomon's son was able to steal the Ark from the Holy-of-Holies which was so amply guarded. The Temple was forbidden to strangers on pain of death. But it would not seem at all impossible that Solomon should have had a copy...made...of the Ark, to hand to his son, no doubt after due instruction."[4] If so, then the object revered today in Axum, although not the Ark itself, may be an authentic copy dating back almost 3,000 years, and therefore an invaluable artifact. But even this generous interpretation of the *Kebra Nagast* collapses when we realize that "Ethiopia" did not exist at the time of the events the manuscript portrays. The region was then known as Napata, an Egyptian colony in upheaval, and did not become a kingdom, the biblical Kush, until 755 B.C., 165 years *after* Menelik supposedly returned from Israel with an ark, real or otherwise.

Author Graham Hancock tried to lend some credibility to the idea of the Ark in Ethiopia by reinterpreting its story in the light of ancient history. He postulated that Levite priests spirited it away from Jerusalem around 650 B.C., some 130 years before Nebuchadnezzar destroyed the First Temple, because Israel's wicked king, Manasseh, had profaned the Holy-of-Holies with the introduction of Babylonian cult-statues. Via either a long water route and land passage from Upper to Lower Egypt, or southward through the Arabian peninsula, the Levites arrived with their sacred burden at the small island of Elephantine, in the Nile River.

Here, they raised a new temple for the Ark, in which it was enshrined until the building was destroyed during the 5th century B.C. Once again, the priests picked up their charge and headed south, crossing the border into Ethiopia, where it was installed at a simple tabernacle constructed on another island, Tana Kirkos, for the next 800 years. Sometime during the late 4th century A.D., the first Christian bishop mentioned in the Byzantine theologian's account, Frumentius, removed the Ark to Axum, the capital city, and set it up in a church dedicated to Saint Mary, the Mother of Christ, its present location.

Or maybe not. That Ark may be a replica of a replica, because some traditions state that the Ark (or its facsimile) was destroyed in the 16th century, when Axum fell to the Somalian armies of Ahmed Ibn Ibrahim, also called Ahmed Gran, the Left-Handed. Jesuit missionaries in Ethiopia likewise claimed to have demolished the Axum Ark as a blasphemous counterfeit.

Rather than taking the Ark of the Covenant out of Jerusalem, the Levites would have far more likely hidden it somewhere within Israel's borders, most probably through the debir's trapdoor, purpose-built into the Temple for just such an emergency. Who would have dared assume responsibility for risking the Ark across bandit-ridden Arabia, much less down the length of the Nile in the very country from which the Ben-Ben Stone, now masquerading as the Aron ha-Berit, had been stolen by Moses? For Jews, Egypt represented the worst enemy territory, the land from which, after all, the Exodus had taken place. No one in his right mind would have considered reentering Egypt, and certainly not with the Ark of the Covenant.

Japan

While Ethiopia has been long touted as the Ark of the Covenant's final resting place, its alleged existence in Japan is far less well-known. In 1990, Nobuhiro Yoshida (Professor of Languages, International University, Hiroshima), followed up on local legends about the artifact's location on a mountain in the Tokushima prefecture. To determine what, if anything, might be found as the basis for such a wild claim, he led 15 members from Kitakyushu's Japan Petrograph Society to the summit of Mount Tsurugi, 6,000 feet above sea level. It was here that peculiarly

dressed foreigners were said to have arrived in several large vessels by sailing up the Yoshino River during the remote past. The flotilla passed through the Kii Channel to land at a small village, Funa-hate, where the strangers disembarked after destroying their ships. Interestingly, *funa* is Japanese for "ship," and *hate* signifies "final mooring."

From Funa-hate, the visitors moved on to Mount Tsurugi, or Sword Mountain, carrying a kind of palanquin, common in Asia as a covered litter, usually for one passenger, transported by poles on the shoulders of four men. The mountain derived its name from a ceremonial sword said to have been interred with the Ark in a cave, the entrance to which was sealed and concealed. Over time, all trace of the strangers vanished when they were absorbed into the native population.

The Tokushima myth has been researched by regional scholar Hiroshi Ohsugi, who believes it relates the arrival of Levite priests fleeing occupied Jerusalem in 589 B.C., and their subsequent arrival on Japanese shores with the Ark of the Covenant. In the course of his investigations during the late 20th century, he learned a variant of the tradition that has the Hebrews setting themselves up at Mount Kami-yama, literally God's Mountain. Its summit is crowned by the ruins of a small shrine that used to draw area worshippers, who believed their prayers for good fortune were answered by the Ark of the Covenant buried there. Local historians confirm that voluntary guards stood watch over some kind of secret site atop Mount Kami-yama until after World War II. Even today, villagers at its foot preserve curious flags emblazoned with faded Hebrew letters as part of their town treasury.

Mr. Ohsugi's investigations were preceded in 1911 by ethnologist Takatarou Kimura, who concluded that the people in the Uwajima district, on the southeastern part of Shikoku Island, and likewise in the Tokushima prefecture, were the mixed though direct descendants of ancient Semites. He based his conclusion on alleged dialectical affiliations between the language of Uwajima residents and Hebrew. Other comparisons included the royal attire of Japan's first emperor, Tenno Jimmu, and his warriors, with traditional garments worn by the Levite priests. Kimura also found that the imperial household's funeral ceremonies, which differ radically from common mortuary practices, bore striking similarities to Hebrew rites for the dead.

Following the Second World War, in 1947 an American rabbi visited Tokushima prefecture with special permission from General Douglas MacArthur to look for the lost Ark of the Covenant, and found nothing. Professor Yoshida's expedition some 50 years later was somewhat more productive, when he and his JPS colleagues climbed to the summit of Mount Tsurugi. There, they found ancient rock art previously unknown to Japanese archaeology. While the enigmatic petroglyphs did not suggest any Hebrew influence, the images confirmed that the peak was revered as a sacred site in prehistory. At the mountaintop, Professor Yoshida and company visited the Shrine of the Sword, which still exists. Nearby, to the northwest, beneath the summit, a guide took them to the Gyouja-ana, or Mountain-Priest's Cave, some 60 to 90 feet deep. Gyouja-ana is one of Mount Tsurugi's numerous, mostly unexplored caves, which Professor Yoshida speculates may contain the lost Ark.

The Ark's relocation to Japan seems far-fetched, until we realize that Solomon operated his own fleet of ships eminently capable of navigating trade routes along the Indian subcontinent and southeast Asia, into the Pacific Ocean. Their voyages to Lebanon for cedar and more-distant Ophir, probably South Africa, returning to Israel with gold, were frequent and well-attested. A plausible scenario has the Levites boarding one of their long-range freighters with the Aron ha-Berit before Jerusalem fell to Nebuchadnezzar, then sailing as far as Japan. Their selection of Mount Tsurugi likewise makes sense, because it is a dormant volcano still prone to the kind of seismic activity the Ark would have required to function as intended.

Otto Rahn's Obsession

Perhaps the most controversial explanation of the Grail/Ark's fate concerns a great, if troubled scholar who lost his life in the search. From early childhood, Otto Wilhelm Rahn's fascination for the Holy Grail developed into an obsession undeterred by his university studies in jurisprudence, philosophy, and history. After years of passionate investigation, he grew convinced that the Grail Knights were none other than the Cathars, who concealed the Mani Stone somewhere in the Pyrenees Mountains just prior to their immolation. Beginning in 1928, the 24-year-old Rahn traveled widely throughout Switzerland, Italy, France, and Spain, researching the Albigensian period at public and private libraries, and visiting important historic sites in the Perfecti drama.

By the early summer of 1929, he had headquartered himself at Lavelanet, a small village in the Languedoc, from which he conducted his scientific expeditions to the ruins atop Montségur and related locations in the vicinity. Rahn was at first resented by the natives, known for their fiercely provincial pride, not the least because he was German. Residents suspected his interest in their land was less archaeological than military, and some toughs beat him badly enough to send him to the local hospital for a few days. Immediately following his release, he resumed his quest, made somewhat easier after the inhabitants learned he was fluent in their dauntingly insular Occitanian dialect. There was a slight thaw in local animosity, as a few old-timers volunteered what they knew of the region to the indomitable stranger. He regarded their oral traditions most highly, and later credited them with important contributions to his investigations.

Back in Paris, Rahn found that all his patrons had been ruined by the deepening economic depression sweeping the industrialized world, and he was unable to find a publisher for the French edition of his book, *Das Kreuzzug gegen den Gral*, or *Crusade Against the Grail*. In serious financial straits now, more fundamental concern for food and shelter made him despair of ever being able to further pursue his life's mission. He did not realize it at the time, but the world was about to change radically and forever. On January 30, 1933, Adolf Hitler became the third Reich's Chancellor, and the head of his elite SS (*Schutzstaffel*, or Protection Squads) began searching for an appropriate facility to serve as an officers' training school. When Heinrich Himmler was shown Welwelsburg Castle the following November 3, he decided that very night that it was an ideal setting.

The late Gothic-style fortress was an unusual, triangular configuration with massive walls connected to a trio of equidistant, round towers, its plan conforming to a delta-shaped plateau sloping above the floor of Westphalia's Alma Valley, in Central Germany. Raised between 1603 and 1609, it was originally intended to serve as a second residence for the Prince Bishop of Paderborn. But the construction site was steeped in far more ancient origins. Himmler had them in mind when he said of the Welwelsburg, "May in this castle the spirit of the most ancient past be the spirit of the future!"[5] To reaffirm that spirit at Welwelsburg, he called in experts from the Ahnenerbe.

In 1935 Himmler established a scientific foundation, the *Deutsches Ahnenerbe—Studiengesellschaft für Geistesurgeschichte* (German Ancestry—Research and Teaching Society) to investigate the anthropological and cultural history of the German folk. By then, he knew of Otto Rahn's work, had offered him much-needed financial assistance, and now invited him to renew his Grail quest with the Ahnenerbe. The young scholar henceforward devoted every waking hour to his investigations and the completion of his book. Its publication in 1937 created something of a sensation, and the author found himself invited to give public lectures about his conclusions. Rahn combined his Ahnenerbe membership with rank in the SS, and his future seemed assured.

The last two years of Rahn's life, however, were so enigmatic, biographers have been hard-pressed to determine precisely what happened. They do know he began work on another book about the Inquisition's persecution of the Cathars, *Luzifers Hofgesint*, or *Lucifer's Court*, eventually published just before the outbreak of World War II. But the sharp turn in his fate is largely mysterious. Rahn was suddenly demoted and ordered to perform disciplinary duties for a short time at a concentration camp. After his release, he resigned from the Ahnenerbe, then took his own life in March of 1939. Suggestions were made that the cause of his misfortune was his homosexuality, Jewish origins, or both. These speculations are groundless, however, because SS men discovered as homosexuals were not demoted and sent to a concentration camp for a few weeks, but executed by firing squad, and all memory of their former existence expunged. Background checks of applicants, especially their genealogical roots, were very strict. In the unlikely event an SS man's Jewish ancestry was uncovered, he would have been simply expelled. Rahn was supposed to have become disillusioned with the Third Reich, and killed himself in despair.

In late spring of 1938, Rahn was granted permission to undertake a secret expedition to the Languedoc accompanied only by six young cadets, one older officer, and a professor. Relations with France were far from exemplary at the time, so the nine Germans traveled under civilian passports as archaeology students and teachers from the University of Munich, where the professor taught classes in medieval history. During their lengthy train trip, Rahn could barely contain his enthusiasm. Against orders and the only officer's frustrated protestations, he told his companions that the cause of their covert journey was on behalf of an apparent breakthrough in his research; namely, to verify his conclusion concerning the whereabouts of Wolfram von Eschenbach's Stone of Exile.

He recalled that during his previous expeditions to Languedoc, he learned from an old shepherd, "Long ago, when the walls of Montségur were still standing, the Cathars kept the Holy Grail there. Their citadel was in danger. The armies of Lucifer had besieged it." One of them "threw the sacred jewel into the depths of the mountain. The mountain closed up again, and in this manner was the Grail saved. When the devils entered the fortress, they were too late. Enraged, they put to death by fire all of the Pures, not far from the rock on which the castle stands, in the Field of the Stake."[6]

Rahn's line of investigation was directed by this and other similar local accounts, until he believed he had sufficiently narrowed his research to justify an expedition for possible recovery of the Holy Grail. "My duty is to find it," he earnestly instructed his companions, "Yours, to help me bring it safely to the Reich." While the cadets were thrilled by the prospect, swearing to die protecting the lost Stone of Exile, their commanding officer in mufti was sullenly incredulous, and the accompanying professor quietly amused.

No sooner had the Germans detrained near Lavelanet, where Rahn spent his first Occitanian summer nine years before, than he led them straight beyond Ornolac-Ussat-les-Bains on the highway leading from Toulouse to Barcelona. They hiked and climbed into the Sabarthes of the Pyrenees Mountains, exploring caves and peering down crevices, but finding nothing of significance and encountering no other hikers for more than a week. On the 10th day of their expedition, they arrived at a kind of overhanging rock shelter, high up a mountain slope facing the morning sun. Rahn studied the sheaf of unbound notes always stuffed in his pockets, then entered the low-ceilinged formation. At its far end, perhaps 30 feet from the narrow entrance, the others were surprised to see him suddenly attack the back wall with a mountaineer's pick. Grabbing their own, three cadets joined him in hammering away, to what purpose they could not guess. After perhaps 15 minutes of sweaty labor, however, everyone was shocked to see the entire wall abruptly collapse, exposing a small chamber, approximately 10 feet wide and 5 feet deep, but relatively high, at about 10 feet. The room gave every appearance of having been a natural space slightly modified or terra-formed by the hand of man a very long time ago.

At its center was a crude, though unquestionably artificial, rock altar supporting just one object: an exceptionally large quartz crystal. After pausing in silence before it for some moments, Rahn quietly ordered the stone carefully placed in the special carrier brought along just for this purpose. The stone was heavier than expected, requiring two cadets to lift it at either end into the container. The crystal's overall length was a few inches more than 2 feet, and approximately 10 inches at its widest point, but was most memorable for its exceptional clarity.

From the moment of discovery, Rahn was a changed man. His ordinarily ebullient good nature grew somber, he spoke little, and seemed lost in his own thoughts most the time. On their homeward journey, the men wondered among themselves if he was disappointed with the results of his quest. When one of them ventured to ask him if the crystal they found was, in fact, the Holy Grail, he snapped, "What else?!"

An experienced smuggler, the SS officer overseeing the little operation had no difficulty getting their prize past French customs via a false-bottom valise, and soon the crystal was set up on its own pedestal in the Welwelsburg.

The object did not "officially" exist. After all, it had been removed illegally from a foreign country already hostile to the Third Reich. Even after the fall of Paris in 1940, the real origins of Rahn's find could not be acknowledged, because the German authorities would tolerate nothing that might upset their important collaboration with the Vichy French.

Although its recent, commandeered origins were entirely classified, virtually everyone in residence at the castle—even many visitors who passed through the Welwelsburg gates—had heard at least something about the mysterious item locked in the so-called King Arthur Room, to which only Rahn held the key. Shortly after returning from the Sabarthes with his find, he sometimes yielded to requests from dignitaries curious about the alleged Grail. On one occasion, a high-ranking SS commander remarked after seeing it that the quartz was indeed a fine specimen, but obviously did not merit the diplomatic risks to obtain a mere crystal, as superior examples were on public display in the mineralogy wing at Berlin's German Museum of Natural Sciences. Rahn responded hautily, *"Hic lapis exilis extat precio quoque vilis spernitur a stultis, amatur plus ab edoctis."* He was quoting a line from the *Rosarium Philosophorum*, by Arnold di Villanova, a 13th century contemporary of Wolfram von Eschenbach, to the effect, "This stone of exile is indeed of trifling value to fools, therefore all the more precious to the wise." His arrogance got him into trouble, as the SS commander was fluent in Latin, and reported him in unequivocal German to the Reichsführer.

Himmler himself began developing grandiose notions about Welwelsburg and its stone. No longer interested in the old fortress as a mere school, he envisioned it as the seat of a knightly order embodying the highest, purest conception of National Socialism (Nazism) in the elite of the elite—the SS leadership. In time, the castle would become a Teutonic mecca with its own Kabah, eventually developing into the spiritual center of the entire Aryan world. Plans were laid and architectural models created for an extensive expansion project that featured the citadel as the hub of an ideal administrative center as large as a town. Perhaps patterned after Plato's 4th century B.C. description of Atlantis, it was to be arranged in concentric rings, but the war prevented construction of Himmler's Grail city.

He had already established its metaphysical focal point in Welwelsburg's north tower, where a stone-lined chamber, known as the Gruppenführersaal, or Group Leaders' Hall, featured a massive oaken roundtable seating a dozen leaders. At the center of this Arthurian piece of furniture stood Rahn's crystal Grail on its wrought-iron pedestal over a large, stylized swastika of 12 SS runes forming a sun-wheel floor design. Himmler often referred to the Gruppenführersaal as *das Mittelpunk der Neuen Welt*, the Center of the New World.[7] In this, he echoed the millennia-old association between a power-gem and the Navel of the World that resulted wherever it was set up. His consciousness had been altered into the same kind of spiritual megalomania close proximity to the crystal formerly engendered in the Cathars, Templars, Moses, Akhenaton, and all those other custodians of the Fire Stone deep into prehistory.

The Welwelsburg Stone, as it became known, was moved throughout the north tower from one room to another, as occasion demanded. A provision for its temporary placement was provided in a ceremonial crypt, the Walhalsaal, or Valhalla Chamber, located directly below the Gruppenführersaal. At the precise center of a sunken area in the middle of the room, directly beneath a stylized swastika in relief at the apex of the overhead dome, was a concentric circle for the quartz crystal from Languedoc. Of this strange "Realm of the Dead" Stephen Cook and Stuart Russell write, "Although known to be the quintessence of Himmler's dream, its exact purpose still remains an unsolved mystery. Thus, even today, the North Tower is surrounded in a veil of secrecy and suspense."[8]

Otto Rahn could not escape the influence of that mystery. As punishment for his disrespect to a superior officer, he lost his rank as Unterscharführer (although not his SS membership), and was ordered to serve a three-week tour of duty at the Dachau concentration camp outside Munich. Worse, he was banned from the Welwelsburg—and from the presence of his beloved Mani Stone—until and unless his behavior significantly improved. Shortly after completing his disciplinary sentence, he tendered his resignation from both the Black Corps and the Ahnenerbe in early 1939, then hiked alone into the Tyrolean Alps, where he died of exposure amid the snows of the Wilderkaiser. As Christopher Jones observes in his English translation of *Crusade Against the Grail*, "he ended his life in the style of the ritual Cathar endura."[9]

Rahn had written in that same book about the Albigensians:

> *Their doctrine allowed suicide but demanded that one did not put an end to his life because of disgust, fear, or pain, but in a perfect dissolution from matter. This kind of endura was allowed when it took place in a moment of mystical insight into divine beauty and kindness. For them, death was nothing more than changing dirty clothes, a little like butterflies abandoning the chrysalis to lose themselves in the radiant springtime....The transit from one state to the other is not at all as cruel as it may appear.*[10]

The timing of Rahn's endura, as was his death, was deliberate. It took place on March 13, the day before the Cathars celebrated their last Manisola, prior to their mass immolation at the prat des cramats, 695 years before.

The World War that erupted six months following Rahn's endura did not inhibit the transformation of Welwelsburg into a 20th century Navel of the World. On July 12, 1940, Adolf Hitler himself issued a directive authorizing Himmler to carry out whatever he deemed "necessary for the completion of his task,"[11] which would continue almost to the end of hostilities. When Himmler was given charge of the SS in 1929, it had just 280 followers. After the Third Reich went to war against the Soviet Union, it numbered almost 2 million, nearly half of whom were not German. Foreign volunteers from all over Scandinavia, the Baltic, the Balkans, the Ukraine, Spain, Italy, and even former enemies from France and Russia filled out entire divisions of Waffen-SS, or Armed-SS. Himmler's dream of Welwelsburg as the metaphysical hub of the Aryan world seemed to be coming true.

But in late March of 1945, troops of the 1st U.S. Army's Third Armor Division, Spearhead, penetrated Westphalia, and were about to surround his Grail castle. On the same day an evacuation order was given, Himmler dispatched demolition experts headed by SS-Hauptsturmführer Heinz Macher to deprive the Americans of the dream fortress. At 1600 hours, March 31, it was virtually destroyed by a series of powerful explosions that left only the unfinished north tower relatively undamaged. From it Macher or one of his men had rescued the Gruppenführersaal's crystal, a foresightful move, as the smoldering ruins were almost immediately thereafter plundered by souvenir-hungry soldiers and local villagers made desperate by the war for anything of value.

So extensive was the damage to Welwelsburg that its reconstruction, begun in 1949, needed 30 years to complete. Today, it is a popular tourist attraction, showcasing some surviving artifacts and photographs from its checkered past, although the north tower, site of Himmler's "Center of the New World," is off-limits to the public. Whatever became of the Welwelsburg Stone has so far not been determined with any degree of certainty, beyond unconfirmed reports that one of Heinz Macher's men buried it deep in a glacier of the Bavarian Alps. There it supposedly remains and will continue undiscovered until the ice concealing it melts.

The White Lady of the Pyrenees

A less radical, although hardly less provocative possibility for the Ark of the Covenant's present whereabouts contends it is still functioning properly and impacting the lives of millions of people. Its modern history began in 1858, when a common French girl, Bernarde-Marie Soubirous, claimed to have made numerous sightings of a mysterious "White Lady" in a grotto at the foot of the Pyrenees Mountains. Her visions took place at Massabielle, Lourdes, not far from Montségur where the Perfecti met their fiery deaths 614 years before. Return appearances by Soubirous to the grotto were attended by ever-growing throngs of spectators, not all of them devout, who witnessed her kneel to speak, sometimes for an hour or more, with, she always insisted, the Mother of God. Meanwhile, the apparition was invisible to hopeful onlookers.

After some five months of one-on-one meetings with the Blessed Virgin, the teenager was subjected to rigorous civil and clerical inquiry. Popular sentiment on behalf of Soubirous's credibility accelerated until the Catholic Church officially admitted to the validity of her claims and recognized the Cult of Our Lady of Lourdes. Since then, about three million persons visit the pilgrimage-town each year, many seeking relief for various ailments from the allegedly curative powers of the freshwater spring that runs by the grotto.

This is the famous story of Bernadette of Lourdes, which may help explain what became of the Cathars' Mani Stone after they smuggled it out of their doomed fortress. According to Bernadette, "And one day, she told me to eat a plant that was growing at the same spot where I was to drink, only once."[12] These instructions from the White Lady were identical to ritual procedure at Delphi, where the Pythia chewed a laurel leaf and drank "only once" from the holy spring before Apollo spoke through her. Mary would then direct Bernadette to dig in the earth for a sacred spring. Although no such water source, miraculous or otherwise, was known to exist at Massabielle, the girl scratched a few times in the ground to bring forth the first drops of an unsuspected gusher that was soon producing some 25,000 gallons every 24 hours. As was the sacred spring at Delphi, the one at Lourdes is thought to be curative by the 50,000 sufferers who annually seek its waters, just as Apollo's spring attracted patrons from all over the civilized world. Furthermore, Bernadette's first vision took place on February 11, the seventh day of Bysios in ancient Greece—the birthday of Apollo.

The scene of her otherworldly encounters was a grotto—a Navel of the World, the Delphic "womb." The White Lady told Bernadette that a regular procession should be instituted to the grotto, reminiscent of the processions at the Grail Castle and at Delphi. A chapel to the Cult of Our Lady of Lourdes was erected at the grotto, just as the original oracle of Apollo in Greece was worshiped at a shrine near the watery Korykion cave, after Kore, the Virgin. Both Bernadette and the Delphic Pythia

were naïve young virgins who fell into divine ecstasies, during which they uttered words attributed to a supernatural being of light.

Statue (near 2,000-year-old burial mound in Ridgeland, Wisconsin) of the blue-robed "White Lady" associated with the Navel of the World, Holy Grail, Delphic Pythia, Blessed Virgin, and earth-energies.

Some of these Pythian elements are partially revealed in local folklore that long predated events at Lourdes. One such story told how a boy was directed by the White Lady, disguised as an old woman, to find a laurel flower near a special stone at a fountain; the early 20th century mythologist, Andre Massignon, discovered no less than 36 versions of this tale in the Pyrenees.[13] They go back in France to the last day at Montségur, when the Perfectae Esclarmonde de Foix perished with her fellow Cathars at the prat des cramats. Since then, her spirit, in the form of a pure-white woman, has been reportedly seen by numerous Pyrenees inhabitants, mostly children.

There also appears to be a connection between the White Lady and the Holy Grail. As Lohengrin's did, the Virgin Mary that Bernadette saw refused to identify herself until asked repeatedly. Also, in Wolfram von Eschenbach's *Parzifal*, the whiteness of Repanse de Schoye, the Grail queen, is emphasized: "So radiant was her countenance that everyone thought the dawn was breaking."[14] He portrayed her as the bearer of a vessel containing the Stone of Exile, the world's most powerful source of regeneration. As such, she bears a striking resemblance to the Keltic goddess Cerridwen, the White Mare, who possessed a cauldron of renewal from lost Avalon. As the "Island of Apple Trees," Avalon's resemblance to Atlantis, with the Hesperides' "Tree of Life" at its center, is unmistakable.

In his *Kritias*, Plato stated that the primeval woman of Atlantis was Leukippe, likewise a White Mare. He wrote that the most sacred ceremony of her society featured golden cups and a communal meal identical to the ritual Grail feast in *Parzifal*. And on the other side of the Atlantic Ocean, the Mayas revered Ixchel, the White Lady, as a culture-bearer and sorceress who arrived on the Yucatan island of Cozumel after the Great Flood. In temple art, she is often portrayed holding a magical vase. The cauldron, cup, or platter was one of the Holy Grail's changing shapes—together with the cave, stone, womb, and skull—symbolic of a vessel or container for the Perfection of Paradise.

These earlier manifestations of the White Lady were linear forerunners to the apparition Bernarde-Marie Soubirous experienced in the mid-19th century, hallucinations brought about by exposure to the power-crystal's mind-altering influences. Her uncanny comparisons with the Pythia of ancient Delphi were the results both women shared when subjected to its behavior-modifying energies. If true, then the continued presence of the Cathars' Mani Stone in the Pyrenees is clear.

The four Perfecti who carried the Ark of the Covenant away from Montségur days before the citadel capitulated may have hidden it not so very far away, in one of the innumerable caves at or near Massabielle. There it has remained for the last eight centuries, occasionally radiating outbursts of negative ions triggered by seismic stress, for which the Pyrenees is well-known. Bernadette and her precursors who encountered the White Lady ever since Esclarmonde perished in the flames of 1244 have been responding to the Ark of the Covenant her fellow Perfects concealed so successfully in its subterranean hiding place. From there, it continues to perform as it was originally intended, energizing higher human consciousness—the crown chakra—with transforming visions of godhood, and healing of the afflicted.

CHAPTER 13

Is the Ark in America?

The Grail...there was nothing on Earth so precious...

—Wolfram von Eschenbach,
Parzifal, Book X, 519

During his years of intense research, Otto Rahn amassed a considerable library of information about the Holy Grail, following every conceivable lead to its whereabouts. Some clues pointed to an old Scottish church a little more than 7 miles from Edinburgh. Half a century before the structure became world-famous for its role in the Grail quest, and early in his association with the Ahnenerbe, Rahn visited Rosslyn Chapel, but came away disappointed, because the evidential trail seemed to end there.[1] Other questors since Rahn are convinced he was on the right track after all, but overlooked some revealing facts that would have otherwise influenced the further course of his investigation. They argue that the Grail/Ark of the Covenant had been slipped out of Montségur by the Knights Templar defending the last Cathar citadel, while the Perfecti went to their fiery doom content at least in the awareness that their most

sacred object was in safe hands, spirited away to Paris, where la milice du Christ was headquartered.

For the next 63 years, the grail was supposedly locked in innermost secrecy, but, as with all such classified objects, word of its existence leaked to the outside world. Whispers circulated of a severed human head or defleshed skull used by the Templars in their admittedly arcane initiations. Although such rumors missed the mark, they were nonetheless in the target area, because one of five popular Grail manifestations or symbols was, in fact, a skull—regarded simultaneously as a sacred vessel, a container of the infinite human spirit, and the image of mortality, signifying an alchemical mix of life and death, the exilir from which true eternity is brewed. Moreover, the skull of Dagobert II, The Merovingians' sainted king, was preserved in a silver reliquary. But it does not appear to have ever been used by the

Templars for any purpose, nor removed to the French capital from Mons at the convent, where it is still kept. Even so, general suspicion that the Knights revered some macabre cult-object was a distorted rendition of the Cathars' Manisola that had been criminalized by the Inquisition, but still conducted in the private chambers of the Templars' Paris fortress.

Their alleged interest in cranial rituals did not concern the king of France until 1307. Years earlier, before he was crowned Philip IV, he sought refuge from a murderous mob behind the walls of the same castle, and subsequently applied for membership in la milice du Christ. Aware of the prince's flaws, the Grand Master turned him down, but Philip would never forget the perceived insult. When he eventually ascended the throne, he involved his country in a costly war with England, a military adventure that threatened to bankrupt him. Desperate for funds, he unexpectedly ordered the Templars' mass arrest on October's Friday the 13th, brought charges against them of numerous felonious counts, and had them tortured until they told their tormentors whatever they wanted to hear. Such worthless, though by the standards of the time entirely legal "confessions" absolved the king from his obligation to repay huge loans received from the Knights. The courts additionally informed him that, in view of the criminals' confessed heresy, he was authorized to impound all their assets "for the good of France." The judges also decreed that the Templars' extensive real estate holdings should be transferred to another military order, the Hospitallers. But Philip the Fair, as he was then called, ignored them, and confiscated the lands for himself. These disgraceful deeds climaxed after seven years of manhunts and torture, when the Grand Master, Jacques de Molay, and two other Templar leaders publicly recanted statements they made under severe duress. For refusing to admit their guilt, they were burned alive at the stake.

While Philip's henchmen sacked de Molay's Paris headquarters for any valuables they could lay their hands on, Inquisitors rooting among the scattering debris were unable to find the severed head or skull they had heard so much about. The object of their search for evidence of heresy had, in fact, been removed months before, when the Order's deteriorating relations with the king were becoming apparent. As the Cathars did before them, the Knights kept transferring the Grail from one of their numerous castles to another, making it difficult for the royal authorities to locate at any particular moment.

To Scotland and North America

With the Templars' proscription on the Continent, however, some made use of their private fleet of merchant ships, and sailed en masse for the last European country where they could find refuge: Scotland. According to Grail researcher William Mann, they "came under the protection and patronage of Henry Sinclair, Earl of Orkney and Baron of Rosslyn during the 14th century." Mann writes that Henry "was a known patron of refugee Templars...So many Templars fled to Scotland that they actually formed the bulk of Scottish cavalry at the Battle of Bannockburn."[2]

In time, however, the hospitable earl began having second thoughts about his needy guests. What if the pope were to launch a crusade against him for harboring such unrepentant heretics? Scotland could become another Languedoc. Anxious to avoid such a catastrophe, he loaded them aboard 13 ships and sailed the Atlantic Ocean to the eastern seaboard of North America in 1398, nearly a full century before Columbus.

Templars at Oak Island

Unacceptably wild as the story may seem to conventional scholars, it does not lack foundation. Known since earliest colonial times, a boulder outside Westford, Massachusetts is decorated with the faded image of a European warrior from the Middle Ages, with the broadsword and shield insignia of the Sinclair clan. During the 1960s, Thomas Letherbridge, Cambridge University's curator of archaeology in Britain, "identified the shield as a 14th century emblem of a Scottish knight."[3] Sinclair's transatlantic crossing was no voyage of discovery, however, as Scotsmen had already been traveling to North America for 388 years. According to the medieval *Greenlanders' Saga*, two Scottish "rangers" belonged to the crew of Thorfinn Karlsefni, when the Norse captain landed in Vinland, somewhere along the upper New England coast, in 1010.[4]

But what of the Grail supposedly carried by the Templars? Speculation concerning its American whereabouts has drifted to little Oak Island, off the coast of Nova Scotia, site of the so-called Money Pit. Accidentally discovered by three boys in 1795, the depths of the man-made shaft have never been plumbed, despite many thousands of dollars and several lives lost in its exploration for the treasure believed buried within. At least since 1804, the seemingly bottomless pit has been suspected to have Templar origins because it continually flooded to within 33 feet of the top; "the highest level in the Masonic Scottish Rite is the 33rd degree."[5] And after all, Oak Island is part of Nova Scotia, "New Scotland." Investigators wondered if such a complex engineering feat without parallel could have been undertaken by Templars from Scotland as an impenetrable vault for their most precious treasure, the Holy Grail, also known as the Ark of the Covenant.

If so, then the mystery might find elucidation in the enigmatic architecture, sculpture, and carvings of Sinclair's Rosslyn Chapel, which Wallace-Murphy and Hopkins describe as "a memorial to the heretical order of the Knights Templar".[6] But work at Rosslyn only began in 1446, 248 years after the Templars supposedly left Scotland for North America. Steven Sora, whose research of the Oak Island site is definitive, concludes, "There is no evidence that the guardian families in Scotland ever had the Ark of the Covenant. In fact, there is evidence to the contrary. In 1768, James Bruce, who claimed to be a direct descendant of Robert the Bruce, the king, made his own search. His expedition to find the Ark took him to Ethiopia."[7]

None of this deprives the Money Pit of its possible medieval significance; evidence for the Templars' impact on pre-Columbian America is persuasive. The leading engineers of their time, the Templars were entirely capable of creating such a complicated shaft, and certainly had the motive for removing themselves from beyond the grasp of their European enemies. King Philip never did find the Knights' treasury he coveted, nor the Order's extensive banking records and other, secret documents. Perhaps these precious items lie at the as yet inaccessible bottom of Oak Island's mysterious site.

The Ark in Tennessee?

Stories of the Ark of the Covenant in America are not confined to its arrival with the Templars, however. Native oral tradition contends that the sacred object has not only been venerated for time out of mind, but is still the center of worship. Late in life, William Pacha, a former Cherokee chief and medicine man, told how his grandfather, a "high-high priest," took him to a cave near Gattenburg, Tennessee, in the early 20th century.

There, the young boy was shown the Ark, in which the spirit of Yowa, the supreme being, was believed to dwell, as evidenced by the bright light it emitted. He recalled that the rectangular vessel was covered with strange letters, some of which resembled Egyptian hieroglyphs for water, a shepherd's crook, and human-like stick-figures holding hands. Although not allowed to look inside, his grandfather told him the large box, which he alluded to as the Tree of Life, contained special crystals. Guards were under orders to immediately kill anyone who approached the coffer too closely or attempted to touch it.

Sometime after Pacha's visit, the Ark was removed to an ancient Cherokee burial ground, where it remained only a few years before construction of a federal dam project to provide electrical power for the residents of eastern Tennessee during the 1930s threatened to flood the area. Finally established at a secret location in northern Georgia, the coffer was subsequently carried on rare occasions to other parts of the Midwest, as the centerpiece of a special, annual ceremony. To Pacha's knowledge, the last such event took place in Kentucky in 1973.

Although he contends that the Cherokees are the Ark's tribal stewards, the Iroquois, Pacha believes, have known of its existence for countless generations. To both peoples it was so holy, no one is allowed to speak openly of it, and Pacha himself violated a "death oath" he was made to swear after having been shown the object, never to discuss it with anyone. He did so late in life not to boast of his covert knowledge, but because of his membership in the Church of Jesus Christ of Latter Day Saints. When joining, he learned that its doctrine recounts the arrival of Semitic peoples in America about 2,600 years ago. As a devout Mormon, he felt obligated to share the secret heritage with his coreligionists,

because it tended to confirm their belief in transoceanic contacts from the Near East during pre-Columbian times. *The Book of Mormon*, upon which his faith rests, tells of Prince Mulek, son of King Zedekiah, who led a migration of followers from Israel across the North Atlantic to America, circa 600 B.C.

Critics scoff that the tale is without factual basis, but a closer look does reveal some provocative historical parallels. Although none admittedly exist for Mulek, his father's role in 6th century B.C. Jerusalem is well attested. Zedekiah became the last king of Judah in 597 B.C. Just 10 years later, as the city was being seized by Babylonian forces, he and his minions escaped before it capitulated, but they were captured soon after on the plains of Jericho, and taken in chains to Riblah. There, after his children were executed before his own eyes, the fallen monarch was removed to Babylon, where he eventually died in prison.[8]

The Book of Mormon version differs only from the Old Testament in claiming that one of Zedekiah's sons did, in fact, successfully flee the invasion with his own followers by traveling as far as North America. The remarkable feature of Mulek's alleged voyage is its coincidental timing with the destruction of the First Temple and disappearance of the Aron ha-Berit. If there is something to *The Book of Mormon* story, then it may refer to Hebrew survivors of the Babylonian conquest who made good their escape with the Ark of the Covenant aboard Israel's considerable merchant fleet.

One year after *The Book of Mormon* was released, in 1844, Oxford scholar Edward Kingsborough published the first installment of his pioneering, nine-volume investigation of Mesoamerican archaeology, *The Antiquities of Mexico*, which provided some substance for William Pacha's claims:

"As among the Jews, the Ark was a sort of portable temple in which the deity was supposed to be continually present, so among the Cherokees an Ark was held in the highest veneration, and was considered an object too sacred to be touched by any but the priests."[9]

If the Ark of the Covenant was really enshrined in Tennessee, it would not be the first ancient Jewish artifact found in that state. When archaeologists from Washington, D.C.'s Smithsonian Institute excavated a large burial mound at Bat Creek outside Knoxville in 1885, they broke into two crypts connected by corridors in the Dynastic Egyptian style. Each contained the remains of one man, whose forensic reconstruction revealed distinct racial differences from the local indigenous population. The central chamber also contained a small tablet inscribed with an inscrutable text. It was finally translated the following century by Dr. Cyrus Gordon, professor of Mediterranean Studies at New York's Brandeis University. After noticing that the Bat Creek writing resembled 2nd century A.D. script found on Judean coins, he was able to read the tablet: "A comet for Judea," or "A star for the Jews."[10] Having been included in the burial chamber, the words were apparently intended to refer to its male skeleton.

Professor Gordon's estimate of the Bat Creek stone's age was confirmed in 1989 by Smithsonian archaeologists who radio-carbon-dated a piece of wood removed with the tablet. Their results showed a chronological spread from 32 A.D. to 769 A.D. These time-parameters were further validated by sheet-copper bracelets discovered in the crypt; they had been made from a zinc-copper alloy commonly in use during Roman imperial times, between 45 B.C and 200 A.D.

Chemical and linguistic dating procedures combined with the text itself to con-vince Professor Gordon that the Bat Creek stone was an artifact from a dangerous insurrection against Rome instigated by the Jewish leader Simon Bar Kochba in 132 A.D. His short-lived revolt having failed, "the Hebrews fled across the sea to *Epeiros Occidentalis*, a land unknown to them before," according to the contemporary Jewish historian, Flavius Josephus.[11] Epeiros Occidentalis indicates a land far away in the west.

Simon Bar Kochba was supposed to have perished in his misguided attempt, but he may have disguised his death and fled across the North Atlantic to America with some followers. Although his name meant "Son of a Star," he was also known as Simon Bar Kozba, "Son of the Lie," implying he was skilled in deceit. Human remains inside the Georgia mound may be those of the Jewish revolutionary. In any case, the ancient earthwork's identification with a 2nd century rebellion against Rome received additional supportive evidence when Judean shekels dated to another Jewish uprising from 132 to 135 A.D. were unearthed in Tennessee.

While all these scientifically attested discoveries go back 600 and more years after the possible arrival of Mulek with the Ark, they nonetheless document an ancient Jewish presence in the American Midwest, thereby lending credence to claims for earlier voyages from Israel.

On its own merits, the old Indian chief's account featured enough internal evidence to give skeptics pause. His name for the supreme being that inhabited the secret coffer, Yowa, seems parallel to a Cherokee rendition of the Hebrew Yahweh, who made his will known through the Aron ha-Berit. Both objects gleamed with a bright radiance, and neither was to be touched or even approached on pain of death. The special, annual ceremony he said attended the Native American box parallels Yom Kippur, the Day of Atonement, when the Hebrews reaffirm their covenant between Yahweh and his Chosen People. Although it's possible that he may have gleaned all of this from a meticulous reading of the Old Testament, Pacha's insistence that the vessel he saw as a child was inscribed with Egyptian-style hieroglyphs infers an Ark association with the Great Pyramid, something he would have been unlikely to consider. His grandfather's reference to the Ark as the Tree of Life containing special crystals harks back to even earlier and more esoteric origins in Atlantis.

Particularly enlightening is Pacha's statement that "no one is allowed to speak openly of it"; an admonition particularly characteristic of Midwestern tribal societies. When, for example, Chief Fun-maker, a Ho Chunk elder from Wisconsin, was asked by a reporter for Fox Television in 1997 about the validity of a particular ceremonial site, Rock Lake, outside the state capitol at Madison, he replied, "there are some things too sacred for us to talk about."

The Crystal Skull from Mexico to Canada

Another good case for the Grail in the Americas is a remarkably lifelike carving of a human skull in clear, quartz crystal. It is 29 to 32 inches wide, by 13 to 16 inches high, 7 to 8 inches long, and weighs 9 pounds. The workmanship is of an extraordinarily high level, far surpassing the dozen or so other crystal skulls touted as archaeologically or mystically genuine. Known as the Mitchell-Hedges Crystal Skull, it is not, however, well-endowed with unimpeachable provenance. Contrary to fantastic tales of its discovery in the jungles of British Honduras (modern Belize), the object appears to have actu-

ally been obtained from Mexico in 1936 by a London antiquities dealer. Eight years later, he put it up for auction with Sutteby's, when it was sold to a wealthy adventurer, F.A. Mitchell-Hedges. After his death in the late 1950s, the Crystal Skull passed to his adopted daughter, Anna, a resident of Kitchener, Ontario, where, in her 90s, she is still its constant custodian.

Despite the refusal of mainstream scholars to even consider the Crystal Skull as a pre-Columbian find due to an utter lack of archaeological pedigree, its ancient authenticity is nonetheless supported by a number of observations: Surface marks were made by fire-hardened, wooden dowels— pre-Conquest instruments, not modern tools. Barely perceptible holes in the detachable lower jaw and at the cranial center of gravity, forward of the ear cavity, indicated it was probably used as an oracular device for a seer. In 1989, forensic reconstruction was undertaken by Dr. Clyde Snow (professor of Anthropology at the University of Oklahoma, at Norman), Dr. Irwin Kirschner (head of the Cook County Medical Examiners Office in Chicago, Illinois), Peggy C. Caldwell (consulting forensic anthropologist for the Office of the Chief Medical Examiner in New York City), and Frank J. Domingo (composite artist for the New York City Police Department). Their combined investigation revealed that the Mitchell-Hedges Crystal Skull was the accurate copy of an actual human skull belonging to an American-Indian woman in her early 20s with distinctly Aztec or Toltec facial features.

To the Maya (circa 200 B.C. to 900 A.D.), a crystal skull was the emblem of Ixchel, the White Lady, who arrived at Cozumel, an island off the coast of Yucatan, as a flood-survivor from the destruction of her homeland in the Atlantic Ocean. Temple art and surviving codexes depict her angrily wielding a sky-serpent, or comet, with which she threatens to bring about a deluge for the destruction of sinful mankind. Other portrayals show her overturning a vase to drench the world with water, likewise suggesting the Flood. She was the goddess of prophesy, as signified by the crystal skull, symbolic of the full moon, and hence, psychic powers. Centuries after the Maya, the Toltecs and Aztecs knew her as Coyolxauqui, or Coyote Woman. A large, sculpted disk portrays her body dismembered in the configuration of a *sauvastika* (a reversed *swastika*), the Hindu lunar emblem, thereby demonstrating a cross-cultural connection between the Indian subcontinent and Mexico in pre-Columbian times. Included in the Coyolxauqui disk is the image of a white skull.

These Mesoamerican attributions of the Crystal Skull—its allegedly paranormal powers and Atlantean origins—compliment medieval European notions of the Holy Grail. The Grail itself was an exceptionally clear crystal, likewise able to induce altered states of consciousness. And the White Lady apparition associated with the Grail in the French Pyrenees seems reflected in the Maya Ixchel. But if, as her myth describes, she brought the power-crystal directly from lost Atlantis to Cozumel, where the ruins of her temple still stand, then how are we to account for very similar traditions in Western Europe?

CHAPTER 14

The New Jerusalem

It is not an extraordinary thing to say that those who start
something are not the ones who finish it.
—Jean-Jacques Olier, 1643,
Les vértables motifs des Messieurs et Dames
de la Société de Notre-Dame de Montréal

A more bizarre explanation for the Ark of the Covenant in America, but far better documented than stories of Levites in Ethiopia or Templars in Newfoundland, begins just before the surrender of Montségur. When the four Perfecti slipped with the Ark through the lines of the surrounding royal army, they made their way across the Pyrenees into Spain, traveling the same route traced 713 years later by Otto Rahn during his final quest for the Holy Grail. Arriving outside Barcelona, they climbed halfway up Catalonia's 4,054-foot mountain to the monastery of Montserrat. A Benedictine abbey, it had been chosen long before by the Cathars for its Montségur-like inaccessibility as a contingency against the catastrophe that eventually overwhelmed them in France. The name, "jagged mountain," derived from Montserrat's serrated profile, as seen from a great distance. Not without cause, the abbey was the basis for Richard Wagner's Grail Castle—Montsalvat—in both *Lohengrin* and *Parsifal*, and has been popularly known since the 13th century as a repository for the Perfection of Paradise.

Effects characteristic of the Ark/Grail soon manifested themselves in an upsurge of spiritual illuminations experienced by visitors to the mountainside retreat. Among them was Íñigo López de Loyola, a Basque soldier badly wounded on May 20, 1521, at the Battle of Pamplona, when a cannonball struck his legs. After long months of recovery, he visited the Montserrat abbey, where he underwent a life-changing catharsis, hung up his military uniform before an image of the Virgin, and 12 years later founded the Society of Jesus, the Jesuits. During the next century, they were to play a major role the fate of Montserrat's sacred object that had so utterly transformed de Loyola's life.

Today, only some ruins of the original abbey are still visible near a replacement monastery built at the same site during the 19th century. Still, a memory of the Ark's former residence survives in Montserrat's modern logo: an image of the mountain topped by a mysterious box.

In this legend, the Cathars' irreplaceable Mani Stone was safe in Spain, where it continued to exercise its power, but their ideology had been dealt a mortal wound with the surrender of Montségur. Despite the long-term, eminently successful efforts of the Inquisition to extirpate any suggestion of opposition in Languedoc, its masters of the rack and the stake continued an apparently needless, though intense, investigation of the area, long after all contrary views, together with the men and women who held them, had been wiped out. "The troubling fact is the interest constantly displayed by the kings of France in the Cathar region," Markale observes, "after they had done everything in their power to destroy the Cathar heresy and take possession of the country."[1]

The explanation: The authorities were trying to find something. The non-Cathar defenders of Montségur had been granted immunity from prosecution upon surrender, but Arnaud de Miglos was, for no obvious reason, made an exception. A nobleman, he served the Albigensian cause as a common soldier, although he was imprisoned in the dungeons of Carcassone to be interrogated for the rest of his life.[2] His tormentors tried, unsuccessfully, to determine the precise whereabouts of "the Cathar treasure" they suspected had been hidden in the caves of Ornoloc, just 3 miles from the de Miglos estate. Ornoloc had been, in fact,

the first stop made by the four Perfecti after escaping with the Ark of the Covenant from Montségur prior to its capitulation; the same site investigated by Otto Rahn in his quest for the Grail. Given the close proximity of the imprisoned man's home to these events, he must have been privy to them, or so the Inquisitors believed. But poor Arnaud de Miglos almost certainly knew nothing about any "treasure."

While Catharism withered under relentless suppression, its attendant organizations simply went underground. Their adherents could not stop being what they were, just because their convictions had been criminalized, even if exercising a sense of identity meant violating the law and undergoing martyrdom. The Templars suffered similar persecution beginning in 1307, but at once formed a *sub rosa* organization that perpetuated their way of life. The group behind them and the Cathar mainspring was so well-connected in high places, from Paris to Rome, its aristocrat officers and members—all from France's leading families—needed only brush aside any suggestion of collusion with the heretics to escape censure or worse. The venerable and prestigious Order of the Holy Sepulcher established by Godfroi de Bouillon after the Crusader conquest of Jerusalem in 1100 had become, following the Templars' demonization 200 years later, an organizational iceberg: 1/10 visible, 9/10 below the surface.

Despite the collapse of their highest hopes—to establish Chartres Cathedral as a French temple for the Ark of the Covenant, the centerpiece of a New Jerusalem, and the medieval Navel of the World in a radically reformed Europe—Order directors consoled themselves with the sacred object's safekeeping in Spain. There it must remain until conditions in France allowed for its return. But given the climate of the times, that did not appear imminent. The abbey at Montserrat, it seemed, would forever be the home of the Holy Grail.

Christopher Columbus

During the last decade of the 15th century, however, a new possibility came under serious consideration. A Genoese sailor was making the rounds of Europe's crowned heads, trying to win support for his proposed voyage of a new route to India by sailing around the globe. Among the numerous and so far unsubstantiated benefits that would result from such an undertaking, Christopher Columbus promised his patrons the possible discovery of new lands and the wealth they might provide the crown.

When Spanish royalty at last underwrote his venture, among the first volunteers was Bernat Boil from the Montserrat abbey. Welcomed aboard as a knowledgeable observer, he was a crew member with the admiral's premiere voyage to the Americas, and an eyewitness to the planting of King Ferdinand's flag in the beach at El Salvador. As some measure of the influence the monk exerted on Columbus, he named a Caribbean island "Montserrat" after the Catalonian monastery. Returning to Spain, Boil reported to his superiors that new lands had indeed been found, though none appeared suitable for relocating the Ark of the Covenant. Further exploration, however, might reveal better possibilities.

To that end, another operative for the Order was aboard during the second voyage to the New World, in 1493. Martin Garcia was not only Ignatius Loyola's brother, but also a Templar—although banned in France, the Knights remained unpersecuted by the Spanish authorities. Garcia's influence was likewise apparent in the red croix pattée that emblazoned the mainsails of Columbus' ships. He later expanded upon Boil's conclusion, adding that the newly discovered territories were far broader than anyone could imagine. Garcia urged that a trusted member of the Order, who would know precisely what he was looking for, be given the opportunity to find ideal refuge for their secret treasure.

Montréal

Such a man was found in Jacques Cartier. In 1534, he had just returned from his first voyage to Canada, where he was among its earliest explorers. While Spain was actively claiming all lands in the south, he hoped to find undiscovered territories that France might colonize further north. The following year, on May 13, he was at sea again in three ships carrying 110 Frenchmen and two native boys from his previous visit aboard the *Emerillon*, her mainsail billowing with the Templars' crimson cross. Cruising down the Saint Lawrence River, Cartier came upon an unusually beautiful island. It was actually a 760-foot-high dormant volcano, still occasionally wracked by earthquakes, its base wreathed in lush forest and topped by a rectangular, truncated pyramid.

Archaeological excavations undertaken in 1997 revealed that the man-made structure of densely compacted, rock-hard clay originally stood 90 feet tall. This outsized earthwork was the focus for aboriginal ceremonies beginning circa 1500 B.C., making it the oldest structure of its kind in Canada, and contemporary with North America's most ancient urban center, Louisiana's Poverty Point, some 1,325 airline-miles to the southwest. The Canadian mound was surrounded by a large village its native residents called Hochelaga, from which more than a thousand Hurons descended to greet the foreign strangers at the river's edge. When Cartier first gazed up at the mountain in the stream on October 2, it seemed to be a vision of the Grail island itself, and he gave it the name by which the sacred object's fortresses had been known in the Holy Land and France: Montréal.

But native hospitality alternated with unexpected outbursts of murderous violence, exacerbated by the onset of scurvy. Although the Frenchmen were the first Europeans to have penetrated the interior, eastern regions of the continent, they departed Canada with little more than their lives and a description of Hochelaga's mountainous island. The intention of Cartier's third and final return voyage was to establish a permanent colony there in 1541. Things went badly almost from the beginning, however, when the Indians attacked and cannibalized about 35 settlers before Cartier and his men could retreat behind their improvised fortifications. Realizing their numbers were simply insufficient to cope with an entire population of hostile natives, they shipped out in early June of 1542, arriving back in France the following October.

For almost the next 100 years, prospects for moving the Ark of the Covenant to Montréal were put off by impossible conditions in the New World, but improved firearms throughout the early 17th century alone made settlement feasible. During the summer of 1608, after Samuel de Champlain arrived in Canada, he and two other Frenchmen, together with 60 native allies, were confronted by 200 Iroquois warriors at what is now Crown Point, New York. Calmly leveling his new, cannon-like arquebus at three chiefs leading the attack, Champlain fired, killing two of them with a single shot. The attacking Indians turned and fled. Over the next several decades, native numerical superiority contended with European superior weapons technology for the fate of North America,

until gradually the French established relatively successful settlements along the St. Lawrence. In the summer of 1611, Champlain secured Montréal, cleared the land, and built a fortified wall. Just 13 years later, he laid the first stone at Quebec City, although this important population center would not be considered safe for permanent inhabitation until 1634.

Conspiring for the Ark

When word of Champlain's success spread to Europe the following year, two of his fellow countrymen back in the homeland had already undergone kindred life-changing events with far-reaching ramifications: Jean-Jacques Olier and Jérome Le Royer de La Dauversiére both claimed to have experienced similar visions of the Blessed Virgin, who desired a rebuilding of the Ark of the Covenant's First Temple as the center of a New Jerusalem at Montréal. Olier was a Jesuit priest, a confidant of St. François de Sales; La Dauversiére, a prominent aristocrat. Together, they determined to fulfill their shared sense of mission by finding supporters in the *Compagnie du Saint-Sacrament*, a secret society of influential persons founded eight years earlier by Henri de Levis Duke de Ventadour, nephew of a Grand Master of the Knights Templar. After the Inquisition relinquished its hold on Montségur, around 1260, his Languedoc family occupied the former citadel for the following centuries. Henri and his wife, Marie-Louise de Luxembourg, had been similarly transformed by some spiritual incident, after which they renounced their own conjugal love, as perfect Cathars, and formed the Compagnie for covert purposes. In fact, it was a front for a much older, secretive institution, the Order of the Holy Sepulcher, founded immediately after the First Crusade, 528 years before.

Many French historians—Jean Marqués-Riviére, Heni Probst-Biraben, A. Maitreot de la Motte-Capron, and others—have identified Godfroi de Bouillon's enduring, resilient organization as the unseen "interior group" behind the formation of the Templars and the direction taken by the Ark of the Covenant from its discovery in Jerusalem to its relocation in France, culminating in its escape to Spain.

The Order's effective method of camouflage, as ever, was to hide in plain sight. "During the 17th century, there was tremendous prestige associated with chivalric orders," observes Francine Bernier, a leading authority on the early history of Montréal, "particularly the Order of the Holy Sepulcher."[3] Pope Urban VIII himself "pledged that the cross of the Knight of the Order of the Holy Sepulcher be conceded only to the noble ones who made the pilgrimage to the Tomb of Christ in Jerusalem."[4] Thus, by way of brilliant public renown, its directors achieved their ulterior agendas through a number of openly unaffiliated groups such as the Compagnie du Saint-Sacrament.

The very real operation of these secret societies should hardly be cause for skepticism or doubt, given the times responsible for their creation and the events that preceded them. More than a million people had died in the Church's Albigensian Crusade to liquidate heretics. Tens of thousands had been imprisoned, tortured, burned at the stake, and deported during King Philip the Fair's extermination of the Templars. Although the Inquisition was no longer "officially" operative, its spirit of suspicious vigilance still lurked in the power centers of Europe. Bernier is correct in observing that "secrecy was formally required from all members" of the Order and its affiliates.[5] "Their constitution," she adds, "actually forbade members to keep records."[6] To avoid a recrudescence of recent horrors and the miscarriage of their plans for the Ark of the Covenant, members in the Order of the Holy Sepulcher and its related associations, such as the Compagnie du Saint-Sacrament, and a new class of missionaries, the Sulpicians, operated under a thick veneer of respectability well within the system.

The Sulpician brotherhood was founded in Paris just as the first settlers—known as Montréalistes or the Ville-Maries— arrived at Montréal by the same Jean-Jacques Olier whose shared vision was the impetus for their quest. His choice of the name, *Societas Presbyterorum a S. Sulpitio*, or the Society of Saint-Sulpice, seemed innocent enough, but it concealed the secret agenda of which he was a part.

A Merovingian theme was sounded as early as 640 in St. Sulpice, or Sulpitius the Pious, who intervened with King Dagobert on behalf of his subjects, easing their tax burden. At the request of the same monarch, he performed services for the "See" or Bishop, of Cahors, and was a protégé of Dagobert's grand vizier, Eloi, a leading goldsmith and alchemist. As shown by his uncommon influence with the king, Sulpice may have been Merovingian himself.

The emblem Olier chose for his Sulpicians was a variant of the Templar cross "directly associated with the Holy Sepulchre in Jerusalem from the first crusade," according to a modern Sulpician at Montréal.[7]

The single-minded goal of these missionaries and their colleagues in other fronts for the Order was to establish a New Jerusalem with its secret Holy-of-Holies at Montréal under the guise of a "city of the Virgin," Ville-Marie. They were fused together by a shared inspiration as fanatical as it seemed miraculous. Beginning with de Ventadour's catharsis in 1627, literally dozens of France's outstanding noblemen and ladies underwent a shared spiritual transformation that turned them from ordinary aristocrats into zealots possessed by an all-consuming sense of high purpose.

Most of these zealots were directly or indirectly associated with places connected to the Templars (Troyes, Champagne, and so on) and the Cathars (Languedoc) or affiliated with Godfroi de Bouillon's Grail family. Many cashed in their fortunes to give themselves over entirely to the project. Francine Bernier herself was scarcely less astounded:

> We should perhaps underline that it was quite, if not completely abnormal, particularly in the bourgeois French noble circles of the 17th century, that so many people would enter a monastic, religious life—particularly late in life. Something literally "happened" to them, which made them change their priorities, abandon a "normal life," and instead choose a life devoted to God—or soul-searching. It happened to all the people involved with the foundation of Ville-Marie...they all had revelations from God, and, as such, they considered themselves touched by Grace and closer to God and the mysteries of the faith than the average Christians.[8]

To her, this mass transformation was "unique in history."[9] Or was it?

The same inexplicable change overcame the Cathars, Templars, Baudoin II, Solomon, Moses, Akhenaton, and anyone exposed to the Fire Stone and lucky enough to escape death. Just as were their predecessors, the Ville-Maries (as the enthusiastic proponents of the Compagnie du Saint-Sacrement called themselves) were allowed to behold the Great Secret. Directors of their parent organization, the Order of the Holy Sepulcher, wanted them to fulfill a dream preserved since the four Perfecti stole out of doomed Montségur with the Ark, over the Pyrenees and Spanish frontier, into the Benedictine abbey outside Barcelona. That dream began with Jacques Cartier's discovery of another Montréal on the opposite side of the sea, far removed from the clutches of popes or kings. But de Champlain's success in settling New France made a transatlantic relocation possible for the first time. In preparation, the Ark of the Covenant was transported from Montserrat, its home for the previous 403 years, back across the Languedoc border to Montréal-de-Sos, which had sheltered it until the approach of the Albigensian Crusade, and owned, conveniently enough, by Duke Henri de Ventadour's family. Its return to this old Grail castle occurred in 1627, when he experienced his vision and formed the Compagnie du Saint-Sacrement. Others followed, as the Perfection of Paradise transformed curious aristocrats into dedicated Ville-Maries.

But the dream they hoped to materialize—the creation of a New Jerusalem in Canada—was a costly proposition. Their wealth—especially considerable when pooled for the common cause—was sufficient to inaugurate the enterprise, but could not sustain it. In the King of France, they were especially fortunate to have found their most important supporter. Louis XIII was desperate for people willing to resettle in New France, because his English enemies were ambitious to take it over for themselves. Canada was rich in minerals and furs, both vital to the French treasury, whose supplies were almost depleted through lengthy wars with the British Empire over imperial rights on the other side of the Atlantic Ocean. Although de Champlain had declared much of the St. Lawrence River region secure for colonization, very few Europeans were actually convinced enough to take him up on his suggestion, as the New World had an indissoluble reputation for native violence. King Louis was, therefore, overjoyed to learn that this group of religious activists expressed enthusiasm for permanently establishing themselves in Montréal.

However, his right-hand man, the second most powerful—on occasion, *the* most powerful—man in France, threatened to abort the Ville-Maries' plans. Armand Jean du Plessis, Cardinal de Richelieu, understood the necessity of populating Canada with enough Frenchmen to prevent the English from seizing it. But he was not about to allow a gaggle of unconventional aristocrats outside mainstream Catholicism (in other words, beyond his control) to arrogantly set themselves up over the Church in a distant land, where they might reveal their true, heretical tendencies he already suspected. Richelieu seized Montréal-de-Sos, and had it dismantled stone by stone. But he did not find the sacred object of his search, as spies for the Compagnie du Saint-Sacrament in the royal palace discovered his intentions in time to forewarn the castle. Learning of the Compagnie's foundation in 1627, the Cardinal sought to negate its effectiveness at the same time he formed his own Compagnie de la Nouvelle France, which, through influence of the *éminence grise* with the King, obtained a monopoly on Canada's fur trade, and forbade settlement there by anyone other than Roman Catholics—a pointed reference to the doctrinally questionable Ville-Maries. When they were finally about to depart for New France, the Cardinal dispatched Sieur de Montmagny, the former governor of New France, to stop them. But the Order of the Holy Sepulcher's reach was long, and its directors prevailed upon the Vatican to cancel out Richelieu's interference.

While both the Order and the Compagnie du Saint-Sacrament worked largely behind the scenes to create the New Jerusalem, a more aboveboard group was needed to organize the personnel, material, supplies, and ships that would constitute the settlers and their complex enterprise. Such an organization established in 1639 was the Société de Notre-Dame de Montréal, a cover, according to many historians such as Alain Tallon, professor at the Paris Sorbonne, for the Compagnie du Saint-Sacrament, "one of many companies created by the Compagnie to facilitate their operations in perfect anonymity."[10]

Clues Hidden in Paintings

After years of preparation and opposition, the Montréalistes at last sailed from the port of Larochelle in July of 1641, the same year Nicolas Poussin settled in Paris. Among the greatest and most famous artists of his times, his apparent relationship with the departing Ville-Maries was as enigmatic as his personal invitation by their powerful enemy to live in the capital was confusing. Did Richelieu want to keep an eye on Poussin because of hidden suggestions in his paintings, secrets the Cardinal was determined to learn?

The work under suspicion was finished shortly after Poussin returned to Paris from Rome, just as the Ville-Maries arrived in New France. Entitled *Les bergers d'Arcadie*, or *The Shepherds of Arcadia*, his large oil on canvas portrays a rugged country scene, at the center of which stands an aboveground tomb visited by three shepherds. A young man on the right gazes up at the standing figure of a woman in flowing robes, while he points to a Latin inscription that reads, *Et in Arcadia ego*, or "I am in Arcadia." These words imply that death may be found in even the most perfectly tranquil site. That, at any rate, is the painting's exoteric interpretation. But its esoteric side was apparently obvious enough to have alarmed Cardinal Richelieu. "Under the stark, external, classical stillness," observes William Mann, referring to *Les bergers d'Arcadie*, "there is evidence of a more mysterious, vibrant, inner life."[11]

Arcadia was a pastoral district in the central Peloponnesus of ancient Greece synonymous for any rural place of ideal peace and simplicity. But Acadia was also the name given by the French to their colonial territories in northeastern North America that included Montréal, where the long-concealed Ark of the Covenant was to be eventually installed. At the absolute center of Poussin's painting, the kneeling figure points at the first three letters of the inscription's third word, *Arc*adia. If the name is a play on Acadia, the artwork might be telling us that the Ark of the Covenant is in New France: I am in Arcadia (Acadia). The actual burial site Poussin used as a reference was located on the outskirts of a village with the singularly appropriate

name of Arques, where it stood until the modern-day landowner had it demolished. The tomb's inscribed implication seems underscored by the standing woman, who appears to be pregnant, thereby emphasizing her navel, the old Navel of the World.

All this might be so much unsubstantiated speculation, except for the painting's simultaneous completion with the Ville-Maries' arrival in Montréal, and Poussin's own connection with their covert organization. According to Baigent, Leigh, and Lincoln, the artist was visited 18 years after finishing *Les bergers d'Arcadie* by Abbé Louis Fouquet, whose mother "was a prominent member of the Compagnie du Saint-Sacrament."[12] They quote a letter the Abbé wrote about Poussin to his brother, Nicolas Fouquet, the French superintendent of finances, to the effect that the artist possessed information concerning an unparalleled discovery of the greatest significance which will, in any case, never be found again. Bernier states that Nicolas Fouquet too belonged to the Compagnie du Saint-Sacrament."[13] Poussin himself was a Freemason, going so far as to depict himself prominently wearing a Masonic ring in his self-portrait of 1650. He believed, as many Masons still do, that Freemasonry was directly descended from the Order of the Knights Templar.

Nor was *The Shepherds of Arcadia* his first or only painting of its kind. With less subtlety, his *Le Peste D'Azoth* boldly presents the Ark of the Covenant between a pair of massive columns on a stone plinth, as though it were in the process of being moved out of Solomon's Temple, while a Christ-like figure addresses a crowd, and a young child lies in the center foreground. The imagery implies a new life or rebirth for the Ark. Azoth was sought by alchemists as the universal medicine, a cure-all to wipe out illness, and symbolized by the Caduceus, the Tree of Life wand carried by Thoth (Thaut), the Egyptian god of healing from whom Azoth derived its name. The inclusion of Azoth in the title of Poussin's painting indicates he understood the revivifying, consciousness-expanding, perhaps even Atlantean dimensions associated with the Ark of the Covenant. Moreover, he began work on *Le Peste D'Azoth* in 1630, just when the Compagnie du Saint-Sacrament was formally organized to undertake its secret mission; namely, the creation of a New Jerusalem in Canada. It would seem that these paintings were meant to celebrate that mission among fellow cognoscenti, of whom Poussin, as a proud Mason, was one.

Crisis

The Ark, however, had not yet traveled to Acadia. In this, *Les bergers d'Arcadie* and *Le Peste D'Azoth* heralded its future relocation to Montréal. Until then, the colonists needed time to build their settlement, become self-sufficient, and construct the temple. The sacred object would remain concealed at a secret repository in the Languedoc until the Ville-Maries were ready to receive it for safekeeping, and not before. Their arrival in Quebec City could not have been more ill-timed, as the French and Iroquois wars had only just begun a few months before, while the pilgrims were still at sea. Against constant native threat and frequent attacks, they finally reached the island of Montréal in May of 1642. Building the New Jerusalem was continuously interrupted by material shortages, disease, and hostile Indians. Just 10 years after a representative from the Order of the Holy Sepulcher raised a cross over Ville-Marie, its population numbered just 2,000 men, women, and children. Even so, the first, tentative step away from mainstream Christianity was taken as early as 1660, when the Sulpicians

succeeded in arranging a pontifical Bull making Montréal independent from both the Church of France and the Archbishop of Nouvelle-France.

The break was not without drastic consequences, however. That same year, the Compagnie du Saint-Sacrament was dragged by royal authorities before public scrutiny for the first time, all its voluminous records destroyed, its regional leaders in the city of Caen formally accused of overt anti-Semitism—then a criminal offense. A year later, Nicolas Fouquet, the once-powerful finance minister under Louis XIV and Poussin's connection to the Compagnie, was imprisoned for life, and the Compagnie du Saint-Sacrament disappeared. In 1663, the Société de Notre-Dame de Montréal relinquished far-off Montréal, which was saved for the future when the Compagnie du Saint-Sulpice, in Paris, took over ownership. These disturbing events convinced Order of the Holy Sepulcher directors that conditions in Europe were threatening their overseas' enterprise. The long-awaited moment was approaching when the priceless centerpiece of Ville-Marie's Holy-of-Holies must leave France for the New Jerusalem.

Father Baudoin

Only one of the elect, the equivalent of a 17th century Levite priest, could have been honored with such a uniquely historic responsibility. Jean Baudoin, as his name suggests, was descended from Jerusalem's Crusader Kings, which included Baudoin I, who built the first Montréal in the Holy Land, and Baudoin II, royal founder of the Knights Templar, and under whose auspices they found the Ark of the Covenant. As such, entrusting it to Jean's care was entirely appropriate.

Due to a number of male relatives also named Jean who became missionaries in the 17th and early 18th centuries, historians often confuse him with these other kinsmen, particularly Abbé Jean Baudoin, who followed his cousin during 1688 to Nouvelle-France, but was diverted to New Brunswick's Beaubassin on the Bay of Fundy. He kept a detailed journal, regarded as important source material describing contemporary conditions in Newfoundland, where he was Commander Pierre Le Moyne d'Iberville's chaplain before dying at 36 years of age.

The older Jean Baudoin, similar to Ignatius Loyola, began as a professional military man, joining the French Army as a 17-year-old cadet in 1641, just when the Ville-Maries left for Canada. A year following the conclusion of his training, he rose rapidly through the ranks to become a musketeer in His Majesty's Guard. The prestigious unit was regarded as a springboard for ambitious, young careerists with their eyes on officer positions. While on leave in 1645, however, he suddenly resigned his promising place as a guardsman to join Loyola's Jesuits. The transformation from warrior to priest seemed inexplicable to his friends and comrades, to whom he had been known as something of a hedonist. As was said of those similarly struck with zeal for the New Jerusalem, "something happened."

Indeed it did. That same year, Jean had traveled to the Languedoc on undisclosed business. But the abrupt alteration in lifestyle that came over him was consistent with the radical changes experienced by anyone admitted into the presence of the Ark of the Covenant. As a Baudoin earmarked by the Order of the Holy Sepulcher for its "Grail-bearer," its directors impressed upon him the significance of his mission by exposing him to its ionic radiance.

Jean was one of many de Bouillon family members deeply involved in the Ville-Marie project. Relatives such as Maurice Godefroy de la Tour de Bouillon and Madame Angelique Faure de Bouillon were not only generous contributors to, and effective fundraisers for the New Jerusalem, but high functionaries in their crusader-ancestor's Order of the Holy Sepulcher and its associated companies. It was through them that the young man had been introduced to the Ark, and given his mission to install it in the New Jerusalem. They were also his financial backers, and supported his transatlantic voyage, which landed him in Montréal in 1667. The Ville-Maries were convinced that once placed inside the Temple, the restored Ark would activate a spiritual revolution that must bring heaven on Earth. He was appalled, therefore, to see that the less-than-half-finished structure was far from built, 10 years after Marguerite Bourgeoys laid the first stone of the Bon-Secours Chapel, a cover-name for the temple. She apologized that the exigencies of survival and the absence of money to purchase materials from Quebec City were responsible. Father Baudoin sent her to France on a fundraising mission, providing her with valuable contacts in the Order of the Holy Sepulcher and his own family, particularly Marie-Anne, the Duchesse de Bouillon.

Meanwhile, a proper place for his golden treasure had to be secured until the temple/chapel was completed. He found it on the *seigneurie* (a kind of feudal holding or plantation) at the western end of Montréal belonging to René-Robert

Cavelier. He too had joined the Jesuits as a young man in his native France, but resigned to follow an older brother, Jean Cavelier, a Sulpician priest, to Ville-Marie in 1667. René-Robert fell in love with the New World, becoming fluent in Iroquois and the languages of several other native peoples. They told him of a large river known to them as the Ohio that flowed into the even greater Mississippi. Intrigued, he set out with five canoes and 15 men during the spring of 1669, exploring new territories as far away as what is now Louisville, Kentucky. The expedition's success brought him a fur trade concession and a title of nobility. Henceforward, he was known as René-Robert Cavelier, Sieur de La Salle. His seigneurie prospered, and he fortified it with a village of armed guards to protect it against the Indians' unpredictable behavior. As such, Lachine, as he liked to call his beloved estate, was the ideal, temporary setting for Father Baudoin's charge. The two men became collaborators and close friends.

By 1672, Bourgeoys was back at Montréal with sufficient donations to renew construction. Completed in 1678 and renamed Notre-Dame-de-Bon-Secours, its interior chapel duplicated Solomon's Temple, including replicas of the two great pillars named Boaz and Jachin in the Old Testament. As was Bon-Secours Chapel's other precursor, the Great Pyramid, Montréal's structure was carefully oriented "on the perfect east-west axis."[14]

The perennial Navel of the World was reaffirmed in that Grail figure, the pure maiden, revered at Notre-Dame-de-Bon-Secours as the Black Virgin, a thinly veiled Christian version of a very ancient Mother Earth goddess. She personified "the energy hidden and contained in the Earth, the ultimate symbol of telluric activity."[15] Her iconic presence at Montréal, with its dormant but not dead volcano and frequent

tremors, was particularly appropriate. According to her autobiography, Bourgeoys recorded nine earthquakes in as many hours on February 5, 1663, a "swarm" signalling the beginning of geologic upheavals that persisted intermittently over the next eight months. "The island of Montréal," observes Bernier, "was a centre of great telluric activity and frequent earthquakes, which still occur today."[16] Thus, as with old Jerusalem's Mount Moriah or ancient Egypt's Giza Plateau, Ville-Marie had been deliberately selected for its inherent seismicity, the natural, chthonic force that would power the Ark of the Covenant, or, more accurately, the Fire Stone contained therein. Montréal "represented that age-old symbolism of the centre of the New World, the omphalos, like the Temple Mount of Jerusalem formed the axis mundi of the Old World...*Mont Réal* was indeed a reflection of a new Holy Land, with all its symbolic topography, far away from the absolutism of the king and his libertine court."[17]

In 1678, Notre-Dame-de-Bon-Secours stood finished at last. During a special ceremony, the Ark of the Covenant was brought under guard from de La Salle's Lachine and placed in its chapel, a reproduction of King Solomon's Holy-of-Holies, with Marguerite Bourgeoys as its Grail maiden and Father Baudoin the Levite high priest. The New Jerusalem could now begin to unfold its transforming radiance.

Cathar Resurgence

Almost at once, however, Father Baudoin noticed a disturbing alteration in his parishioners. The expanding distortion of their earlier attitudes, which he previously let pass as eccentric, now seemed alarming. As with all their predecessors overexposed to the Perfection of Paradise, the Ark exercised a degenerative effect on the state of their mental health. They began to resemble that other group of heretical extremists, the Cathars, especially in their growing disavowal of sexual relations. Paralleling the Albigensian distinction between Perfecti and Credentes, leaders of the Société de Notre-Dame de Montréal distinguished themselves from mere members by vows of chastity. "The virtual equality between the men and women involved in the foundation of Ville-Marie" mirrored the Cathars.[18] "This rare equality in social status between Christian men and women in Montréal was something completely new during the 17th century."[19] But not in 13th century Languedoc. They endeavored "to restore the purest—if not Gnostic—form of Christianity."[20]

These comparisons between the Montréalistes and the bons hommes demonstrate that both groups were equally impacted by prolonged contact with the Ark of the Covenant. Their deterioration was similar, if not identical, because the object's profusion of negative ions, while initially salubrious in moderation, was ultimately harmful, as are all forms of euphoric stimuli with excess. Addiction warps personality by inflating the ego into an absolute center of the universe: the Navel of the World's dark side.

For all its esoteric orientation to achieve that cosmic centeredness, Notre-Dame-de-Bon-Secours was built without any defenses, allowing Iroquois warriors laying in wait to pick off at ease any parishioners walking from the settlement to the half-finished church. The Ville-Maries never made any provision to protect this "sacred way," imagining they trod a direct passage to heaven, if they were blest enough to get killed while undertaking their little pilgrimage. In this, they especially resembled the Cathars, whose endura, which provided sanctioned escape from the bonds of Satan's world, was virtual suicide. As attrition began to gnaw away at their already insubstantial numbers, surviving Montréalistes were convinced their purity laid the only acceptable foundation for the coming New Jerusalem.

To Jean Baudoin, the ex-soldier, they were insane. But even more alarming was the basis for their chastity: In refraining from sexual relations, they made possible the Second Coming, for any Ville-Marie woman who became pregnant would repeat the virgin birth, having conceived, not by man, but through the Holy Spirit, as a kind of Canadian Mother of God. Hence, her child must be Jesus reborn in the flesh. His earthly destiny this time was not death on the cross, but as the world-acknowledged head of his revived church in the new Holy Land.

Their radical devotion began to strike Father Baudoin as the lunatic blasphemy of an overly pious community unraveling in isolation. Its settlers had already been abandoned by the French king, who was more interested in the commercial and military value of Quebec City because of its opposition to British designs on Nouvelle-France. With dissolution of the Compagnie du Saint-Sacrament and other fronts for the Order of the Holy Sepulcher, Villa-Marie, never more than minimally self-sufficient, could depend on outside support from only a few, aging aristocrats such as the Duchesse de Bouillon. The gnostic utopians were without a future. In time, either English troops or French authorities must absorb the metaphysical experiment at Montréal. In fact, it would linger for little more than 20 years, expiring after the turn of the next century, when, in 1705, the name was forever changed from Ville-Marie to Montréal. Less than 50 years later, the Bon-Secours Chapel, the intended duplicate of ancient Jerusalem's most sacred shrine, was burned to the ground. British forces were to capture Montréal in 1759, their occupation legalized in another four years by the Treaty of Paris, which turned over New France to the king of England.

Abscondng with the Ark

None of this was what Jean Baudoin had crossed the ocean for with the world's most important object. How he himself had managed to avoid being adversely effected by his golden charge, we do not know. But returning in its company to Europe was out of the question; no less so than leaving it with unhinged fanatics. An alternative location had to be found in North America, and soon, before either Quebec City ambition or British imperialism moved to seize the New Jerusalem. Father Baudoin's only alternative was the assistance of his longtime confidant and closest friend at Montréal: La Salle, who was inspired at the prospect of renewing his explorations while searching for the Ark's new home. He unhesitatingly liquidated all his holdings at Lachine to organize a large, properly provisioned and well-armed expedition. When everything was in readiness, Father Baudoin and three assistants stole late one night into the newly made Bon-Secours Chapel, from which they lifted the Ark of the Covenant on its twin carrying poles, took their precious burden outside, and mounted it on a waiting cart, wheels muffled with rags against alerting the sleeping Ville-Maries.

Over the next week, covering some 250 miles, Father Baudoin and company made their way without incident down the St. Lawrence River, stopping along the southern shores of Lake Ontario to Fort Conti, near Niagara Falls. There, they completed construction of a new, capacious vessel that shoved off on August 7, 1679. *Le Griffon* carried the first Europeans to navigate the Great Lakes by sailing ship, scudding across Lake Erie, northward through Lake Huron, then down the length of Lake Michigan. On November 1, her crewmen built a fort at the mouth of the St. Joseph River in what is now Michigan, where they remained for more than a month to hunt for fresh meat. Reentering the St. Joseph on December 3, they followed it until arriving at a portage to the Kankakee River, which carried them into the Illinois River. After a wearying passage, La Salle paused to build a military establishment he called Fort Crèvecoeur near present-day Peoria, Illinois. The expedition was getting low on supplies and near exhaustion, so further exploration was halted for more than two years.

In all these extensive, trail-blazing travels, Father Baudoin was forever alert for a potential location for his rescued Ark, but nothing seemed remotely suitable. During the long pause in the expedition, he hoped to find clues among the native peoples from all over the region attracted by the presence of powerful strangers at Fort Crèvecoeur. A few Christian converts in the Yuchi tribe from the southeast, along the western banks of the Wabash River, particularly attracted his attention. They said that neither he nor his companions were the first bearded, literate white men to visit these prairie lands, as La Salle and the others wrongly imagined. Very long ago, the Indians said, their forefathers were host to another group of fair-skinned people "with writing" from across the Great Water, in the east. Over several generations, the foreigners were wiped out through a combination of disease, warfare, and intermarriage. But before disappearing, they left behind many holy relics entombed in a cave that the Yuchi have ever since revered as their most sacred site. The converts invited Father Baudoin to accompany them to the subterranean location, where he could contribute his own "writing" to the underground collection.

Although their story sounded far-fetched, something about the Yuchi themselves suggested ancient, alien influences. However slightly, they differed physically from the plains Indians he knew, with paler complexion, lighter eyes, wavier hair, and less prominent facial features. They spoke a linguistic isolate, unrelated to any other known Native American tongue, and, as he was later to learn, were a separate people from other tribes. If all these differences indeed formed the lingering legacy of deeply prehistoric contacts with some white foreigners, then the Yuchi story of their memorial cave may have been based on at least a real location of some kind. Perhaps the Ark could be temporarily sequestered at such a remote place until some future time when another recreation of Solomon's Temple in the New World was built on firmer ground than the Bon-Secours Chapel at Ville-Marie—or so Father Baudoin imagined.

In any case, he promised to accompany the Yuchi Christians at his earliest opportunity, and they agreed to remain at Fort Crèvecoeur until then. The long-burdened Jesuit priest was by then fatigued with his mission, which he hoped to at least interrupt with a proper storage place, however impermanent. He and La Salle alone knew what lay concealed beneath the piles of skins and furs. To have exposed it to the crew would have certainly led to serious disorder, and neither of them could have guessed how the indigenous peoples, who outnumbered them by a thousand to one, might have reacted. The Indians, after all, seemed to offer a possible solution to the problem posed by indefinitely dragging an invaluable but ultimately hazardous item across North America.

When La Salle returned with much-needed supplies from Ontario's Frontenac in 1682, Father Baudoin told him they may at last have found a proper place to dispose of their secret cargo. Late that spring, 23 Frenchmen accompanied by 18 Native Americans left *Le Griffon* behind forever at Fort Crèvecoeur, canoeing their way down the Illinois River. Where the Mississippi and Ohio Rivers meet at the bottom of Illinois, the explorer and the priest parted company. They had shared more than 1,000 miles of discovery together, but La Salle felt drawn irresistibly to investigate the Gulf of Mexico, while Jean Baudoin wanted only to relieve himself at long last of his clinging responsibility. Off what is today Fort Defiance State Park, Illinois, the two men pursued their separate destinies, one toward the south, the other in the east. La Salle spared eight of his best marksmen to protect Father Baudoin, who was led by two Yuchi into the Ohio River. Nearly three days later, the trio of long canoes reached the Wabash, following its zig-zag meandering to a point just below the future Vincennes, Indiana, not far beyond an important Jesuit headquarters for preaching among tribal peoples in the central Midwest. It was here that the native guides directed their French guests to enter a much smaller river leading back into Illinois. They paddled up the eerily quiet Embarras (pronounced "ahm-bra"), as it was later called, until a populous Indian village appeared on the left bank, less than a week after the 11 travelers separated from La Salle.

While his weary men were well treated and refreshed after their long journey, Father Baudoin was taken alone to the Yuchi sacred site on a thickly forested cliff overlooking a bend in the river. He was led into a low-ceilinged rock shelter where torches were lit to reveal apparently man-made chambers connected by a series of narrow corridors. They seemed to spread in various directions, but fallen debris often cut off their passage. This was, after all, seismically active territory, part of the

New Madrid Fault, with a long history of violent earthquakes. Doubtless, the collapsed fill resulted from similar geologic violence in the years since the subterranean complex was made—when and by whom, Father Baudoin could not guess. Until now, as far as he knew, he was the only European to have ever visited this part of the world. Yet the finely chiseled masonry over which he ran his appreciative hand did not seem typical of the Indians' craftsmanship. Indeed, they themselves claimed the underground structures were hewn by others—white foreigners, during the deep past.

The priest was at last convinced, when his hosts brought him dozens of strange black stones illustrated with the portraits in profile of European men wearing headgear uncannily reminiscent of Roman era helmets. His amazement deepened when he was shown stone tablets covered with long, neat texts in a written language he could not read. Truly, someone had sailed up the Embarras long before himself. But who these stern faces represented and when they left their images here seemed beyond speculation. The Yuchi urged him to contribute his own record to the strange collection, and showed him how it had been made. They cut oval sections of dark clay from the river bank, padded them into smooth, uniform shapes, then gave him a sharp-pointed stone. Using it as a stylus, he could write and draw on the moist surface with ease. Finding the task engaging, he covered first one, then several more of the crude tablets with French sentences. They may have recounted his recent travels, or reproduced prayers to bless the underground location. On a leftover piece too small for writing, he sketched a crude likeness of the Ark.

Whatever the real origins of the peculiar cave, remoteness and inaccessibility eminently qualified it as at least a temporary hiding place for Father Baudoin's secret. On his command, the weighty object was lifted, still concealed by piled pelts, from his canoe by four Indian converts, who alone accompanied him back into the subterranean structure. At his request, they led him into the deepest corridor, which terminated in a small chamber barely spacious enough to accommodate their burden. After carefully setting it down, he ordered them to kneel before the golden vessel, and swear on their immortal souls never to tell anyone—Yuchi or white man—anything about the "big box," especially its location. Having pledged their solemn word, they got to work at once, piling up fallen rubble in front of the chamber entrance until it was thoroughly and compactly sealed. Whether the priest ever returned to the site, or what his ultimate plans for the concealed treasure may have been is not known. Jesuit strongholds at Vincennes and St. Louis did not yet exist, and the entire region consisted of a largely unexplored wilderness. Making use of the cave probably seemed his only alternative. The longer he kept the sacred object with him during his extensive travels, the greater the odds against escaping some terrible mishap. God had preserved it, and him, over many thousands of miles and the previous 15 years since Jean Baudoin left France with his sacred charge for Montréal. This place, it seemed, hidden underground and utterly unknown to the outside world, had been revealed to him for a divine purpose.

The Yuchi proved true to their sworn promise, keeping their secret from missionaries and fur traders who passed along the Embarras River in ever greater numbers, as European settlement grew across southeastern Illinois. In time, the Indian village became a French hamlet known as Verde Gras for its green prairies. Much later, under increasing Anglo-American influence, the name was changed to Stringtown, whose most famous visitor was General "Mad Anthony" Wayne, during the War for Independence. Today, however, Stringtown is a ghost-town, its spooky, late 19th century cemetery an infrequent haunt of hopeful antiquarians swinging handheld metal-detectors in search of old buttons or coins.

After stashing the Treasure of the World inside the Yuchi cave, Jean Baudoin became the most prominent missionary of his time. For the next 30 years, he traveled the Midwest's extensive river systems, making Christian converts among native peoples throughout the Mississippi Valley. According to his biographer and mid-20th century descendant, Kenneth Lawrence Beaudoin, "He led a strange, lonely life, but he must have had a great, human understanding, and considerable personal magnetism, for there was not an Indian village between Quebec and New Orleans in which he was not respected....Toward the end of his life, he was made Superior of all the Jesuits in America, and, as such, he was the ranking churchman in New France. His headquarters in later years was in St. Louis," where he died in 1709 during his 75th year. "But his grave has been lost. His bones are probably resting in pleasant anonymity beneath the great, new city which has grown over the city of his primitive, provincial see."[21]

For his own sake and that of his covert mission, Father Baudoin was right to part from La Salle. In 1684,

the intrepid explorer attempted to establish a French colony on the Gulf of Mexico, at the mouth of the Mississippi River, with 300 settlers loaded onto four transports; one of which was blown off course and captured by pirates in the West Indies. His flagship, *La Belle,* sank in the inlets of Matagorda Bay, where the third vessel ran aground. The survivors straggled to an area near Victoria, Texas, where they built Fort Saint Louis, while La Salle led a group eastward on foot during three separate expeditions in a fruitless search for the Mississippi River. In the last attempt, mutiny infected his 36 followers, four of whom murdered him not far from present-day Navasota, Texas. Fort Saint Louis survived him by only two years, when Karankawa-speaking Indians massacred its 20 remaining adults and took their five children as captives. Remarkably, La Salle's ill-fated *La Belle* was discovered under the muck of Matagorda Bay in 1995, and has since become the subject of archeological dives.

In late September of 1811, the most violent seismic event in North American history jolted southern Illinois, temporarily reversed the course of the Mississippi River, and rang churchbells as far away as Boston, 950 miles to the east. But the New Madrid earthquake refortified Father Baudoin's concealing work, when the corridor that led to the chamber in which he and the four Indians concealed their "big box" totally collapsed, rendering any access to it impossible. By then, the entire Yuchi tribe had been pushed to the brink of extinction by a combination of foreign-introduced diseases, intermarriage with outsiders, and the genocidal intentions of fellow natives, the Cherokee. Survivors evacuated the Wabash area to resettle in the eastern Tennessee River valley, from which they were forcibly removed 100 years later to Georgia and Oklahoma to make way for large-scale European settlement.

By 1956, their population had dropped to less than 3,000 tribal members, when Chief Brown, perhaps sensing the demise of his people, shared the old secret with Dr. Joseph Mahan, professor of history at the University of Georgia, in Columbus. This last elected leader of the Yuchi told him that very long ago white men sailed up the Embarras to a bend in the river just below an old Indian village the French later called Verde Gras. There, the foreigners modified a natural cave, terra-forming it into a subterranean network of tunnels and rooms. In one of them was an inestimable golden treasure. His tribal kinsmen had sworn by God never to divulge its existence, let alone its whereabouts. But Chief Brown felt the story should not be allowed to die with his people. During their wars of extermination with the Cherokee and migrations under duress it had become more fireside myth than oral history, in which the precise location of the cave was no longer remembered with certainty. Consequently, the cave was still safe from intruders.

The Cave Discovered

Some 26 years after Dr. Mahan learned the old Yuchi secret, Russel. E. Burrows, a woodworker from West Virginia, hiked through the backcountry of southern Illinois, where he had married a local woman. During his spare time, Burrows searched for pioneer relics and the occasional Indian rock-art that collectors still found in the area. While walking along

the left bank of the Embarras River to the overgrown ruins of Stringtown in the spring of 1982, he stumbled upon an entrance to the Yuchi sacred cave. For the next seven years, Burrows removed an estimated 3,000 artifacts, mostly black stones incised with the line-drawings of helmeted men and inscribed texts in unknown written languages.

The incised illustration of what appears to be the Ark of the Covenant on a stone from the southern Illinois cave.

Although mainstream scientists took no interest in his discoveries, unconventional investigators began buying individual pieces from Burrows they believed amounted to credible, physical evidence for an ancient Old World presence in pre-Columbian America. He found the trade brisk, all the while resisting constant appeals to disclose the location of the cave. He felt proprietary about the site, and desired its protection from looters who, in their greed for artifacts, might destroy it. Among those he sold to Wayne N. May, publisher of *Ancient American*, a popular archaeology magazine, was a black, roughly oval "mud-stone" measuring 3.25 inches across by 3 inches high. An illustration on one side depicts the image of two winged figures facing each other atop a rectangular box resting on a platform of some kind. Floating above them is a wide, shallow cup or bowl containing a single cuneiform glyph of five strokes for the Hebrew name of God, Yahweh.[22] The illustration suggests the mercy-seat from which God manifested his radiant energy. Descending from the underside of the vessel toward the twin winged figures are three lines, possibly signifying rays. Is this the stone etched by Father Baudoin in his attempt to to portray the Ark of the Covenant that he installed in the Embarras River cave?

Several other stones Burrows recovered from the underground complex were not for sale. These included tablets inscribed in the French language and adorned with crucifixes. Convinced they somehow tended to discredit the authenticity of the cave's apparently Roman era items in the minds of his customers, he destroyed the untypical specimens with a ball-peen hammer before they might taint the body of his collection with buyer uncertainty. Ironically, if the French tablets were, after all, inscribed by Father Baudoin, they would have gone far toward validating the controversial site.

In early 1989, with the imminent passage of a harsh state law against the unauthorized retrieval and sale of premodern artifacts, several terrific gunpowder explosions occurred inside the cave, permanently sealing its entrances. During the decade that followed, Burrows continued to sell specimens from his large collection, all the while refusing to divulge their subterranean source. In the spring of 1999, Wayne May arranged for a ground-penetration radar investigation of the site's suspected location near the Embarras River. Almost at once, electronic imagery revealed a network of large rooms and smaller chambers connected by a series of artificial corridors 60 feet beneath the surface of a farmer's private property. With the owner's permission, surveys continued over the next three years, painstakingly probing for an entrance. Instead, May's readouts showed the blast effects of at least one explosion that had collapsed an unspecified number of tunnels and interior spaces. Worse, the detonation might have ruptured a deep aquifer, flooding the remainder of the complex. This suspicion was underscored in 2002 and again in the years following, when core-drilling into several targets erupted like Yellowstone geysers the moment their drill-heads broke through. All the rooms were filled to their ceilings with water.

While electronic sweeps sought for other, unflooded chambers, improved equipment brought to light some features not seen before, such as the perfectly squared, obviously man-made configuration of several buried rooms and corridors, and what appeared to be standing statues and neat piles of metal. The most arresting result of its kind was made in 2004 under the auspices of Ralph Wolak, a project liaison manager at the time. The radar image he retrieved quite clearly showed a small cavity—approximately 8 feet long by 5 feet wide—and an adjacent, narrower corridor entirely filled with debris, save for about 3 feet connecting to the precisely cut space. Inside the chamber was what instrument operators concluded was a rectangular box with a pair of attached staves running along its length, a pole on either side. One end of the apparent vessel was obscured by what seemed to be fallen material, up to perhaps 1/5 of its top. "It sure looks like the Ark of the Covenant to me," Wolak said, "although I just can't believe it's the real thing. Maybe it's a replica. Even that would be something, if only we could get at it."

In late 2004, all research at the site was suspended when one of the property owners of the land on which the cave is located passed away, throwing her heirs into probate proceedings. Not until fall of 2006 were the investigators permitted to resume their search for an elusive entrance that might gain them access to the underground complex. They pursued their painstaking quest through the autumn, until early winter froze the ground too hard for further excavation. A warming phase in early January, 2007, inspired hopes for their return, but the only access road leading to the site was transformed into a quagmire of mud by unseasonably torrential rains, preventing deployment of the drill-rigs. As prolonged dry-weather conditions are imperative for the operation of such heavy equipment, investigators realistically plan to restart their digs of the subterranean network in midsummer, 2007.

So far, the buried objects continue to show up as tantalizing radar images that are still beyond reach. If and when their physical reality is ever validated by recovery, not even Wayne May and his dauntless researchers are willing to guess. As for Ralph Wolak's electronic portrait of a subterranean "box," the Ark of the Covenant may have found its final resting place under 60 feet of Illinois limestone.

The Real Meaning of
the Ark

*How fares it with your search for the Grail? Have you at last
discovered its true nature?*

—Sigune in Wolfram von Eschenbach's
Parzifal, Book IX, 441

There are many credible accounts for the Ark of the Covenant's whereabouts, but they can't all be true. Or can they? The ancient technology responsible for its creation would not have produced just one specimen, any more than *Challenger* alone emerged from the rocket science that made the space shuttle possible. So too several power crystals were used over time, as reflected in the traditions and even archaeological evidence of numerous cultures around the world. Some of those traditions themselves mention more than one "ark" and several "grails."

The Ark as a Shared Experience

The consistency of such mostly oral accounts among disparate peoples often unknown to each other, sometimes separated by thousands of miles and years, can only mean that they were all referring to the same kind of sacred object, a physical artifact revered as the most valued heirloom a folk could possess. It was a stone, usually a jewel, and more often a crystal, or a metamorphic rock with crystalline veins, commonly associated with earthquake activity, luminous, and most importantly, able to connect human beings with the direct experience of God. The many names this object (and its variants) received while passing among various peoples all derived from and reflected its qualities: Phoenix Stone, Emerald Tablets, The Jewel That Grants All Desires, Transformer of the World, and so on. In whatever form, it is invariably associated with light: the Fire Stone, Phoenix Stone, Shining Trapezohedron, Navel of Light, Sun Stone, the *radiant* Grail, the *glowing* Aron ha-Berit. Its closest attendants were often practioners of a solar cult, such as Amenhotep IV's Atonism, or the Cathars' dualistic worship of light.

The sacred object always had its special guardians: the Tuaoi Stone's Atlantean brotherhood, Rosthau Watchers at the Giza Plateau, U Mamae keepers of the Maya Giron-Gagel crystal, the Ark of the Covenant's Levite priesthood, the Templars, the Cathars, the Grail knights, the Order of the Holy Sepulcher, and Canada's Ville-Maries. They most often preserved their holy charge on a centrally located mountain, mountain-like structure, or ceremonial city: the Great Pyramid; Akhenaton's Horizon of the Sun; Moses' Mount Sinai; the Delphic omphalos atop Mount Parnassus; the Delian omphalos at Mount Kynthos; the Temple Mount at Solomon's Mount Moriah; Malory's Grail City of Sarras; Chartres Cathedral; the Montréals of Baudoin I, Henri de Ventadour, and Jacques Cartier; the Cathars' Montségur; von Eschenbach's Muntsalvatch; von Scharffenberg's Munsalvaesche; Loyola's Montserrat.

When the mythic Japanese hero, Kashima Daimyojin, pressed the Kaname-ishi into a giant carp to prevent earthquake violence, his Navel Stone performed the same service rendered on the other side of the world by the Great Pyramid's Ben-Ben Stone to counter seismic upheaval throughout the Nile Valley. As its most important single artifact, such a stone was society's sacred center, becoming for its owners the Navel of the World, a characterization inseparable from the object itself. Whatever plot of ground set aside for the Pearl Beyond Price became an axis mundi, engendering profound sensations of centeredness in anyone touched by its ionic aura. These locations were each its own Navel of the World, a spiritual womb for the soul's rebirth, because it had been transformed by some mystical encounter. The resulting epiphany was a life-changing catharsis brought about when God suddenly became supreme reality.

Understandably, a balance between inspiration and indulgence was difficult to strike. The abuse of devotion is fanaticism, and virtually everyone exposed to the Perfection of Paradise succumbed to its transforming power. Similar to 1960s' anti-establishment hippies overdosing on LSD, Amenhotep IV changed his name to Akhenaton, and instituted a monomaniacal religion around a Stone of Destiny in the desert; Baudoin de Bourcq changed his name to Baudoin II, and abdicated the throne of Jerusalem for life as a monk in the Tomb of the Holy Sepulcher after the Ark was dug out of his palace grounds; Hughes de Champagne, leader of the excavation, changed his name to Hughes de Payn and exchanged court luxury for vows of poverty, chastity, and obedience in "Christ's poor Fellow Soldiers of Solomon's Temple," the Templars; Count de Champagne's coconspirator, Bernard de Fontaine, changed his name to Bernard de Clairvaux and claimed he saw God in the configuration of the Ark; in Thomas Malory's medieval epic, *Le Morte d'Arthur*, a Grail hero finds the object of his quest, but "as soon as he casts his eyes upon it, he started to tremble, for his mortal flesh perceived spiritual things," Galahad fell to his knees and died; Esclarmonde de Foix put aside the rich garments of her noble ancestry for a martyr's robe, and together with 204 other Cathars, preferred death at the stake to renouncing their Mani Stone; at Barcelona's "Grail monastery," a professional soldier, Íñigo López de Loyola, changed his name to Ignatius of Loyola and founded the Jesuits, one of whom, Jean Baudoin, likewise gave up his military career to become Father Baudoin, and was entrusted with the Ark itself; literally hundreds of French aristocrats gave up their wealth, and sometimes their lives, to build a New Jerusalem in Canada; Bernarde-Marie Soubirous became Saint

Bernadette after experiencing visions of the White Lady near the Cathars' Grail castle; Otto Rahn killed himself in the manner of the Cathars, because he was prevented from further exposure to the Mani Stone.

A Background of Ancient Technology

A common theme connecting these individuals suggests that the focus of their quest must have been a real, material object that energized an area of the brain, the hippocampus, associated with the human subconscious. That such a device could have been invented and applied millennia before the industrial world came about seems impossible. It is generally assumed that our scientific age is alone capable of technological achievement, and that all previous societies simply lacked the means or know-how for the kind of material progress to which we are accustomed. Yet this myopic view of the past fails to recognize that men today are, in evolutionary terms, no different than their ancestors tens of thousands of years ago, and that each generation has always given birth to its equivalent Leonardo da Vinci and Thomas Edison.

To the contrary, old Stone Age cave paintings at Lascaux in France and Spain's Altamira are as sophisticated and finely executed as any artwork created since. More than 5,000 years ago, someone built the Great Pyramid, which today's construction engineers are still unable to duplicate. The ancient Egyptians once used a common pregnancy test, lost with the fall of their civilization, and not reinvented for another 3,000 years. They were skilled optometrists and brain surgeons millennia before professional medicine resurfaced in modern times. The so-called Antikythera Device, found amidst a Roman

shipwreck in the Eastern Mediterranean Sea and dated to circa 80 B.C., is a mechanical analog computer designed to calculate astronomical positions. Another instrument far ahead of its time was discovered in the village of Khuyut Rabbou'a, near the Iraqi capital in 1936 by the German director of the National Museum of Iraq. Four years later, Wilhelm König identified the curious jar as a galvanic cell for electroplating gold onto silver objects. Fruit juice or vinegar had been originally used as an acidic agent to jump-start the electrochemical reaction between both metals. Electroplating was not rediscovered until the 19th century, some 1,600 years after the "Baghdad Battery" was made.

Numerous similar examples from antiquity abundantly demonstrate: 1) that human beings during the ancient past achieved material greatness equal to, and occasionally in advance of, modern science, and (2) many of their high accomplishments have been lost. Among these still undiscovered marvels was perhaps early civilized man's greatest technological exploit—a colossal geo-transducer able to discharge the Earth's potentially destructive seismic energy into useful electrical energy. The resulting profusion of negative ions generated by such discharges had the secondary effect of stimulating cathartic reaction in the hippocampus of the human brain.

The Crystal and the Ark

Discovering the connection between activated crystals and altered states of consciousness could have been made by early, preliterate islanders during the course of simple observation, as suggested by the ritual practices of another tribal people: the Ute Indians. In the mountains of Utah and central Colorado, the Uncompahgre Ute Indians still collect piezo-electric quartz for their seances. So too the

Lemurians, who dwelt within the Pacific Ocean's seismically vibrant Ring of Fire, witnessed crystal's relationship with geophysical forces and human spirituality.

Their use of certain stones selected for telluric and psychic resonance was preserved in the mythic traditions of Easter Island's Te-pito-te-Kura, Hawaii's Pohaku-o-Kane, New Zealand's Puna-Mu, Japan's Kaname-ishi, Peru's Paypicala, Tibet's Chintamani, and among numerous other societies from Pacific coastal America, across Polynesia and Micronesia, to Australia and Asia—that vast area of the world impacted by the Lemurians during their florescence, and later in their flight from a natural catastrophe that closed the last ice age. Fleeing far from their ravaged archipelago, they arrived on the other side of the world at a large, temperate island in the mid-Atlantic Ocean, some 250 miles west of Gibraltar. Immigrant spiritual heritage combined with Western European influences, resulted in a new people, the Atlanteans, their name derived from the island's foremost mountain, the "Up-Holder," Atlas. Centuries of uninterrupted development gave birth to a high culture where metaphysical growth was not contradicted by, but melded with, technological and material sophistication.

Toward the close of the 4th millennium B.C., however, the approach of four comets showered meteoric debris over the Earth, badly damaging early civilization. While the reconstruction of Atlantis began, its scholars were determined to prevent, or at any rate ameliorate, the worst consequences of another global cataclysm. They fashioned a large crystal, the Tuaoi Stone, as the leading component part of a geodetic device that would discharge seismic energy into electricity. Surveying the planet, they determined that the absolute center of its land mass was located at the Nile Delta, the optimum location for a geotransducer. Pharaonic Egypt then emerged from the cooperation between Atlantean designers and native laborers required for its massive construction. Placement of the electronic quartz, now known as the Ben-Ben stone, in the Great Pyramid completed the public works project, which made possible the establishment and function of Dynastic society for the next 1,800 years.

During the mid-14th century B.C., King Akhenaton transferred the crystal capacitor to his new capital, "Horizon of the Aton," down the Nile, where it became the centerpiece of his solar monotheism. Then, 17 years later, his former general, Ay, restored the Ben-Ben to its original position inside the Great Pyramid. During 1227 B.C., the Delta was partially occupied by a piratical coalition of Sea Peoples, who temporarily expelled the Egyptian authorities. Taking advantage of their absence, a vizier and former high priest, Ramose Khamenteru, broke into the Great Pyramid and stole its power-crystal. The invaders' unexpected rout and Pharaoh's unwelcome return forced him to flee with the Ben-Ben and his followers into the desert, an escape many centuries later recounted in the biblical *Exodus*. It describes the Ark of the Covenant's construction, intended actually as a vessel for the requisitioned pyramid stone. Under Joshua's leadership, it was converted for military application and deployed with dramatic success against targets such as the walls of Jericho.

But the crystal capacitor proved treacherously capricious, indiscriminately taking Jewish and Gentile lives alike, until it was captured by enemy Philistines. They too found the Ark so unreliable, it was returned to the Israelites. After they mopped up Canaanite resistance around Jerusalem, Solomon built the first temple for the Aron ha-Berit, as the Egyptian Ben-Ben was called in Hebrew, which he sequestered from potentially lethal contact with the outside world. His mid-10th century B.C. completion of the Holy-of-Holies provided a stable home for the Ark, until Jerusalem fell to Babylonian forces in 587 B.C. Before the invaders reached the temple, the Ark was lowered through a trapdoor into a shaft deep beneath the shrine room. Despite the conquerors' thorough efforts to loot Jerusalem and utterly demolish its sacred center, they never found the Aron ha-Berit.

It was concealed for the next 1,714 years, until the first nine members of the Knights Templar, acting on rabbinical information, located the lost Ark under the al Aqsa mosque, at the Temple Mount of Jerusalem's Mount Moriah. Returning with their discovery to Europe in 1127 A.D., they secretly preserved it at Flanders' Castle de Bouillon, while a permanent repository was prepared at Chartres Cathedral. Undue interest shown by political and papal authorities, however, forced abandonment of the project, and a new group of elite custodians took charge of the Ark. In Cathar hands, its identity began to merge with native European traditions of the Holy Grail, as it was transferred from one castle to another, always at least one step ahead of the royal and Church authorities. By 1208, those authorities succeeded, however, in launching a "crusade against the Grail" that eventually pushed the Cathars back to their fortress in the Pyrenees. Days before Montségur capitulated in 1244, four of them slipped through enemy lines with the Ark of the Covenant, and hid it in a deep cave somewhere not far from the scene of capitulation and immolation.

This reconstructed story of the Stone of Destiny, from Lemurian and Atlantean origins to its disappearance after Montségur's surrender, represents a straightforward narrative. With the castle's surrender, however, the story takes off in a dozen different directions, many of them plausible, because at least some appear to describe more than one ark, and other grails. But our interest is in *the* Ark of the Covenant; the Tuaoi Stone custom-built by Atlantean culture-bearers for their reconstituted civilization in the Nile Valley, and hence, the greatest power crystal of its kind ever created; the Great Pyramid's Ben-Ben; the Templars' Holy Grail. The object of our quest comprises all these artifacts; they are one and the same Fire Stone.

Where is the Ark?

Belief that it still lies hidden in Jerusalem's Mount Moriah after the First Temple fell nearly 2,600 years ago, or its willful destruction by Visigothic barbarians after the collapse of the Roman Empire, seem contradicted by numerous traditions and abundant material strongly suggesting the Aron ha-Berit's reappearance in other parts of the world.

England's Glastonbury Tor or Hawkstone Park are unconvincing alternatives, if only because both locations allegedly feature the Grail as a cup (in the latter case, an insignificant unguent jar) from Christ's Last Supper, a contrivance superimposed by Robert de Boron in 1195 A.D. on original, much older accounts of Grail-like stones or cauldrons that do not allude to Jesus.

Limiting the Ark or Grail to his bloodline is opposed by the weight of evidence identifying it as a physical object; namely, a gemstone that assumes other manifestations, all symbolic of its mystical functions.

Although Ethiopia's Ark is certainly not King Solomon's original Aron ha-Berit, it may be nonetheless an invaluable replica going back to perhaps the late 4th century A.D., during the Christian Church's earliest attempt to convert East Africans.

The Japanese too may have an ancient facsimile at Sword Mountain, one of several arks Israelites fleeing from the Babylonian invasion may have carried in their eminently seaworthy ships to the other side of the world.

Less believable is the Templars' transatlantic deposit of the Ark in Oak Island's Money Pit, off Nova Scotia shores, although artifacts such as Westford, Massachusetts' faded image of a Scottish knight indicate they visited North America's Eastern Seaboard during the 15th century or even earlier. But placement in such an inaccessible location would have been tantamount to destroying it, something the Templars were unlikely to allow. On the other hand, Native American oral traditions of at least *an* ark in Tennessee are compelling, because they were meant to be secret, yet long ago documented by Edward Kingsborough, an important early compiler of Indian folk accounts. They are also supported by authenticated Jewish artifacts in a pre-Columbian context.

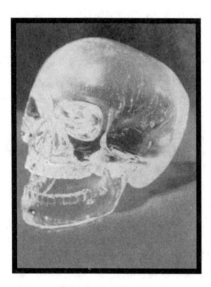

The Crystal Skull. Photograph with permission of William R. Corliss.

The Mitchell-Hedges Crystal Skull actually does exist, and its ancient association with the Mesoamerican lunar goddess of psychic power is discernible. While it cannot be *the* Stone of Destiny, the Crystal Skull is more likely the Maya specimen of an unknown number of grals, similar power-crystals carried by culture-bearers from Atlantis into the various lands impacted by survivors of the catastrophe that overwhelmed their homeland.

Otto Rahn's Welwelsburg Stone was no less real, and perhaps the Cathars' Mani Stone he found in the Pyrenees. If so, however, what became of the golden Ark in which the four Perfecti carried it away from the fall of Montségur? While Rahn's scholarship in Albigensian matters is not to be doubted, nothing connects the Welwelsburg Stone to the Holy Grail, save his own dissolution. Similar to its Ethiopian, Japanese, and Cherokee counterparts, the Welwelsburg Stone may have been one of several Perfections of Paradise fashioned by the Atlanteans or their descendants, but was probably not the original Tuaoi that passed from Atlantis to the Great Pyramid, Solomon's Temple, and Montségur.

If that supremely sacred object never left the Pyrenees following the Cathar martyrdom, then the Ark's continued presence there is borne out by sensitive persons such as Bernarde-Marie Soubirous, whose visions of a White Lady appear to a receptive mind stimulated by the crystal's negative ion radiance in a seismically active zone. More convincing is the incomparable aura of physical and emotional healing sufferers by the tens of thousands continue to experience at Lourdes, where the Ark may have been hidden more than six centuries ago and could still exist, unseen but strongly felt. If so, it continues to fulfill its original mission. If not, both the White Lady visions and spiritual cures could result from yet another power crystal, not *the* Mani Stone in the immediate area.

The Ville-Maries' attempt to establish a New Jerusalem at Montréal and the Great Lakes' explorations undertaken by

The Crystal Skull depicted on a sculpted, stone disk as the emblem of Coyolxauqui, the Aztec "White Lady."

Sieur de La Salle with Father Jean Baudoin are recorded history. Southern Illinois' cave, its black stone bearing the illustration of the Ark of the Covenant, and Ark-like electronic images retrieved from one of its deepest chambers are no less real. Such material evidence, especially in the context of the Frenchmen's experiences throughout New France, seem to make sense only if the sacred object is indeed interred near the banks of the Embarras River.

Even so, the Ark of the Covenant has not yet been found. Perhaps for the better, in view of its historic abuse, the blood shed over its possession, and its overpowering effect on consciousness. Unable to adequately process such potent input, the human mind's capacity for spirituality can degenerate into religious intolerance. Such a device, either rediscovered or reinvented,

must be held at a proper distance, making its possible location at Lourdes positively optimum.

The Way of the Ark

The Grail's dual role as a former capacitor in Egypt's geo-transducer—harmonizing contrary forces—and subsequent psychic transformer—vitalizing mankind's spiritual essence—complements its esoteric identity as the elusive ideal. Within its radiant aura, the previously unenlightened upper four energy centers of compassion, expression, insight and spirituality, respectively in the human heart, throat, brow, and crown chakras, are activated. Hence, the meaning of Richard Wagner's foremost leading motif in *Parsifal*: "*Durch Mitleid wissen, der reine Tor,*" or "Through compassion made wise, the pure fool." The lower three centers of survival, pleasure, and control in the root, sacral, and navel chakras anchor us in physical reality, but failure to simultaneously use and rise above them confines us to the level of beasts, and cuts us off from our higher destiny. Dwelling exclusively in the sphere of everyday concerns is the wasteland described by Wolfram von Eschenbach and T.S. Eliot. Humanity's real purpose withers without a radiant ideal to inspire it. Emphasis shifts from the higher chakras of the heart, voice, mind, and spirit to the body's obsession with material security, transient happiness, and ephemeral power.

An upsurge of current interest in the Stone of Destiny and its better known manifestations as the Ark of the Covenant or the Holy Grail implies a popular longing for its return. So too growing dissatisfaction with the mostly feckless values of our tinsel culture signifies a concomitant restlessness for something universally uplifting that can transcend present vulgarity into future nobility. A fellow countryman of Godfroi de Bouillon, M. van de Walle, stated that a "consciousness of history," a "consciousness of eternity" is striving for expression in the modern soul: "One must become fully what one is" echoes the Grail's implicit command. Van de Walle's perception was carried further by a more famous 20th century contemporary, the American mythologist, Joseph Campbell, who declared that pursuing the Grail was a quest for "the authentic life" amidst the wasteland of modern society.

In view of what we have learned about it, the rediscovery of that supremely sacred object would make the most profound impact on our world, and point us toward its promised Perfection of Paradise. Kings and knights, pharaohs and popes, saints and scoundrels have searched for the Ark of the Covenant over the last several thousand years, mostly in vain. Even those who found it lost it sooner or later. It is at once eternal and elusive. But even someone who fruitlessly pursues the Stone of Destiny possesses at least something of it. That, perhaps, is the real meaning of the Grail quest. Indeed, those few who did win it mostly went mad and/or died. Others changed it from a benign device for geophysical and spiritual healing into a killing machine that backfired on its operators.

If the crystal Navel of the World lies hidden near Lourdes, its mere existence is a great, continuous blessing for legions of sufferers. But if, after all, it awaits eventual rediscovery in southern Illinois, the world may or may not be ready to open the Ark of the Covenant.

An Ark of the Covenant Timeline

Whoever can make sense out of all these turns of chance has been well treated by Wisdom.

—Wolfram von Eschenbach, *Parzifal*, Book I, 2

40,000 Years Before Present—Prompted by rising sea-levels, missionaries sail from the Pacific Ocean Motherland throughout the world, spreading the gospel of their nature religion. Some arrive in Western Europe, where Paleolithic cave art at places such as Lascaux and Altamira is sparked by the negative ion influence of Lemurian power crystals on the Cromagnon inhabitants. First evidence of spirituality represented by ivory statuettes of the White Lady phenomenon appears in the Pyrenees Mountains, at Lespuque and Brassempouy. Lemurians settle on a large, fertile island about 220 miles due west from the Strait of Gibraltar, where they merge with the Cromagnon inhabitants to initiate a new, hybrid culture—Atlantis.

11,600 Years Before Present—The violent end of the last ice age inundates extensive areas of Mu, in the Pacific. Some flood-survivors seek refuge in distant Atlantis, swelling its population and significantly contributing to its civilized development.

6,500 Years Before Present—Megalith-building begins in Atlantis, spreading to Britain and France, where the earliest such tombs on the European continent appear. The standing stones, usually granite and veined with resonant quartz, are planted directly over fault zones, where the great monoliths transform Earth-energies into electrical discharges to interface with the bio-circuity of the human brain, thereby inducing mystical experiences.

Late 4th Millennium B.C.—The close pass of Comet Encke, in company with three other comets, showers Earth's northern hemisphere with a destructive barrage of meteoric material, severely damaging early civilization. To prevent or at least ameliorate the worst effects of another global cataclysm, the Atlanteans craft a large, highly sensitive, electronic quartz-crystal—the Tuaoi, or Fire Stone—for use as a capacitor to transmute and direct seismic energy into electricity.

3100 B.C.—On the Giza Plateau, at the Nile Delta, Atlantean culture-bearers locate the precise center of the world's land mass in order to fully harness telluric power for a geo-transducer. Recruiting the indigenous population as a work force, they raise the first and greatest of some 100 similar pyramids down the length of the earthquake-prone Nile Valley. The resultant fusion of native labor and Atlantean technology gives birth to Dynastic civilization in a colossal public works project, completed when the extraordinary crystal capacitor is installed in the so-called King's Chamber of the Great Pyramid. No longer known as the Tuaoi, its meaning as the Fire Stone remains unchanged in its new Egyptian name, the Ben-Ben.

1355 B.C.—In the sixth year of his reign, Pharaoh Amenhotep IV (a.k.a., "Akhenaton") has the Ben-Ben stone removed from the Great Pyramid and brought to his city, Akhetaton, Horizon of the Aton. The power-crystal is set atop a pillar in the Hwt-bnbn, the Mansion of the Ben-Ben, at the Great House of the Aton, as the centerpiece of his solar monotheism.

1334 B.C.—With the death of Akhenaton and the collapse of his religious experiment, Pharaoh Ay restores the Ben-Ben capacitor to its original position in the Great Pyramid.

1227 B.C.—Sea Peoples conquer the Nile Delta, displacing the Egyptian authorities. During the invasion, Ramose Khamenteru, a high-ranking vizier, makes common cause with the enemy, winning a large following of fellow collaborators, who loot the temples. Riding to regional power on a wave of popular violence, and using his knowledge of the Great Pyramid from his former days as a high priest, he and his accomplices break into the King's Chamber, from which they remove the Ben-Ben. At Pharaoh Merenptah's unexpected return and expulsion of the Sea Peoples, Ramose Khamenteru and his compatriots escape over the Egyptian frontier, far into the eastern desert.

1220 B.C.—Using the former Egyptian Stone of Destiny (now enclosed in the Ark of the Covenant) as a weapon, the Israelite commander, Joshua, destroys the walls of Jericho.

1210 B.C.—The Philistines capture the Ark, but find it too erratically dangerous, and soon after return it to the Israelites.

950 B.C.—King Solomon completes the construction of Jerusalem's First Temple, and the Ark is moved into its Holy-of-Holies.

587 B.C.—Jerusalem falls to King Nebuchadnezzar II, whose Babylonian troops obliterate the First Temple in their fruitless search for the Ark of the Covenant, which lies hidden in a deep shaft directly below the Holy-of-Holies.

439 B.C.—The Jews return to Jerusalem from the Babylonian Captivity, but are unable to find any trace of the Ark after the passage of 150 years.

515 B.C.—The Temple is rebuilt, minus the Ark of the Covenant.

65 A.D.—After years of scouring the Temple Mount, Herod the Great fails to find the Ark of the Covenant for his construction of the Second Temple.

398—A Byzantine theologian writes that the Ark of the Covenant is in Axum, Ethiopia.

1103—Baudoin I, the Crusader king of conquered Jerusalem, learns of local reports locating the Ark of the Covenant on his palace grounds atop the Temple Mount. For verification, he dispatches an emissary to his friend, Hughes de Champagne, at Troyes, France, where rabbinical tradition confirms the rumors. Baudoin and the Count begin careful preparations for excavation.

1127—During mid-summer, after nine years of excavating beneath the Temple Mount, Knights Templar unearth the Ark of the Covenant. In the fall, they carry it aboard ship for Europe, arriving at the port of Brindisi, then journey to northern Italy, where they winter with their discovery at the abbey of Seborga.

1128—The Ark is taken to the Cistercian monastery of Citeaux, in France, while its permanent home is being built at Chartres, the first Gothic cathedral. But the abbot, Bernard de Clairvaux, proves to be a security risk, and the Templars remove the Ark to the Castle of Boullion, in Flanders. They entrust it to a special order of caretakers, the Cathars, who some years later carry the Ark to a more remote fortress near the foot of the Pyrenees Mountains, Montréal-de-Sos.

1204—The Ark is transported to the Cathar stronghold, Montségur, which is continuously refortified over the next 40 years, making it the best defended castle in Europe.

1244—After a nine-month siege, Montségur surrenders to the forces of Catholic France. Two days before the capitulation, the Ark is smuggled through enemy lines by four Cathars, who carry it across the Spanish frontier to the abbey of Montserrat, just outside Barcelona.

1492—A Montserrat monk accompanies Christopher Columbus on his first voyage to the New World in the hope of finding a secure hiding place for the Ark of the Covenant an ocean away from popes and kings.

1493—After joining the admiral's second transatlantic voyage, Templar Martin Garcia decides that a proper location for the Ark should be explored further north, beyond the expanding sphere of Spanish influence.

1533—In Canada's St. Lawrence River, Jacques Cartier discovers a large island he names Montréal, as a possible site for relocating the Ark of the Covenant. But native resistance renders permanent settlement impossible until the advent of improved firearms during the first half of the next century.

1550—During the sack of Axum, Ethiopia, the Ark or its replica is allegedly destroyed by the Somalian forces of Ahmed Ibn Ibrahim.

1642—The Ville-Maries, volunteers dedicated to establishing a spiritual utopia with the Ark at its center in New France, arrive at Montréal. Building and securing their settlement, however, requires more decades of effort.

1667—A Jesuit priest, Jean Baudoin, finally arrives with the Ark of the Covenant in Montréal.

1678—Montréal's facsimile of the original Holy-of-Holies, the Notre-Dame-de-Bon-Secours chapel, is completed and enshrines the Ark of the Covenant. Realizing that the New Jerusalem experiment is doomed by internal problems and external threats, Father Baudoin absconds with the Ark, aided by fellow Montréalist, the famous explorer, Sieur de La Salle.

1679—La Salle builds a ship for navigating the Great Lakes at Niagara Falls, from which *Le Griffon*, carrying the Ark of the Covenant, departs with its steward, Farther Jean Beaudoin, on August 7th. Five months later, they arrive in north-central Illinois, where Fort Crèvecoeur is built near what is now the town of Peoria.

1682—After learning from regional Indians of a possible location for the Ark, the Frenchmen canoe away from Fort Crèvecoeur, down the Illinois River, into the Mississippi. Where it meets the Ohio River, De La Salle continues southward, while Father Baudoin, accompanied by a few native guides and French guards, paddles with the Ark east, then north to the Wabash River until it connects with the smaller Embarras. Another day's journey brings them to a Yuchi Indian village. Just beyond it, on the west bank of the Embarras, Father Baudoin is escorted to a cave he judges a proper hiding place for the Ark, which he seals inside.

1811—The New Madrid Earthquake collapses the entrance to the southern Illinois cave and some of its internal passageways, trapping the Ark, still relatively undamaged in his own chamber, under thousands of tons of limestone.

1858—Bernarde-Marie Soubirous experiences visions of the White Lady at Massabielle, Lourdes, near the foot of the Pyrenees Mountains, where the Mani Stone was alleged to have been hidden in a cave by four Cathars fleeing the downfall of Montségur.

1938—In the Pyrenees, Otto Rahn finds a large quartz crystal he believes is the Cathars' Mani Stone, which he smuggles into Germany. It is enshrined in the Grail room of an early 17th century Westphalian castle, where it is known as the Welwelsburg Stone.

1945—To prevent it from falling into enemy hands, the Welwelsburg Stone is allegedly transported to the Bavarian Alps, where it is buried in a glacier.

1982—The southern Illinois cave used by Father Baudoin as a last refuge for the Ark of the Covenant is entered by a local woodworker after its accidental discovery.

1989—Gun powder explosions reseal the cave and obscure its precise whereabouts.

1999—The lost cave is rediscovered.

2004—Ground-penetration radar images reveal what appears to be a man-made chamber containing the Ark of the Covenant, 60 feet beneath collapsed limestone.

2007—Excavation efforts to access the subterranean complex, badly damaged by earthquakes and demolitions, continue, so far without success.

Dramatis Personae

Aicart, Amiel—One of four Cathars carrying the Ark of the Covenant away from Montsègur before its capitulation in 1244.

Akhenaton—The former Amenhotep IV removed the Great Pyramid's power-crystal for his monotheist experiment.

Arcis, Hugh de—Commander of the French royal army besieging Montsègur.

Ay—The Pharaoh who restored the power stone to its original position in the Great Pyramid.

Baudoin II—King of Jerusalem, he formerly recognized the Templars and allowed them to dig in his palace grounds for the Ark of the Covenant.

Baudoin I—The first Crusader king of Jerusalem, he learned of the Ark's possible existence on his palace grounds, and initiated its excavation.

Baudoin, Jean—Jesuit priest, bearer of the Ark from France to Montrèal and Illinois.

Belcaire, Escot de—Cathar who alerted his coreligionists in besieged Montsègur that their Mani Stone had been successfully evacuated.

Boil, Bernat—A monk who accompanied Christopher Columbus on his first transatlantic voyage to scout for a possible new hiding place for the Ark.

Bouillon, Godfroi de—Flemish duke of Lower Lorraine, leader of the First Crusade, the conqueror of Jerusalem, where he instituted the Order of the Holy Sepulcher, a semi-secret organization to care for the Ark of the Covenant.

Bourgeoys, Marguerite—Builder of Montrèal's Bon-Secours Chapel for the Ark of the Covenant.

Brown, Chief—Last, elected leader of the Yuchi tribe, who told of the southern Illinois cave where the Ark may have been hidden, 26 years before the site was actually found.

Burrows, Russell E.—Discoverer of the southern Illinois cave in which the Ark is allegedly concealed.

Cachi, Ayar—Pre-Inca flood hero who arrived on the shores of Peru, where he was transformed into a power-stone.

Cartier, Jacques—Discovered Montrèal.

Castelnau, Pierre de—The Pope's representative whose assassination was the incident needed by Innocent III to launch, as scholar Otto Rahn saw it, a "Crusade against the Grail."

Cavelier, Rene-Robert, Sieur de La Salle—Mid-17th century French explorer of the Great Lakes, who brought the Ark from Montrèal to Illinois.

Cayce, Edgar—An early 20th century American psychic, he envisioned the Atlantean Tuaoi Stone.

Cerridwen—Keltic goddess, the White Mare, associated with a Grail-like object: the cauldron of abundance.

Champagne, Hughes de—Early organizer of efforts to find the Ark of the Covenant and bring it to Europe.

Champlain, Samuel de—His early 17th century settlement of New France made possible the Ark's new home in Canada.

Childeric I—Merovingian king buried with artifacts suggestive of the Holy Grail.

d'Arnave, Guillaume—The Templar founder of Montrèal-de-Sos, twice the refuge of the Ark of the Covenant, which was virtually obliterated by Cardinal Richelieu in his frustrated search for the treasure.

Dagobert II—Sainted Merovingian king, ancestor of Godfroi de Bouillon.

Dagon—Philistine god whose statue was broken up by the Ark of the Covenant.

Daimyojin, Kashima—Japanese sea-god, possessor of the anti-earthquake Navel Stone.

Eschenbach, Wolfram von—Early 13th century Bavarian author of the foremost Grail romance, *Parzifal*.

Flegetanis—A minor but revealing character in Wolfram von Eschenbach's *Parzifal*, he "wrote the adventure of the Grail" just after the final destruction of Atlantis.

Foix, Esclarmonde de—Daughter of Ramon de Pereille, a Cathar Perfectae burned at the stake following the fall of Montsègur in 1244, thereafter associated with mystical appearances of *La Dame Blanche*, or the White Lady.

Fouquet, Nicolas—French King Louis IX's finance minister, jailed for his secret efforts to remove the Ark to Canada.

Galahad—A knight in quest for the Holy Grail, he is only one of three knights who found it.

Himmler, Heinrich—Head of the SS, he had Westphalia's 17th century fortress transformed into a 20th century Grail castle.

Isaac, Solomon Ben—Also known as "Rabbi Rashi," he related Jewish tradition generally locating the lost Ark of the Covenant to Hughes de Champagne.

Ixchel—The Mayas' White Lady, whose crystal skull has been associated with the Holy Grail.

Josephus, Flavius—2nd century Jewish historian for important information concerning Jerusalem's First Temple.

Joshua—Israelite commander who attacked Jericho's walls with the Ark of the Covenant.

Khamenteru, Ramose—Originally Irsa Beya (a.k.a., Irsu or Iarsu Beja), a Syrian who rose through the ranks to become Chief Vizier by making himself indispensible to the Egyptian authorities. With their temporary expulsion from the Nile Delta by foreign invaders, he broke into the Great Pyramid to remove its power stone, with which he fled into the eastern desert accompanied by his followers, who called him Moses.

La Dauversière, Jèrome Le Royer de—Envisioned recreation of the Ark's original First Temple in New France.

Leukippe—According to Plato, the White Mare of pre-civilized Atlantis, a theme extending to the Holy Grail's White Lady.

Lohengrin—The Swan Knight of the Holy Grail, Parzifal's son, and the mythic ancestor of Godfroi de Bouillon.

Loyola, Íñigo López de—Ignatius Loyola, transformed by close proximity to the Ark during its prolonged stay at Spain's Montserrat abbey.

Matua, Hotu—In Polynesian tradition, the flood-survivor who landed with his family and followers at Easter Island with the Navel of Light.

Melchizedek—In *Genesis*, Noah's adopted son, Shem, who received the sacraments of an antediluvian mystery cult practiced at Jerusalem's Mount Moriah, scene of the Ark's Holy-of-Holies.

Menelik—Son of King Solomon and the Queen of Sheba, he allegedly absconded with the Ark to Ethiopia, where it is believed to still exist.

Merenptah—Pharaoh of the Exodus.

Meryey—Libyan king who invaded western Egypt in concert with Sea Peoples attacking from the north.

Miglos, Arnaud de—Imprisoned by the Inquisition for his assumed knowledge of the Ark's whereabouts.

Mirepoix, Peter Roger de—The last commander of Montsègur.

Molay, Jacques de—Last Grand Master of the Knights Templar, burned at the stake.

Mulek—Israelite prince alleged to have escaped the Babylonian conquest of Jerusalem with the Ark of the Covenant to North America.

Nebuchadnezzar II—The Babylonian conqueror of Jerusalem in 587 B.C.

Olier, Jean-Jacques—Prime mover behind relocating the Ark to Canada.

Pacha, William—The 20th century Cherokee chief and medicine man stated that the Ark of the Covenant was in the American Midwest at least until 1973.Pereille, Ramon de—Defender of the Cathars, renovator of Montsègur.

Philip IV—Known as Philip the Fair, he outlawed the Templars, seized their properties, and had their leaders executed.

Plato—The Classical Greek philosopher whose account of Atlantis is the first of its kind.

Plèssis, Armand Jean du, Cardinal de Richelieu—Tried to prevent the Ark from being spirited out of France.

Poussin, Nicolas—Leading, mid-17th century painter of artworks hinting at the clandestine removal of the Ark from France to Canada.

Rahn, Otto Wilhelm—Leading Grail expert of the 1930s, discoverer of the Welwelsburg stone.

Roerich, Nikolay Konstantinovich—Early 20th century Russian artist, discoverer of the Chintamani Stone.

Scharfenberg, Albrecht von—Late 13th century German author of *The Younger Titurel*, describing the first Grail king.

Sinclair, Henry—The Earl of Orkney who allegedly sponsored the Templars' removal of the Ark from Scotland's Rosslyn Chapel to Oak Island, off the coast of Nova Scotia, in 1398.

Soubirous, Bernarde-Marie—Saint Bernadette, envisioned the White Lady in the vicinity of the Ark's last known location.

St. Bernard—Originally Bernard de Fontaine and Bernard de Clairvaux, founded the Order of the Knights Templar along with Baudoin II and Hughes de Champagne, and temporarily kept the Ark of the Covenant at his Cistercian abbey.

Thaut—The ancient Egyptian god of civilization, the Greek Thoth or Hermes, bearer of the Emerald Tablets from his sunken homeland in the distant west, mythic builder of the Great Pyramid.

Troyes, Chretien de—Author of the first Grail romance, circa 1190.

Urban II—The Pope who inaugurated the First Crusade in 1095.

Uzzah—A Jewish attendant killed by the Ark of the Covenant.

Ventadour, Hènri de Levis de—Founded the Compagnie du Saint-Sacrament, a secret society for the relocation of the Ark to New France.

Wolak, Ralph—Wondered if his ground-penetration radar located the Ark of the Covenant in 2004.

Zedekiah—Last Jewish king of Jerusalem before the Babylonian conquest in 589 B.C.

Glossary

Albigensians—The name applied, mostly by their enemies, to the Cathars, because the French town of Albi was an early Cathar stronghold.

Amarna—The Post-Dynastic, Arabic name for the ruins of Akhetaton, Horizon of the Sun, the capital of Amenhotep IV's heretical revolution.

Aron ha-Berit—The Hebrew Ark of the Covenant.

Asert Tree—The Egyptian counterpart of the biblical burning bush at the Great Pyramid.

Axis mundi—The World Axis, the center of being around which the universe appears to revolve.

Baraita—An ancient collection of oral Hebrew traditions depicting the Ark of the Covenant as an electrical device.

Ben-Ben—Also known as the Bennu Stone, or Phoenix Stone, the Stone of Destiny inside the sarcophagus of the King's Chamber in the Great Pyramid.

Bons hommes—The "good men," by which name the Cathars were commonly known.

Bon-Secours Chapel—A 17th century recreation at Montréal of the Holy-of-Holies (the Debir) in Solomon's First Temple, where the Ark of the Covenant was enshrined. Bon-Secours Chapel was later renamed Notre-Dame-de-Bon-Secours.

Chintamani Stone—The Shining Trapezohedron, an Asian crystal, the Jewel that grants all Desires, associated with floods and a sunken kingdom.

Chwarna—In ancient Persia, a magical jewel virtually identical to the Grail.

Compagnie du Saint-Sacrament—A secret society created to establish the "New Jerusalem" in Canada, with the Ark of the Covenant as its centerpiece.

Comet Encke—Periodic comet that made close passes to the Earth around 3100 B.C., 1628 B.C., and 1198 B.C., corresponding, respectively, to the sudden birth of civilization in the Nile Valley, the arrival of the Hyksos at the Nile Delta, and the final destruction of Atlantis.

Consolamentum—A Cathar ceremony in which Credentes were upgraded into Perfecti.

Coricancha—Also known as the Incas' Inticancha, "the Enclosure of Gold," surrounding the Holy Place (Holy-of-Holies), the Huacapata, where a sacred stone, the Paypicala, was venerated.

Credentes—"Believers" in Catharism, its lay supporters.

Croix pattée—The Templars' distinctive red cross, it also occurred in the Cathar caves of the Pyrenees Mountains and among regalia of Godfroi de Bouillon's Order of the Holy Sepulcher.

Debir—The Holy-of-Holies in Solomon's First Temple where the Ark of the Covenant was enshrined.

Ehecailacacozcatl—The Aztec Wind Jewel, symbolic of the Feathered Serpent's mystical power.

Endura—In Catharism, refusal to prolong life when approaching death and a means of escaping the bonds of reincarnation.

Ephod—A protective outer garment worn by the Levite high-priest, the Cohen Gadol, when attending to the Ark of the Covenant.

Fayra—The Fire Stone sacred to the original inhabitants of the Canary Islands, the Guanche.

Fayracan—The Guanche high-priest alone permitted to serve the Fayra Stone, just as the Levite high-priest was the Ark of the Covenant's sole attendant.

Fréres casaliers—"Rural brothers," Cathars who served in the Order of the Knights Templar, performing non-military duties. They were also known as the fréres de métiers, "serving brothers."

Giron-Gagal—The Quiche Mayas' crystal power stone brought by the U Mamae, "the wise men" of Patulan-Pa-Civan, to Yucatan from their homeland across the sea before it was destroyed by a natural catastrophe.

Gruppenführersaal—"The Group Leaders' Hall" in the North Tower of Heinrich Himmler's Grail Castle, where the Welwelsburg Stone was kept.

Heimholtz resonators—Spheres of varying sizes to determine the specific frequency at which each resonates. Their purpose in the Great Pyramid was to step up the vibrational energy, converting and concentrating the vibrations into airborne sound.

Heka Khasewet—"Rulers of Foreign Lands," better remembered today as the Hyksos, a collection of various Semitic peoples driven by drought conditions en masse from their Palestinian homelands into the eastern Nile Delta, circa 1625 B.C.

Kaname-ishi—Japanese keystone said to prevent earthquakes.

Lachine—Sieur de La Salle's estate at Montréal.

Lapis Exilis—"The Stone of Exile," the Holy Grail in Wolfram von Eschenbach's *Parzifal*.

Laurel—The emblem of the Cathars, equally associated with the ancient Greek pythia and apparitions of the White Lady in the Pyrenees Mountains.

Levites—A kind of Hebrew Grail family, tribal members who alone had access to the Ark of the Covenant.

Lia Fáil—The Stone of Destiny carried by the Tuatha da Danann to Ireland from the final destruction of Atlantis.

Mani Stone—The Cathars' Holy Grail and Ark of the Covenant.

Manichaeism—A 3rd century Persian dualism whose adherents regarded existence as a struggle between pairs of opposites, especially between light and darkness, spirit and matter.

Manisola—The Cathars' holiest ceremony, in which Perfecti were irradiated with the aura of the Holy Grail.

Mercy Seat—A platter-like fixture atop the Ark of the Covenant directly between twin representations of cherubim, where God appeared as fire or a bright light. The Mercy Seat was equivalent with the Holy Grail, from the Old French word, *grazala*, for a serving dish or platter.

Merovingians—A Frankish tribe who formed Europe's first dynasty after the collapse of Classical civilization in the late 5th century.

La milice du Christ—"The Poor Knights of Christ," the Order of the Knights Templar.

Montserrat—Spanish abbey where the Ark of the Covenant was taken by Cathars after the fall of Montségur.

Mount Moriah—In Jerusalem, its summit is the Temple Mount, the scene of Solomon's Temple.

Mount Parnassus—Above the Gulf of Corinth, site of the Greek Omphalos. (Such power stones are usually found atop seismically active, sacred mountains: the Holy Grail's Monsalvat, the Ark of the Covenant's Mount Sinai, the Cathars' Montségur, Japan's Sword Mountain, the Ville-Maries' Montréal, the Mohave Indians' Hawlopo at the summit of Mount Avikome, the Ben-Ben in the Great Pyramid, and so on.)

Mount Tsurugi—Japan's Sword Mountain, alleged site of the Ark of the Covenant.

Mu—Also known as Lemuria (Rome), Hiranyapura (India), Helani, Kahiki (Hawaii), Hiva (Easter Island), and so on, the sunken Motherland of mankind, where geo-metaphysical crystallography originated.

Munsalvaesche—Mount of Salvation, also known as Salvas, or Montsalvatch, a play on the Cathars' Montségur, the Grail castle.

Omphalos—The Greek navel stone at the center of Delphi.

Order of the Holy Sepulcher—A semi-secret society founded by Godfroi de Bouillon after his conquest of Jerusalem to restore his Merovingian bloodline to power, and, later, promote the discovery and reactivation of the Ark of the Covenant.

Perfectae—A female Cathar.

Perfecti—Cathar clergy.

Perfectus—A Cathar priest.

Piezo-electricity—The transformation of mechanical stress into electrical energy, as occurs in a quartz crystal when subjected to physical pressure.

Pohaku-o-Kane—The Hawaiian Stone of Kane, the sacred crystal of drowned Kahiki; in other words, Mu or Lemuria.

Sarpay—The Inca version of the Greek pythia, a virginal priestess who experienced an altered state of conscious while officiating for an antediluvian crystal, the Paypicala, at the Incas' Enclosure of Gold in Cuzco, literally, the Navel of the World.

Seborga—A northern Italian monastery where the Templars brought the Ark of the Covenant soon after its discovery.

Shekhinah—In the Hebrew Kabala, the materialization of spiritual energy in the physical world associated with the Ark of the Covenant.

Shugs—A psycho-spiritual energy coursing through the Chintamani Stone.

Societas Presbyterorum a S. Sulpitio—The Society of Saint Sulpice, a semi-secret organization aimed at recruiting and training men for missionary work in the New Jerusalem.

Te-pito-te-Kura—The Navel of Light, a power stone rescued from sunken Hiva (Lemuria) and taken to Easter Island, which derived its name, Te-pito-te-Henua, The Navel of the World, from the sacred object.

Transformer of the World—A prophetic crystal belonging to the Inca progenitor, Pachacutec.

The Tree of Life—Analogous for the human spinal column entwined with the serpentine energy of spiritual power, associated in myth with the sacred center, the axis mundi, the Navel of the World, and identified with specific locations: Lemuria, Atlantis, Giza, Crete, Delphi, Troy, Rome, Cuzco, Jerusalem, and so on, where such inner enlightenment is attained.

Tuaoi—Described by Edgar Cayce as the Fire Stone, a power crystal engineered in Atlantis.

Umbilicus Urbis Romae—The Navel of Rome, Troy's sacred stone, the Palladium; earlier, the Umbilicus Mundus, the Navel of the World, enshrined behind Rome's Temple of Saturn.

The Urna—A green gem from the forehead of the Hindu god Shiva, associated with the brow chakra's spiritual perception and the Western European Holy Grail.

Ville-Marie—The House of Mary, the New Jerusalem's original name at Montréal. The early settlers were known as Ville-Maries, or Montréalistes.

Yonaguni—Off the shores of this southernmost Japanese island a large ceremonial center was discovered 100 feet beneath the surface of the Pacific Ocean.

Notes

Introduction
1. Pinkham, *Guardians*, 57

Chapter 1
1. Charpentier, *The Mysteries*, 12

Chapter 2
1. Kimura, *Diving Survey Report*
2. Ibid.
3. Heyerdahl, "Reports"
4. Brown, *The Riddle*
5. Beckwith, *Kumulipo*
6. Alexander, *North American*
7. Ibid.
8. Lanning, Edward, *Peru*, Pt. I, Ch. 87
9. Brundage, *Aztec Myth*, 11
10. Lanning, Edward, *Peru*, Pt. I, Ch. 100
11. Bierhorst, *Mythology*
12. Andersen, *Myths*
13. Davis, Frederick, *Myths*
14. Roerich, *Shambhala*
15. Ibid.
16. Ibid.
17. Ibid.
18. Ibid.
19. Ibid.
20. Ibid.
21. Ibid.
22. Roerich, *Heart*
23. Decter, *Messenger*

Chapter 3
1. Braghine, *Shadow*
2. Taylor, *Plato's*, 2, 108
3. Ibid., 2, 24
4. Ibid., 2, 25
5. Ibid.
6. Ann, *Goddesses*
7. Fragione, *De immenso*, Volume I, 5
8. Cook, Roger, *Tree*, 9
9. Greier, *Odyssey*, Chapter XVIII
10. Myhill, *Canary*, 27
11. Markham, *Guanches*, 133
12. Schliemann, *Ilios*
13. Nuttall, *Fundamental*, 496
14. Ibid.

15. Vincent, *Mahabharata*

16. Ibid., 137

17. Le Plongeon, *Sacred*, 53

18. Nutall, *Fundamental*, xii, 53

19. Blackett, *Lost History*, 193

20. Galde, *Crystal*, 10, 11

21. Brundage, *Aztec*, 5

22. Horcasitas, *Book of the Gods*, 474

23. Taylor, *Plato's*, 4. 6,7

24. Ibid., 22

25. Bailey, *Natural Catastrophes*, 212

26. Ibid., 177

27. Ibid., 179

28. Taylor, *Plato's*, 2, 24

Chapter 4

1. Petrie, *Pyramids*, 131

2. Fix, *Pyramid*, 128

3. Braghine, *Shadow*, 237, 238

4. Tompkins, *Secrets*, 43

5. Farrell, *Giza*, 62

6. Lemesurier, *Decoding*, 22

7. Seis, *Great*, 149

8. Braghine, *Shadow*, 41

9. Hapgood, *Maps*, 79

10. Tedlock, *Popol*, 99

Chapter 5

1. Tompkins, *Secrets*, 137

2. Ibid., 138

3. Ammianus, *Roman*, 162

4. Jackson, *Building*, 24, 25

5. Crowley, *My Life*, 102

6. Houseman, "Pyramid,"70, 72

7. Corliss, *Lightning*, 186

8. Budge, *Book of the Dead*, 235

9. Devereux, "Fault," 89

10. Devereux, *Earth Lights*, 23

11. Malkowsky, *Egypt*, 123

12. Bauval, *Orion*, 235

13. Farrell, *Giza*, 75

14. Pinkham, *Guardians*, 58

15. Dunn, *Giza*, 134

16. Ibid., 23

17. O'Hara, *Earth*, 49

18. Ellis, *Thoth*, 98

19. Nelson, *Life*

20. Tunstall, "Pyramid," 6

21. Radka, *Electric*, 145

22. Turner, *Ute*

23. Farrell, *Giza*, 88

24. Ibid., 83

25. Collins, *Gods*

26. Bauval, *Orion*, 101

27. Taylor, *Plato's*, 2, 22

28. Clark, R.T. Rundle, *Myth*, 132

29. Gardiner, Gnosis, 86

30. Budge, *Book of the Dead*, 248

31. Farrell, *Giza*, 72

32. Cayce, *Atlantis, The Edgar Cayce Readings*, 877-26 M.46 5/23/38

33. Ibid., 218

34. Ibid., 440-5 M.23 12/20/33

35. Ibid., 519-1 M.39 2/20/34

36. Ibid., 263-4 F.23 3/6/35

37. Ibid., 2072-10 F.32 7/22/42

38. Ibid., 440-5 M.23 12/20/33

39. Charpentier, *Mysteries*, 44

40. Ellis, *Thoth*, 173

41. Nuttall, *Fundamental*, 521

42. Ibid.

Chapter 6

1. Devereaux, *Shamanism*, 209
2. Devereaux, *Earth Lights*, 47
3. Hunt, *Shamanism*, 23
4. Buckalew, "Negative," 22
5. Fornof, "Stress," 43
6. www.electrostaticsolutions.com
7. Ivanhoe, "Geometric," 32
8. Dusch, "Baraboo," 28

Chapter 7

1. Caroli, Kenneth
2. Ibid.

Chapter 8

1. Christy-Vitale, *Watermark*, 101
2. MacPherson, *Known Plays*, 194
3. Edwards, A.E., *Complete Works*, 138
4. Mercatante, *Who's Who*, 143, 144
5. Ellis, *Tempest*, 114
6. Osman, *Moses*, 128
7. Ibid., 130
8. Redford, Donald B., *Akhenaten*, 235
9. Osman, *Moses*, 131
10. Mercatante, *Who's Who*, 18
11. Lauton, *Giza*, 160
12. Fornof, "Stress," 4
13. Lauton, *Giza*, 160
14. Aldred, *Akhenaten, King of Egypt*, 104
15. Schulman, "Military," 52
16. Aldred, *Akhenaten and Nefertiri*, 142
17. Budge, *Dwellers*, 235
18. Weigall, *Life*, 105
19. Mercatante, *Who's Who*, 196
20. Brier, *Murder*, 193
21. Greier, *Odyssey*

22. Edwards, *Complete Works*, 122
23. Wadell, *Manetho's*, 76
24. Murnane, *Le Papyrus*, 89
25. Ibid., 90
26. Childress, "Great Pyramid," 18, 21
27. Traver, *From Polis*, 73
28. Aldred, *Tutankhamun's*, 186
29. Malamat, *History*, 43
30. De Moor, *Rise of Yahwism*, 102
31. Fisher, *Tacitus'*, lib. v, c.2
32. Justinus, *Epitoma*, lib. XXXVI, c.2.
33. *Saint Joseph Edition, Exodus* Chapter III, 21, 22
34. Ibid., Chapter XII, 36

Chapter 9

1. Dunn, *Giza*, 173
2. Bailey, *Natural*
3. Lindy, *Geology*, 44
4. Joseph, *Destruction*, 122
5. Bailey, *Natural*, 156
6. Schachermeyr, *Griechische*, 112
7. Budge, *Ancient Egyptian Amulets*, 218
8. Ibid., 226
9. Ibid., 227
10. Ibid., 227
11. Ibid., 312
12. Ibid., 183
13. Ibid., 157
14. *Saint Joseph Edition, Exodus* Chapter 10: 22, 23
15. Bailey, *Natural*, 347
16. Childress, "Great Pyramid," 21
17. Ibid., 15
18. Ibid., 25, 10
19. Ibid., 22

20. Ibid., 21

21. Ellis, *Solomon*, 141

22. Edwards, *Complete Works*, 138

23. *Saint Joseph Edition, Exodus* 24:12

24. Ibid., 24:15

25. Ibid., 24:18

26. Ellis, *Solomon*, 172

27. Ibid., 148

28. *Saint Joseph Edition, Exodus* 3:1

29. Ibid., 3:2, 3

30. Ellis, *Solomon*,161

31. Budge, *Ancient Egyptian Amulets*, 42

32. *Saint Joseph Edition, Exodus* 19:12,13

33. Ellis, *Solomon*, 157

34. Budge, *Ancient Egyptian Amulets*, 42

35. *Saint Joseph Edition, Exodus* 12:36

36. Ibid., 14:21,22;24

37. Cavendish, *Genesis*, 130

38. Fillon, "Science," 66

39. *Saint Joseph Edition, Exodus* 20:3

40. Ibid., 32:26, 27; 28

41. Radka, *Electric*, 123

42. *Saint Joseph Edition, Kings* 8:8

43. Ibid., 8:9

44. *Saint Joseph Edition, Exodus* 16:34

45. Ibid., *Numbers* 17:25

46. Ibid., *Hebrews* 9:4

47. Hancock, *Sign*, 8

48. Ellis, *Solomon*, 196

49. Ibid., 6

50. *Saint Joseph Edition, Joshua* 6:24

51. Ibid., *Samuel* 4:7

52. Ibid., *Joshua* 3: 14-17; 4:18

53. Frydman, "Geotechnical"

54. Ibid.

55. *Saint Joseph Edition, Leviticus* 9:22-10:7

56. Ibid., *Kings* 26:3

57. Ibid., *Samuel* 4:2

58. Ibid., 4:10,11

59. Ibid., 4:18

60. Ibid., 5:3,4

61. Ibid., 6:4

62. Ibid., 6:19

63. Ibid., 7:1

64. *Saint Joseph Edition, Chronicles* 13:11

65. Ibid., *Samuel* 7:1,2

66. Department, "Research"

67. Floderus, "Occupational," 2

68. Rao, "Regulation," 2

69. *Saint Joseph Edition, Samuel* 6:1-11

70. Ibid., *Chronicles* 13:1-13

71. Cayce, *Atlantis, the Edgar Cayce Readings*, 2072-10 F.32 7/22/42

72. *Saint Joseph Edition, Chronicles* 21:25

73. Ibid., *Samuel* 24:24, 25

74. Ibid., *Genesis* 14:18

75. Bernier, *Templars'*, 199

76. *Saint Joseph Edition, Book of Enoch*, 7:71-73

77. Ibid., *Deuteronomy* 17:8

78. Matthews, *Grail*, 31

79. Halley, *Halley's*, 159

80. Hasel, *Biblical*, 4

81. Bailey, *Natural*, 285

82. Sora, *Lost Treasure*, 122

83. Frydman, "Geotechnical," 5

84. *Saint Joseph Edition, Kings* 19:11

85. Edey, *Sea Traders*,122a

86. Mercatante, *Who's Who*, 87, 88

87. Bernier, *Templars'*, 200

88. Michell, *View*, 79

89. *Saint Joseph Edition*, *Kings* 1:4, 29-31

90. Ibid., 2 *Kings* 25:1

91. Ibid., 2 *Kings* 25:3; *Lamentations* 4:4, 5, 10

92. Ibid., *Jeremiah* 52:16

93. Ibid., 2 *Kings* 25:22, 24; *Jeremiah* 40:1, 2, 5, 6

94. King, *Legends*

95. *Saint Joseph Edition*, *Jeremiah* 3:16

96. Ibid., *Revelations* 11:19

97. Ibid., *Maccabees*, 2:4-10

98. Ibid., *Deuteronomy* 34:1

99. Charles, *Apocalypse*, Chapter 6, 10

100. Sora, *Lost Treasure*, 124

Chapter 10

1. Gibbon, *Decline*, vol.I, 274

2. Prawer, *Crusader's*, 36

3. Addison, *History*, 2

4. Prawer, *Crusader's*, 36

5. Pinkham, *Guardians*, 132

6. Markale, *Montségur*, 277

7. Wallace-Murphy, *Rosslyn*, 64

8. Baigent, *Holy Blood*, 268

9. Bernier, *Templars'*, 54

10. Addison, *History*, 38

11. Charpentier, *Mysteries*, 49

12. Ralls, *Templars*, 33

13. Charpentier, *Mysteries*, 49

14. *Saint Joseph Edition*, *Maccabees* 2:4-10

15. Ibid., *Deuteronomy* 34:1

16. Ibid., *Maccabees* 2:4-10

17. Sora, *Lost Treasure*,169

18. Charpentier, *Mysteries*, 50

19. Ralls, *Templars*, 31

20. Baigent, *Holy Blood*, 87

21. Prawer, *Crusader's*, 269

22. Charpentier, *Mysteries*, 49

23. Kenyon, J. Douglas, "Templar," 11

24. Ralls, *Templars*, 32

25. Prawer, *Crusader's*

26. Addison, *History*, 12

27. Charpentier, *Mysteries*, 69

28. Ibid., 13, 37, 72

29. Ibid., 161, 162

30. Ibid., 29

31. Mann, *Knights*, 259

32. Markale, *Montségur*, 110

33. Ibid., 148

34. Douzet, *Wanderings*, 69

35. Fines, *Who's Who*, 37, 38

36. Ibid., 41

37. Lambert, *Cathars*, 67

38. Shea, *Perfect*, 55

39. Lambert, *Cathars*, 144

40. Ibid.

41. Ashbridge, *First Crusade*, 32

42. Lambert, *Cathars*, 87

43. Ashbridge, *First Crusade*, 98

44. Markale, *Montségur*, 89

45. Douzet, *Wanderings*, 69

46. Ibid., 227

47. Fanthorpe, *Mysteries*, 178

Chapter 11

1. Staines, *Complete*, 33

2. Mustard, *Parzifal*, Book V, 235

3. Ibid., Book IX, 495

4. Ibid., Book IX, 471

5. Ibid., Book IX, 493

6. Ibid., Book XV, 778

7. Ibid., Book IX, 474

8. Ibid., Book IX, 470

9. Markale, *Grail*, 137

10. Matthews, *Grail*, 21

11. Ibid., 22

12. Passage, *Titurel*, 144

13. Markale, *Grail*, 275

14. Mustard, *Parzifal*, Book IX, 471

15. Rahn, *Crusade*, 153

16. Passage, *Titurel*, H-309, 1

17. Bryant, Nigel, *Merlin*, 79

18. Markale, *Grail*, 158, 276

19. Mustard, *Parzifal*, Book IX, 473

20. Ibid., 471

21. Ibid., Book XV, 737

22. Ibid., 495

23. Ibid., Book IX, 468

24. Ibid., xlii.

25. Ibid., Book IX, 469, 471

26. Pinkham, *Guardians*, 46

27. Matthews, *Grail*, 124

28. Mustard, *Parzifal*, Book IX, 470

29. Passage, *Titurel*, 50

30. Markale, *Grail*, 134

31. Ibid., 128

32. Tribbe, *Holy Grail*, 79, 98

33. Hoyle, *Delphi*, 44

34. Matthews, *Grail*, 16

35. Ibid., 15

36. Nuttall, *Fundamental*, 469

37. Kearsley, *Mayan*

38. Blackett, *Lost History*, 235

39. Hoyle, *Delphi*

40. Matthews, *Grail*, Volume IX, 493

41. Mustard, *Parzifal*, Chapter V, 121

42. Taylor, *Plato's*, 171

43. Mustard, *Parzifal*

44. Taylor, *Plato's*, 198, 211, 319

45. Rahn, *Crusade*, 157

46. Mustard, *Parzifal*, 453, 454

47. Markale, *Grail*, 138

Chapter 12

1. Phillips, *Templars*, 182, h,i

2. Markale, *Montségur*, 65, 66

3. Childress, "Great Pyramid," 30

4. Charpentier, *Mysteries*, 64

5. Cook, Stephen, *Heinrich*, 23

6. Mustard, *Parzifal*, 191

7. Cook, Stephen, *Heinrich*, 199

8. Ibid.

9. Rahn, *Crusade*, 13

10. Ibid., 91, 148

11. Cook, Stephen, *Heinrich*, 46

12. Fitzgerald, *Bernadette*, 253

13. Markale, *Grail*, 229, 230

14. Mustard, *Parzifal*, Book V, 235

Chapter 13

1. Wallace-Murphy, *Rosslyn*, 22

2. Mann, *Knights*, xi, xii

3. Thompson, *American*, 319

4. Mallery, *Rediscovery*, 122

5. Mann, *Knights*, 19

6. Wallace-Murphy, *Rosslyn*, 1

7. Sora, *Lost Treasure*, 125, 126

8. *Saint Joseph Edition*, 2 *Kings* 25:1-7; 2 *Chronicles* 36:12; *Jeremiah* 32:4,5; 34:2, 3; 39:1-7; 52:4-11; *Ezekiel* 12:12

9. Kingsborough, *Antiquities*, vol. viii, 250

10. Thompson, *American*, 2

11. Edwards, A.E., *Complete Works*, 178

Chapter 14

1. Markale, *Grail*, 271
2. Douzet, *Wanderings*, 65
3. Bernier, *Templars'*, 281
4. Ibid.
5. Ibid., 26
6. Ibid., 28
7. Ibid., 223
8. Ibid., 160, 280
9. Ibid., 160
10. Ibid., 25
11. Mann, *Knights*, 90
12. Baigent, *Holy Blood*, 44, 45, 178
13. Bernier, *Templars'*, 296
14. Ibid., 34
15. Ibid., 210
16. Ibid., 21
17. Ibid., 131
18. Ibid., 75
19. Ibid.
20. Ibid., 31
21. Beaudoin, *Family*, 6
22. Deal, "Mystic," 14

Bibliography

Addison, Charles G. *The History of the Knights Templars*. Kempton, Ill.: Adventures Unlimited Press, 2001.

Aldred, Cyril. *Akhenaten and Nefertiri*. New York: Brooklyn Museum, 1973.

———. *Akhenaten, King of Egypt*. London: Thames & Hudson, 1988.

———. *Tutankhamun's Egypt*. New York: Scribner's, 1972.

Alexander, William. *North American Mythology*. New York: Harcourt Brace, 1935.

American Journal of Forensic Medicine and Pathology, The. *www.amjforensicmedicine.com*.

Ammianus, Marcellinus. *Roman History*. London: Bohn, 1862.

Andersen, Johannes C. *Myths and Legends of the Polynesians*. London: Harrap, 1928.

Andressohn, John C. *The Ancestry and Life of Godfrey of Bouillon*. Bloomington: Indiana University Publications, Social Science Series No. 5, Indiana University, 1947.

Ann, Martha, and Dorothy Myers Imel. *Goddesses in World Mythology*. New York: Oxford University Press, 1993.

Asbridge, Thomas. *The First Crusade, A New History*. London: Oxford University Press, 2004.

Baigent, Michael, Richard Leigh, and Henry Lincoln. *Holy Blood, Holy Grail*. New York: Bantam Doubleday Dell Publishing Group, Inc., 1983.

Bailey, Mark E., Michael Baillie, Lars Franzen, Thomas B. Larsson, Bruce W. Masse, Trevor Palmer, Benny Peiser, and Duncan Steel. *Natural Catastrophes During Bronze Age Civilizations: Archaeological, Geological, Astronomical and Cultural Perspectives*. Oxford, England: Archaeo Press, 1998.

Ballinger, Bill S. *Lost City of Stone, The Story of Nan Madol*. New York: Simon and Schuster, 1978.

Barber, Malcolm. *The New Knighthood: A History of the Order of the Temple*. Cambridge, UK: Cambridge University Press, 1994.

Bauval, Robert, and Adrian Gilbert. *The Orion Mystery, Unlocking the Secret of the Pyramids*. New York: Crown Publishers, 1994.

Beaudoin, Kenneth Lawrence. *The Family of Napoleon Beaudoin of Cadillac, Michigan, With a Brief Account of the Beaudoin Family on the North American Continent Since 1667: 282 Years of Continued Residence*, privately published, 1949.

Beckerath, Jürgen von. *Chronologie des Pharaonischen Ägypten*. Mainz: Philip von Zabern, 1997.

Beckwith, Martha W. *The Kumulipo, A Hawaiian Creation Chant*. Chicago: Chicago University Press, 1951.

Ben-Dov, M. *In the Shadow of the Temple, The Discovery of Ancient Jerusalem*. Jerusalem: Keter Publishing House, 1982.

Bernbaum, Edwin. *The Way to Shambhala: A Search for the Mythical Kingdom Beyond the Himalayas*. London: Creuzer Press, 2001.

Bernier, Francine. *The Templars' Legacy in Montréal, the New Jerusalem*. Kempton, Ill.: Adventures Unlimited Press, 2001.

Bierhorst, John. *The Mythology of South America*. New York: William Morrow and Company, Inc., 1982.

Blackett, W.S. *The Lost History of America*. London: Truebner, 1883.

Blashfield, Jean F. *Cartier: Jacques Cartier in Search of the Northwest Passage*. New York: Compass Point Books, 2001.

Bonwick, James. *Irish Druids and the Old Irish Religions*. London: Dorset Press, 1986.

Bourn, G.P.F. Van Den. *The Duties of the Vizier*. London: Kegan Paul, 1988.

Boylan, Patrick. *Thoth, the Hermes of Egypt*. London: Oxford University Press, 1922.

Braghine, Alexander. *The Shadow of Atlantis*. Kempton, Ill.: Adventures Unlimited Press, 1997.

Breasted, James Henry. *Ancient Records of Egypt*. London: Histories & Mysteries of Man, ltd., 1988, 204.

———. *A History of Egypt*. New York: Scribner's & Sons, 1909.

Brier, Bob, Ph.d. *The Murder of Tutankhamun*. New York: Berkley Books, 1999.

Brown, John MacMillan. *The Riddle of the Pacific*. Kempton, Ill.: Adventures Unlimited Press, 2003.

Brundage, Henry. *Aztec Myth and Symbol*. New York: Doubleday, 1960.

Brunton, Paul. *A Search in Secret Egypt*. London: Hall House, 1936.

Bryant, Alice, and Phillis Galde. *The Message of the Crystal Skull*. Woodbury, Minn.: Llewellyn Publications, 1989.

Bryant, Nigel, trans. *Merlin and the Grail: Joseph of Arimathea, Merlin, Perceval: The Trilogy of Arthurian Prose Romances Attributed to Robert de Boron*. New York: D.S. Brewer, 2005.

Buckalew, L.W., and A. Rizzuto. "Negative Air Ion Effects on Human Performance and Physiological Condition." *Aviation, Space, and Environmental Medicine*, 55, Part 8, 731-734, Aug 1984.

———. "Subjective Response to Negative Air Ion Exposure," *Aviation, Space, and Environmental Medicine*. 53, (8) 822-3, August 1982.

Budge, E.A. Wallis. *Ancient Egyptian Amulets and Talismans*. New York: University Books, 1968.

———. *Dwellers on the Nile*. New York: Dover Publications, Inc., 1967.

⸺. *Osiris and the Egyptian Resurrection*. New York: Dover Publications, Inc., 1966.

⸺. *The Book of the Dead*. Boston: Dover Books, 1966.

⸺. *The Gods of the Egyptians*. New York: Dover Publications, Inc., 1965.

Burland, C.A., and Werner Forman. *Feathered Serpent and Smoking Mirror*. New York: G.P. Putnam & Sons, 1975.

Burland, C.A. *The Gods of Mexico*. London: Eyre & Spottiswoode, 1970.

Butzer, Karl W. *Early Hydraulic Civilization in Egypt, A Study of Cultural Ecology*. Chicago: University of Chicago Press, 1976.

Cameron, Norman, trans. *The Gods of the Greeks*. New York: Grove Press, 1960.

Camp, L. Sprague de. *The Ancient Engineers*. New York: Ballantine Books, 1960.

Caroli, Kenneth. Personal correspondence, 1989 to 2006.

Carter, Howard, and A.C. Mace. *The Discovery of the Tomb of Tutankhamun*. New York: Dover Publications, Inc., 1967.

Cavendish, Marshall. *Genesis and Exodus*. New York: Marshall Cavendish, 1961.

Cayce, Edgar. *Atlantis and Lemuria*. Virginia Beach, Va.: A.R.E. Press, 2001.

⸺. *Atlantis, The Edgar Cayce Readings*, Vol. 22, compiled by the Readings Research Department, Association for Research and Enlightenment, Inc., Virginia Beach, Va., 1987.

Charles, R.H. *The Apocalypse of Baruch*. Boston: Destiny Publishers, 1988.

Charpentier, Louis. *The Mysteries of Chartres Cathedral*. London: Thorsons Publishing Group, Limited, 1988.

Childress, David Hatcher. "The Great Pyramid and the Ark of the Covenant," *World Explorer*, vol. 2, no. 2.

⸺. "The Kamanawa Wall." *World Explorer*, vol. 1, nr. 8, p. 19, 1996.

⸺. *Ancient Tonga and the Lost City of Mu'a*. Kempton, Ill.: Adventures Unlimited Press, 1996.

Christie, Anthony. *Chinese Mythology*. New York: Peter Bedrick Books, 1977.

Christy-Vitale, Joseph. *Watermark*. New York: Paraview Pocket Books, 2004.

Churchward, James. *The Lost Continent of Mu*. Albuquerque, N. Mex: BE, Books, 1987.

Clark, R.T. Rundle. *Myth and Symbol in Ancient Egypt*. London: Thames & Hudson, 1959.

Clark, Rosemary. *The Sacred Tradition in Ancient Egypt*. Woodbury, Minn.: Llewellyn Publications, 2001.

Clayton, Peter A.. *Chronicles of the Pharaohs*. London: Thames & Hudson, 1995.

Clemente, Adriano, and Andrew Lukianowicz, trans. *Narrations, Symbolic Languages and the Boen Tradition in Ancient Tibet*. New York: Library of Tibetan Works and Archives, 1988.

Clube, Victor, and William Napier. *The Cosmic Winter*. Oxford: Basil Blackwell, Inc., 1990.

Collins, Andrew. *Gods of Eden*. Rochester, Vt.: Bear and Company, 2002.

"Color and Its Relation to the Aura." *The Aura and What it Means to You, A Compilation from Many Authorities.* Mokelumne Hill, Calif.: Health Research, 1955.

Cook, Roger. *The Tree of Life, Symbol of the Centre.* London: Thames and Hudson, 1984.

Cook, Stephen, and Stuart Russell. *Heinrich Himmler's Camelot, The Wewelsburg Ideological Center of the SS, 1934-1945.* Andrews, N.C.: Kressmann-Backmeyer Publishing, LLC, 1999.

Cooper, J.C. *An Illustrated Encyclopedia of Traditional Symbols.* London: Thames and Hudson, 1978.

Corliss, William R. *Ancient Structures.* Glen Arm, Md.: The Sourcebook Project, 2001.

———. *Lightning, Nocturnal Lights and Related Electromagnetic Phenomena.* Glen Arm, Md.: Sourcebook Project, 1984.

Cox , Isaac J. *Journeys of LaSalle.* New York: Ams Pr Inc, 1922.

Crowley, Aleister. *My Life.* London: Diabolic Press, Ltd., 1939.

Cunningham, Scott. *Hawaiian Religion and Magic.* Woodbury, Minn.: Llewellyn Publications, 1994.

Davidson, Richard. *The Book of Enoch.* New York: Grosset and Dunlap, 1969.

Davis, Ester Payne. "The Strange Lat'te Stones of Guam." *World Explorer*, vol. 1, no. 2, 1992.

Davis, Frederick H. *Myths and Legends of Japan.* Singapore: Graham Brash Publishing Company, 1989.

De Moor, Johannes C. The Rise of Yahwism: *The Roots of Israelite Monotheism, Second and Revised Edition.* New York: Peeters Publishers, 1997.

Deal, David Allen. "The 'Mystic Symbol' Demystified." *Ancient American*, vol. 1, nr. 5, March/April, 1994.

Decter, Jacqueline, Ph.D. *Messenger of Beauty, The Life and Visionary Art of Nicolas Roerich.* Rochester, Vt.: Park Street Press, 1997.

Department of Environmental Sciences, University of Kuopio, Finland. "Research on cancer-related biological effects of electromagnetic fields (EMF). *www.swan.ac.uk / cget / ejgt / Ghentsummary.doc*

Devereux, Paul. "The Fault of the Earth," *Mysteries of Mind, Space & Time*, vol. VII, 822-825, New Haven, Conn.: H.S. Stuttman, Inc., 1992.

———. *Earth Lights Revelation.* London: Blandford Press, 1989.

———. *Earth Memory.* Woodbury, Minn.: Llewellyn Publications, 1992.

———. *Shamanism and the Mystery Lines.* London: Quantum Books, Ltd., 2001.

Dorson, Richard M. *Folk Legends of Japan.* Rutland, Vt.: Charles E. Tuttle, 1962.

Douzet, André. *The Wanderings of the Grail.* Kempton, Ill., Adventures Unlimited Press, 2006.

Driscoll, Robert. *Technology in the Ancient World.* San Francisco: McVey Publishing Company, 1981.

Dunn, Christopher. *The Giza Power Plant, Technologies of Ancient Egypt.* Rochester, Vt.: Bear and Company Publishing, 1998.

Dusch, Christopher T. J. "The Baraboo Hills Astrolabe: An Ancient Electronic Technology," *Ancient American*, October/November, 2001.

Edey, Maitland A.. *The Sea Traders.* New York: Time-Life Books, 1974.

Edgerton, W.F., and J. Wilson. *Historical Records of Ramses III, the Text of Medinet Habu*. Chicago: University of Chicago Press, 1964.

Edwards, A.E., trans. *The Complete Works of Flavius Josephus*. London: Esterville House, Ltd., 1938.

Edwards, I.E.S. *The Pyramids of Egypt*. London: Penguin Books, 1986.

Eher, Frederick. *Philo Judaeus*. New York: Macmillan, 1970.

Electrostatic Solutions, Ltd. *www.electrostaticsolutions.com*

Ellis, Ralph. *Jesus, Last of the Pharaohs*. Kempton, Ill.: Adventures Unlimited Press, 2001.

———. *Solomon, Falcon of Sheba*. Kempton, Ill.: Adventures Unlimited Press, 2002.

———. *Tempest and Exodus*. Kempton, Ill.: Adventures Unlimited Press, 2000.

———. *Thoth, Architect of the Universe*. Kempton, Ill.: Adventures Unlimited Press, 2001.

Emerson, Nathaniel B. *Unwritten Literature of Hawaii*. Washington, D.C.: Smithsonian Institute, 1909.

Emery, W.B. *Archaic Egypt*. London: Penguin Books, 1971.

Erman, Adolf. *Life in Ancient Egypt*. New York: Dover Publications, Inc., 1966.

Evans, Humphrey. *The Mystery of the Pyramids*. New York: Thomas Y. Crowell, 1979.

Fanthorpe, Lionel, and Patricia Fanthorpe. *Mysteries of Templar Treasure and the Holy Grail*. Newburyport, Mass.: Red Wheel/ Weiser, LLC, 2004.

Farrell, Joseph P. *The Giza Death Star, The Paleophysics of the Great Pyramid and the Military Complex at Giza*. Kempton, Ill.: Adventures Unlimited Press, 2001.

Feinstein, Clarence, ed. *Encylopeaedia Judaica*. New York: MacMillan Co., 1971.

Filby, F.A.. *The Flood Reconsidered*. London: Pickering Press, Ltd., 1970.

Fillon, Mike. "Science Solves the Ancient Myteries of the Bible," *Popular Mechanics*, December, 1996.

Fines, John. *Who's Who in the Middle Ages*. New York: Barnes and Noble Books, 1995.

Fisher, C.D., trans. *Tacitus' Historiae I–V*. New York: Oxford University Press, 1922.

Fitzgerald, Edward, trans. *Bernadette and Lourdes*. New York: Farrar, 1954.

Fix, William F. *Pyramid Odyssey*, New York: Mayflower Books, 1978.

Floderus, Birgitta. "Occupational exposures to high frequency electromagnetic fields in the intermediate range (>300 Hz–10MHz)." *cat.inist.fr / ?aModele=afficheN&cpsidt=14024983*

Fornof, K.T., and G.O. Gilbert. "Stress and Physiological, Behavioral and Performance Patterns of Children under varied Air Ion Ievels," *International Journal of Biometeoro*, 32, 260-270, 1988.

Fragione, Ezio, trans. *De immenso innumcrabili*. London: Pickwick Publishers, Ltd., 1952.

Frydman, Sam. "Geotechnical Problems in the Holyland—Then and Now." Technion Israel Institute of Technology, Haifa, Israel.

Fulcanelli. *Le Mystere des Cathedrales*. Paris: Pauvert, 1964.

Galde, Phyllis. *Crystal Healing, the Next Step*. Woodbury, Minn.: Llewellyn Publications, 1988.

Gambier, J.W. *The History of the Discovery and Conquest of the Canary Islands*. London: Antiquary, 1894.

Gardiner, Philip. *Gnosis: The Secret of Solomon's Temple Revealed*. Franklin Lakes, N.J.: New Page Books, 2006.

Garvin, Richard. *The Crystal Skull*. New York: Doubleday and Co., 1971.

Gaskell, G.A. *Dictionary of All Scriptures and Myths*. New York: Avenel Books, 1981.

Gasten, Theodore H. *Myth, Legend and Custom in the Old Testament*. New York: Harper & Row, 1969.

Gerhard, L., trans. *Parallax*. London: Bartleby House, Ltd., 1950.

Gibbon, Edward, Sir. *The Decline and Fall of the Roman Empire*. London: Crownstall Publishers, 1955.

Görg, Manfred. "Israel in Hieroglyphen," Munich: *Biblische Notizen: Beiträge zur exegetischen Diskussion*, 2002.

Grant, Michael. *The Roman Emperors*. New York: Barnes and Noble Books, 1985.

Graves, Robert, and Raphael Patai. *Hebrew Myths, the Book of Genesis*. New York: Greenwich House, 1964.

———. *The Greek Myths, Vols. I & II*. London: Penguin Books, 1984.

———. *The White Goddess*. New York: Creative Age Press, 1948.

Greier, Florian, trans. *Odyssey*. Chicago: Regnery Press, 1965.

Grossman, Cathy Lynn. "Americans' image of God varies," *USA Today*, September 11, 2006.

Guttenberg, B., and C. Richter. *Seismicity of the Earth and Associated Phenomena*. Princeton: Princeton University Press, 1954.

Halley, Henry H. *Halley's Bible Handbook*. Chicago: Regnery, 1959.

Hancock, Wolfram von Graham. *The Sign And the Seal*. New York: Touchstone, 1993.

Hapgood, Charles, Dr. *The Maps of the Ancient Sea-Kings*. New York: Chilton Books, 1966.

Hasel, Gerhard F. *Biblical Chronologies*. Haversack, Md.: Haversack Press, 1981.

Hawkins, L.H. "Biological Significance of Air Ions," Proc. IEE Colloquium on ions in the atmosphere, natural and man made," London, 1985.

Hesiod. *The Works and Days, Theogony, The Shield of Heracles*. Ann Arbor: The University of Michigan Press, 1968.

Heyerdahl, Thor, Dr. "Reports of the Norwegian Archaeological Expedition to Easter Island and the East Pacific, Volumes 1 and 2." Chicago: Rand McNally and Company, 1965.

Hooten, Ernest. *The Ancient Inhabitants of the Canary Islands*. Cambridge, Mass.: Harvard University Press, 1915.

Hope, Murray. *Atlantis*. New York: Western Tradition Books, 1970.

Horcasitas, Farnando, and Doris Heyden. *Book of the Gods and the Rites of the Ancient Calendar*. Norman, Okla.: University of Oklahoma Press, 1971.

Houseman, Robert. "Pyramid Energies," *Fate*, September, 1995.

Hoyle, Peter. *Delphi*. London: Cassell, 1967.

Hunt, Norman Bancroft. *Shamanism in North America*. New York: Firefly Books, 2003.

Inbar, O., A. Rotstein, R. Dlin, R. Dotan, and F.G. Sulman. "The effect of Negative Air Ions on Various Physiological Functions during Work in a Hot Environment," *Int. J Biometeor*. 26 (2), 153-163, 1982.

Ions, Veronica. *Egyptian Mythology*. London: Hamlyn, 1968.

Ivanhoe, Lytton Francis. "Geometric analysis of seismic fault evidence." AAPG Bulletin, May 1955; 39: 753–761. *www.aapgbull.geoscienceworld.org*

Jackson, Kevin, and Jonathan Stamp. *Building the Great Pyramid*. New York: Firefly Books, 2003.

Jones, Katherine, trans. *Moses and Monotheism*. New York: Vintage Books, 1967.

Joseph, Frank. *Survivors of Atlantis*. Rochester, Vt.: Inner Traditions Press, Inc., 2004.

———. *The Atlantis Encyclopedia*. Franklin Lakes, N.J.: New Page Books, 2005.

———. *The Destruction of Atlantis*. Rochester, Vt.: Inner Traditions Press, Inc., 2001.

———. *The Lost Civilization of Lemuria*. Rochester, Vt.: Bear and Company, 2006.

———. *The Lost Treasure of King Juba*. Rochester, Vt.: Bear and Company, 2003.

Justinus, M. Junianus. *Epitoma Historiarum Philippicarum: Books VII to XII: Excerpta De Historia Hacedonia*. New York: Ares Publishers, 1995.

Kearsley, G.R. *Mayan Genesis, South Asian Myths, Migrations and Iconography in Mesoamerica*. London: Yelsraek Publishing, 2001.

Keller, Werner. *The Bible as History*. London: Hodder & Stoughton, 1970.

Kellogg, E.W. "Air Ions: Their Possible Biological Significance and Effects," *Journal of Bioelectricity*, 3 (1&2), 119-136, 1984.

Kennedy, Gordon. *Nordic Antiquities in the Tropical Atlantic*. Ojai, Calif.: Nivaria Press, 1998.

Kenyon, Douglas. "Great Pyramid Shaft to be Revisited." *Atlantis Rising*, January/February 2006, #55, p. 11.

Kenyon, J. Douglas. "Templar Artifact Found," *Atlantis Rising*, January/February 2006, #55, p. 11.

Kenyon, Kathleen. *Digging Up Jerusalem*. London: Ernest Benn, Ltd. Publishers, 1974.

Kimura, Masaaki. *Diving Survey Report for Submarine Ruins off Yonaguni, Japan*. Okinawa: University of the Ryukyus Press, 2002.

King, Leonard. *Legends of Babylon and Egypt in Relation to Hebrew Tradition*. London: Oxford University Press, 1918.

Kingsborough, Edward King. *Antiquities of Mexico*. New York: University Microfilms International, 1978.

Kitchen, Kenneth Anderson. "The Physical Text of Merenptah's Victory Hymn (The 'Israel Stela')." *Journal of the Society for the Study of Egyptian Antiquities* 24:71-76, 1994.

Kornblueh, I.H. "Aeroionotherapy of Burns in Bioclimatology, Biometeorology and Aeroionotherapy," Gualtierotti, et. al. eds., Carlo Erba Foundation, Milan 1968.

———, G.M. Piersol, and F.P. Speicher. "Relief from Pollinosis in Negatively Ionised Rooms," *American Journal of Physical Medicine*, 37, 18-27, 1958.

Kreuger, A.P., and E.J. Reed. "Biological Impact of Small Air Ions." *Science*, 193, 1209-13. 1976.

Kronkheit, C.A. *A Dictionary of Ancient Egyptian Terms*, Chicago: University of Chicago Press, 1929.

Kunkel, Edward. *Pharaoh's Pump*. Privately published, 1962.

Lambert, Malcolm. *The Cathars*. New York: Blackwell, 1998.

Lanning, Edward P. *Peru Before the Incas*. Upper Saddle River, N.J.: Prentice-Hall, Inc., 1967.

Lansing, Carol. *Power and Purity: Cathar Heresy in Medieval Italy*. London: Oxford University Press, 1998.

Lauton, Ian, and Chris Ogilvie-Herald. *Giza, the Truth*. Montpelier, Vt.: Invisible Cities Press, 2001.

Le Plongeon, Augustus, Dr. *Sacred Mysteries Among the Mays and Quiches 11,500 Years Ago*. New York: Macoy, 1886.

Lemesurier, Peter. *Decoding the Great Pyramid*. Boston, Mass.: Element Books, 1999.

Leonard, R. Cedric. *The Quest for Atlantis*. New York: Manor Books, 1979.

LePage, Victoria. *Shambhala, The Fascinating Truth Behind the Myth of Sangr-la*. Chicago: Quest Books, 1996.

Lichtheim, Miriam. *Ancient Egyptian Literature, A Book of Readings Volume 2: The New Kingdom*. Berkeley, Calif.: University of California Press, 1976.

Lindsay, Jack, trans. *The Golden Ass*. Bloomington, Ind.: Indiana University Press, 1962.

Lindy, James *Geology versus History*. Chicago: Ascension Press, 1954.

MacCana, Prosinas. *Celtic Mythology*. London: Hamlyn, 1970.

Mace, Arthur C. Bulletin of the Metropolitan Museum of Art, The Egyptian Exhibition, 1922-1923, Nr. 112, Vol, 19, 1925.

MacPherson, Andrew, trans. *The Known Plays of Euripides*. Cambridge, UK: Cambridge University Press, 1922.

MacQueen, J.G., ed. *Ancient Near Eastern Texts: The Hittites and Their Contemporaries in Asia Minor*. London: Richter Publishers, Ltd., 1975.

Malamat, Abraham. *History of Biblical Israel: Major Problems and Minor Issues*. New York: Brill Academic Publishers, 2004.

Malkowsky, Edward. *Egypt Before the Pharaohs*. Rochester, Vt.: Bear and Company, 2006.

Mallery, Arlington, and Mary Roberts Harrison. *The Rediscovery of Lost America*. New York: E.P. Dutton, 1979.

Mann, William F. *The Knights Templar in the New World*. Rochester, Vt.: Destiny Books, 2004.

Markale, Jean. *Montségur and the Mystery of the Cathars*. Rochester, Vt.: Inner Traditions, 1999.

———. *The Grail*. Rochester, Vt.: Inner Traditions, 1999.

Markham, Clements, Sir, trans. *The Guanches of Tenerife*. London: Longmans Publishers, 1891.

Martin, Sean. *The Knights Templar: The History & Myths of the Legendary Military Order*. New York: Macmillan, 2005.

Matthews, John. *The Grail, Quest for the Eternal*. London: Thames and Hudson, Ltd., 1981.

McNally, Kenneth. *Standing Stones and other monuments of Early Ireland*. New York: Appletree, 1984.

Mehler, Stephen S. "Was there an Explosion in the Great Pyramid in Antiquity?" *World Explorer*, vol. 3, #4, 2003, p. 27.

Mendelsohn, Kurt. *The Riddle of the Pyramids*. London: Thames & Hudson, 1974.

Mercatante, Anthony S. *Who's Who in Egyptian Mythology*. New York: Clarkson N. Potter, Inc., 1978.

Mercer, A.B. Samuel. *Horus, the Royal God of Egypt*. Cambridge, UK: Society of Oriental Research, 1960.

Michell, Jon. *The View Over Atlantis*. London: Hoover House, Ltd., 1987.

Morford, Mark P.O., and Robert J. Lenardon. *Classical Mythology*. New York: Longman, 1971.

Morison, Samuel Eliot. *Samuel De Champlain: Father of New France*. New York: Little Brown & Company, 1972.

Motet, Pierre. *Lives of the Pharaohs*. New York: World Publishing Company, 1968.

Murnane, William J. *Le Papyrus Harris I, The Journal of the American Oriental Society*. New York: American Oriental Society, 1999.

———. *Texts from the Amarna Period in Egypt*. Atlanta, Ga.: Society of Biblical Literature, 1995.

———. *United With Eternity, A Concise Guide to the Monuments of Medinet Habu*. Chicago: University of Chicago Press, 1980.

Mustard, Helen M. and Charles E. Passage, trans. *Parzifal*. New York: Vintage Books, 1961.

Myhill, Henry. *The Canary Islands*. London: Faber and Faber, 1968.

Naudon, Paul. *The Secret History of Freemasonry*. Rochester, Vt.: Bear and Company, 2005.

Nelson, Dee Jay, and David H. Coville. *Life Force in the Great Pyramids*. Camarillo, Calif.: DeVorss & Co., 1977.

Nutall, Zelia. *The Fundamental Principles of Old and New World Civilizations, Vol. II*, Cambridge, Mass.: Peabody, Harvard University, 1900.

O'Brien, Henry. *The Round Towers of Atlantis*. Kempton, Ill.: Adventures Unlimited Press, 2002.

O'Hara, Cally, and Scarlett Hall. *Earth Facts*. New York: DK Publishing, 1995.

O'Kelly, Claire. *New Grange*. Cork, Ireland: Houston Printers, 1973.

O'Kelly, Michael J. *Early Ireland: An Introduction to Irish Prehistory*. London: Cambridge University Press, 1989.

O'Riordain, Sean P. *Antiquities of the Irish Countryside*. London: University Paperbacks, 1965.

Oppenheimer, Stephen. *Eden in the East, The Drowned Continent of Southeast Asia*. London: Weidenfeld and Nicolson, 1999.

Osborne, Harold. *South American Mythology*. London: Hamlyn, 1970.

Osman, Ahmed. *Moses and Akhenaton*. Rochester, Vt.: Bear and Company, 2002.

Ossendowski, Ferdinand. *Beast, Men and Gods*. London: Hollreiser, Ltd., 1922.

Partner, Peter. *The Knights Templar and their Myth*. Rochester, Vt.: Destiny Books, 1990.

Passage, Charles E., trans. *Titurel*. New York: Frederick Unger Publishing Co., 1984.

Petrakos, Basil. *Delphi*. Athens: Clio Editions, 1977.

Petrie, W.M. Flinders. *A History of Egypt, Vols. I, II and III*. New York: Charles Scribner's Sons, 1905.

———. *The Pyramids and Temples of Giza*. London: Field & Tuer, 1883.

Phillips, Graham. *Atlantis and the Ten Plagues of Egypt*. Rochester, Vt.: Bear and Company, 2003.

———. *The Chalice of the Magdalen*. Rochester, Vt.: Bear and Company, 2004.

———. *The Templars and the Ark of the Covenant*. Rochester, Vt.: Bear and Company, 2004.

Picknett, Lynn, and Clive Prince. *The Sion Revelation, The Truth About the Guardians of Christ's Sacred Bloodline*. London: Simon & Schuster, 2006.

Pinkham, Mark Amaru. *Guardians of the Holy Grail*. Kempton, Ill.: Adventures Unlimited Press, 2004.

Powell, T.G.E. *The Celts*. New York: Praeger Press, 1959.

Prawer, Joshua. *The Crusader's Kingdom*. London: Phoenix Orion, 1972.

Pyeritz, Reed E., and Cheryll Gasner. *The Marfan Syndrome*. New York: National Marfan Foundation, 1994.

Radka, Larry Brian. *The Electric Mirror on the Pharos Lighthouse and Other Ancient Lighting*. Parkersburg, W.V.: The Einhorn Press, 2006.

Rahn, Otto Wilhelm. *Crusade Against the Grail*. Rochester, Vt.: Inner Traditions, 2006.

Ralls, Karen, Dr. *The Templars and the Grail*. Wheaton, Ill.: Quest Books, 2003.

Rao, Sharmila, and Ann S. Henderson. "Regulation of c-fos is affected by electromagnetic fields." *www3interscience.wiley.com / cgi-bin / abstract / 68550 /*

Ratcliffe, J.A. *Physics of the Upper Atmosphere*. Chicago: Henry Regnery Press, 1960.

———. *Sun, Earth and Radio*. New York: Macmillan, 1970.

Redford, Donald B. *Akhenaten: The Heretic King*. Princeton, N.J.: Princeton University Press, 1984.

Redford, Donald Bruce, ed. *The Oxford Encyclopedia of Ancient Egypt, Vol. 2*. New York: Oxford University Press and The American University in Cairo Press, 2001.

Renfrew, Alfred M. *The Flood*. St. Louis, Mo.: Concordia Publishing, 1951.

Roerich, Nicholas. *Heart of Asia, Memoirs from the Himalayas*. Rochester, Vt.: Inner Traditions, 1990.

———. *Shambhala, In Search of the New Era*. Rochester, Vt.: Inner Traditions, 1990.

Rona, P. "Plate Tectonics and Mineral Resources," *Scientific American*, July, 1973, 86-95.

Roscher, Wilhelm Heinrich. *Omphalos*. Leipzig: G. Teubner Verlag, 1913.

Rosenberg, Alfred. *The Myth of the 20th Century*. Newport Beach, Calif.: Noontide Press, 1995.

Rother, Herman. *Ancient Egyptian Medical Science*. Chicago: Regnery, 1977.

Rufus, Anneli S., and Kristan Lawson. *Goddess Sites: Europe*. San Francisco: Harper, 1990.

Runciman, Steven. *The Medieval Manichee: A Study of the Christian Dualist Heresy*. London: Cambridge University Press, 1982.

Rutherford, Alfred, Dr. *Journal of Pyramidology*. Vol. 1, nr. 3, June, 1970.